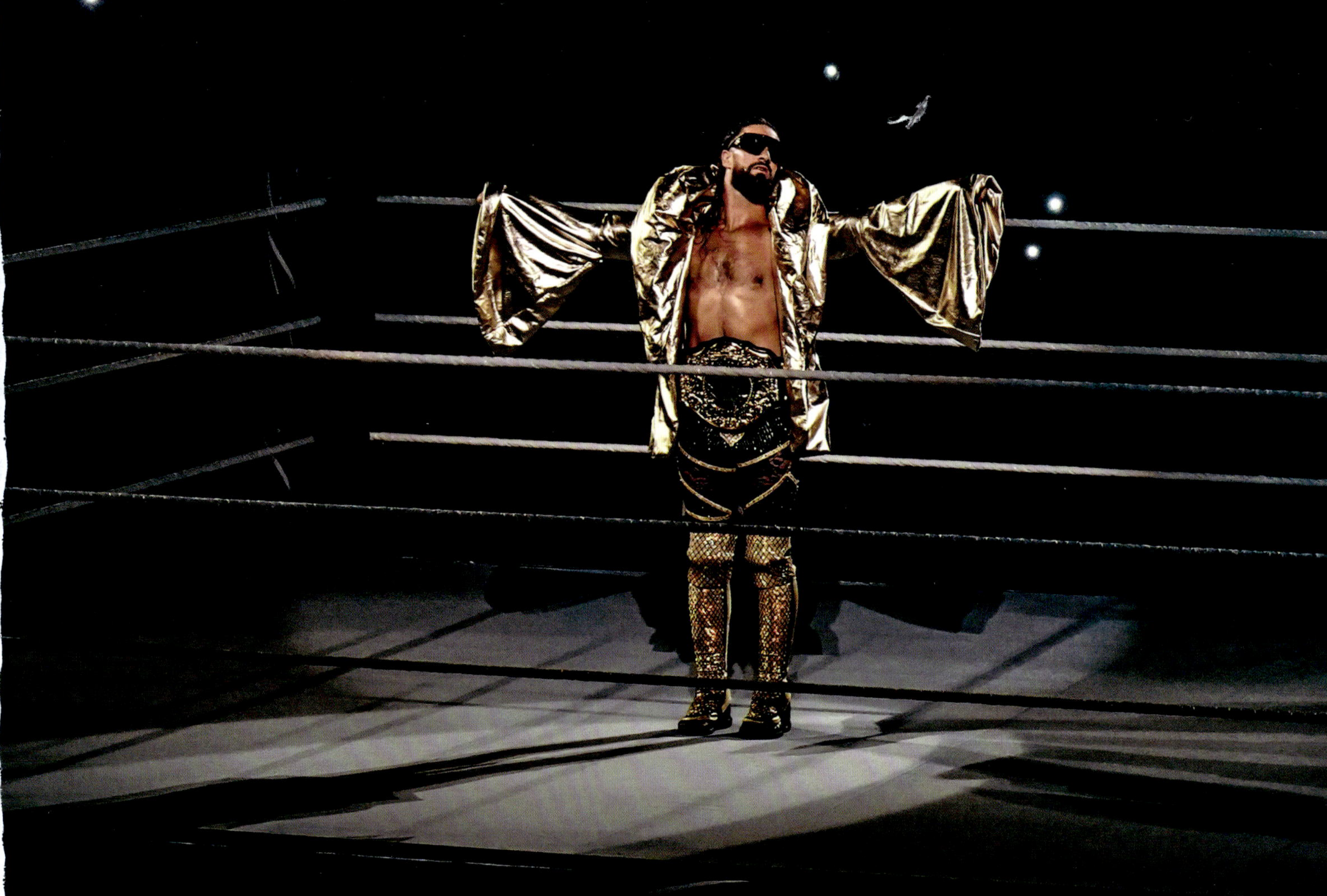

# THREADS of TRIUMPH

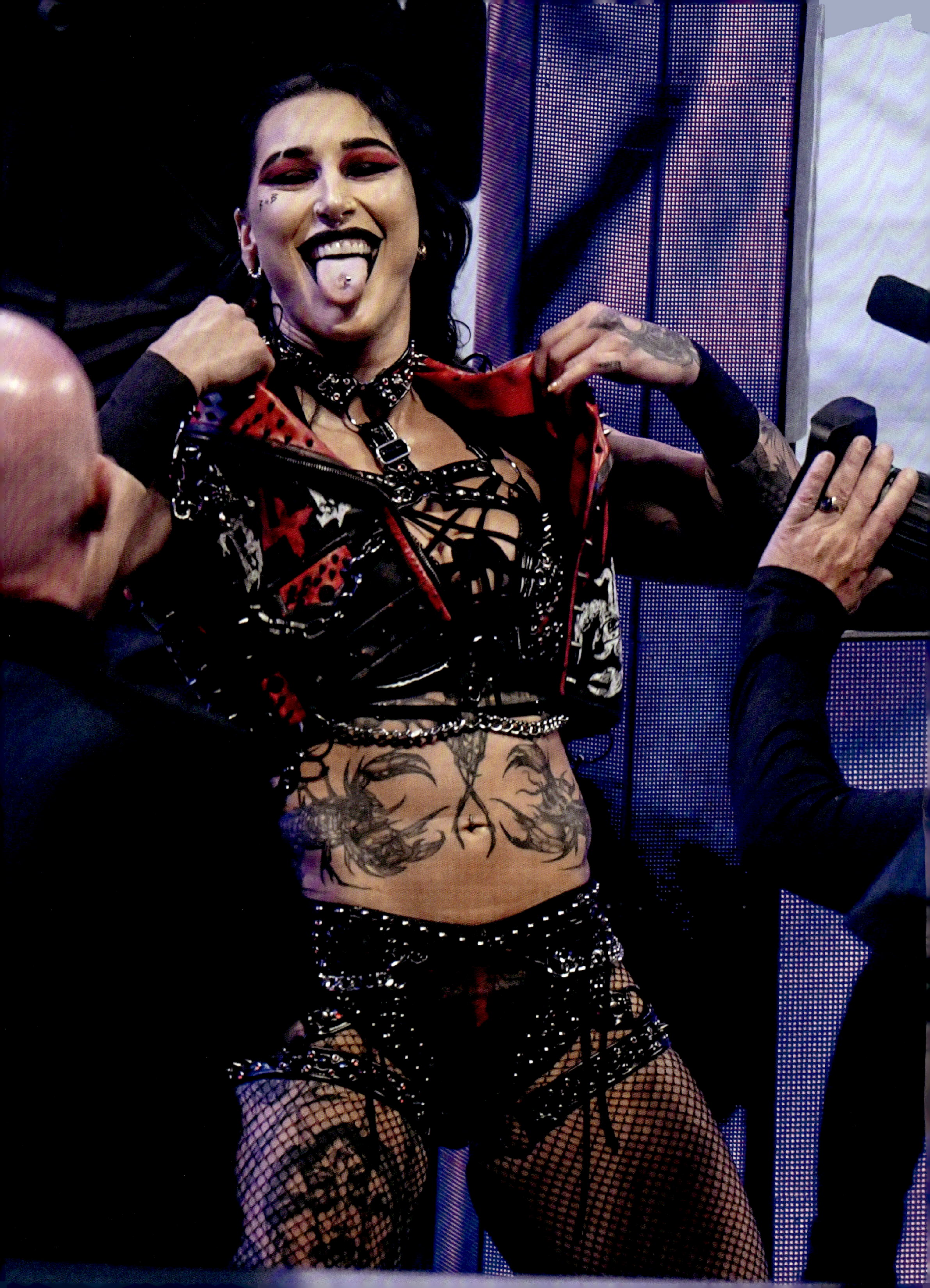

# THREADS *of* TRIUMPH

## PROFESSIONAL WRESTLING'S MOST ICONIC LOOKS

BY **McKENZIE MITCHELL**

FOREWORD BY **MERCEDES MONÉ**

CHRONICLE BOOKS

SAN FRANCISCO

Library of Congress Cataloging-in-Publication Data available.

ISBN 978-1-7972-3897-5

Manufactured in China.

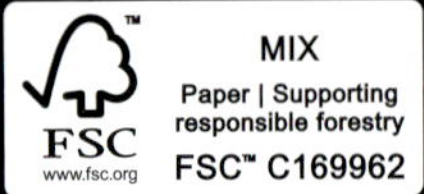



Design by Evelyn Furuta.
Cover by Evelyn Furuta and Neil Egan.
Pages 1, 2, and 8: Photos by Kimberly Morrell.
Pages 4, 6, and 11: Photos by George Napolitano.
Pages 12, 38, 62, 102, and 222: Photos by Basil Mahmud.
Pages 142 and 172: Photos by George Tahinos.

The views expressed in this book belong solely to the author
and those interviewed. A number of featured wrestlers
have been active for many decades. Each wrestler has been
placed in chapters based on their involvement in events
throughout history and their popularity over the years.
The author reserves the right to place athletes in this book
how she sees fit.

10 9 8 7 6 5 4 3 2 1



Chronicle Books LLC
680 Second Street
San Francisco, California 94107
www.chroniclebooks.com

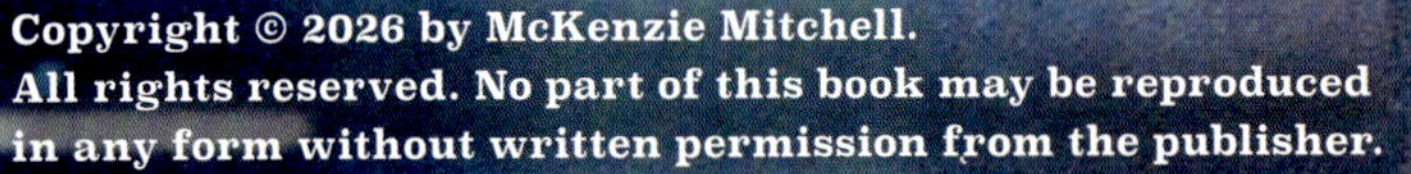

# DEDICATION

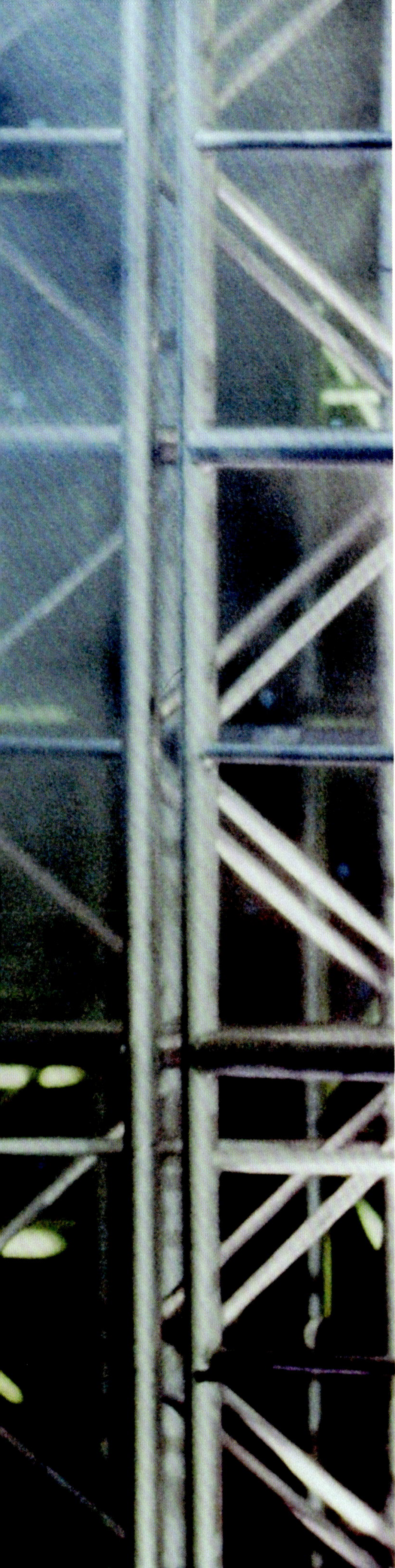

*Threads of Triumph: Professional Wrestling's Most Iconic Looks* is dedicated to:

The icons who came before us and set the tone for the world of professional wrestling as we know it today.

The trendsetters who are currently transcending the industry—boldly, confidently, and in all-capital letters. Who are following the path paved by legends.

Wrestling's next generation of stars. May you be inspired by the work, passion, effort, stories, and time it's taken to achieve the evolved world of professional wrestling that we've come to know in the twenty-first century.

The fans, who wildly and proudly continue to support professional wrestling with all their hearts. Good, bad, or ugly—you are never afraid to share what you believe in . . . and what you don't. Your spirit and passion make the magic we see through a television screen or in person at a show come to life.

PAGE 1: WWE Superstar Seth Rollins at WWE Payback on September 2, 2023. Photo by Kimberly Morrell.

PAGE 2: WWE Superstar Rhea Ripley at WWE Bad Blood 2024 at the State Farm Arena in Atlanta, Georgia. Photo by Kimberly Morrell.

OPPPOSITE: Ric Flair in signature robe at a WCW Live event in 1997. Photo by George Tahinos.

PAGE 6: From left to right: Matt Hardy, Lita, and Jeff Hardy in Team Xtreme. Photo by George Napolitano.

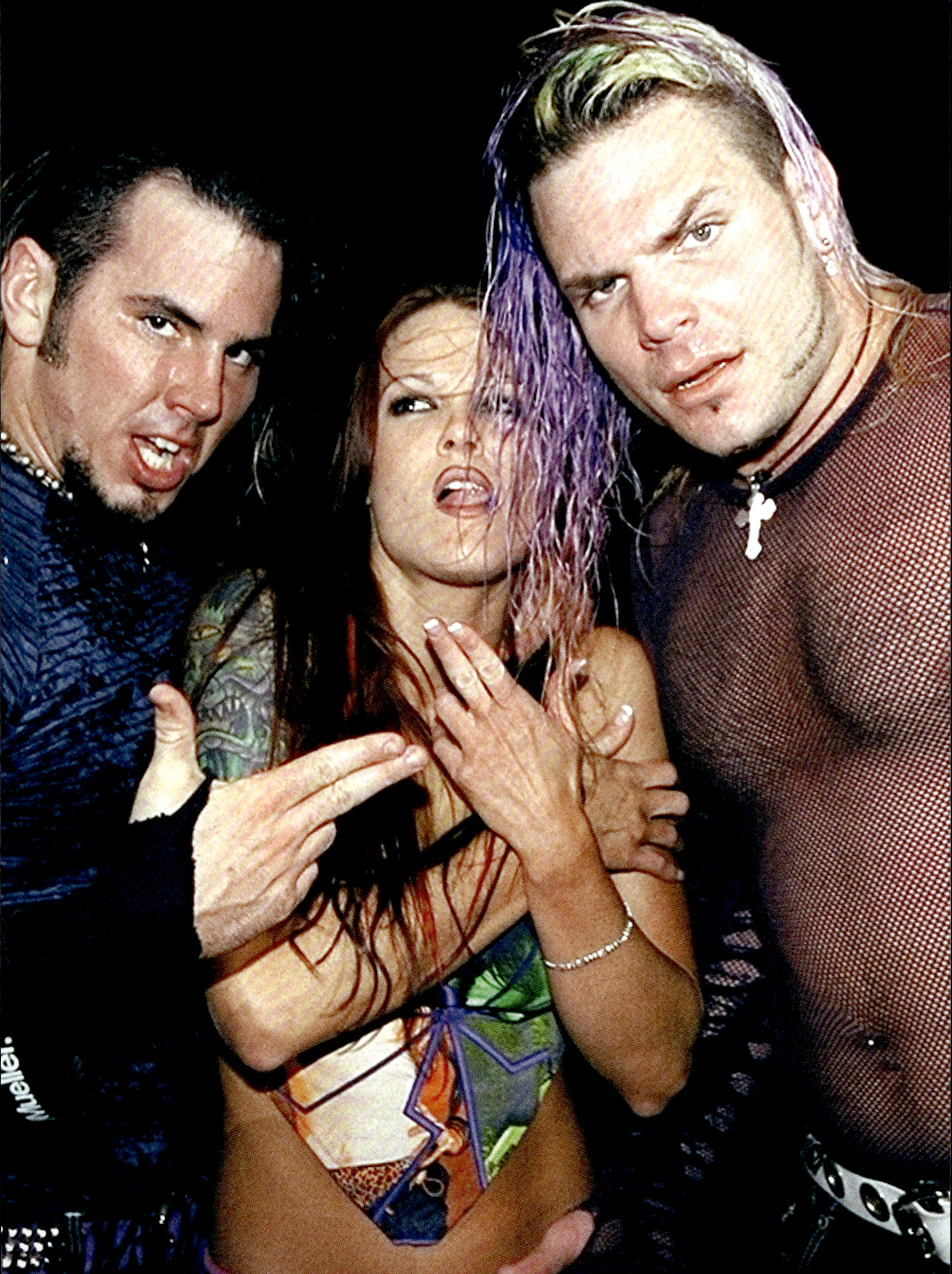

# CONTENTS

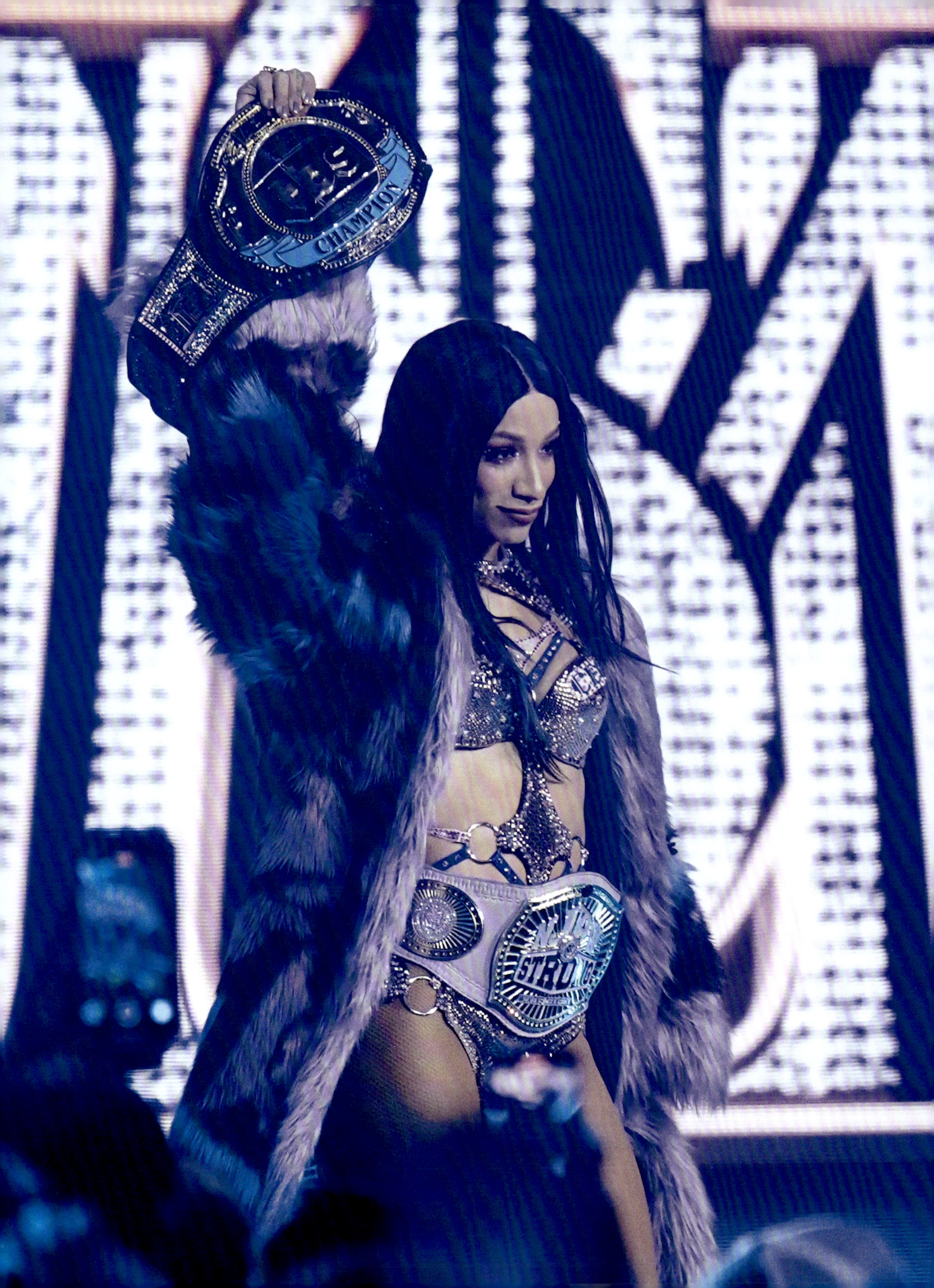

# FOREWORD

**In the world** of professional wrestling, the ring isn't just a place for athletic prowess—it's a grand stage where artistry meets performance, and fashion serves as a powerful means of self-expression. Each superstar embodies a unique persona, and their wardrobe reflects their journey, their character, and their connection to the fans, making their appearances as impactful as their performances. *Threads of Triumph: Professional Wrestling's Most Iconic Looks* captures this essence by celebrating the vibrant tapestry of styles that have defined the industry from the 1940s to today.

Fashion transcends mere fabric and stitching—it's an art form that allows us to communicate without words. As an entertainer, I have always believed that the way we present ourselves can create an indelible impression. My journey from legit boss Sasha Banks to CEO Mercedes Moné has been one of evolution, and each outfit has played a crucial role in shaping my narrative. Like the greats before me, I've strived to push boundaries, redefine norms, and embrace the art of sartorial self-expression. I embrace the power of fashion to stand out in a crowded arena, to tell my story, and to evoke emotion—a dazzling entrance that ignites the crowd and leaves a lasting impact.

Ultimately, fashion is a celebration of individuality. It empowers us to embrace our true selves, to take risks, and to inspire others. As we explore the iconic looks featured in this book, I invite you to appreciate not only the artistry behind each design but also the profound influence these styles have had on the evolution of wrestling culture. Here's to the trailblazers and trendsetters who remind us that in the world of wrestling, style is not just an accessory; it is a vital part of the legacy we leave behind. May you find inspiration in these pages to express your own unique voice and to create a lasting impact in your journey—both inside and outside the ring.

**Mercedes Moné**

Mercedes Moné at AEW Full Gear
2024 in Philadelphia, Pennsylvania.
Photo by Kimberly Morrell.

# INTRODUCTION

**Wrestling dates back** to ancient Greece and Rome, but it wasn't until the late 1800s that professional wrestling as we know it began to take shape. Flashy in-ring attire has become a staple in the industry, but *how* it has evolved also tells an important story.

Let's pull back the curtain and go beneath the seams. Looking back to the 1940s and throughout the decades, *Threads of Triumph* chronicles the stars and styles that have shaped this legendary industry. This book celebrates wrestling's iconic fashions by showcasing some of the industry's most memorable looks over the years, with stunning photography and exclusive and insightful commentary from some of professional wrestling's biggest stars. We'll uncover how pro wrestlers from the early days like "Macho Man" Randy Savage and Shawn Michaels set the blueprints for professional wrestling's modern spectacle and, through their original styles, influenced what we see today. We'll also explore how pop culture, celebrity figures, and generational eras have impacted the sport in undeniable ways.

There's more to a wrestler's gear than meets the eye. What a wrestler wears in the ring plays a large role in evoking emotion, personas, and attitude. Most, if not all, professional wrestlers are responsible for their own gear, including all the costs, the creative process, and how it resonates with fans (and enemies). It's no wonder, then, that gear connects a wrestler to their character, and through their character they connect to their roots, their story, their heritage. Did you know the same seamstress who created outfits for Bret Hart and Jim "The Anvil" Neidhart in the '80s is still creating looks for Jim's daughter Natalya, today? Stories like this show how committed and thoughtful this industry and its athletes can be.

Wrestling fans are as passionate as they come—this book is for you. *Threads* will give you an insider's look at the people and events that have shaped the world of professional wrestling, through the lens of the gear we know and love. *Threads of Triumph* is here to prove that fashion can speak louder than words. It can tell a story without having to speak at all.

"Macho Man" Randy Savage poses for the crowd in neon attire. Photo by George Napolitano.

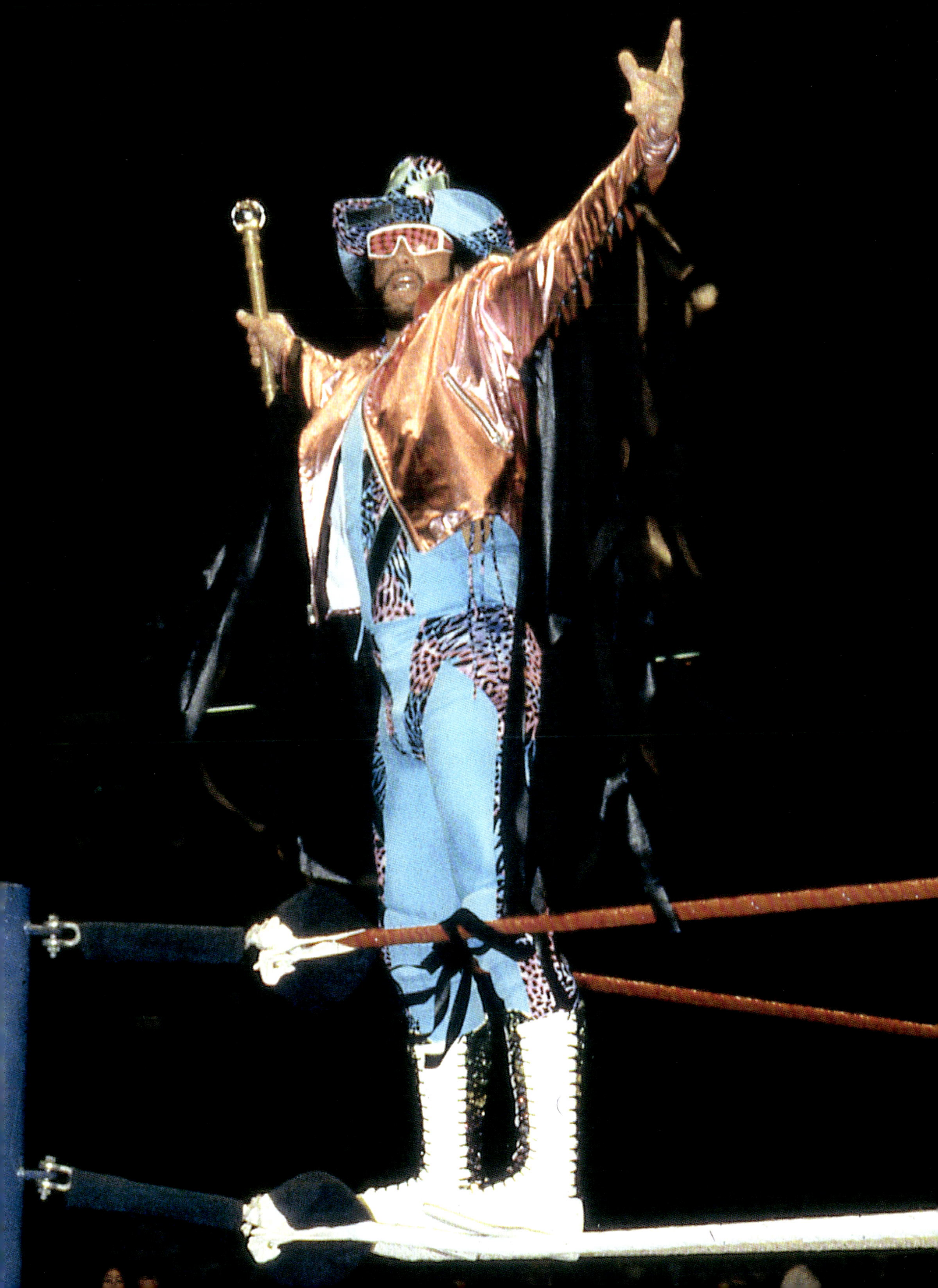

# Prototypes and Blueprints

## (1940s–early 1980s)

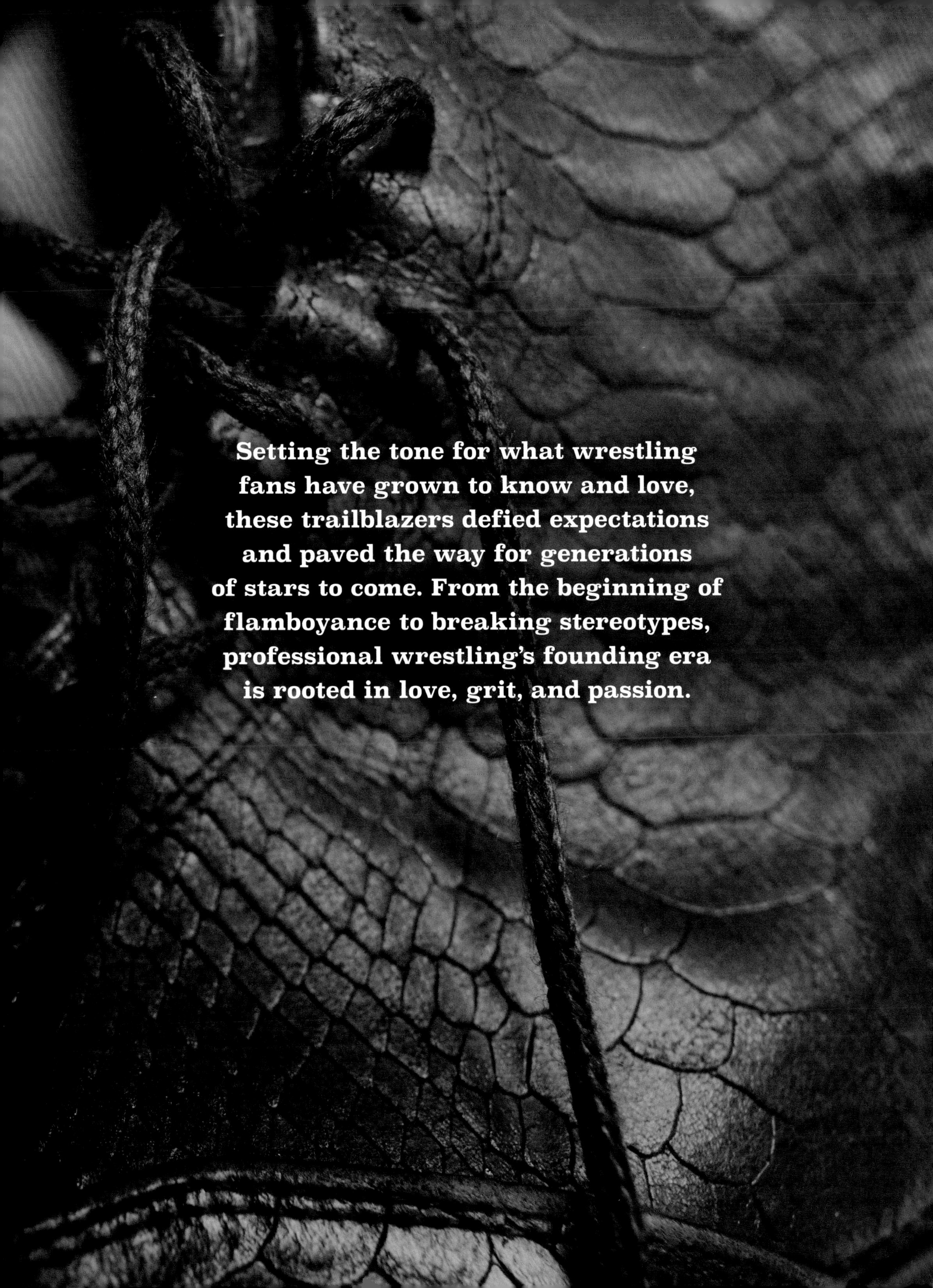


Setting the tone for what wrestling
fans have grown to know and love,
these trailblazers defied expectations
and paved the way for generations
of stars to come. From the beginning of
flamboyance to breaking stereotypes,
professional wrestling's founding era
is rooted in love, grit, and passion.

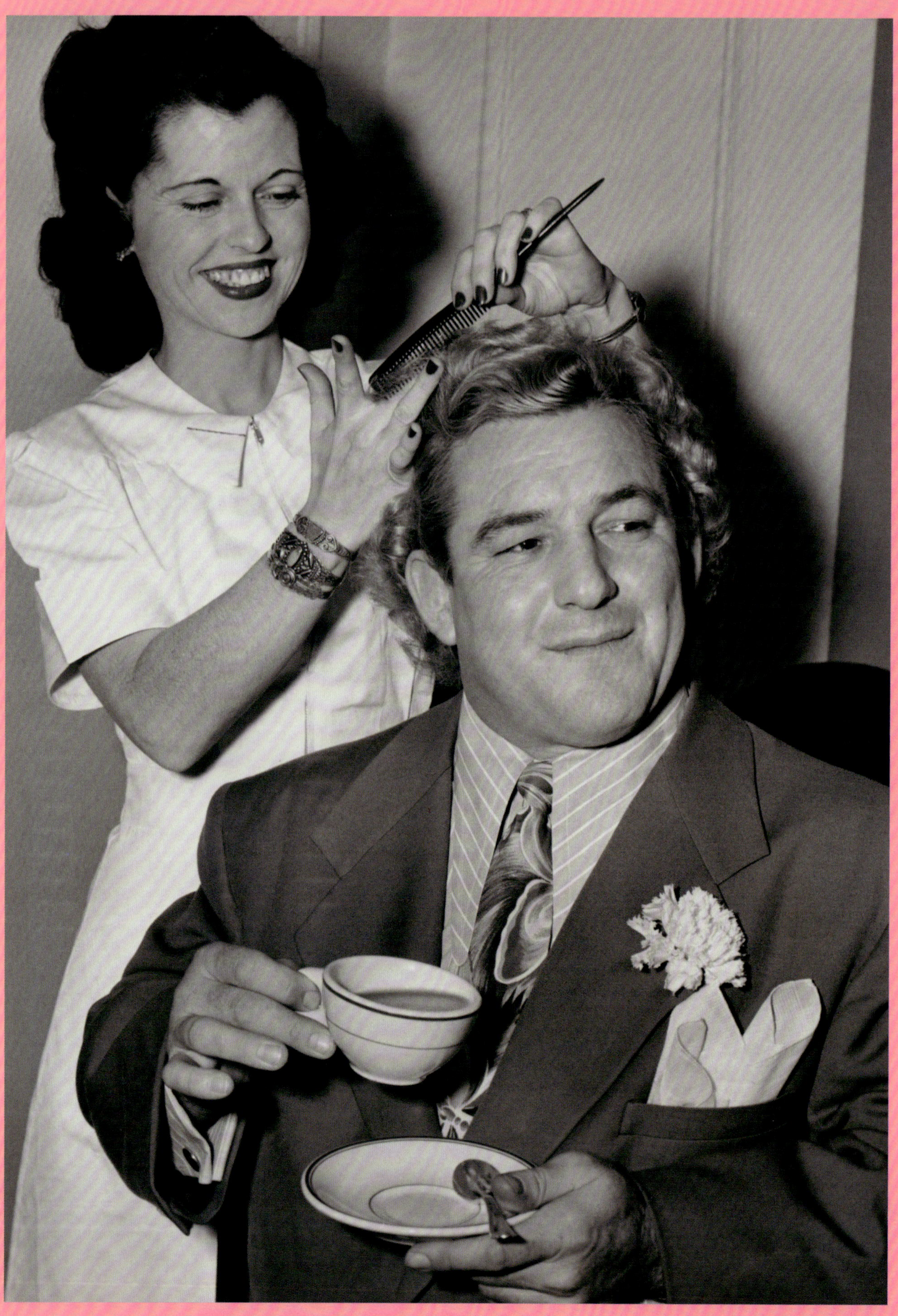

# GEORGE WAGNER
## *GORGEOUS GEORGE*

Active 1932–1962

WWE Hall of Famer

**Gorgeous George was** a trailblazer, trendsetter, and one of the first professional wrestlers to embody what we call stage presence. As extravagant as they come, George understood how to hook an audience and leverage emotions before the crowd even realized what he was doing. He feigned arrogance and took on an almost pompous disposition to rile up the crowd. George's outfits played a key role in selling his persona and inspired the flamboyant style still seen throughout the industry.

Despite standing only 5 feet, 9 inches tall, Gorgeous George made fans believe he was larger than life with his extravagant outfits and mannerisms. While most male wrestlers wore simple trunks and boots, George dazzled in Renaissance-style ruffles, garments made of satin and lace, and long, elegant robes. The rich, luxurious quality of his gear, which he embellished with feathers, flowers, and lipstick, inspired future generations of wrestlers to adopt similar lavish personas. Long before the Flairs were wearing robes, George had made the look his own.

Terry Taylor, who wrestled as The Red Rooster during the early '80s and '90s, was just one of the many young wrestlers inspired by Gorgeous George's groundbreaking character. "George was tough. I appreciated him taking that step out of conformity," said Taylor. "He dyed his hair blond and would walk out spraying perfume. He was way before his time because he would go so far outside of what the norm was."

The younger wrestler also credited George's showman persona with helping take professional wrestling mainstream. "Gorgeous George, along with [fellow athlete] Adrian Street, bet on themselves," said Taylor. "George created this whole different genre, from black tights and very little movement to this flamboyance and showman mentality. That's where people started to say, 'Hey, wrestling's real!' George changed the world."

Gorgeous George studio shoot.
Photo via Alamy / Everett Collection Inc.

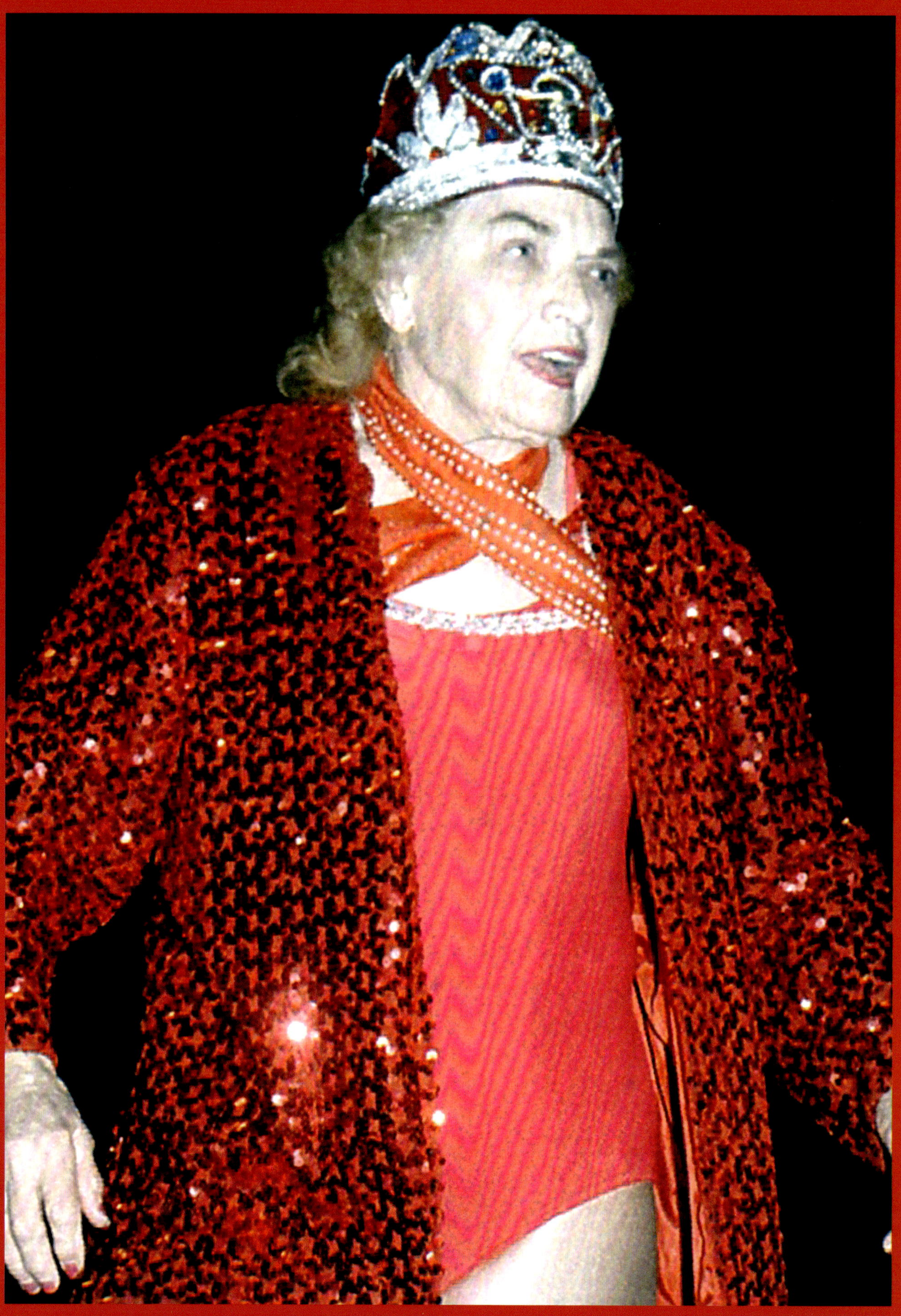

# MAE YOUNG

Active 1939–2010

An Eight-Decade Career
WWE Hall of Famer

**Where would wrestling** be today without Mae Young? One of the strongest and most determined competitors to ever master the art of the sport, Mae increased the popularity of women's wrestling in an era when women had to fight for the right to compete. Proving that women shouldn't be questioned as athletes but instead should be recognized as equal to the men, Mae understood what the future could hold and told her story with grace and grit, influencing generations of women. With unmatched passion, Mae proved that women can compete, and can be strong and refined. Michelle McCool, the inaugural Divas Champion, had the opportunity to work with Mae first-hand. She said, "When I think of Mae Young, I think tough yet classy, sweet but super sassy, hilarious, feisty, beautiful, and *the* epitome of women's wrestling. The mentality she had to have to come up in the business when she did is almost hard to even fathom! She has this swag about her that always drew me in, and her wrestling spoke for itself. Her gear was glamour and glitz, and she wore it well! I think confidence is the sexiest thing a woman can wear, and Mae Young wore it effortlessly."

With Mae, theatrics ran deep. She often wore a velvet ceremonial crown lined with jewels, signaling her fierce and regal elegance. Dressed in simple one-piece leotards, she made timeless appeal feel revolutionary. Her trademark look included a red spandex bodysuit with red boots and a flashy red blazer. This playful monochromatic style showed passion and confidence, as if she was sticking it to this male-dominated industry. In the ring, she always found ways to shock the crowd—nothing was off-limits. "Mae was a jokester and was never afraid to push the envelope," said McCool. "When she was in the bikini contest with me and other Divas, she had myself, Torrie Wilson, and Kristal Marshall all in stitches laughing. After she clearly won the contest, rightfully so, she started dancing around and acting like she was going to take her straps off completely. Not knowing if she was joking or not, we tried to cover her up. The problem was, she was fighting us off and none of us wanted any part of that! No matter the age, she was strong!"

Mae Young wearing her signature color. Photo by George Napolitano.

Later in her career, Mae proved that age is just a number. She never shied away from hardcore moves and crazy stunts, even well into her seventies. WWE Hall of Famer Bubba Ray Dudley developed an extraordinary relationship with Mae when he had to power-bomb her seventy-seven-year-old body through a table weekly. "I've always said that Mae Young is the toughest man that I've ever met," said Dudley. "Mae Young wanted to wrestle on her one hundredth birthday, and she was serious. She went to Vince McMahon and said that she wanted to wrestle when she turned one hundred. She was absolutely fearless. A lot of people have heard this story, but it gets watered down through telling it. When I body-slammed Mae for the first time, I put her down very, very gingerly, delicately, and lightly. It's the world's lightest body slam because I didn't know how a seventy-seven-year-old woman's body was going to react to being body-slammed by a 325-pound man. I had forgotten that Mae Young had been wrestling for fifty years by this point. Her body was a giant callus, impervious to pain, but I was trying to be respectful and gentle and make sure she could get up and, you know, do it again the next day. We get into the locker room, and she walks up to me and grabs my wrist very hard and she looks me in the eyes and says, 'Hey, hotshot! If you're gonna slam me, you slam me like one of the boys!' There was an instant level of respect knowing that this lady was basically telling me, 'If you're gonna do it, you're gonna do it right if you're gonna use me to help you get over.'"

Mae Young was forever young at heart and in spirit. "I'd like to think that when I'm seventy, I'd still be willing and ready to be put through a table on live television with zero hesitation . . . I'd be lying if I said this were the case," said McCool. "Mae just takes things to an unimaginable level of toughness."

From the early days of her career to her final match in 2010, Mae embodied tenacity. There's a reason she's been inducted into the WWE Hall of Fame despite never winning a major world championship. Because of her impact, the Mae Young Classic was born, a tournament that highlights some of the world's best women wrestlers—a fitting tribute to the woman who opened the door in the first place. "It's very easy to look at Charlotte Flair, Becky Lynch, Tiffany Stratton—any of the women that are at the top of the game today in the WWE," said Dudley. "But you have to remember, before those women had an opportunity to get to the top of the game, Mae Young was blazing that trail."

Mae Young proving she could still fight late into her years. Photo by George Napolitano.

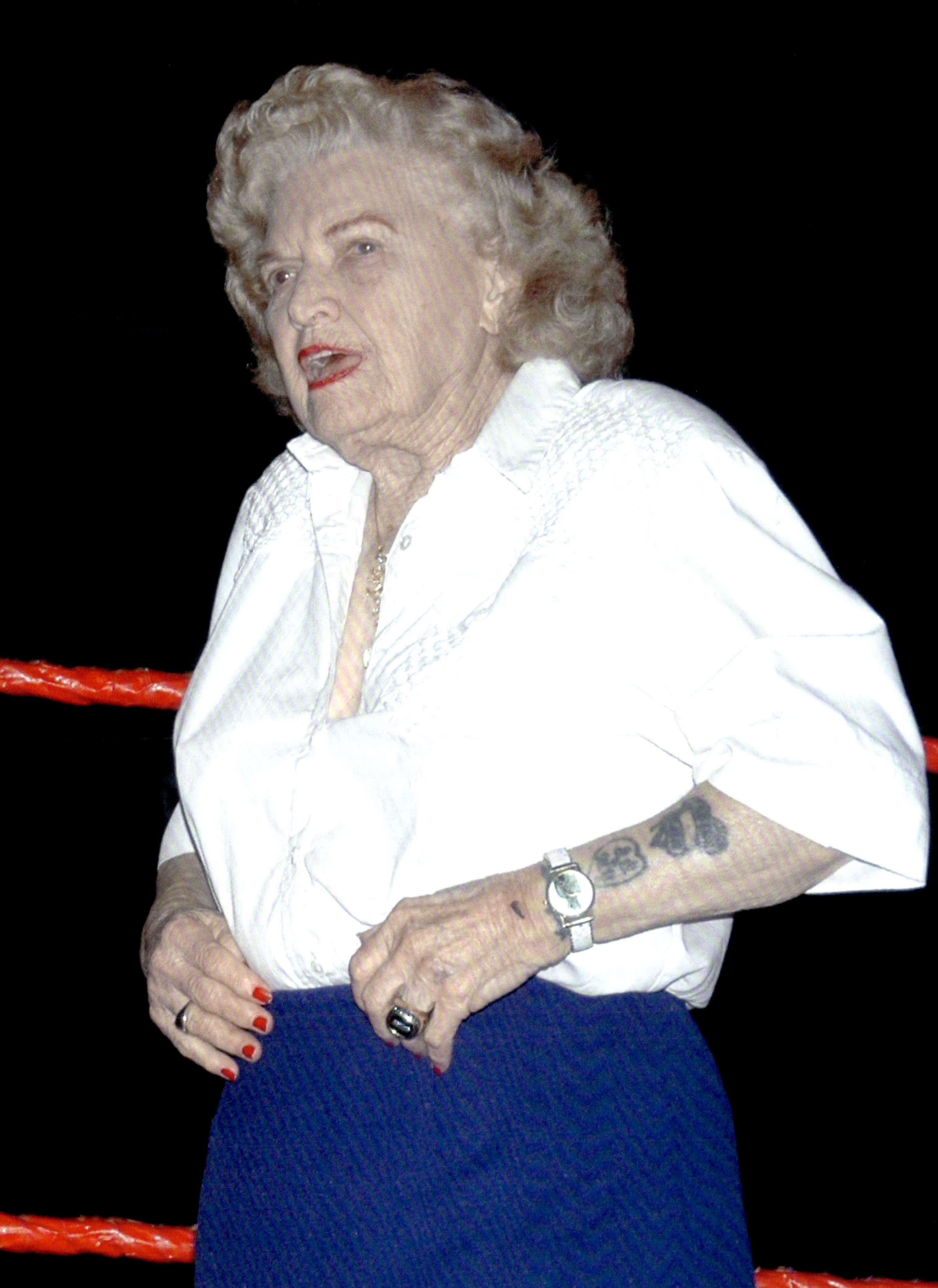

# EDWARD McDANIEL
## WAHOO McDANIEL

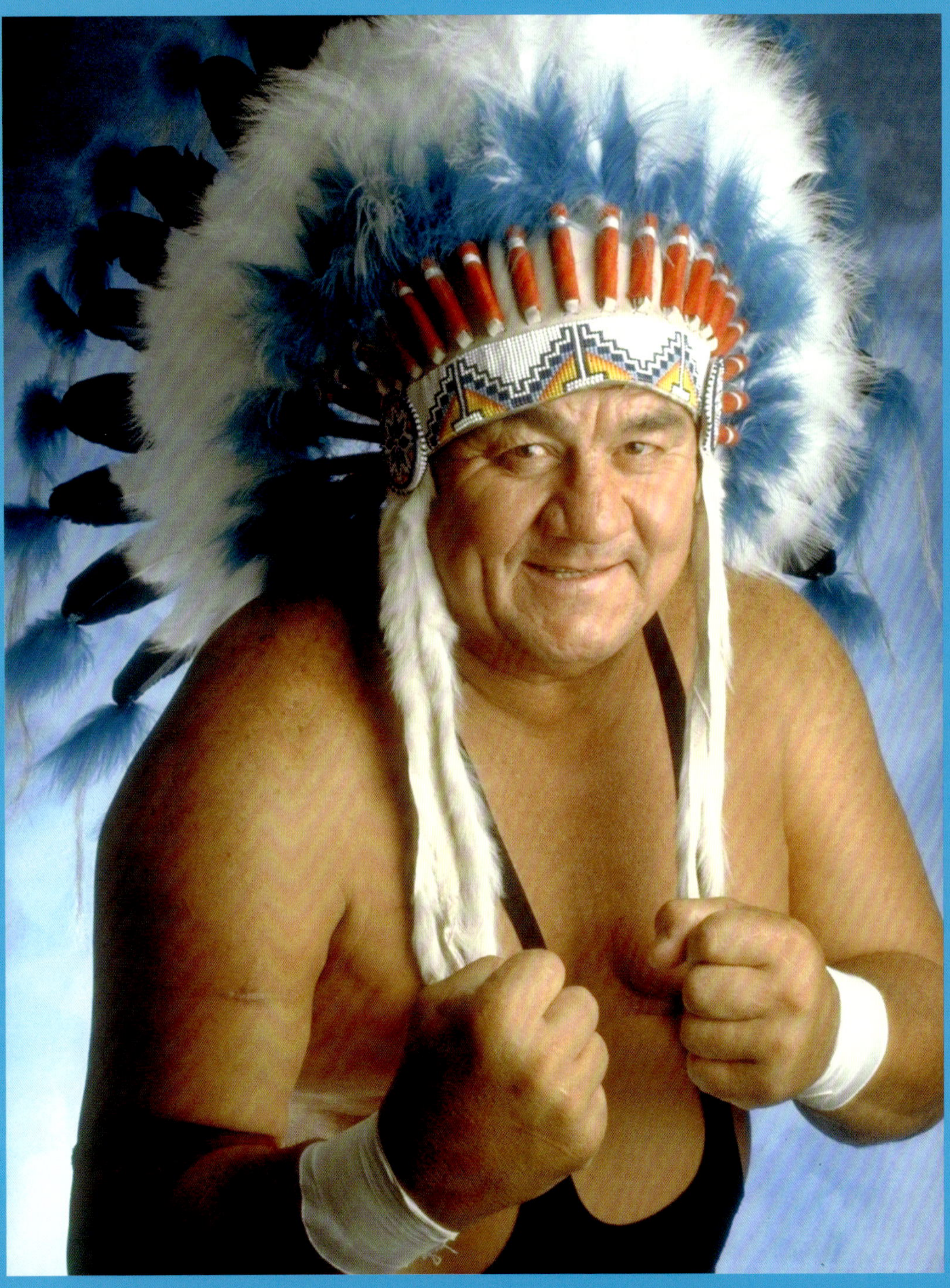

Active 1962–1996

Five-Time NWA Champion
WWE Hall of Famer

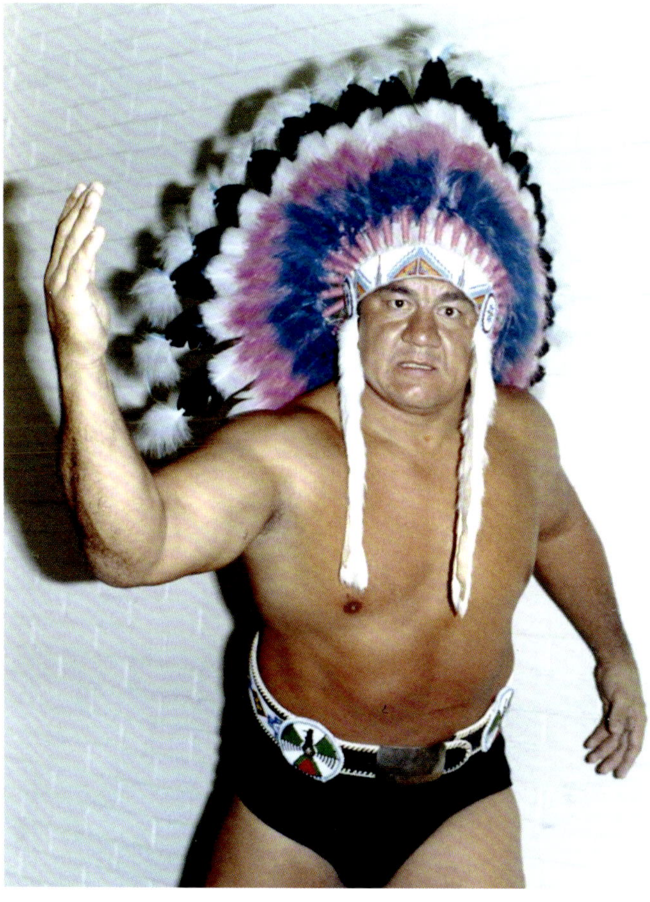

**A warrior inside** and outside the ring, Wahoo McDaniel was tough as nails and a true champion at heart. As a competitor (and former NFL player), he was brutal, strong, and relentless—three words that also sum up his mentality and character. With his large stature, Wahoo would make his way to the ring with a seriousness and purpose. His no-nonsense approach told fans and peers the self-proclaimed chief was always ready for battle.

Wahoo was one of wrestling's first Native American athletes, and his heritage played a central role in his identity. "Wahoo McDaniel was the greatest Native American athlete of all time," said fellow wrestler Terry Taylor, comparing Wahoo to another Native American wrestler, Jim Thorpe. "Thorpe came up in a different time and is more famous, but if you compare the two, Wahoo was amazing. There is a legendary story that's told about Wahoo where he ran a marathon once over a six-pack of beer. Someone bet him he couldn't do it without training, so in dress shoes, Wahoo proved them wrong and won the bet."

Crowds could see Wahoo was rightly proud of his Indigenous background. He wore his heritage with pride, donning beaded tribal belts and necklaces and chiefs' headdresses decorated with colorful feathers. His culture was just a part of him. You could even see it seeping through in the way he carried himself, with the confident swagger of a born warrior.

"There weren't a lot of Native American crossover guys at the time," said Taylor. "He was tough, harsh, rugged, and he beat the crap out of people and got the crap beat out of him. He didn't play up the Native American stuff as much. He wasn't 'I'm a Native American, Wahoo,' he was just Wahoo McDaniel . . . He became this huge character back in the day, and it was because he was being true to himself. He was an ass kicker and opened the door for so many people."

**"Wahoo lived a wide-open, no-holds-barred life in and out of the ring. He was a character, but he was also a man's man and took no crap. He was a nice guy who minded his own business, but the last thing you wanted to do is cross him."**

–Paul Taylor, former colleague and opponent, who wrestled as Terry Taylor and The Red Rooster

OPPOSITE: Wahoo McDaniel poses for studio photos in his iconic headdress. Photo by George Napolitano.

RIGHT: Wahoo McDaniel before action. Photo by George Napolitano.

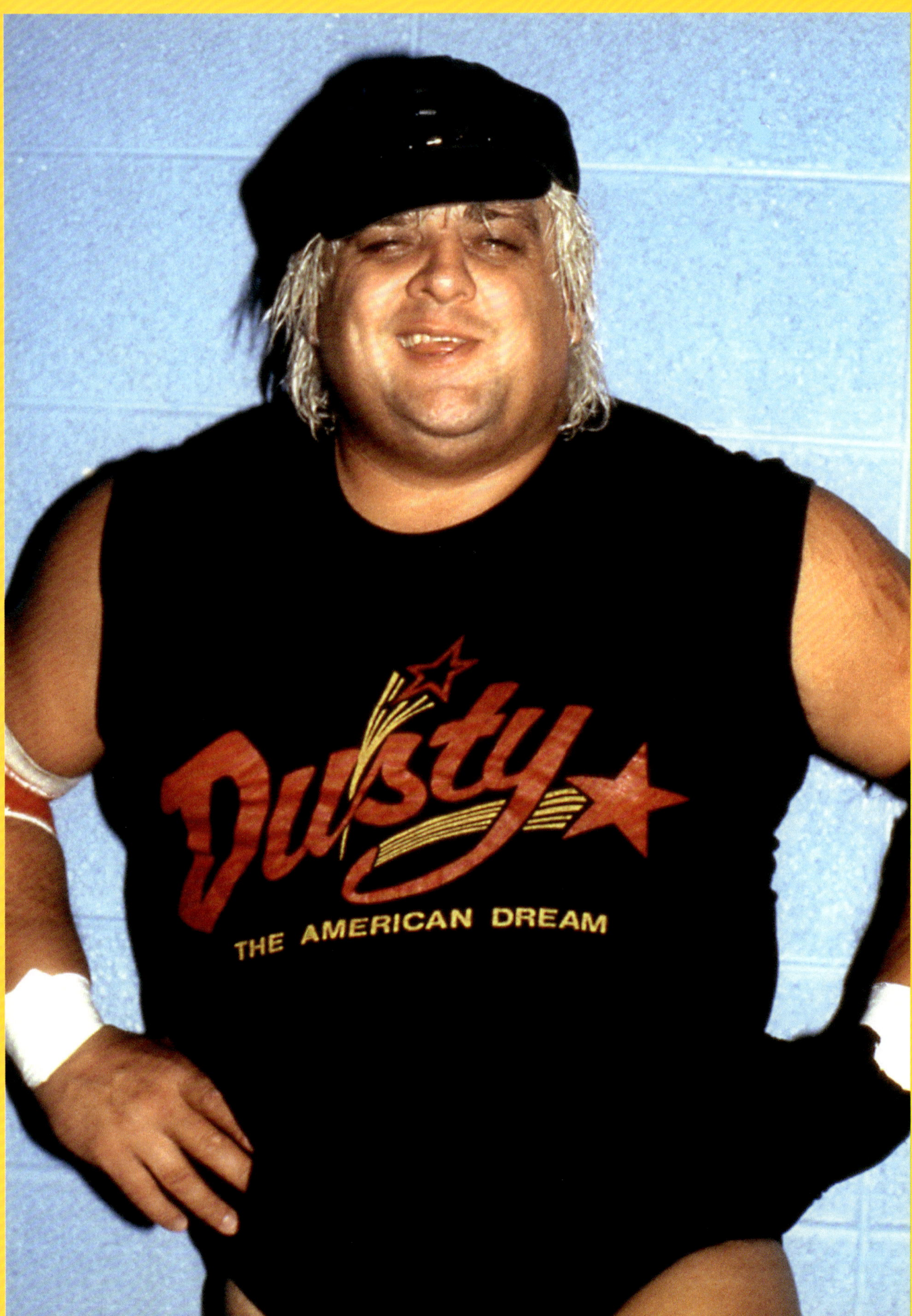

Dusty
THE AMERICAN DREAM

# VIRGIL RUNNELS JR.
## DUSTY RHODES

Active 1967–2010

Three-Time NWA Champion
WWE Hall of Famer

**A simple man,** the everyman, Dusty Rhodes made everyone feel seen and valued. Rhodes didn't need to be draped in sequins or flashy garments to find a special bond with his peers, fans, and the wrestling community. Rhodes's power lay in relatability. He wasn't the biggest or the strongest—instead, he challenged the traditional stereotypes of what a wrestler was supposed to look like. Fans could see themselves in his appearance, as though they were looking at their reflection.

As the son of a plumber, Dusty Rhodes had authentic charm that seeped through the character he portrayed night after night. He epitomized the working class and told stories of real-world struggles, teaching fans that hard work and dedication could take you anywhere you wanted. He proved that you didn't need to have fame or fortune to feel accomplished. As the common man, he was real, raw, and unapologetically human, making his fight the fans' fight. Crowds soaked up every minute in his presence and hung on every word. Dusty Rhodes was the heart and soul of wrestling. Fans of The American Dream, as Dusty Rhodes came to be known, identified with his struggles and loved him even more.

Decades later, Dusty Rhodes has inspired millions of fans across the globe, including the next wave of future Hall of Famers. "Dusty Rhodes is exactly what he was advertised," said hardcore wrestling legend Tommy Dreamer, who credits Rhodes with inspiring his own decades-long career. "He was the common man. He was my hero. I watched him wrestle when I was ten years old, and I could remember it like it was yesterday. There was no ring music; it was just a spotlight on him. I could remember gnats or flies flying around in a smoky arena, and it was as if he floated to the ring.

> **"The clothes don't make the man, the man makes the clothes."**
> **—Tommy Dreamer, professional wrestling hardcore legend and ECW original**

Dusty Rhodes backstage. Photo by George Napolitano.

–Tommy Dreamer on meeting "The American Dream" Dusty Rhodes

He was like a god to me. I watched him wrestle, and while driving home with my father, I said, 'This is what I have to do with my life.' It literally changed my life seeing this man perform, and I've been very blessed for that."

As the American dream personified, Dusty embellished his look with stars or touches of red, white, and blue. But this wasn't what became his signature style—rather, it was an outlandish look that developed years into his career. "As history goes, Vince McMahon put him in polka dots as a joke because Vince said he heard this guy could get away with anything," said Dreamer. "Giant [yellow] polka dots aren't the best or most pleasing, especially with Dusty Rhodes's physique. No one ever said, 'Oh, that's a fat man there.' They said, 'Oh, that's "The American Dream" Dusty Rhodes,' because he made you believe that the clothes don't make the man, the man makes the clothes."

Now Dreamer wears polka dots to honor the man who inspired him and millions of other fans: "For me, I wear them as a tribute to him, but also because of the backstory, that no matter what adversity you're going through, you can overcome it. Someone telling you to go do your job, handcuffing you, wanting you to fail, and you still succeed. I love that about his story."

Dusty Rhodes in signature yellow polka dots with valet Sapphire in 1989. Photo by George Napolitano.

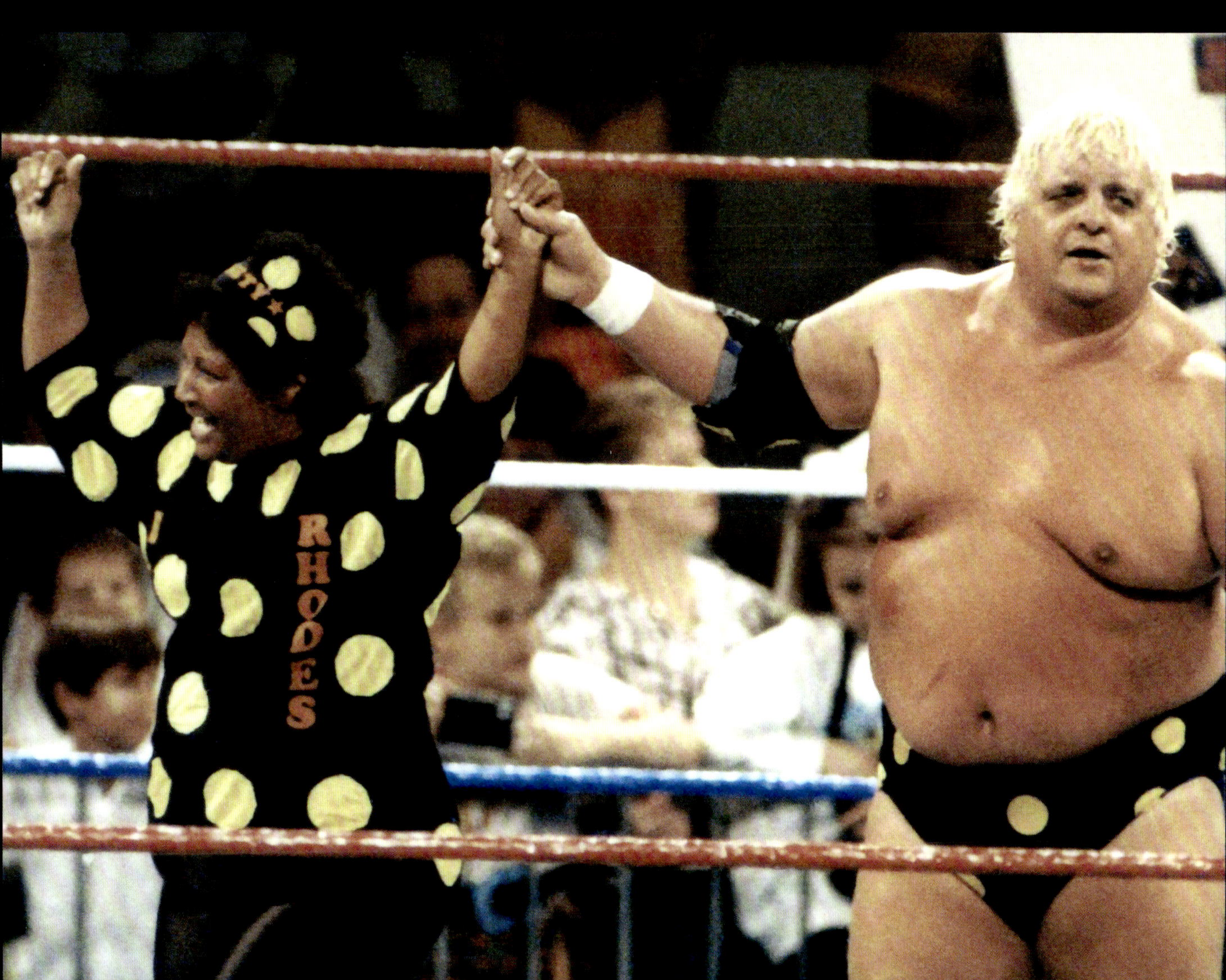
RHODES

# ELDRIDGE COLEMAN JR.
## "SUPERSTAR" BILLY GRAHAM

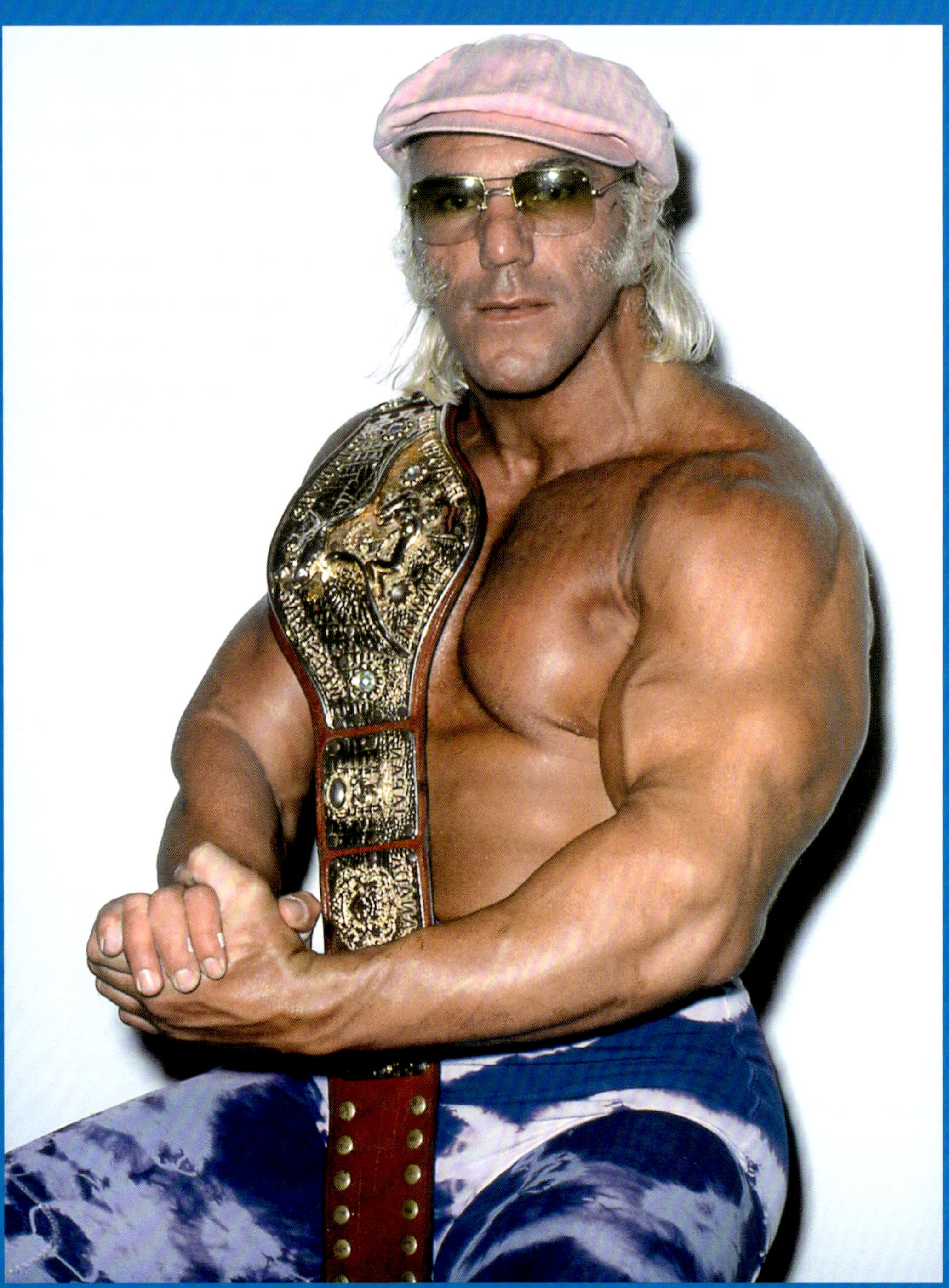

Active 1970–1989

WWF Heavyweight Champion

**"Superstar" Billy Graham** didn't just play a role—he was the role. Full of wit, charm, and other "superstar" qualities, Graham was loud and vibrant at a time when wrestling was quiet and traditional. As a character, he wasn't afraid to embrace his bold, colorful personality by dressing elaborately in bright pinks and purples, breaking stereotypes of the time. Making way for eccentricity, he wrapped himself in feather boas and wore funky sunglasses. As one of the first pro wrestling stars to popularize tie-dye, he embodied '70s style.

Understanding the power of presentation, Graham used theatrics and pizzazz to enhance the way the audience viewed his character. Standing 6 foot 4, Graham made the audience believe he was a giant. With this massive physique, he paraded his looks, flexed his muscles, and hit his signature double-gun pose to really frame moments for fans. With his manager, The Grand Wizard, by his side, Graham built a presence that was further amplified by their dynamic interactions and villainous behavior. In any arena, Graham was the spectacle, the performer you couldn't take your eyes off. Graham had swagger. He looked like a rock star and acted like one, too. And he never took himself too seriously.

Today, Graham's influence is still woven into the fabric of the sport. This true entertainer inspired fans and other wrestlers with his ability to tell stories through his movements, making his fights a must-see attraction.

Legends like Hulk Hogan and Scott Steiner have both credited Graham as an inspiration. Years ahead of his time, Graham knew his appeal wasn't only about what he could do in the ring—it was about the full experience. He reinvented professional wrestling with his forceful nature and ideas. He will always be the Man of the Hour.

OPPOSITE: Billy Graham as WWWF Champion. Photo by George Napolitano.

RIGHT: "Superstar" Billy Graham with manager The Grand Wizard posing backstage. Photo by George Napolitano.

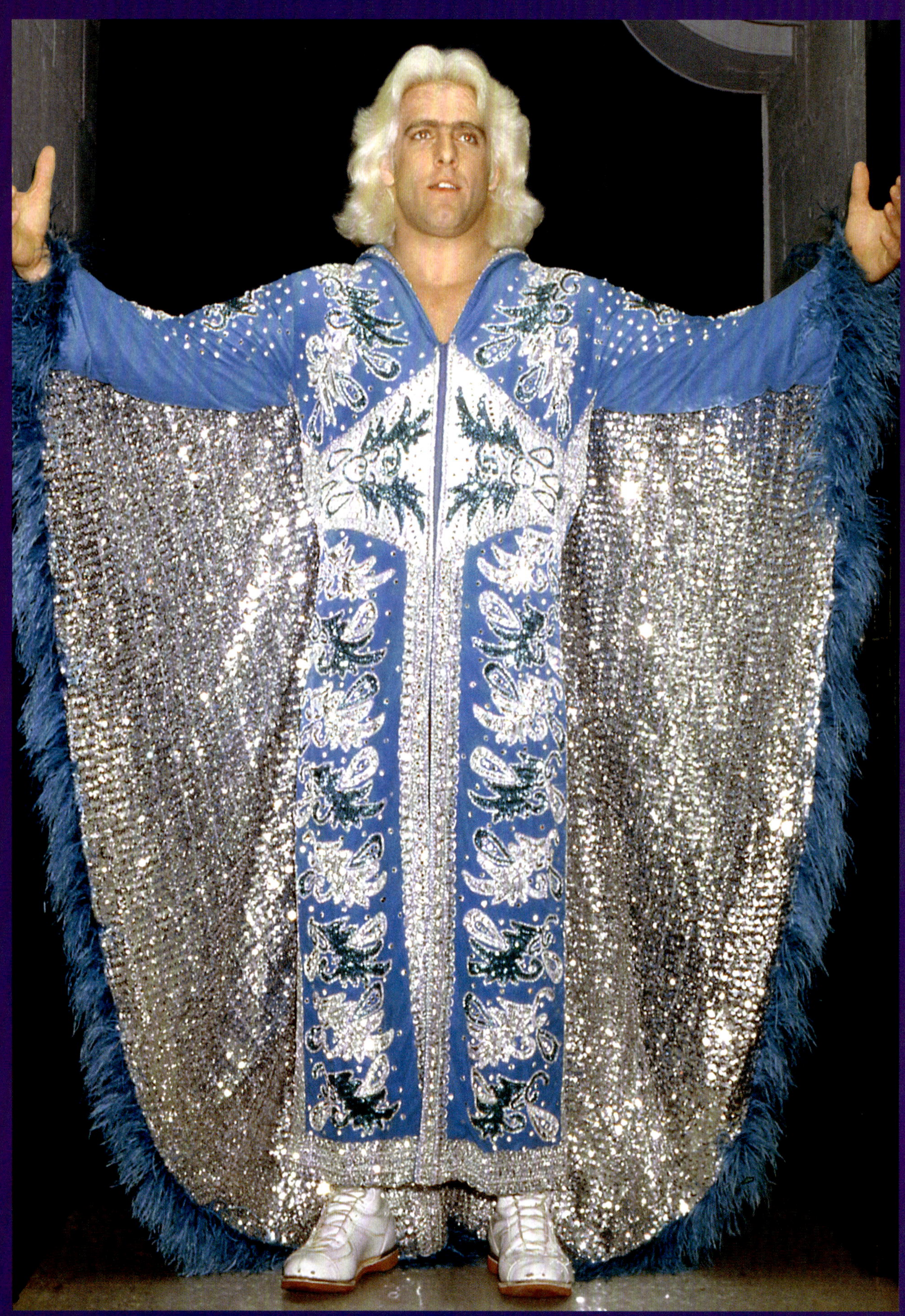

# RICHARD FLIEHR
## *RIC FLAIR*

Active 1972–2022

Sixteen-Time World Champion
WWE Hall of Famer

**Ric Flair is** one of the most celebrated wrestlers in the history of the sport, especially when it comes to grandeur and attire. Wooo-ing his way into the hearts of millions around the world, Flair captivated fans, whether they loved him or loved to hate him. Known as The Nature Boy, he never shied away from flaunting his charisma and excessive lifestyle, both inside and outside the ring. From private planes to luxury cars, he strove to live as large as his in-ring persona. As a limousine-ridin', jet-flyin', kiss-stealin', wheelin'-dealin' son of a gun, Ric oozed pompous confidence—making him one of the best heels in professional wrestling history.

If Ric Flair's actions didn't tell you who he was, his extravagant outfits certainly did. Dressed like wrestling royalty in expensive robes, Flair's moneyed style told his story before he even stepped into the ring. Detailed with feathers, diamonds, sequins, and flashy colors, these elaborate costumes spared no expense. Ric Flair didn't mind splurging on expensive gear, because his lavish attire made fans believe that he was the best.

Ric Flair in signature robe. Photo by George Napolitano.

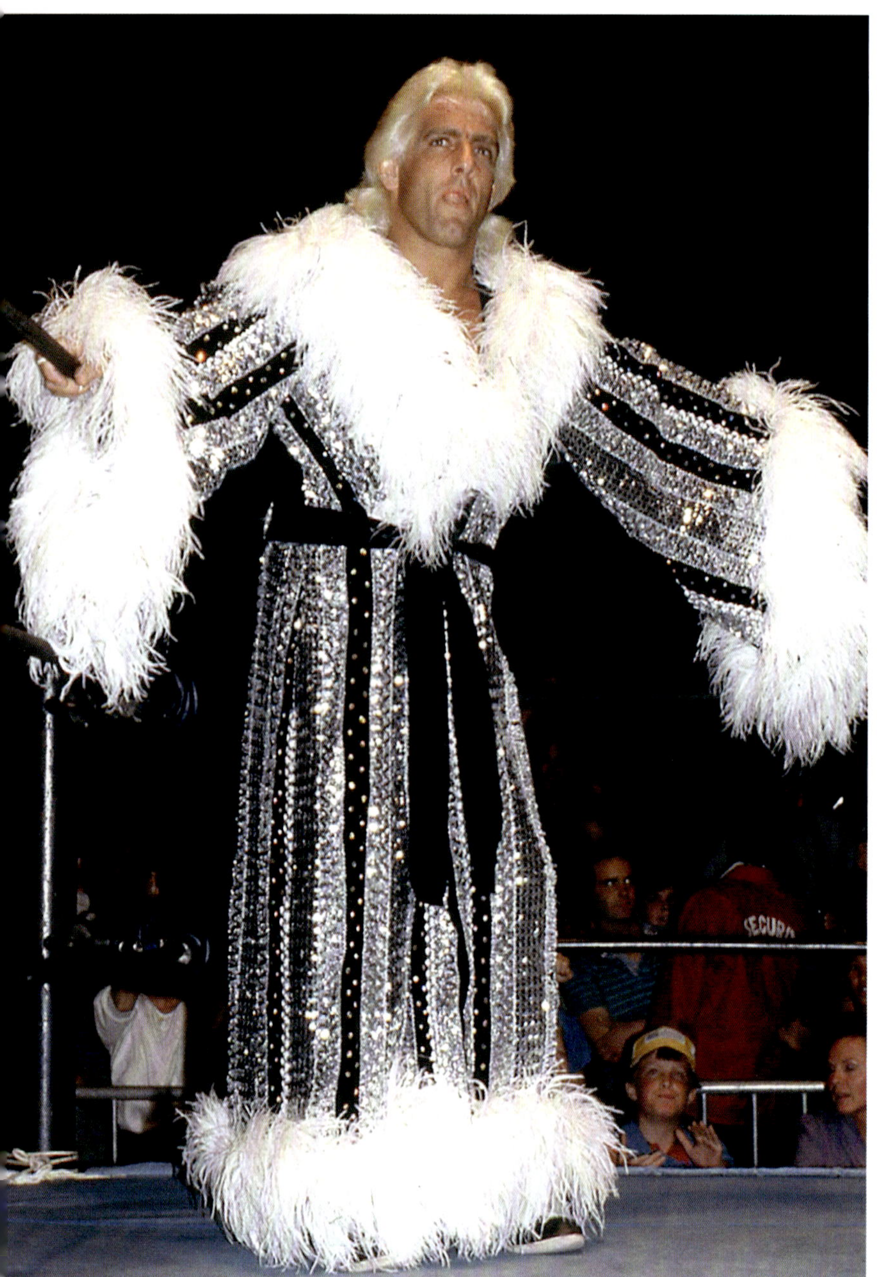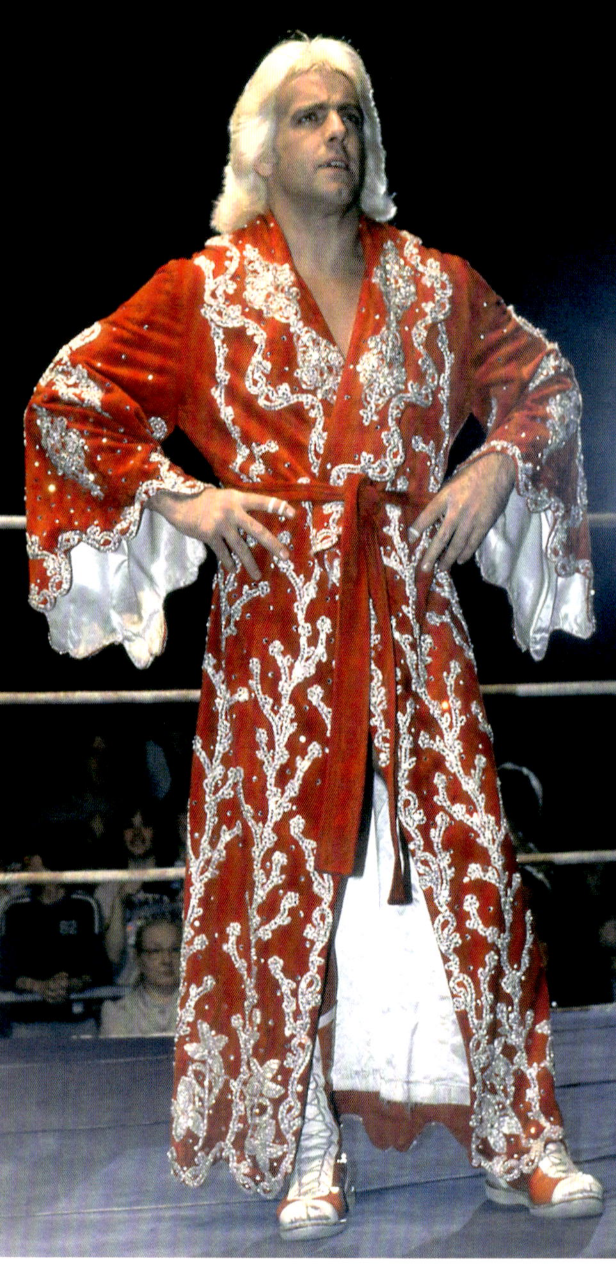

But dressing like a million bucks requires a lot of work. Terry Anderson, the costume designer who created several of Ric Flair's custom robes, said, "Ric would give me a color and I would go for it. I would change up the sleeves and do whatever pattern felt right. I would buy a bunch of different fabrics and things and start placing them. It would take me four days to make a robe, but those days would be twenty-hour days." Fortunately, all that hard work paid off. Not only did Flair's robes cement his status as wrestling royalty, but one of them is even hanging in a Smithsonian museum.

"I made Ric's retirement robe that is in the Smithsonian Institution today," said Anderson. "This robe is really cool because there are shots of him on the stage, coming down the ramp, where his arms are spread out, and there is a giant cape. When [Ric's] daughter Charlotte made her WrestleMania debut, I actually dug through my fabric scraps and found remnants of Ric's robe and

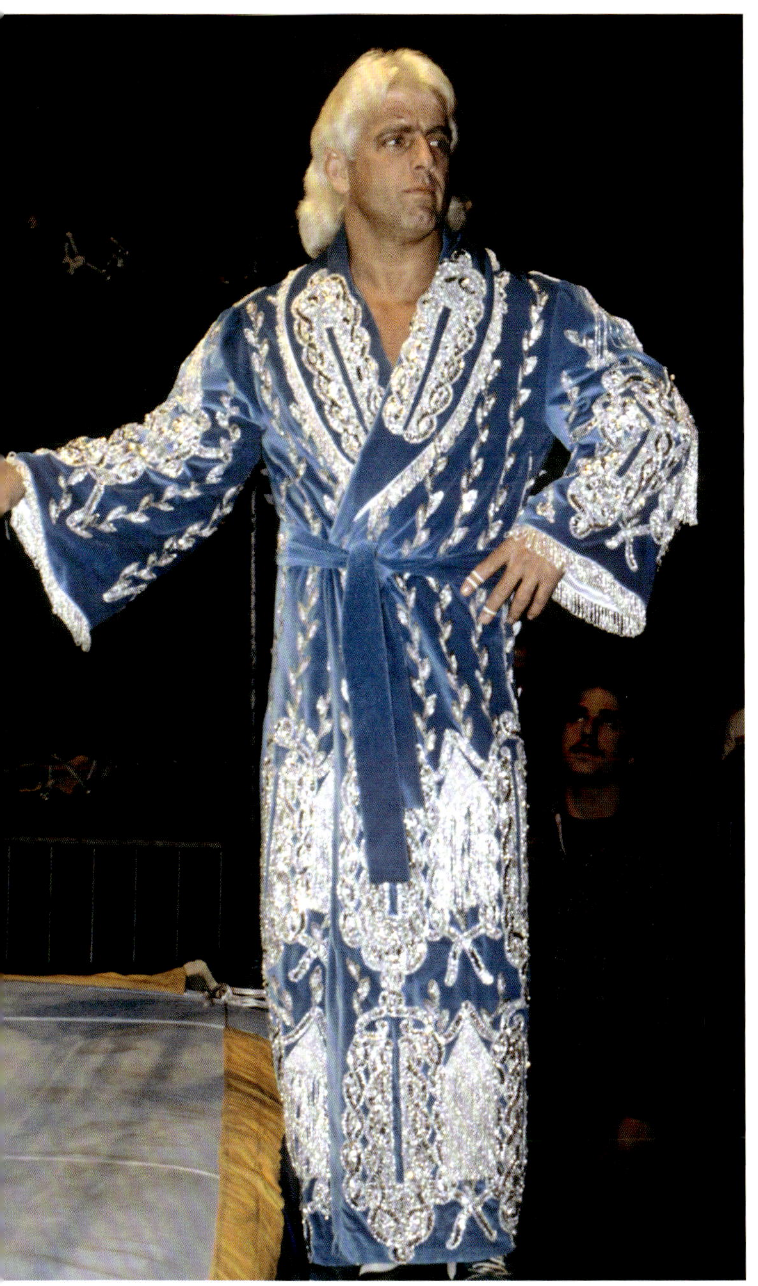

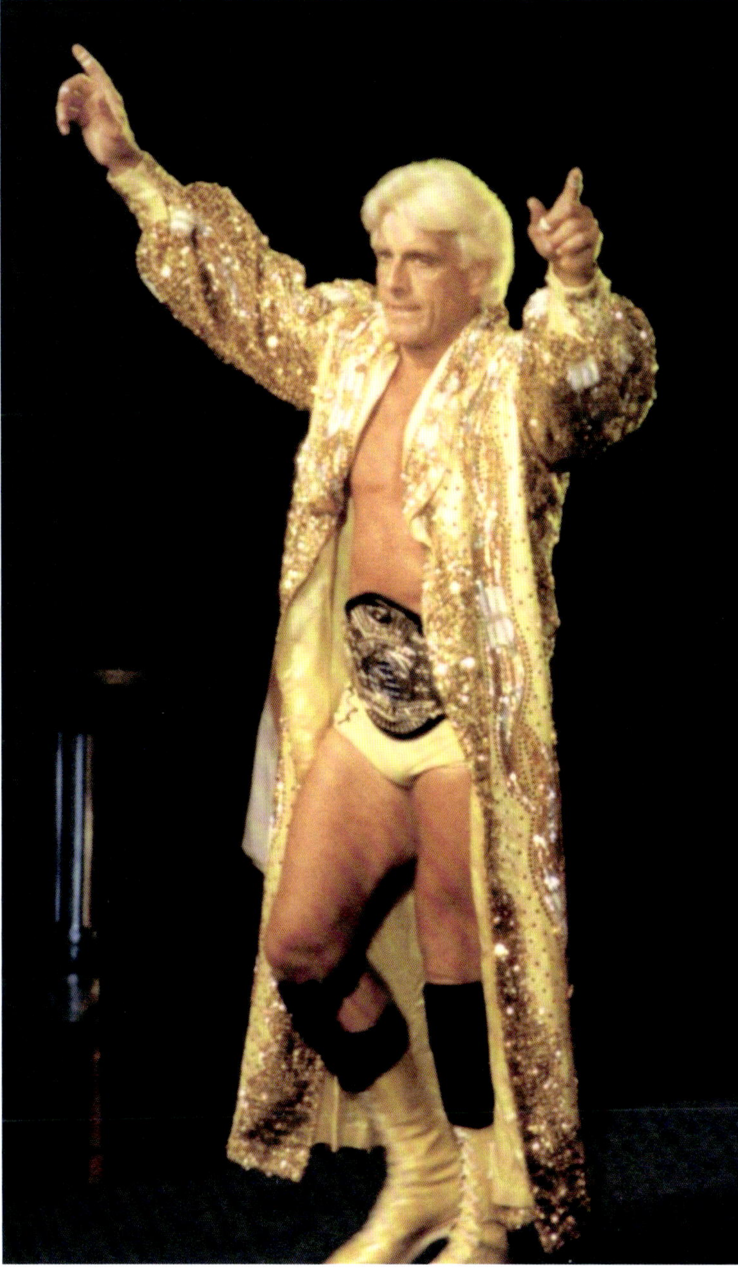



incorporated them into hers. The blue sequin fabric, the trim on the inside, and all of the [other] fabric on the inside were all bits from his robe." This thoughtful gesture served to cement Ric Flair's legacy among the next generation. "I remember hearing Kevin Dunn, who was the executive producer at the time, say, 'This is one of the most iconic photos.' Charlotte was in the same exact position as her dad in his retirement [photo], and no one knew at that point that Ric's fabric was part of her debut."

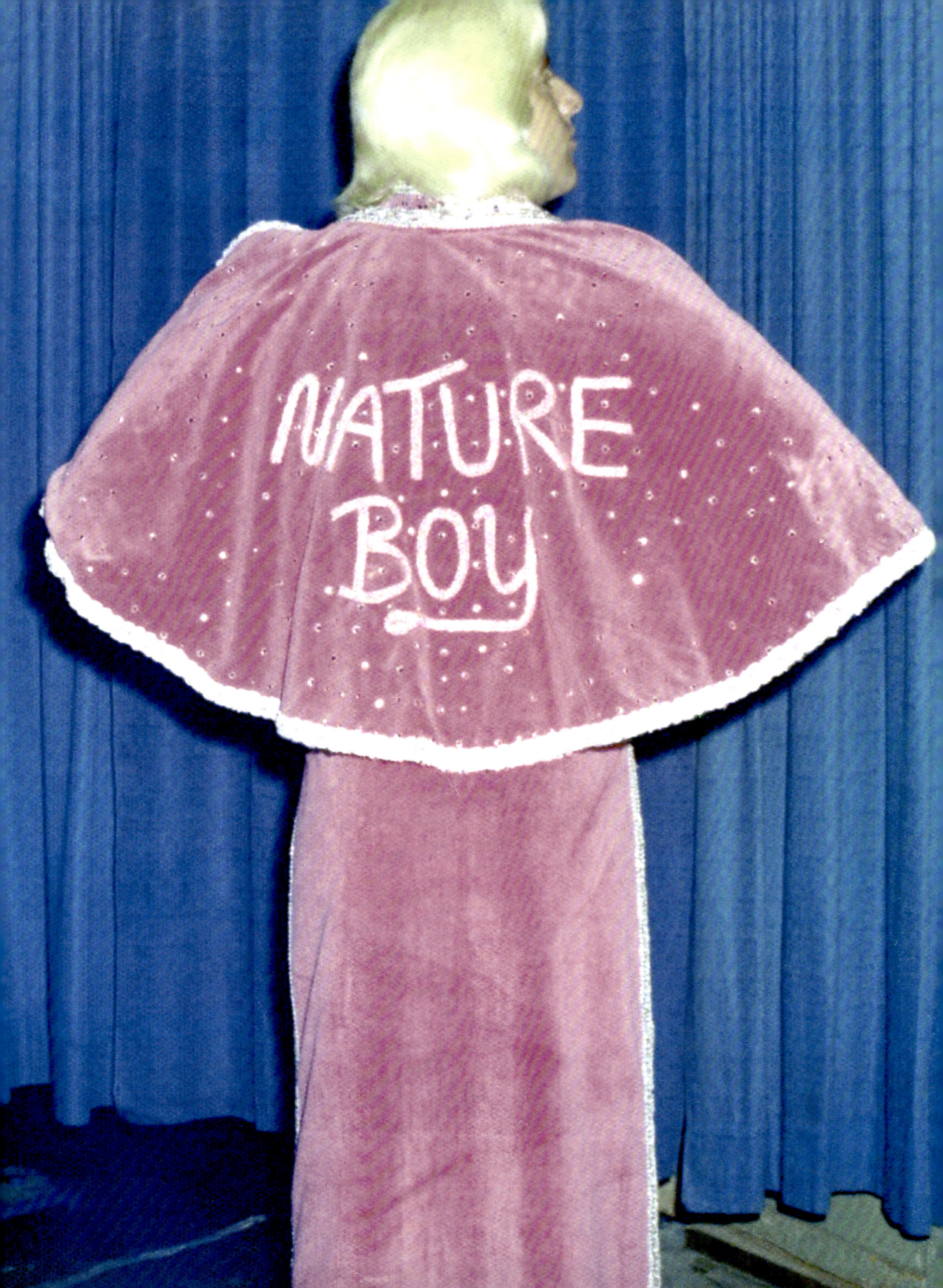

NATURE
BOY

As the leader of The Four Horsemen—alongside Arn Anderson, Ole Anderson, and Tully Blanchard—Ric Flair was also at the center of some of the biggest feuds in wrestling history. His notable rivalry with Ricky Steamboat comes to mind. These dramatically different individuals presented themselves as polar opposites not only in the way they fought but in what they wore. Flair shined in elaborate, embellished overcoats, while Steamboat channeled his martial arts roots with karate-influenced attire. Flair showed us materialism, cockiness, and excess, while Steamboat's minimalism spoke more for morality, honor, and dignity. This is only one example of Flair's excessive attire playing a major role in his being the ultimate showman—a true mark of his overall persona and legacy.

As a sixteen-time champion, the legend lured fans in with his stories and carefully crafted catchphrases, which are still echoed in arenas, at concerts, and on television today. Flair found ways to mesmerize an audience with showmanship. As he strutted down the ramp, he took his time to establish the atmosphere. As he got into the ring, he would slowly drop his robe, indicating that something big was about to happen. With that motion alone, it was as if he was signaling to the audience that they were lucky to witness his greatness. Decades later, Ric Flair is still remembered as one of the best professional wrestlers in history, in part because of his ability to put on a show. "The Nature Boy" Ric Flair will always be The Man.

**Wooo!**

Ric Flair at Madison Square Garden on March 1, 1976. Photo by George Napolitano.

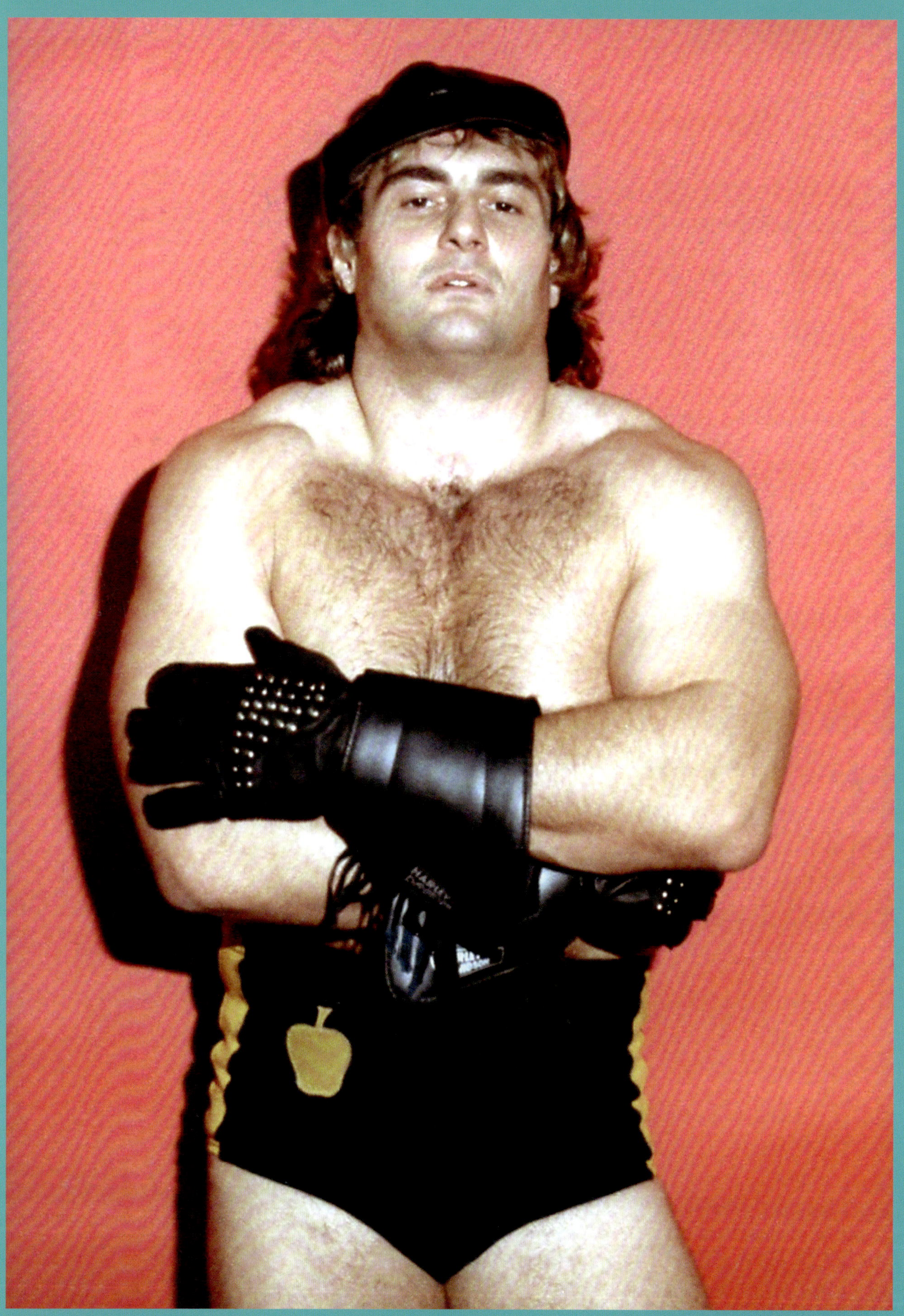

# KEITH ADONIS FRANKE
## ADRIAN ADONIS

Active 1974–1988

World Tag Team Champion

**Adrian Adonis may** be responsible for developing the drastic character evolution professional wrestling is now known for. Adonis started his career as a tough and rugged New York brawler, dressed in leather and streetwear. But after a few years in the ring, the tough-guy wrestler began to reinvent himself as Adorable Adrian Adonis, a flamboyant character. Jimmy Hart managed Adonis for a portion of his career and remembers how the evolution happened: "We were on a TNT show that Vince McMahon hosted, a lot like Johnny Carson, where you would sit on the couch, and they would throw questions at you. Vince knew how talented [Adonis] was, especially for his size, and I think he was at a point in his career where he was getting stale. Vince came up with the idea of him changing to Adorable Adrian Adonis, and they just let us run with it."

Now partial to pastels, sequins, and bleached blond hair with bows and ribbons, Adorable Adonis commanded attention and soaked up the limelight. Inspired by the late Gorgeous George's penchant for makeup, Adorable Adonis also began dabbling with blue eye shadow, blush, and pink lipstick to enhance his new persona. Fans were enchanted by Adorable Adrian Adonis's sequins and vibrant attire, which helped him stand out against his opponents. He wore leg warmers, scarves, capes, and hats, and though he remained a bruiser, Adorable Adonis dared to challenge convention in a world yet to fully embrace diversity—and fans loved him for it.

Adrian Adonis in brawler-style gear before becoming Adorable Adrian Adonis. Photo by George Napolitano.

**"George Scott was one of the biggest bookers back then. He gave me a thousand dollars one day in one of the towns and I went and bought every flower at one of the flower shops we found. We came back to the venue and got two-by-fours and cinder blocks and built the set of 'Flower Shop' that day. I wanted to bring Adrian onto the show like Ed McMahon did for Johnny Carson and go 'Here's Adorable Adrian!' It turned out to be something special, and something no one was doing at that particular time."**

—Jimmy Hart on the "Flower Shop" segment that led to Adrian Adonis versus Roddy Piper at WrestleMania

Adonis, who didn't do anything halfway, delighted in taunting and manipulating opponents to get under their skin. Flaunting his character with exaggerated mannerisms around the ring, Adonis basically begged the crowd to boo him. Adonis was bold and reeked of arrogance, but he believed in himself, causing the crowd to believe in him, too. He strutted alongside the ropes with his manager, Jimmy, and this unstoppable duo knew exactly how to get a reaction from the crowd.

But no matter the character he portrayed, Adonis was a scrapper in the ring who wasn't afraid to fight. Adorable Adrian Adonis only looked easy to beat, shocking opponents as he left them beaten and bruised after a match.

Gone too soon, Adonis deserves to be celebrated for his gusto, vigor, and showmanship. His iconic character paved the way for future generations of wrestlers to fearlessly embrace what makes them unique.

Adorable Adrian Adonis ringside. Photo by George Napolitano.

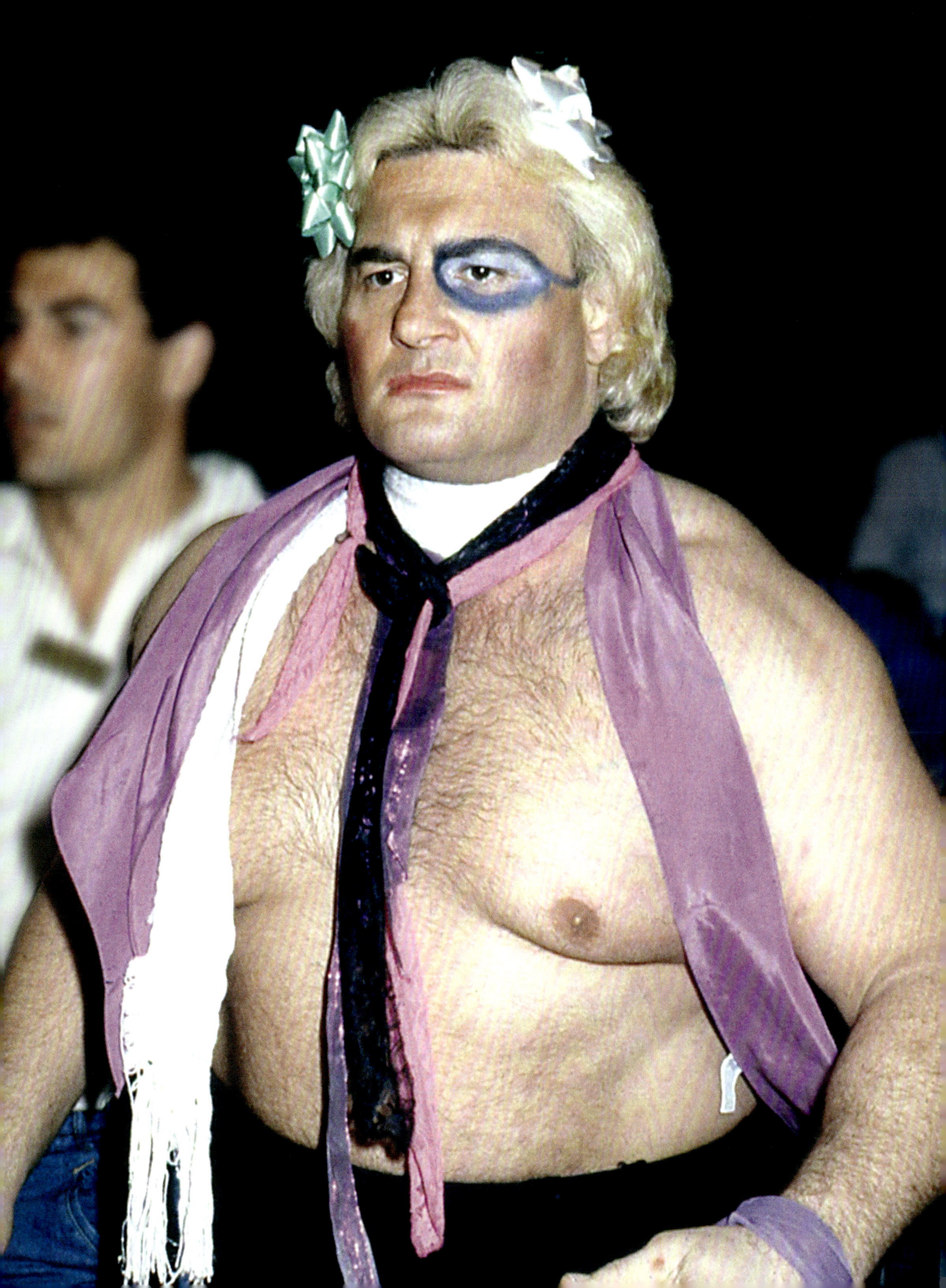

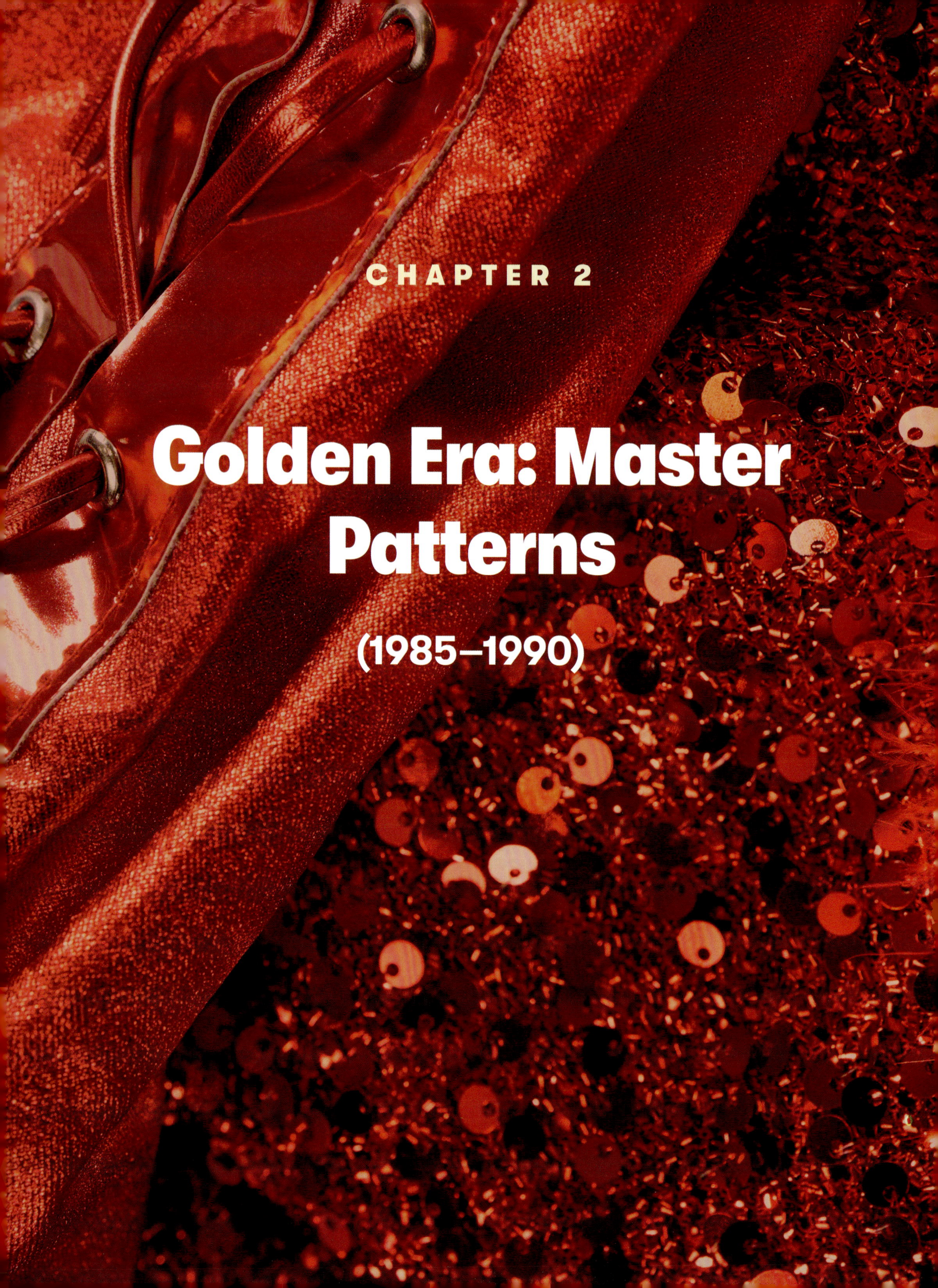


# Golden Era: Master Patterns

## (1985–1990)

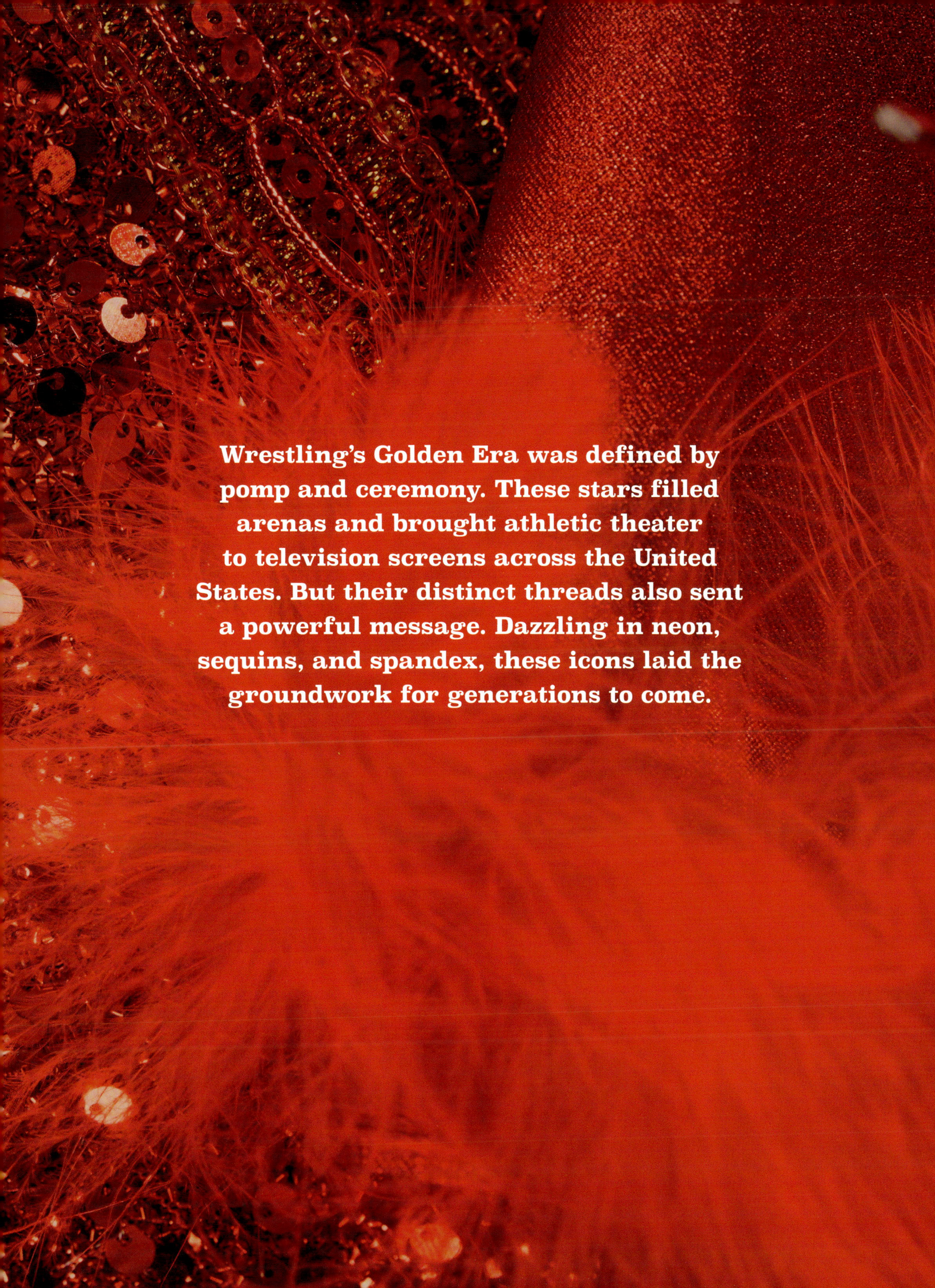
Wrestling's Golden Era was defined by
pomp and ceremony. These stars filled
arenas and brought athletic theater
to television screens across the United
States. But their distinct threads also sent
a powerful message. Dazzling in neon,
sequins, and spandex, these icons laid the
groundwork for generations to come.

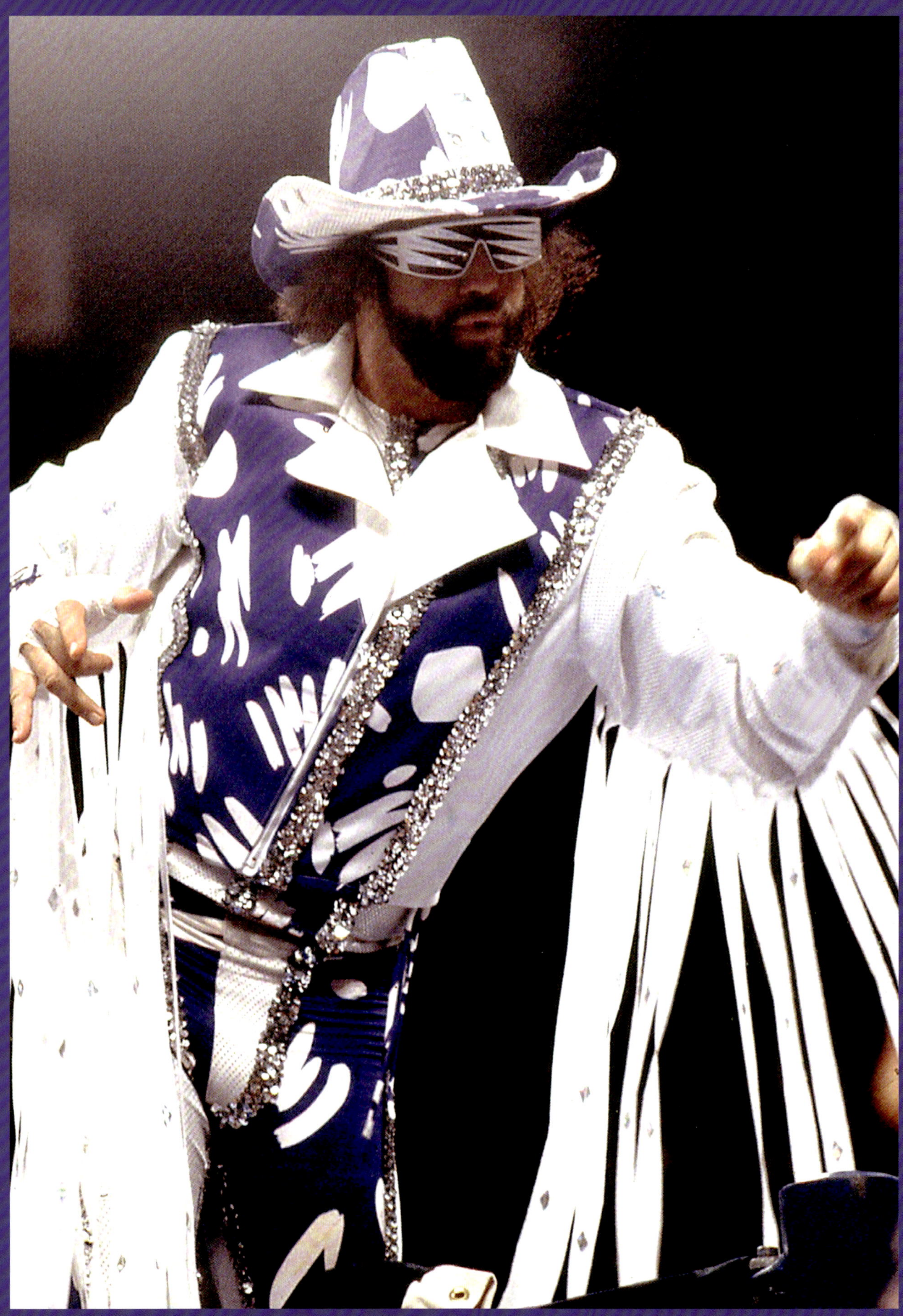

# RANDY POFFO
## "*MACHO MAN*" *RANDY SAVAGE*

Active 1973–2005

Ten-Time World Champion
WWE Hall of Famer

**Ooohhh yeah!!** "Macho Man" Randy Savage was as big of a star as they come. From his signature gravelly voice to his famous catchphrases, Savage was the perfect combination of skill, beauty, and personality. But while Savage's attitude and ability made him larger than life in the ring, his ostentatious neon attire cemented his trailblazing persona. He may also be single-handedly responsible for changing the way sequins are used in the industry. Savage used sequins in ways you wouldn't expect—they weren't just there, they were *everywhere*. From his illustrious capes to his headbands, Savage dazzled. He was also not shy in his utilization of tape, paint, and glitter. "[Randy] came in wearing sunglasses, which were just the ones he was wearing at the time," recalled Michael Braun, the seamster behind Macho Man's iconic looks. "I went and bought the same glasses and put tape and glitter on them."

Braun, who first met Savage early in his career, remembers how Macho Man's style developed over the years. "Randy came in the first time with a pair of shorts," said Braun. "He wanted two-inch letters across his tush that say *Macho Man* with three big stars in the front." But Braun, who was also making clothes for Jimi Hendrix at the time, encouraged Savage to go bigger. "I say, 'First of all, I'm not making any shorts at all. I need real estate from the floor all the way to your head,'" the seamster remembers saying. Savage was initially taken aback but eventually heeded Braun's advice, leading to a decades-long partnership that spanned Savage's thirty-two-year career.

"Macho Man" Randy Savage at WrestleMania 7 against Ultimate Warrior at the Memorial Coliseum in Los Angeles, California, in 1991. Photo by George Napolitano.

**"What I loved about Macho Man was that he could have a great match with anybody, and his promos were so captivating. I was fortunate enough to meet him backstage at a wrestling show, and it was like meeting a superhero. Even in gym clothes, Macho Man was larger than life."**

—Matt Cardona, professional wrestler and multi-time champion

Braun began by making neon shirts with tiny bits of fringe. Then he created five more outfits, including a purple getup with chains that Savage wore on *RAW*. The outfit got an incredible reception, giving audiences a glimpse of the flash and pizzazz that would become Macho Man's signature style. "He told me that he went into a private dressing room and when he came out the boys said, 'Wow, that's great!' He started walking down the hall, and Vince McMahon came up to him and said, 'Where did you get that? That's cool!' As he was standing in the opening about to go to the ring, they put a spotlight on him. In the words of Randy Savage, it really 'popped' and he got over," said Braun, who became Savage's personal seamster and produced hundreds of Macho Man's costumes.

Macho Man's style continued to evolve over the years. Soon aviator-style sunglasses, wide-brimmed hats, and elaborate crowns with amethyst-colored gemstones were part of Savage's stage persona. Braun remembers the day they discovered Macho Man's signature cowboy-esque hat: "He came into the shop one day and said he didn't want to wear the crown anymore because he was phasing out the Macho King look. So I took him to Ybor City in Tampa, which is an old Spanish section of the city. There was a hat store there that had every hat you could imagine because they could make a living off of Gasparilla. We tried on all these hats, from English bowlers to party hats. Cowboy hats were unknown at the time except in the movies on true cowboys. I bought four cowboy hats; some were felt, and others were straw. We covered the hats with fabric to match the outfits, with rings on the side of the brim, and I hand painted *Macho Man* on them. The hats took off."

TOP: "Macho Man" Randy Savage poses for the camera. Photo by George Napolitano.

BOTTOM: Randy Savage at The Match Made in Heaven, marrying Miss Elizabeth at SummerSlam 1991 in New York. Photo by George Napolitano.

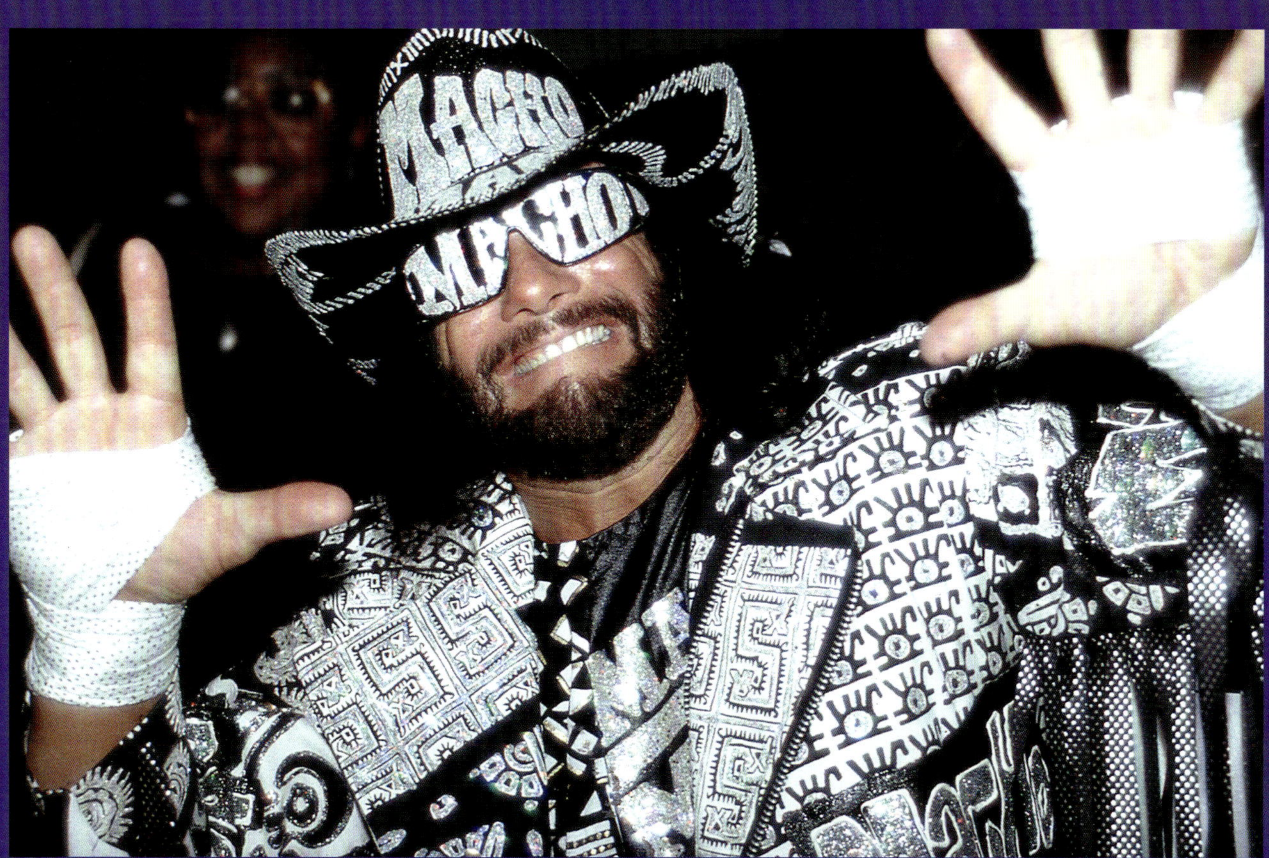

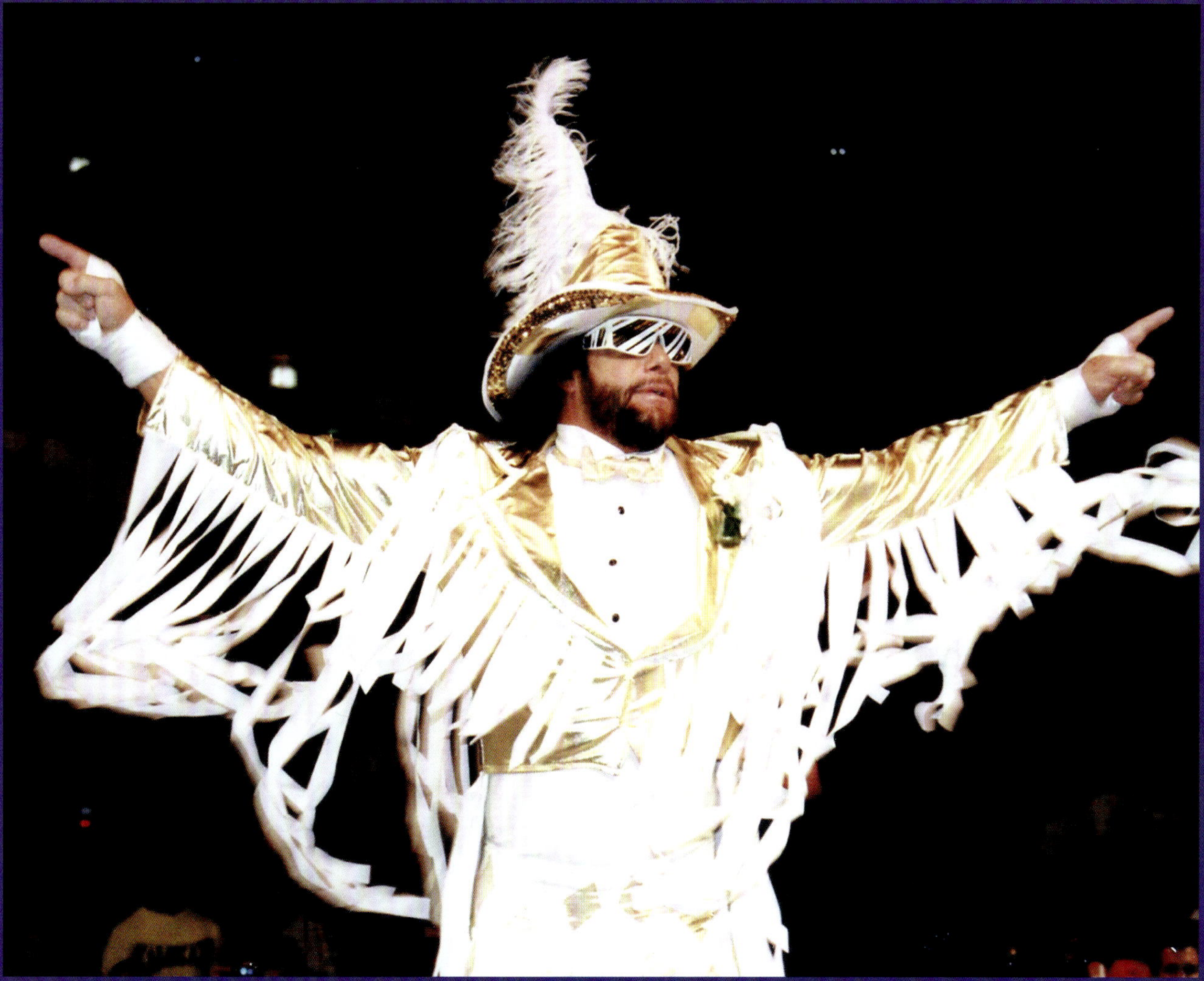

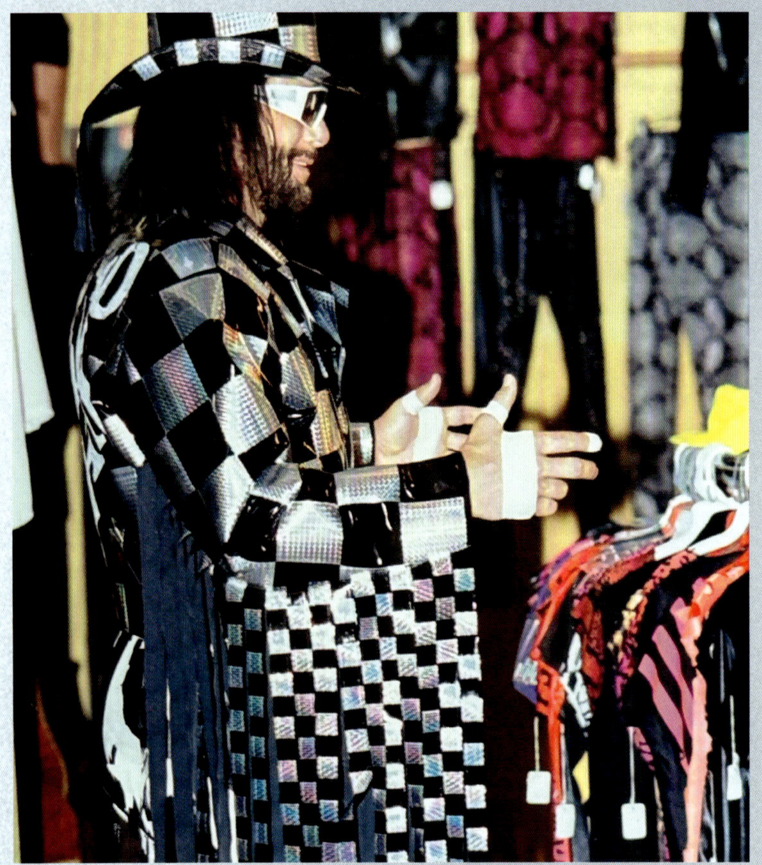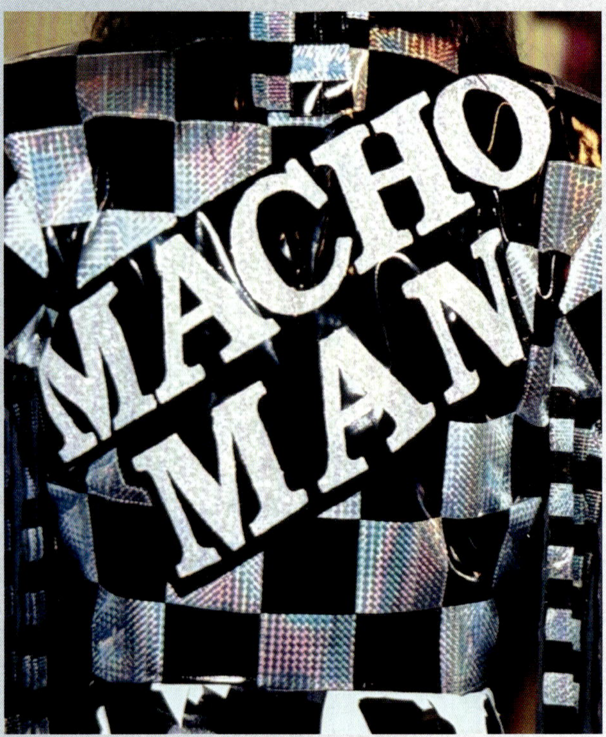



"When Randy would come into the shop, I would take pictures of him in the attire. Sometimes he would be barefoot, other times he would have socks, wrestling boots, or regular shoes on. This would improve my ability to make clothes for him. I needed to see the look in two dimensions. We needed to see what it would look like on television, in a one-hour wrestling show. I needed to compare what every other human that is part of the production looked like opposed to Randy—the audience, other wrestlers, referees, [wrestling valet] Miss Elizabeth, or the commercials. It wasn't about if I made it and I loved it. It was about what was eye-catching. If the commercials were better than Randy, it was no good."

—Michael Braun, personal seamster to "Macho Man" Randy Savage

All personal photos by designer Michael Braun at home in Tampa, Florida.

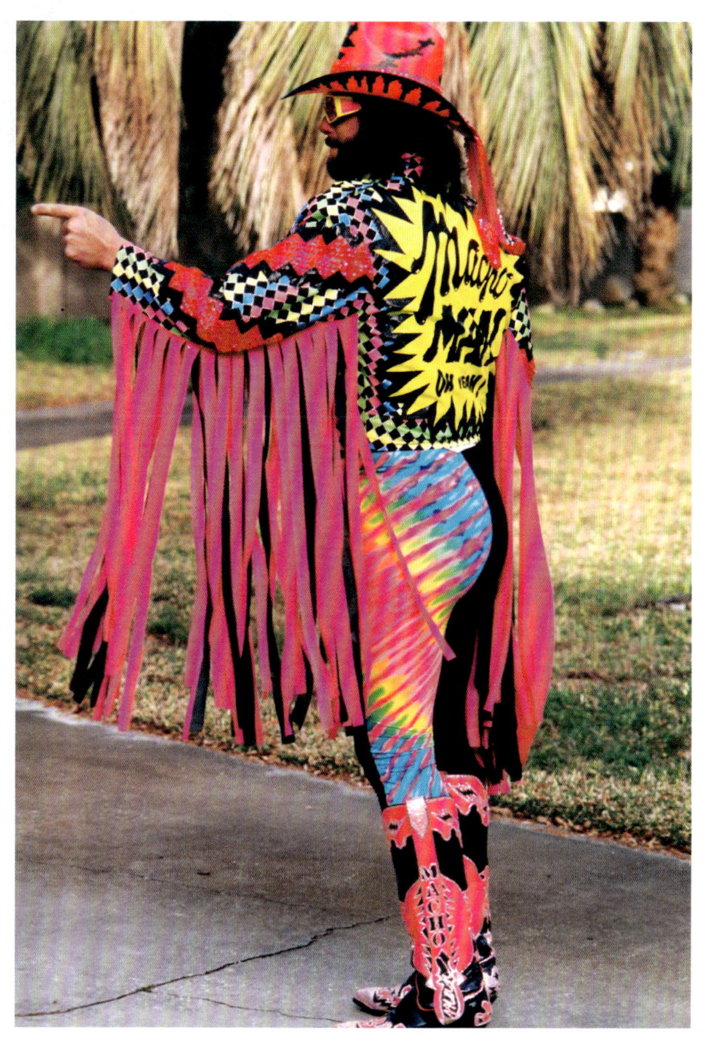
Macho
Man
Oh Yeah

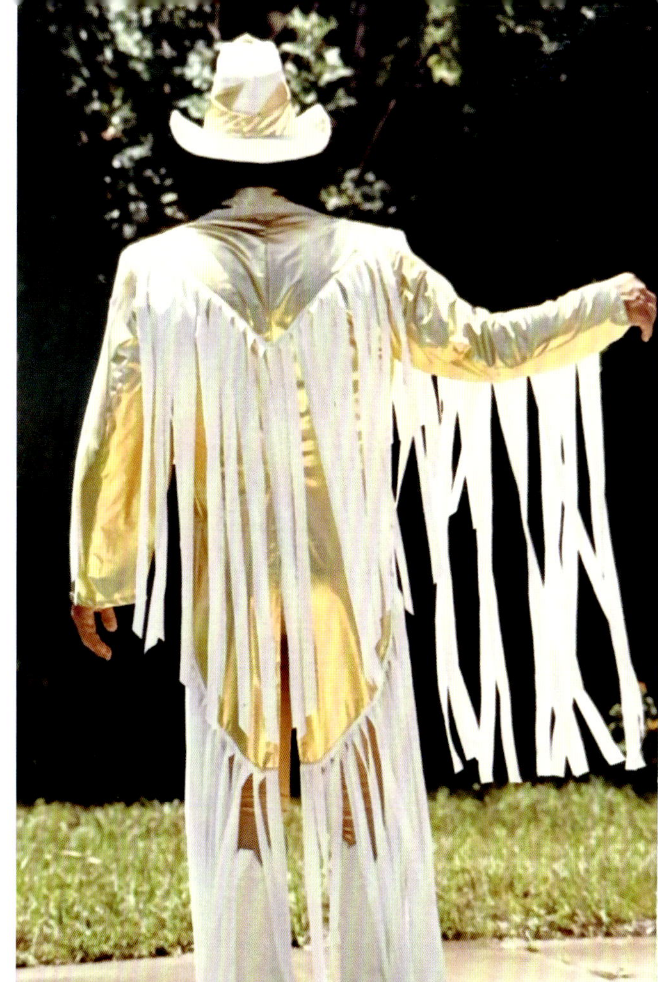

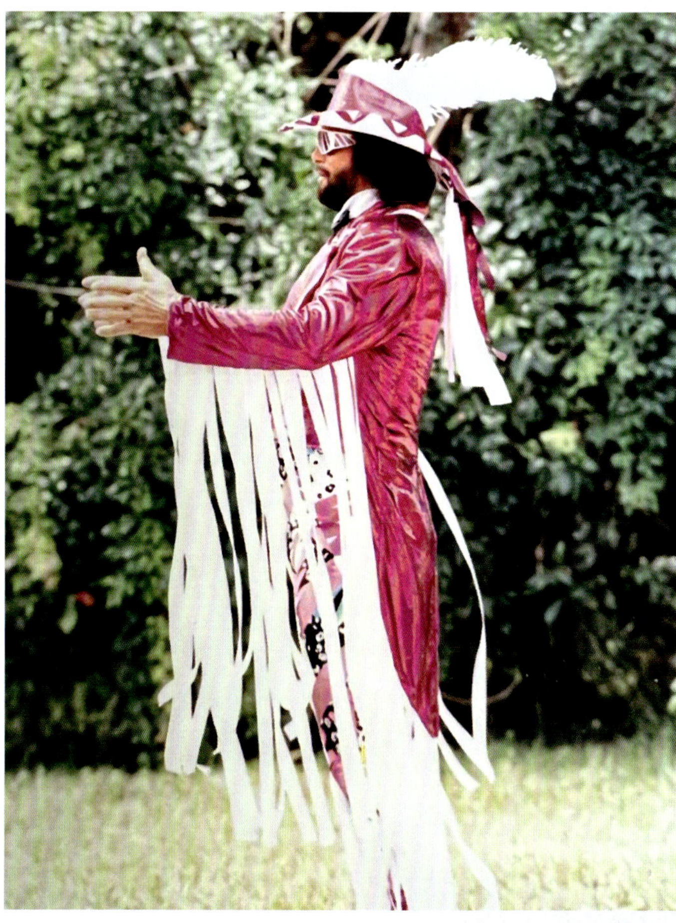

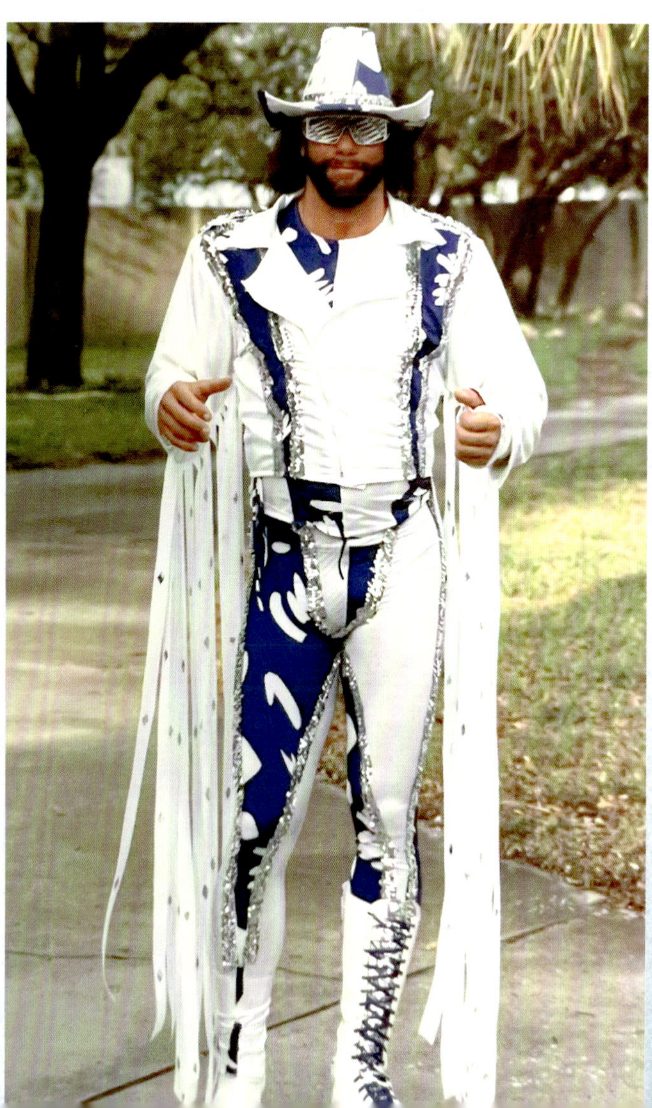

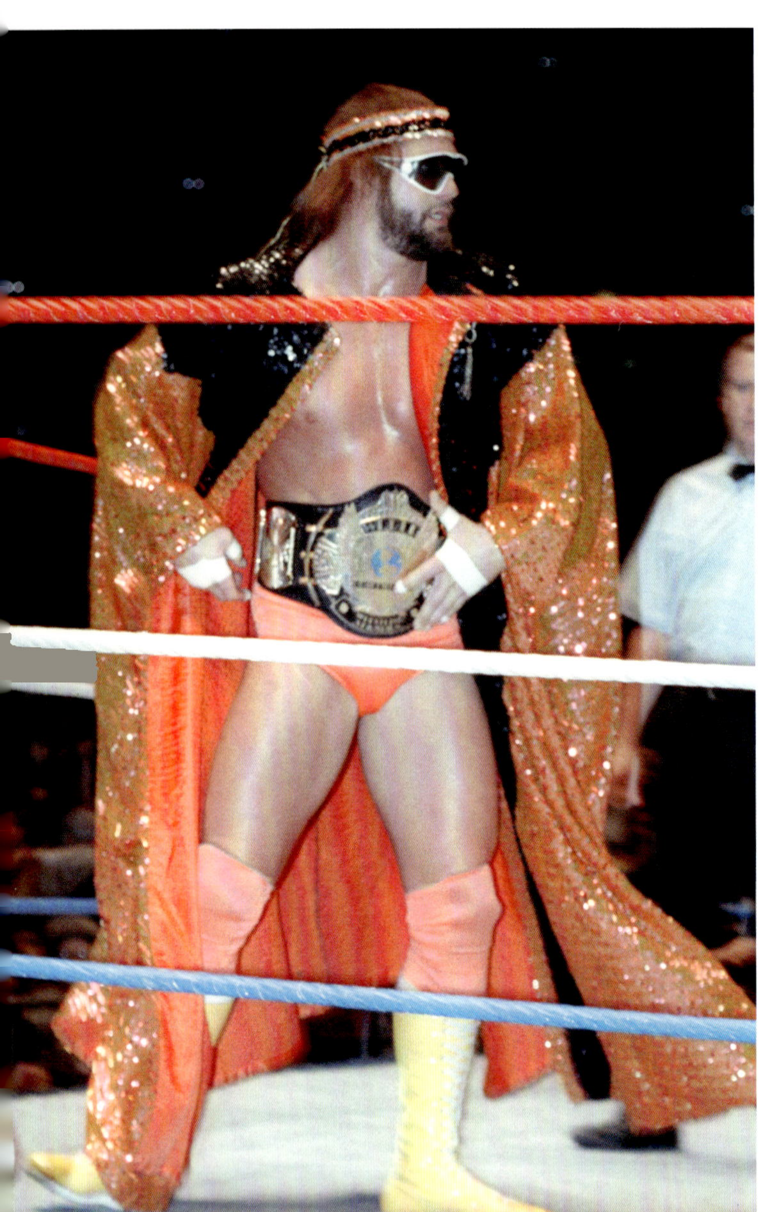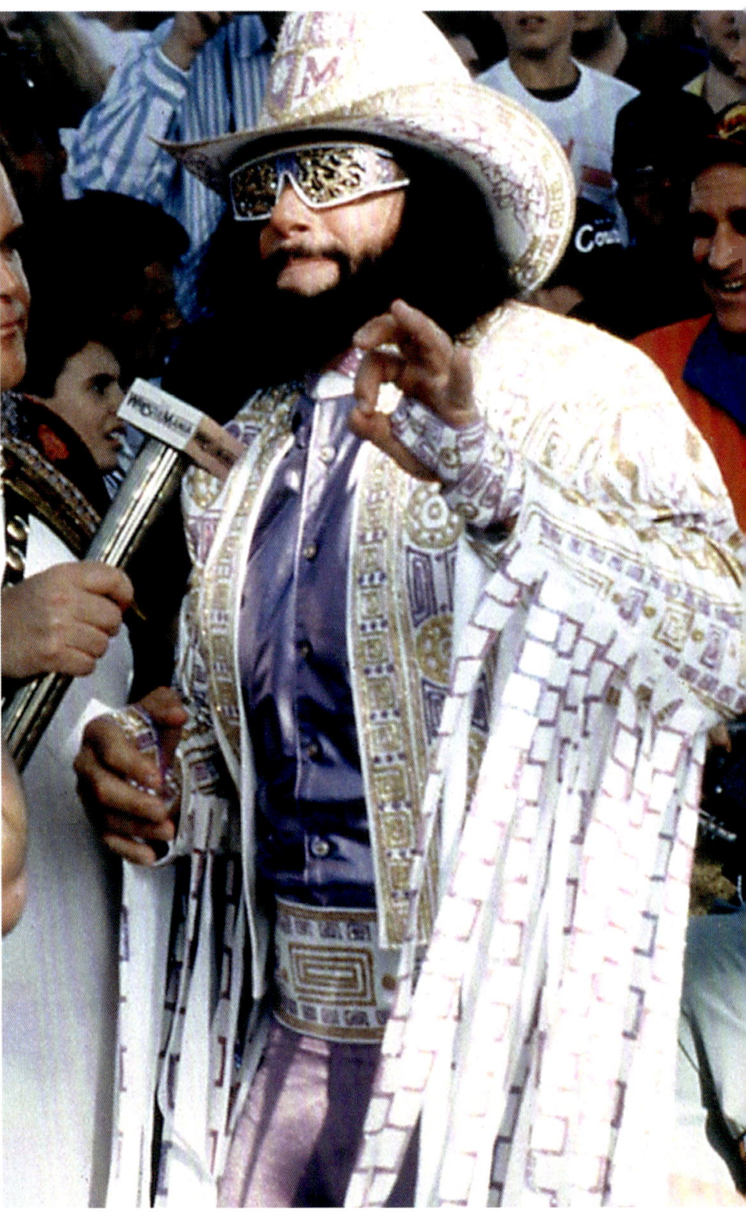

Savage was also distinct because, unlike other wrestlers, he rarely wore the same outfit twice. Savage wanted to stand out, and he didn't mind paying the price for stardom. Luckily for Savage, and all Macho Man fans, he had a visionary seamster in his corner. "There are only fifty-two weeks in a year, and I was making forty to forty-five outfits per year," said Braun, who raced to make new outfits as quickly as he could. "It would take me half a day to go buy fabric and half a day to cut the fabric. I would use another part day to write out everything I was doing for Vera [Braun's bookkeeper and close friend].

The only thing that would hinder the process was finding new, inspiring neon fabrics. I would go to proper ladies' fabric stores that catered to females in Clearwater, St. Petersburg, and Tampa. I would buy every type of bikini spandex fabric I could get my hands on."

Clearly, the gambit worked, and Savage's custom threads created a memorable character. More importantly, Macho Man's flamboyant style paved the way for other wrestlers to step outside their comfort zones and think bigger, louder, and bolder.

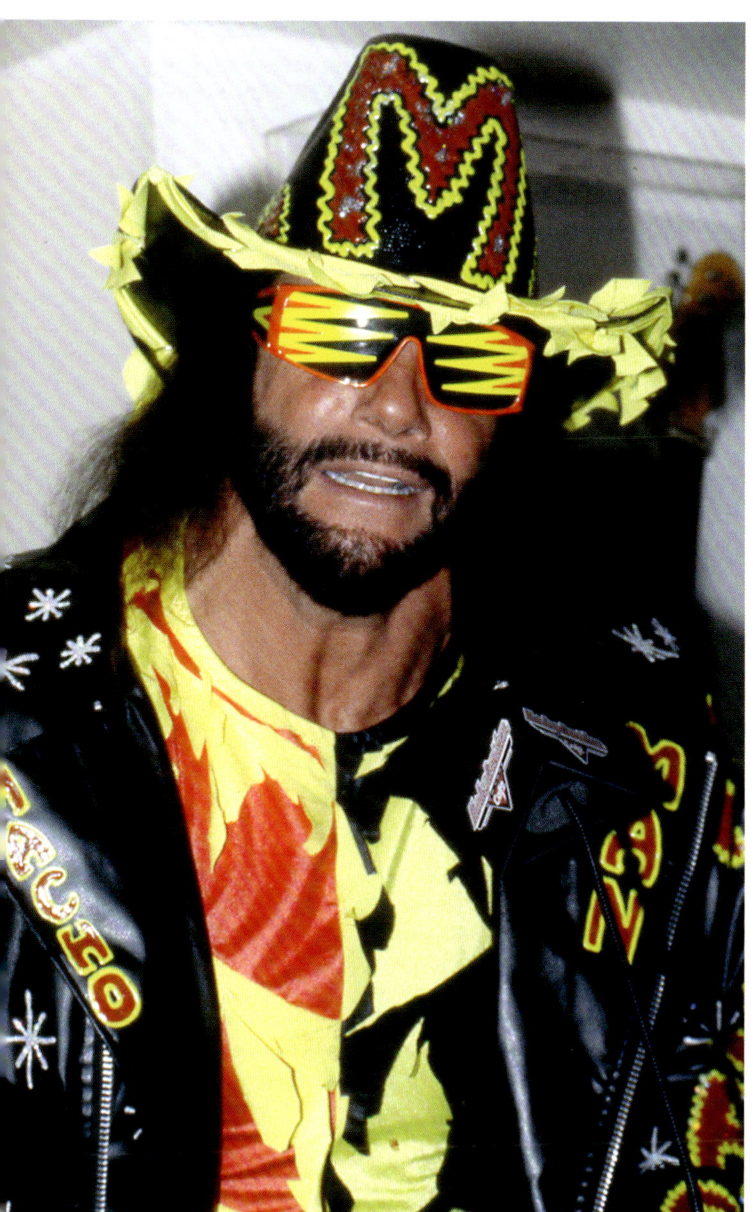

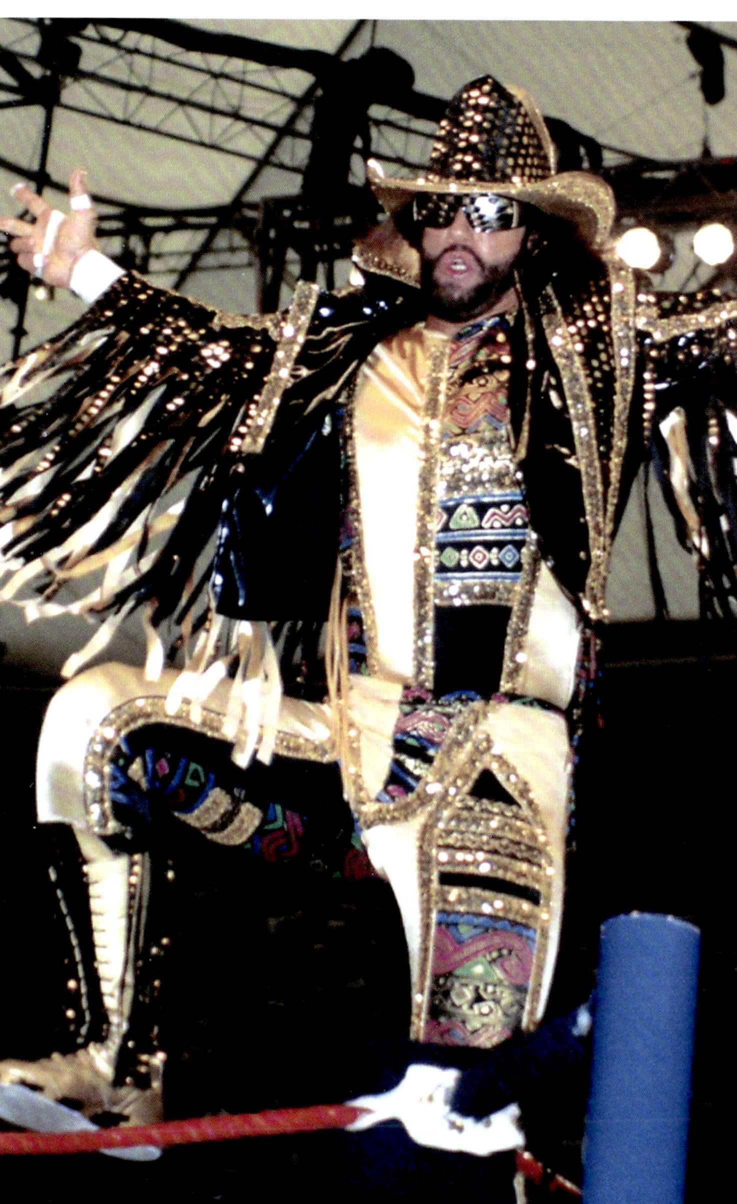



"I don't have one outfit I love the most because, at that time, I didn't have the time to admire the beauty. I just needed to make more clothes. I used to have drivers take me to fabric stores, so I wasn't having to think about driving or how to get there. This was because I wanted to have a free mind to play the game. I was creating art."

—Michael Braun

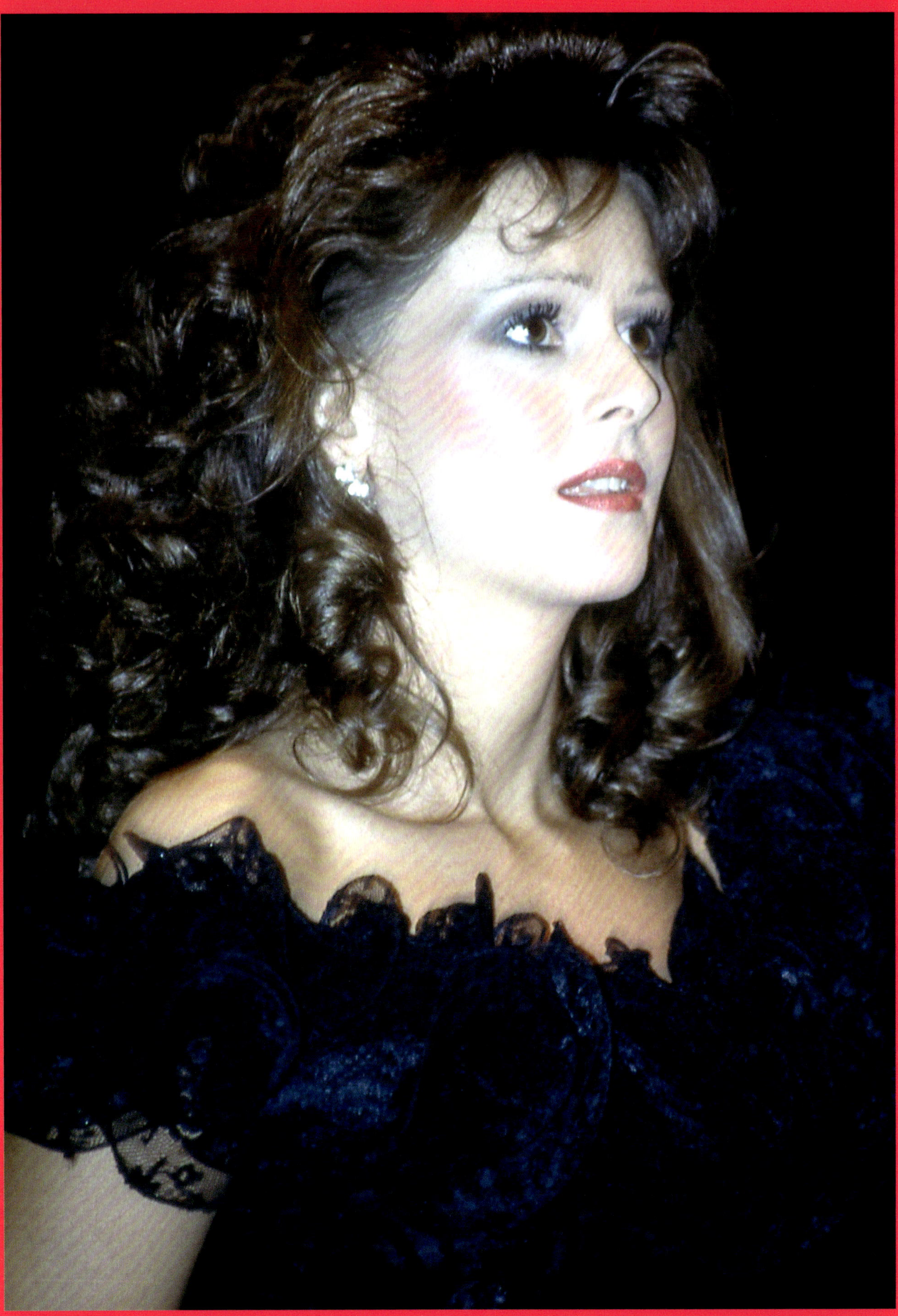

# ELIZABETH HULETTE
## MISS ELIZABETH



**She's beauty and** she's grace; Miss Elizabeth was a timeless icon. Widely acclaimed as one of the sport's most beloved wrestling valets, Miss Elizabeth was often known as the First Lady of Wrestling.

Elizabeth could usually be found with "Macho Man" Randy Savage, whom she managed and married, though she still found ways to hold her own as a star. Every king needs a queen, and with Savage and Elizabeth, this saying proved true. As Macho Man strutted around the ring, Miss Elizabeth became the perfect foil. Macho Man was brash and loud, but Miss Elizabeth quietly elevated each moment with her presence alone.

Miss Elizabeth was much more than just a manager or wrestling valet. She was a trailblazer in her own right. Miss Elizabeth proved women could play a central role in professional wrestling, validating women throughout the industry. Miss Elizabeth's outfits also channeled her vision of what female wrestlers could look like. Wearing elegant gowns, glamorous jewelry, and modest skirts, she showed that women wrestlers didn't have to be scantily dressed to get attention. They could be both classy and sexy.

Miss Elizabeth could pull off just about any look. With her big hair and giant accessories, she was the epitome of an '80s heartthrob. Sometimes she wore satin opera gloves, cutting a glamorous figure in the ring. She often dazzled in diamonds and pearls—in fact, she frequently looked like a Hollywood star, commanding attention through her sophistication. Some women were brash and loud, but Miss Elizabeth took a different approach—she was elegant and poised, making powerful statements through her thoughtful attire and actions.

Elizabeth was a genius at identifying critical flash points in her partner's match, always positioning herself in the right place at the right time to distract opponents with her beauty. A simple smile and wave from Miss Elizabeth made fans and rivals swoon. In times of distress, Elizabeth communicated worry and fret, convincingly playing the damsel in distress—but she knew what she was doing. Every gesture was strategic. In a male-dominated industry that could be rough around the edges, the First Lady of Wrestling provided a refreshing antidote to the usual mayhem with her steady presence and poise.

Miss Elizabeth. Photo by George Tahinos.

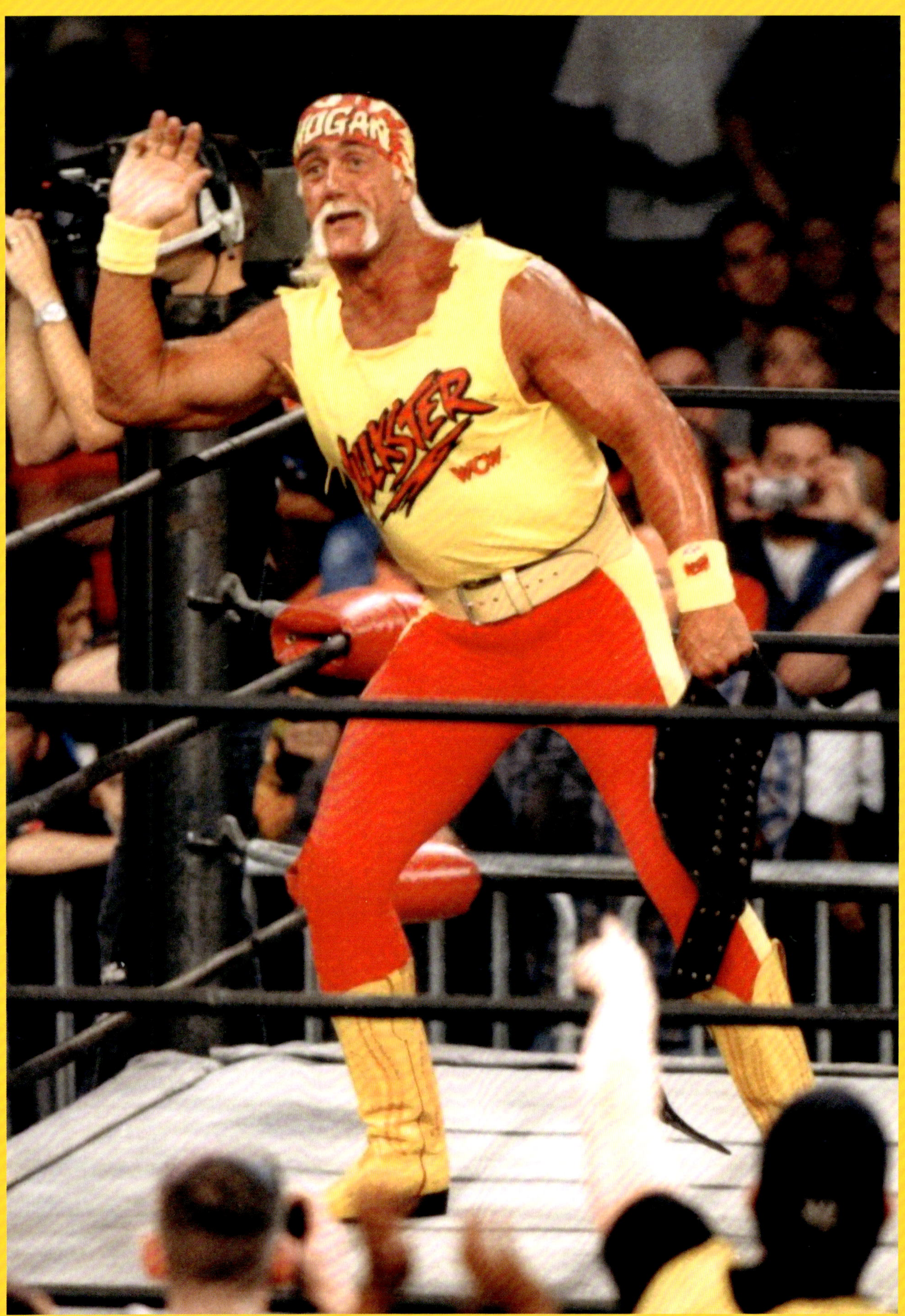
HOGAN
HULKSTER
WCW

# TERRY BOLLEA
## *HULK HOGAN*

Active 1977–2012

Six-Time WWE Champion
WWE Hall of Famer

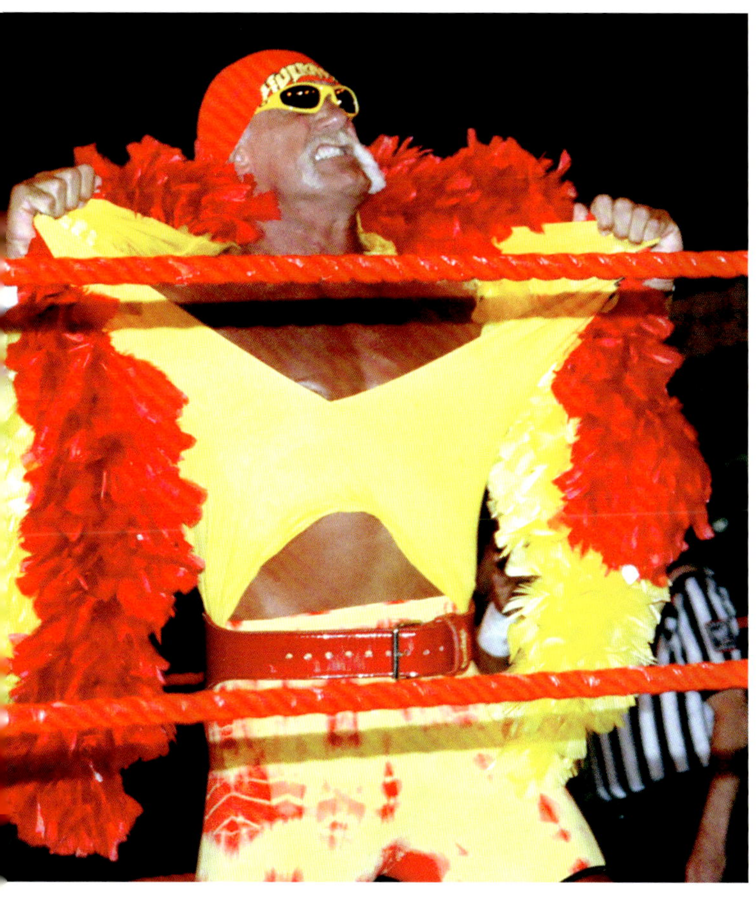

OPPOSITE: Hulk Hogan in WCW.
Photo by George Tahinos.

ABOVE: Hulk Hogan in signature
red-and-yellow attire during his last
WWE run. Photo by George Tahinos.

**With his muscular build,** colorful gear, and patriotic flair, Hulk Hogan often looked like a superhero wrapped in American pride. Exhibiting a large personality and a larger-than-life persona, Hogan wowed fans throughout his thirty-five-year career with his tanned physique and flamboyant style. Whether his T-shirt read *Hulkmania* or *Hollywood*, he created an experience for fans by ripping it in half in front of their eyes. Hogan was known as much for his memorable antics as for his sheer athleticism. Flexing his muscles and striking poses, he allowed fans to bask in his glory as he entered the ring or celebrated a win. Cupping his hand to his ear or iconically pointing his finger at rivals was part of his routine. Hogan flaunted his limitless power as an athlete by taunting opponents with slogans like "Whatcha gonna do, brother?" Meanwhile, he advised young fans to "say your prayers and eat your vitamins."

On top of his skill and showmanship, Hogan was a pro at curating clothes to sell his story. Often wearing red-and-yellow attire that featured big lettering, he created a visual that was easy to read and understand. Today, there are very few wrestlers whom fans immediately associate with specific colors—Hogan is one of them. This speaks to the gravity and impact Hogan had on the industry. He usually wore sunglasses and a bandana, signaling his cool factor and relatability to the everyday working man.

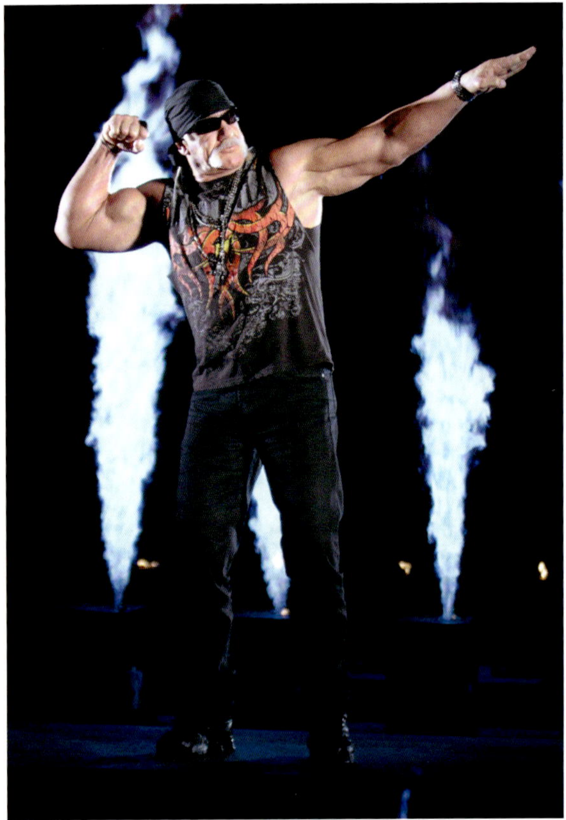

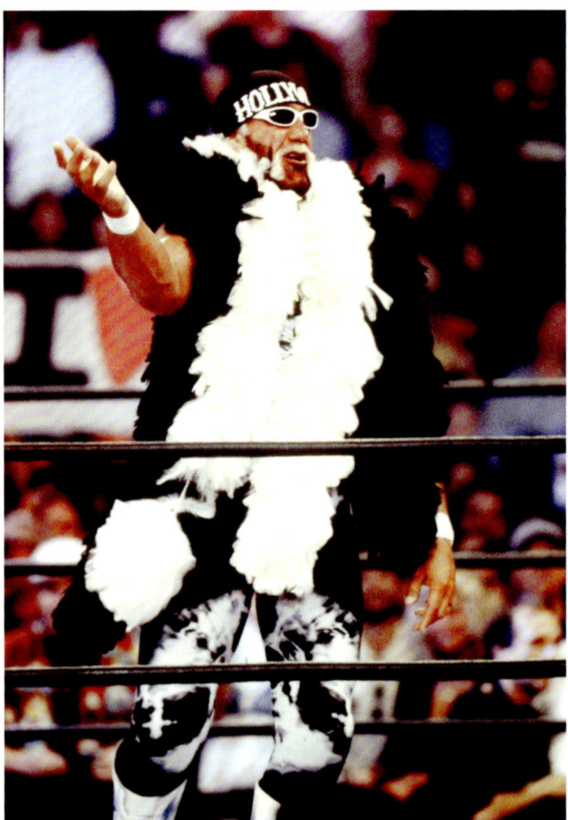

A cross chain dangling from his neck repre-sented his religous beliefs. In the late '90s, Hogan began accentuating his look with a red-and-yellow feather boa, adding even more movement and pizzazz to his over-the-top, rock star persona.

In 1996, Hogan shocked the world by ditching his good guy persona to lean in to a darker side. As "Hollywood" Hulk Hogan, the bad-boy leader of nWo (New World Order), Hogan maintained his signature style but mixed up the way he wore it. Ditching the bright yellows and reds synonymous with his original character, Hogan began wearing black and white to signal his membership in the rebellious wrestling faction. The wrestler still rocked his signature bandanas, but now he wore them in black with spray-painted motorcycle jackets and tactical gloves, giving his look more edge and setting the tone for a new version of Hulk Hogan. Keeping his bleached blond mustache and mullet, he dyed the rest of his facial hair black,

creating contrast that was impossible to miss. By donning bandanas and boas, Hogan maintained his iconic look, but with a different approach.

After leaving nWo in 1999, Hogan reverted back to his iconic red-and-yellow gear, and his celebrity spread from wrestling into acting and then rippled around the world. Hogan's longtime friend and former manager Jimmy Hart compares Hogan's universal recognition to another brand that is known worldwide: "There's a reason McDonald's is still in business after all these years," said Hart, referring to the bright red-and-yellow hues still associ-ated with Hulkamania. "When he landed on the red and yellow, it was a home run. When Hogan was in Minnesota [wrestling for AWA], he was able to make his own T-shirts and sell them out of the trunk of his car. That's when it all clicked for him. Hulk has made so much money in his business. You really don't make money in this business unless you know what the heck you're doing, and he does."

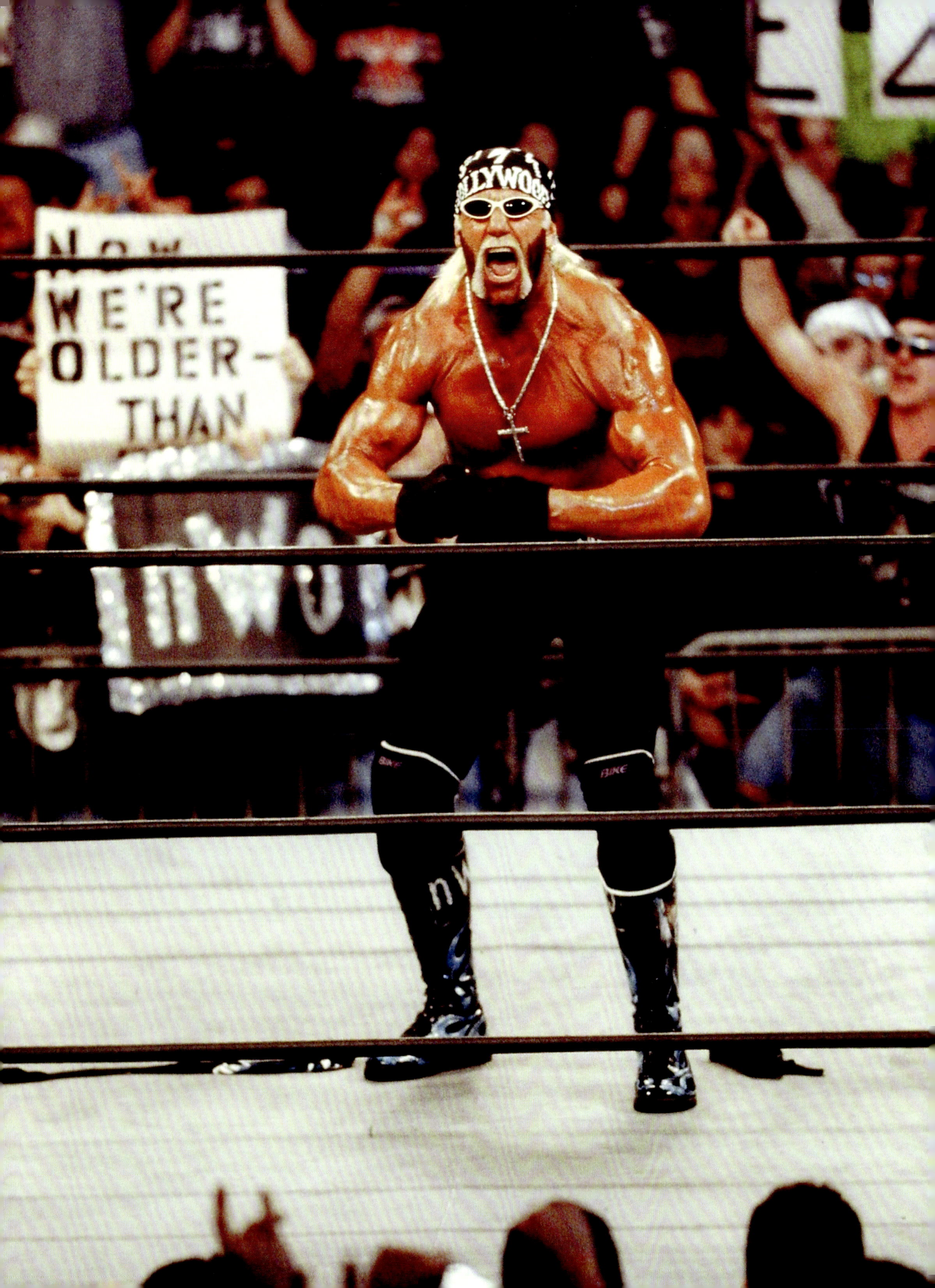

NOW
WE'RE
OLDER-
THAN
nWo

# WAYNE FARRIS
## *HONKY TONK MAN*

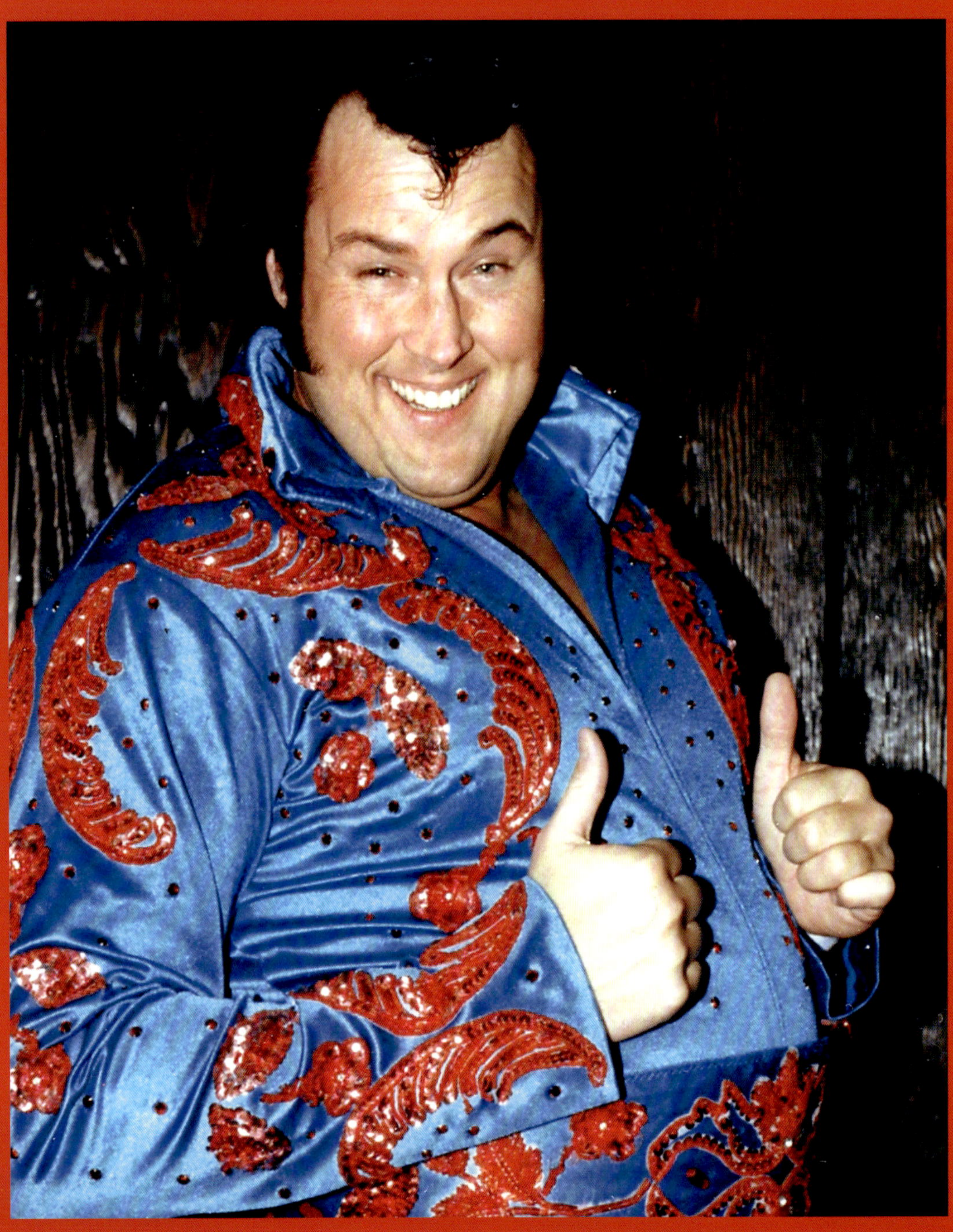

Active 1977–2019

WWE Intercontinental Champion
WWE Hall of Famer

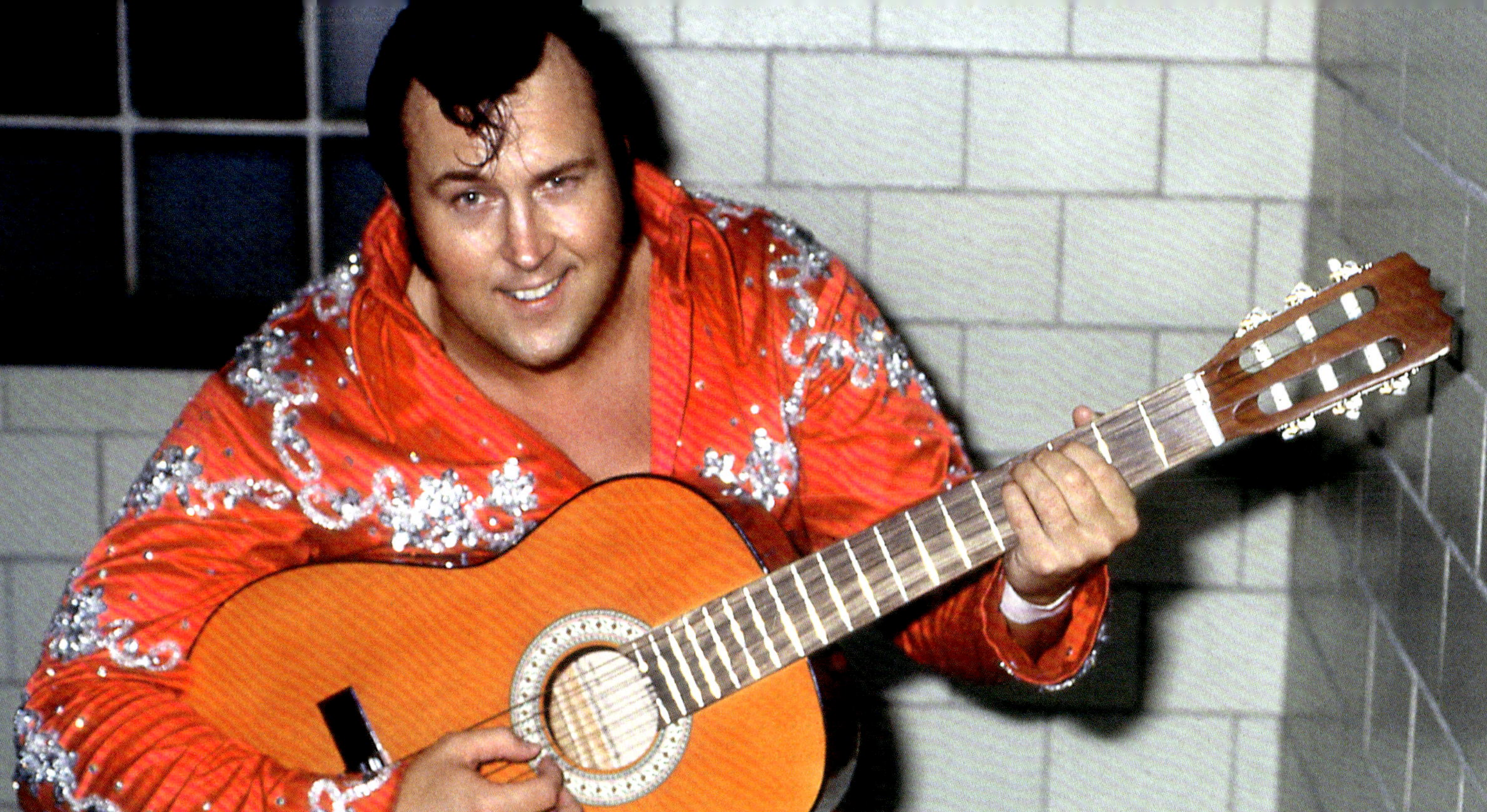



**In the world** of professional wrestling, there are good guys and bad guys. Wayne Farris, globally known as The Honky Tonk Man, was one of the baddest guys to do it. He was a legend fans loved to hate. As a character, Farris captivated people with his haughty attitude and outrageous antics. He took fans on a journey; he wrapped them up in a moment, then left them enraged by his ego. Taking inspiration from The King of Rock 'n' Roll, Farris imitated Elvis's iconic look, sideburns and all.

But though Farris capitalized on The King's appeal, he proceeded to build The Honky Tonk Man into a distinct character. Dazzling in sequins, rhinestones, and one-piece jumpsuits, Farris wasn't afraid to sing his own praises and delighted in playing the bad guy. "He started out as an Elvis impersonator, but Wayne Farris made the character of Honky Tonk Man what it was," said former opponent Terry Taylor. "He took that persona however far to get his foot in the door and then created this whole character. He spoke a certain way, wrestled the way he did, and connected to an audience in a big way."

But unlike Elvis, who had millions of fans worldwide, The Honky Tonk Man carried out antics that weren't usually well received by the audience. Jimmy Hart managed Farris for some of his career and said, "When he became The Honky Tonk Man in Memphis, he was one of The Blond Bombers [tag team with Larry Latham]. When he came to Pensacola, Florida, he had sideburns, jet-black hair, and put the Elvis jumpsuit on. The heat was instant. The way he dressed, the way he looked, wrestled, and interviewed. He stood out more than anything."

In the ring, he would lie, cheat, or sneakily find other suspect ways to win. The legendary bad guy also bragged about his skills and accomplishments, which only amplified the disgust of spectators. Acting as a nuisance came naturally for The Honky Tonk Man, who became one of the biggest villains in wrestling. But unlike other bad guys, Farris had the talent to back up his bravado. No one can deny Farris's success as the second-longest-reigning Intercontinental Champion, a title he held for thirty-five years, while his electrifying appeal, charisma, and guitar smashes revolutionized the sport. Love him or loathe him, The Honky Tonk Man strutted his way into wrestling history with swagger that was cool, cocky, and bad to the bone.

TOP AND OPPOSITE: Honky Tonk Man poses backstage. Photos by George Napolitano.

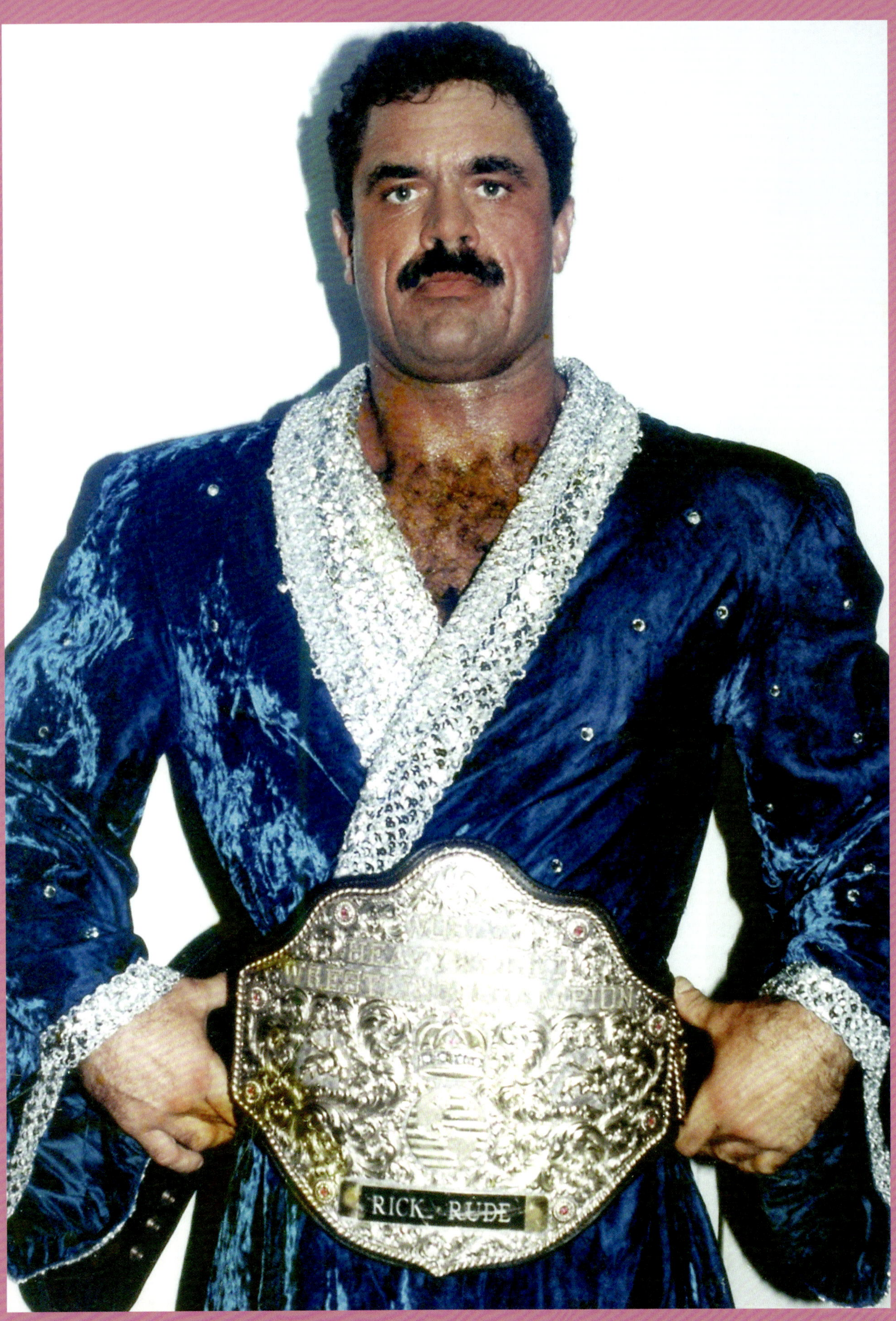

WORLD
HEAVYWEIGHT
WRESTLING CHAMPION
RICK RUDE

# RICHARD ROOD
## *RICK RUDE*

Active 1982–1994

Two-Time Intercontinental Champion
WWE Hall of Famer

**Proving that some athletes** can have and be it all, Rick Rude was as ravishing as he was talented in the ring. Called "Ravishing" Rick Rude for good reason, he used his charm and wit to bond with the ladies in the crowd. This only made men loathe him more—and that's exactly what he wanted. In the Golden Era, he dared to be different, truly *the* example of what a confidence-driven character should be.

Rude was flashy, the cockiest of competitors, and there wasn't a line he wouldn't cross. Terry Taylor, Rude's former opponent and colleague, revealed the genius in this strategy: "Behind the scenes, that guy had no ego and was pretty quiet. You would think with his character, he would be hard to get along with and a bad businessman, but he was one of the easiest guys to wrestle. In front of a crowd, everything he did was to have people boo him. He understood if he could get beat up by the good guy that was the big star, he would be in the mix and make a ton of money. All the stuff he did, I know for a fact, was business. Putting Jake Roberts's wife's face on his tights, kissing a girl as she swooned and laying her down at his feet. Every dude was thinking, 'I hate that guy because I can't do that.' Everything he did was for the good guy to have a foil with the audience so they could get into the good versus evil."

Ravishing Rick Rude as WCW International World Heavyweight Champion. Photo by George Napolitano.

"Ravishing" Rick Rude was a true showman, and as Taylor noted above, he used his looks to great effect. But Rude wasn't *just* a pretty boy—the wrestler was also known for his blood-boiling feuds and intellectual combat. One of his favorite tactics involved employing his gear to tell his story and taunt his opponents. He'd express admiration for himself by wearing tights with boastful sayings like *Out with the Old, In with the Bold*—the "old" being his challenger. Or he might airbrush his pants with the faces of his opponent's loved ones to make the fight more personal. From Ric Flair's wife to his enemies' managers, no one was safe from Rude's psychological warfare. By bringing formerly off-limit topics into the ring, Rude forever changed the way a wrestling heel could behave.

When he wasn't baiting opponents, the ravishing wrestler leveraged his threads to rile up the crowd. Soaking up every minute in the spotlight, Rude made his way to the ring in robes that glimmered and shined as bright as his ego. Insulting city after city, he demanded that crowds keep the noise down as he slowly peeled away layers of capes and sparkly embellishments to unveil his sculpted body. Today, "Ravishing" Rick Rude remains one of the biggest (and best-looking) villains to ever grace the squared circle.

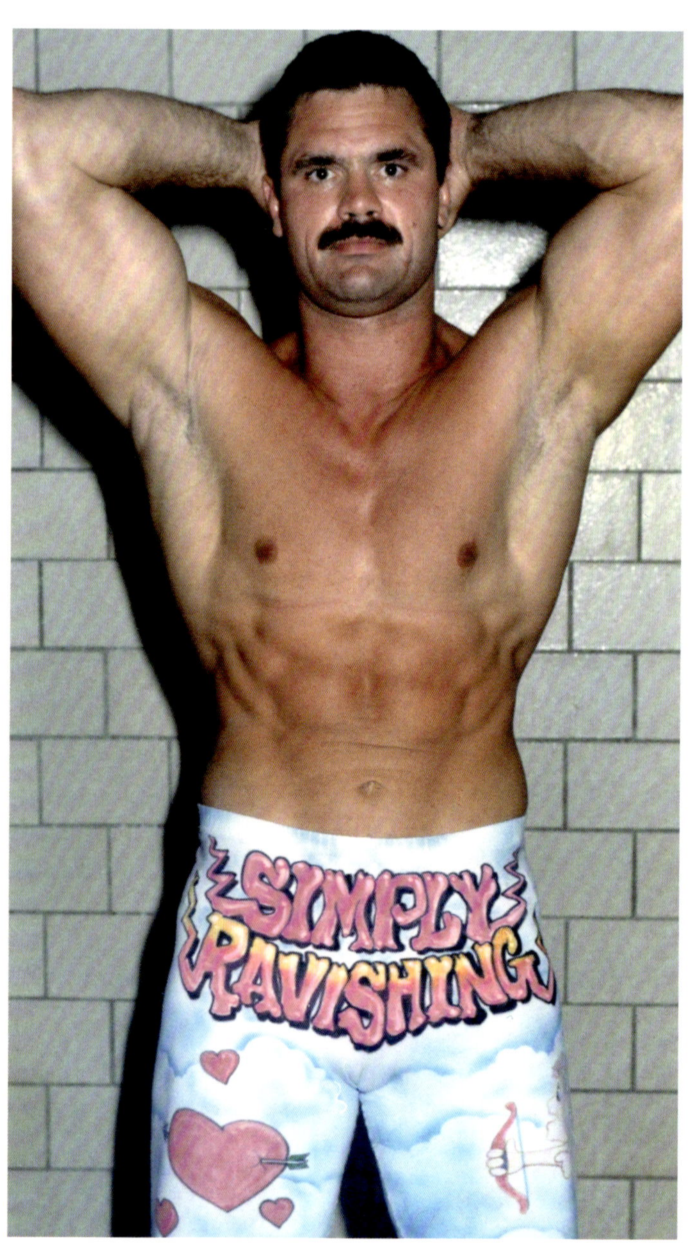

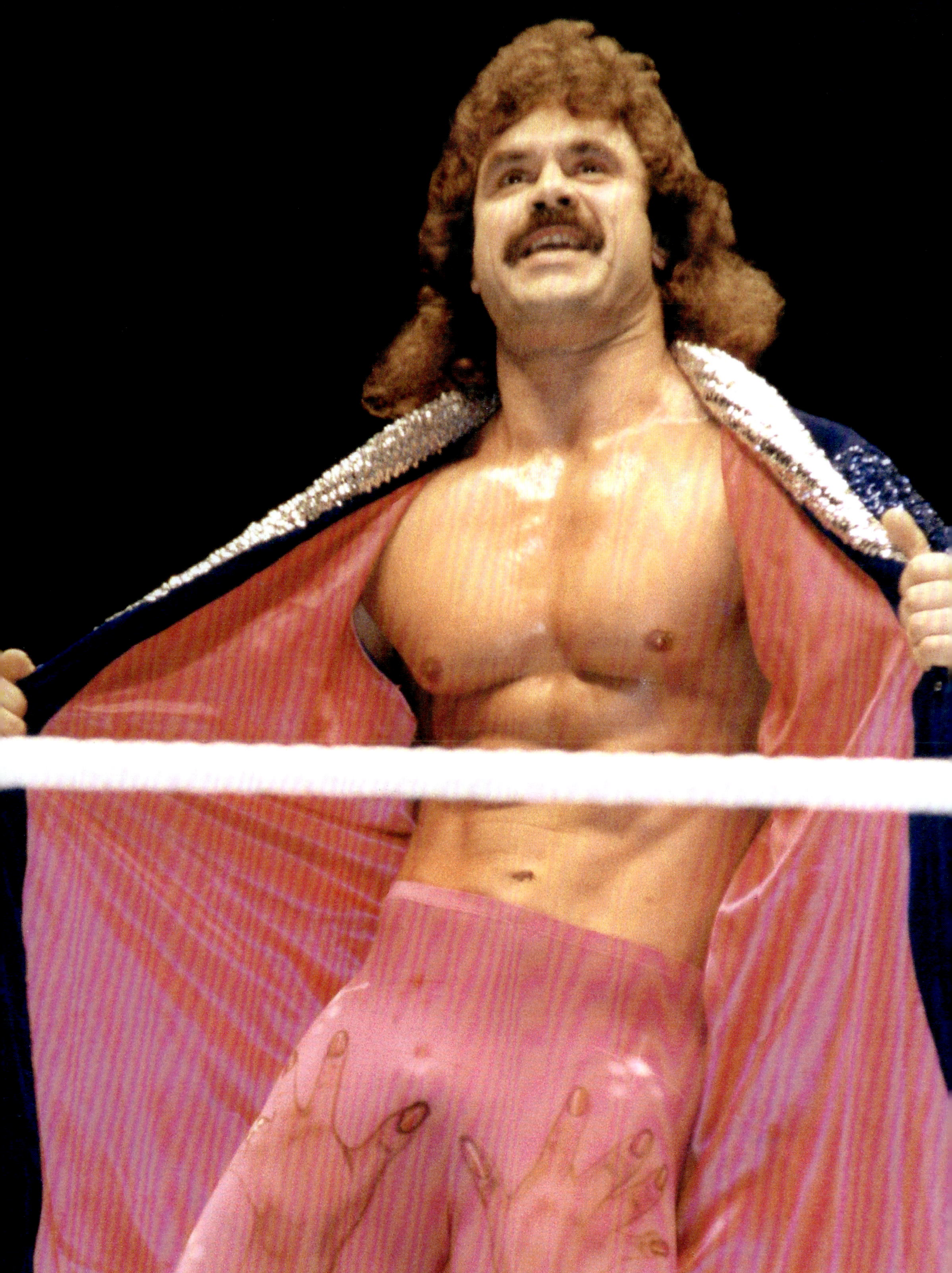

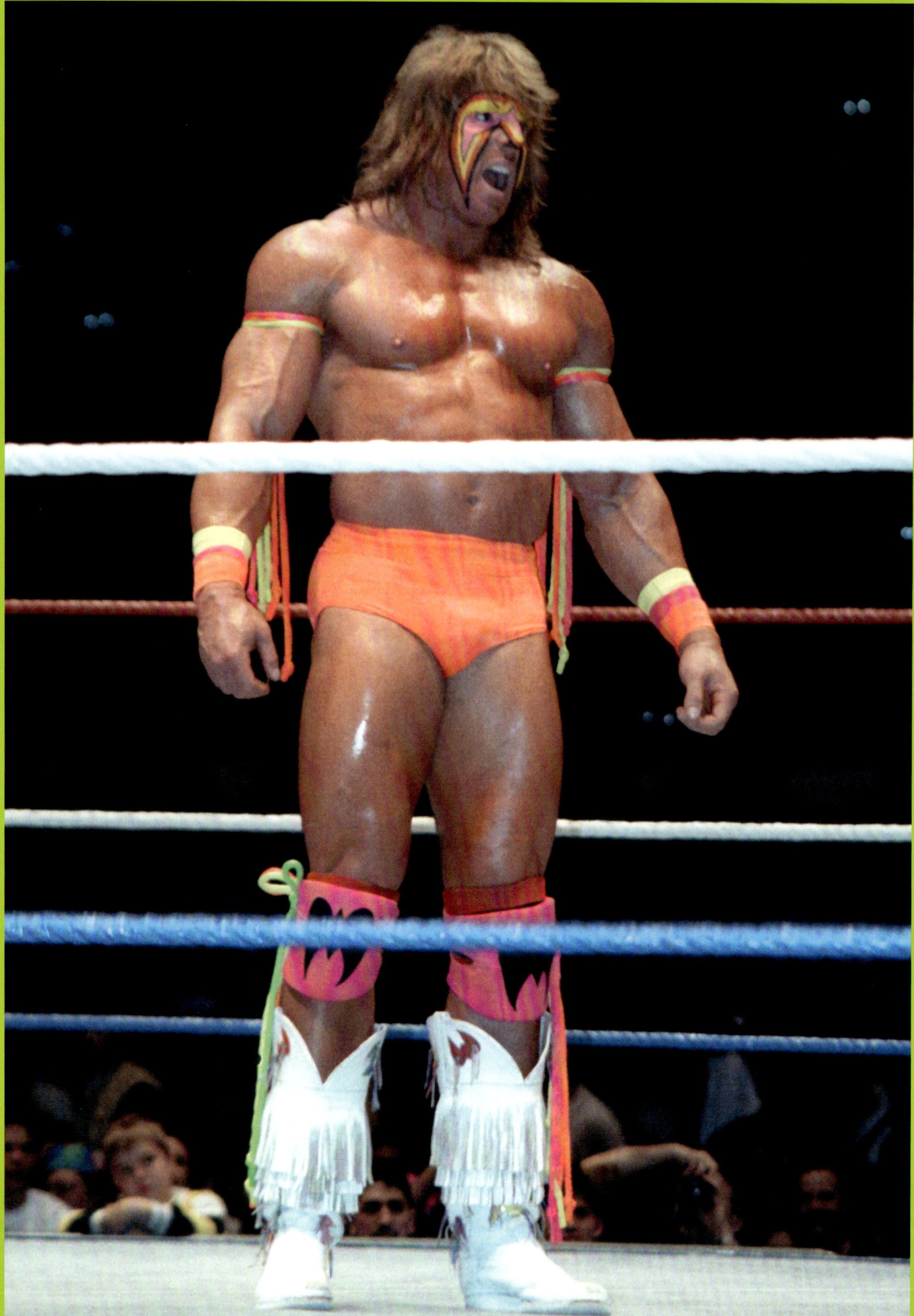

# JIM HELLWIG
## ULTIMATE WARRIOR

Active 1985–2008

WWE Hall of Famer

**The Ultimate Warrior** was a streak of light, exuding vibrancy in every way possible. His untamed energy was rivaled only by his vibrant style, which included colorful face paint that would become his trademark look. Using his body as art, The Ultimate Warrior often wore what looked like a *W* painted across his face. More than just a nod to his name, many fans believed the *W* represented a winged bird or bolt of lightning, symbolizing his character's strength, speed, and resilience.

The Ultimate Warrior's lively garments matched the vigor he brought to the ring. This included mostly neon attire that could be spotted throughout the arena, plus fringe and tassel armbands that accentuated his physique. As his character evolved throughout the years, The Ultimate Warrior added sleeveless painted jackets to further tell his story—a strategic move to accentuate his muscles, intimidate opponents, and signal his force as a competitor. Before every appearance, fans anxiously waited to see what message the star had painted on his body for them that night.

Electrifying in both attire and behavior, The Ultimate Warrior was unapologetically loud. He brought ferocity to the canvas and carried himself with explosive power. He used his intensity and bold movements, including full-throttle sprints and rope shakes, to create an experience for fans. When The Ultimate Warrior stepped into the ring, the whole arena would vibrate with excitement. Fans couldn't take their eyes off one of professional wrestling's most colorful and exciting characters.

Ultimate Warrior in signature bright neon gear at a WWE Live event. Photo by Bob Mulrenin.

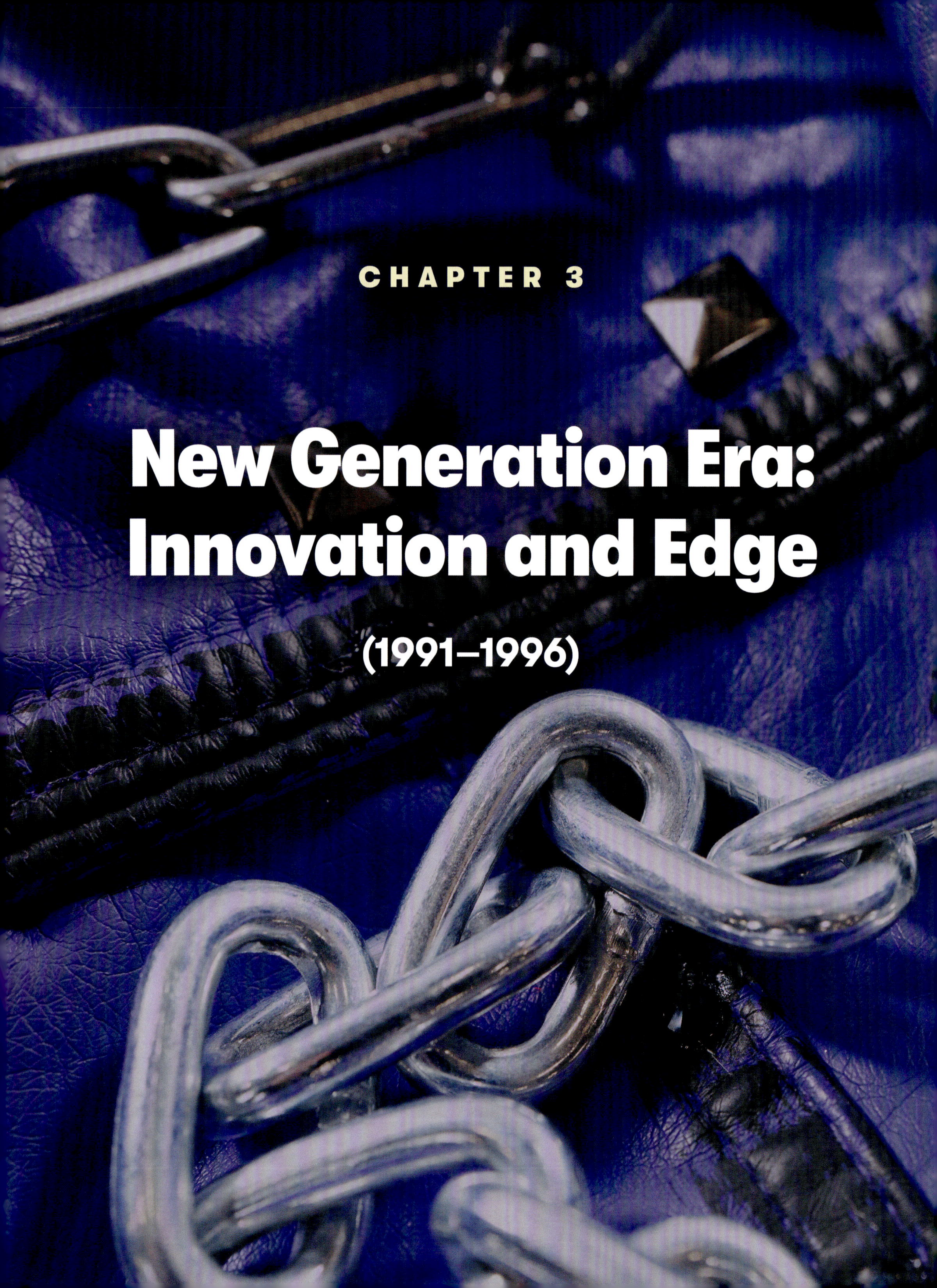


CHAPTER 3

New Generation Era:
Innovation and Edge

(1991–1996)

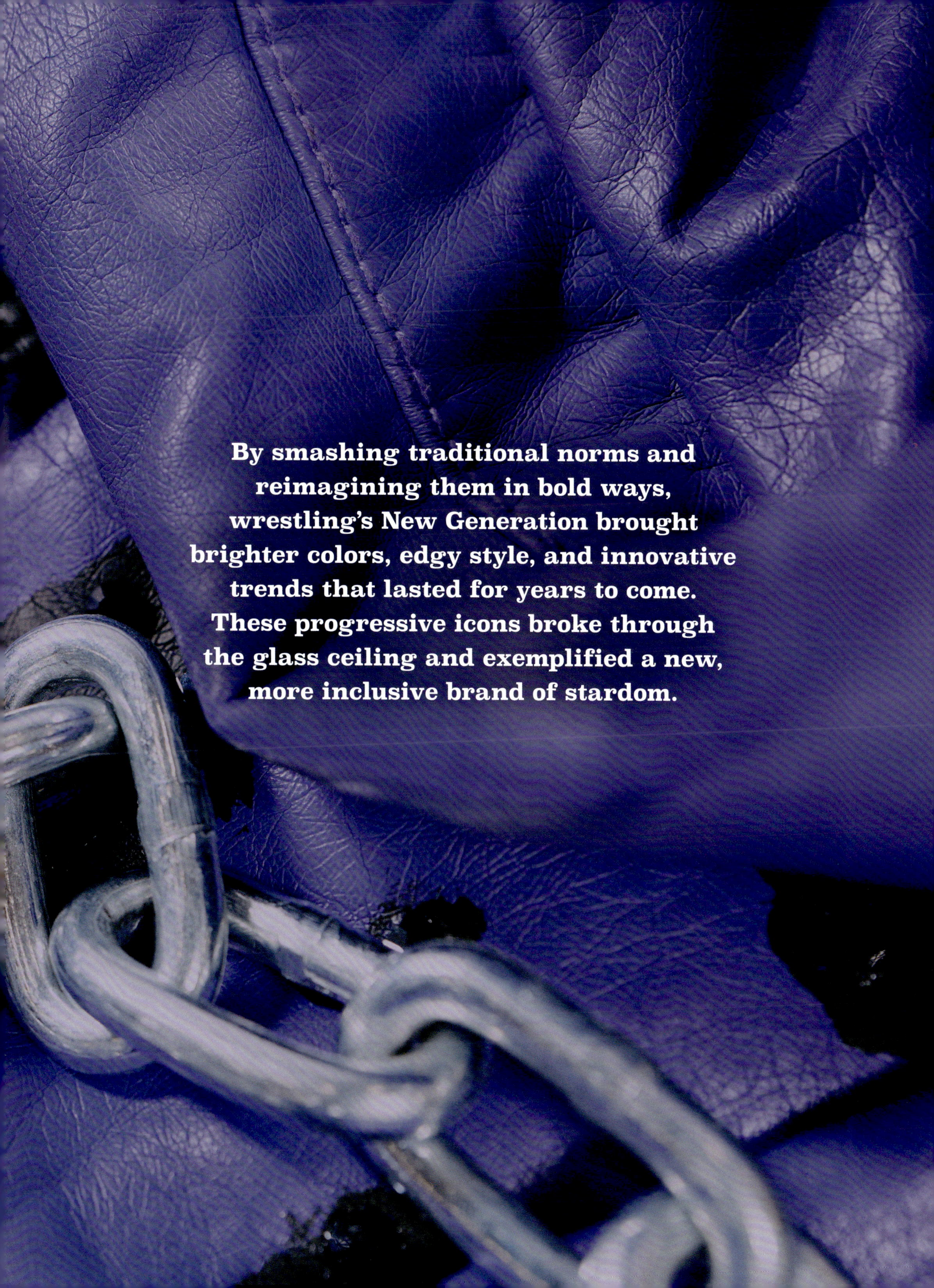
By smashing traditional norms and
reimagining them in bold ways,
wrestling's New Generation brought
brighter colors, edgy style, and innovative
trends that lasted for years to come.
These progressive icons broke through
the glass ceiling and exemplified a new,
more inclusive brand of stardom.

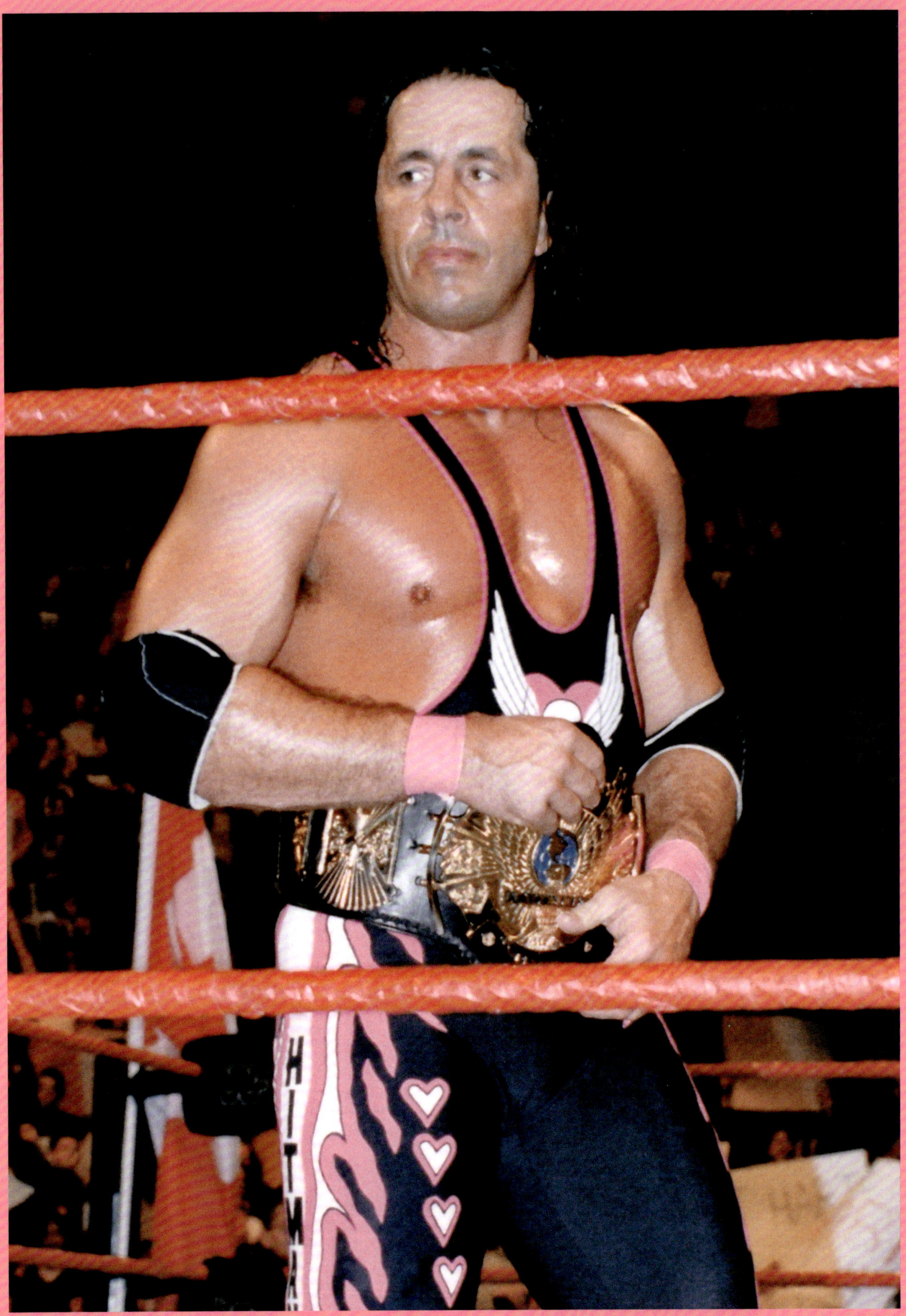

# BRET HART

Active 1978–2000

Five-Time WWE Champion
WWE Hall of Famer

**As the best** there is, the best there was, and the best there ever will be, Bret Hart redefined the color pink in professional wrestling. Not only a world-class athlete with incredible skills, Hart was also a trendsetter. In an era when most male wrestlers wore blacks, reds, and other masculine colors, Bret dared to embrace a color that is widely considered feminine and made it his own. Not only would black-and-pink colors shape Hart's impressive legacy, the vibrant hue would also be passed down from generation to generation within one of wrestling's most influential families.

Terry Anderson, who along with her sister Julie Youngberg made some of Hart's classic looks, recalled how the original concept came together after a chance encounter in Chicago. "We met Bret in Chicago at a bar," said Anderson, who had been talking with Sherri Martel about her and her sister's work with wrestlers Shawn Michaels and Marty Jannetty. "She called Bret over and he asked us to talk in a VIP room," Anderson remembered. "When we went in, Bret pulled out a wrinkled newspaper from his wallet, and it was a picture of a monkey wearing a jacket. I believe it was from The Beatles' [*Sgt. Pepper's*] *Lonely Hearts Club* [*Band*] album. He says, 'Can you guys do this?'" The sisters quickly agreed, although they secretly wondered if they were in over their heads. According to Anderson: "At that time, we had never worked with leather before and we weren't going to say no. We thought, 'What did we get ourselves into?'"

At a time when materials weren't as easily accessible, they found a way to make it work. "We drove from Chicago to St. Louis because we knew there was a great fabric store there. We ended up getting the leather, but it was so thick our sewing machines weren't sewing through them," recalled Anderson. "We ended up borrowing my grandmother's hundred-year-old sewing machine that actually had the foot pedal you have to pump in order to make the needle go through. We were able to sew Bret and Jim's jacket with that very machine."

Those leather jackets embellished with pink details and fringe quickly became part of Hart's trademark look, which is still incorporated into looks worn by members of the family lineage today. The Hart Foundation, a tag team including Bret's brother-in-law Jim Neidhart and managed by Jimmy Hart, identitifed heavily with those colors. Jimmy believes the memorable look played a role in the group's success. "Not a lot of guys back then were wearing pink and black," said Jimmy, who managed The Hart Foundation for six years. "If Bret had his mind set on something, we made it work. We felt like he was the leader of The Hart Foundation. We really believed in him, and we trusted him."

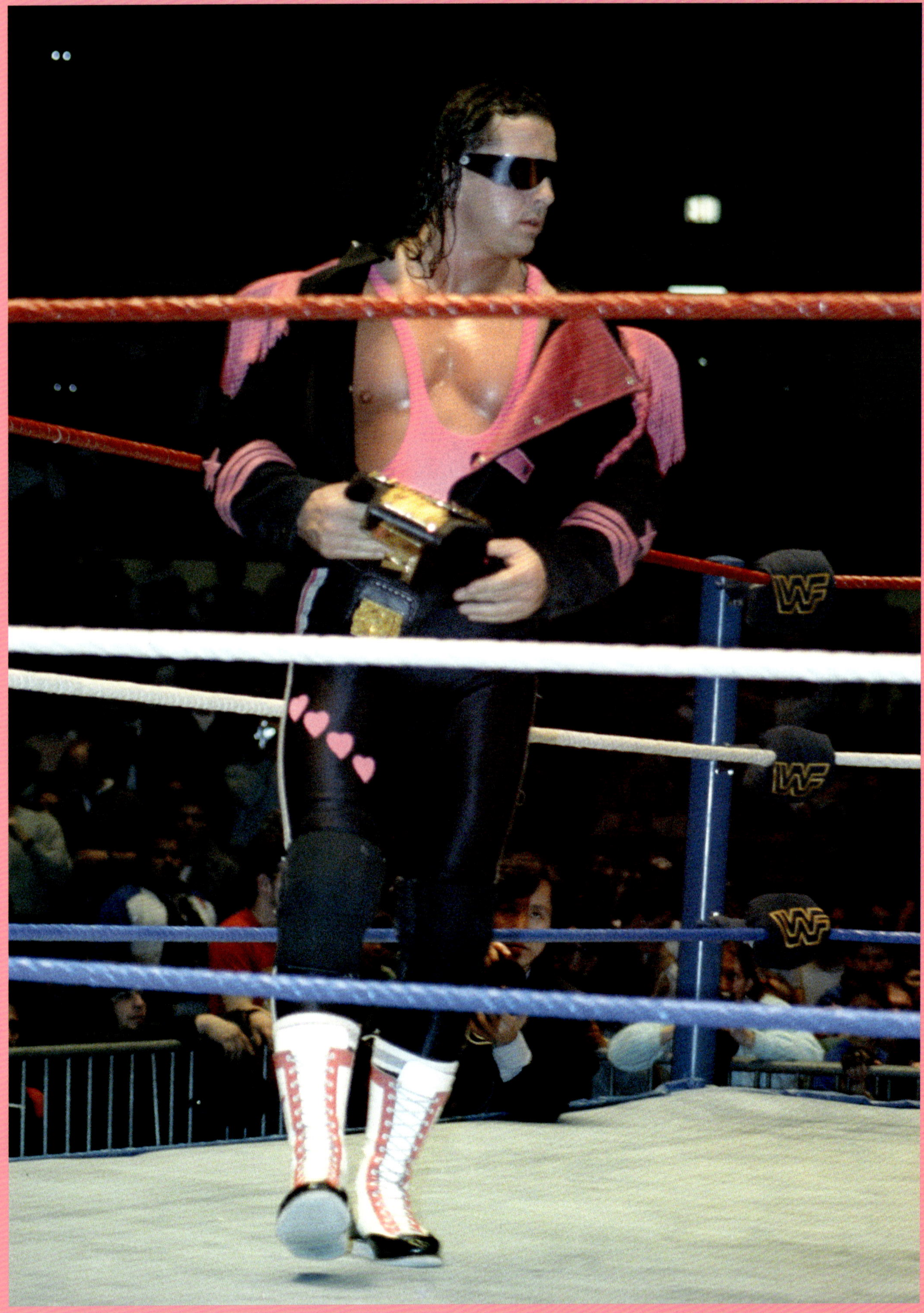

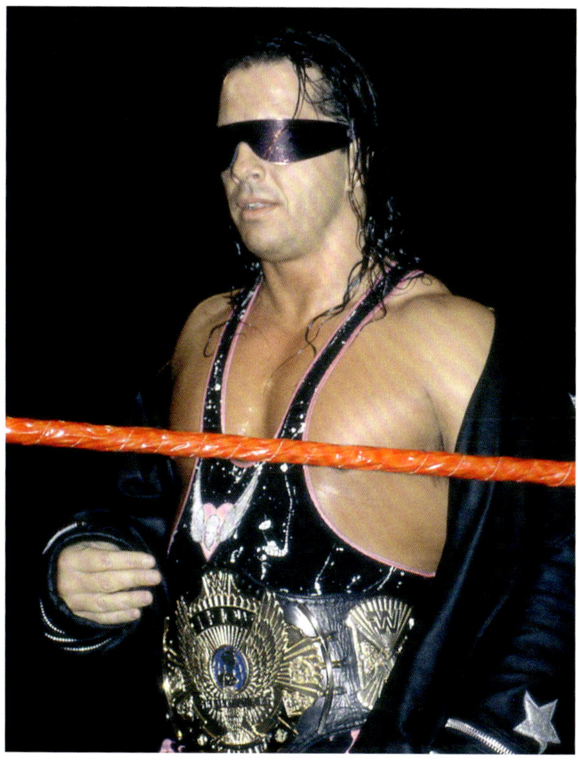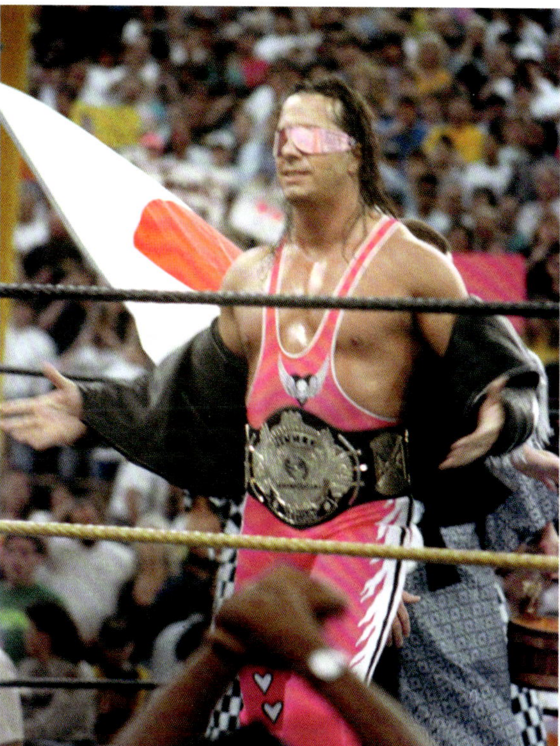

Bret Hart made pink feel powerful rather than soft. Soon, pink-and-black hues were synonymous with Hart's personality, cool yet composed, and so methodical he would become known as Bret "The Hitman" Hart. "We kind of knew it would transcend back then," said Youngberg. "We couldn't make anyone [else] something with the slightest amount of pink and black in it. They knew what they had in the colors," Youngberg said, in reference to the success the color pink had in correlation to the character.

Hart was polished as a performer and delivered outfits that felt intentional. With clean, angular designs, his singlets were as sharp as the Sharpshooter holds he put on opponents. Along with the colors, the Canadian wrestler wove other personal touches into his attire. From hearts to stars, he was thoughtful, and his gear represented different parts of his life. Hart's signature logo—a maple leaf and skull with wings—is one instantly celebrated for its magnitude. "Bret would typically bring me something as inspiration, whether it was a certain skull or something he liked," said

Youngberg, who also made the wrestler's iconic paint-splatter attire. "I made the splatter paint gear for him, and my dad was very angry because there was pink paint all over the basement walls. To create the look, I laid the clothes down on a painting cloth on the floor and made the paint a bit runny and flipped a brush at it."

The paint-splatter gear would become one of the most iconic elements in Hart's wrestling wardrobe, which he enhanced with mirrored sunglasses to create a slick, futuristic appeal. He began the tradition of gifting a pair of his trademark shades to a young fan as he made his way to the ring. This small gesture helped fans connect even more to his character, whose fan base was extending around the world. Decades after he retired in 2000, Bret Hart is still remembered as one of the sport's greatest wrestlers, both for his skill and his iconic sense of style. The Hitman was Excellence in Execution, not just in the way that he moved but in the way that he presented himself as well.

OPPOSITE: **Bret Hart as WWE Intercontinental Champion. Photo by George Tahinos.**

TOP LEFT: **Hart wearing paint splatter gear as WWE World Champion in 1994. Photo by George Napolitano.**

TOP RIGHT: **Hart against Yokozuna at WrestleMania 9 in Las Vegas, Nevada. Photo by Bob Mulrenin.**

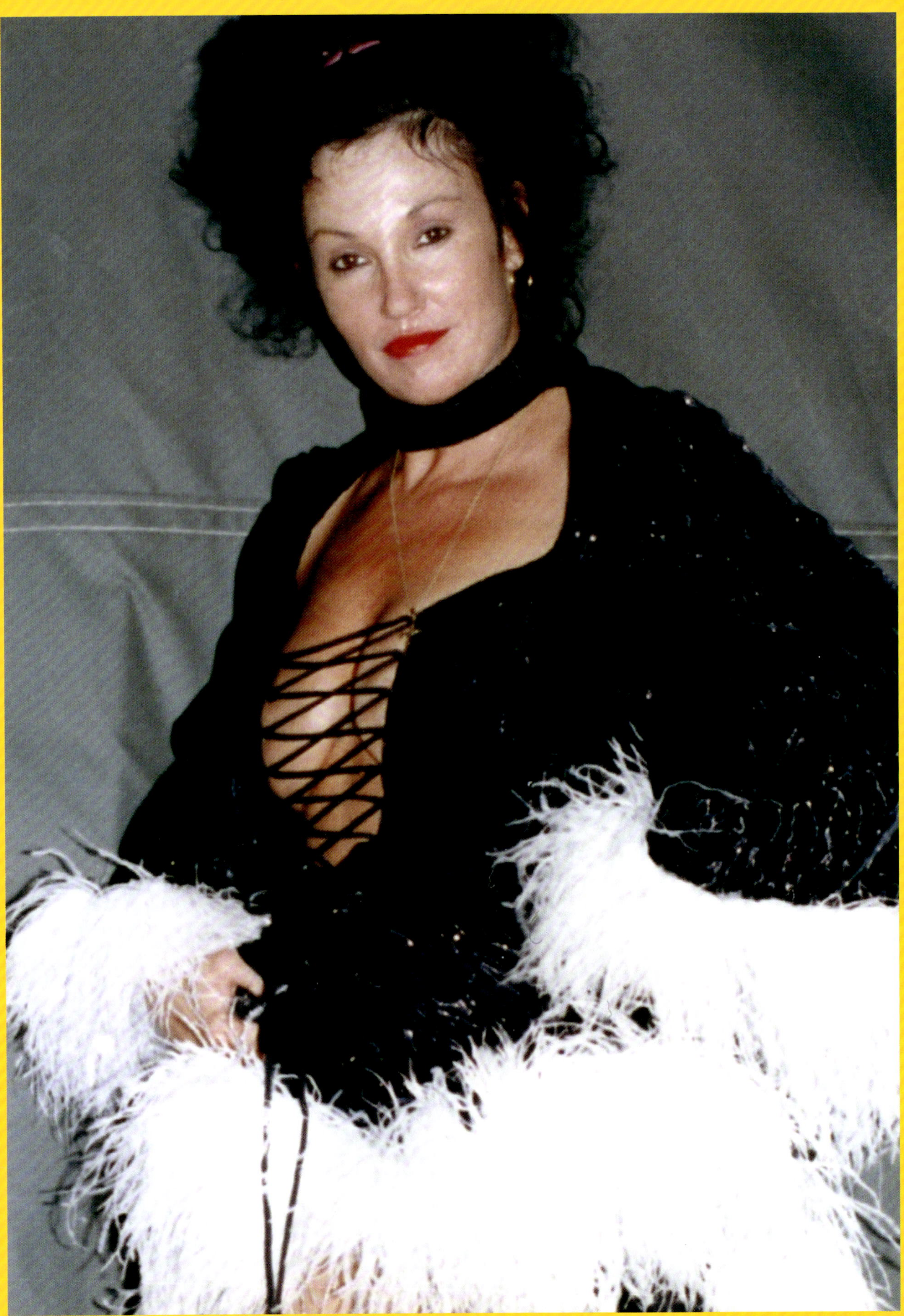

# SHERRY SCHRULL
## SHERRI MARTEL

Active 1980–2006

Four-Time Women's World Champion
WWE Hall of Famer

**Elevating talent after talent** throughout her career, Sherri Martel was an expert at making moments feel bigger. A wrestler in her own right but commonly hailed as one of the best wrestling valets in the history of the sport, Sensational Sherri had a talent for elevating everyone in her orbit. Wrestling fans loved her ability to work the room and bask in the spotlight as a secondary character. Sherri had an undeniable *it* factor, and any wrestler lucky enough to work with her could expect their career to take an upward trajectory.

Shawn Michaels, whom Sherri managed early in his career, remembers the impact she had on his journey: "At that time, she had only been with [Randy] Savage and [Ted] DiBiase, which were guys that were in the main event. They put me with Sherri Martel to raise my stock value. We knew each other from AWA [American Wrestling Association] days, and she always had a sex appeal about her. I asked her if she would be open to wearing white patent leather with high-heeled boots and short shorts to match my look. She said, 'Shawn, I'll do whatever you want.' She was strong, tough, and rugged, and she couldn't have been more supportive. When she started managing me, they had her singing my song. That was the beginning of The Heartbreak Kid and her making me a version of a top guy before I ever was."

Sensational Sherri posing backstage.
Photo by George Napolitano.

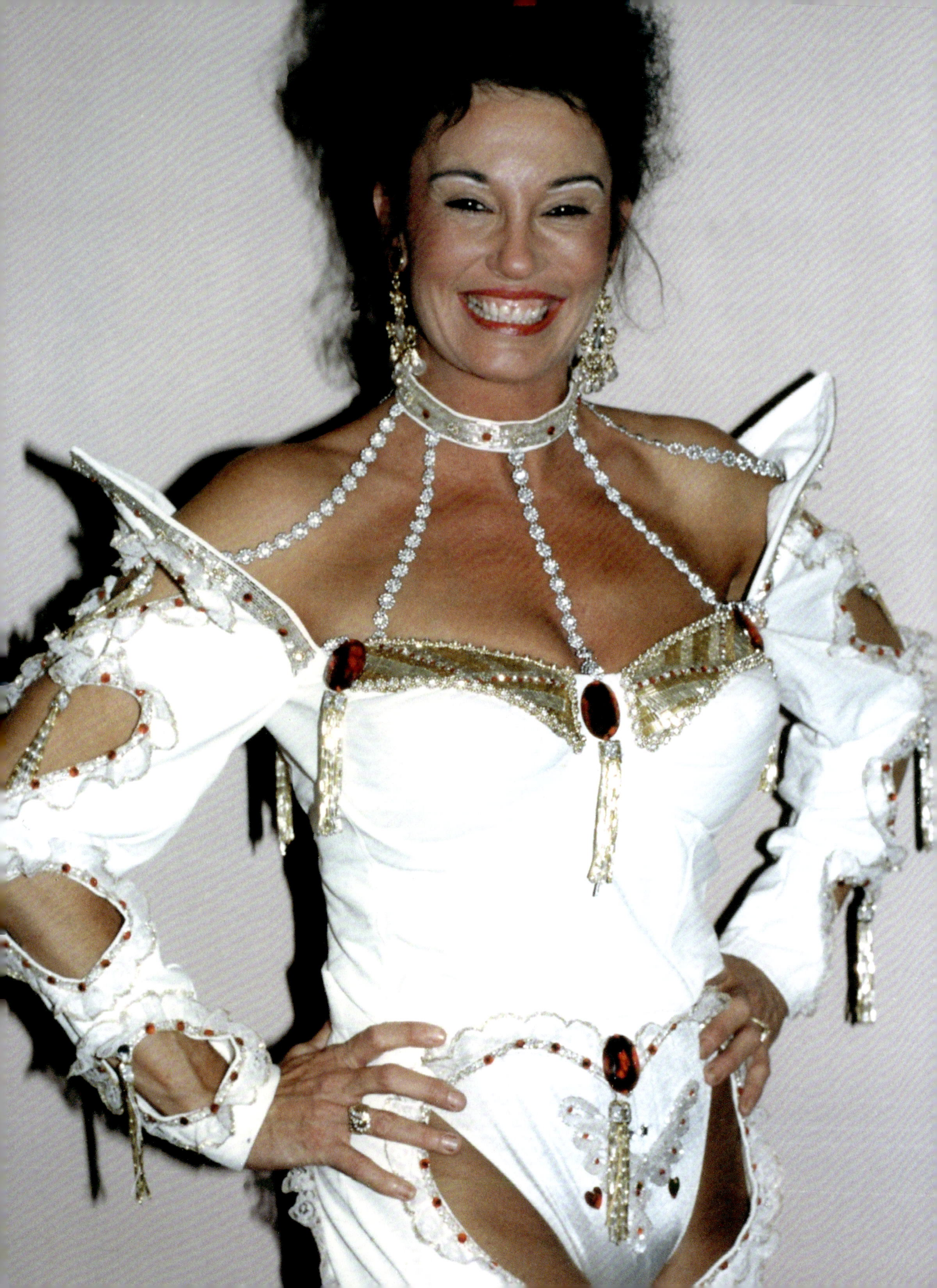

Sherri's outfits—with their symbolic flames and feathers, bejeweled accents, and fabrics that complemented her partner in the ring—made an impact. Sherri used her gear to tell a story that highlighted whomever she was managing. She wore dramatic makeup and bold face paint to convey emotion. She used bright eye shadow, heavy eyeliner, and metallic face paint to exaggerate her features. She was a pro at leveraging her look to tell a larger story.

In the '90s, Sherri began managing The Harlem Heat, a wrestling tag team composed of brothers Booker and Lash Huffman. Booker Huffman (who would become better known by his award-winning persona, Booker T) believes Sherri added excitement and legitimacy to their group: "Sherri oozed confidence, and it was a blessing to have her with us. She was about going out there and creating chaos and causing havoc. She wanted to riot. She wasn't just Sherri Martel with us; she changed her name to be Sister Sherri. I don't know if I've ever thought about it until now, but we were working in the South, and to have two black guys with a beautiful white woman was something totally different. We really created a lot of freaking magic in the early part of my career."

Wrestling personalities come and go, but Sensational Sherri / Sister Sherri is still remembered as a star. With her over-the-top energy and lively ensembles, she helped build the framework wrestling stands on today. "For managers, I don't think she gets the credit that she deserves as far as being one of the greatest of all time. I think she was the pioneer for the women's wrestling movement," said Booker. "She was the one that sparked the women's wrestling movement because she was as real as real could get and was one of the most respected women wrestlers that ever put on a pair of boots."

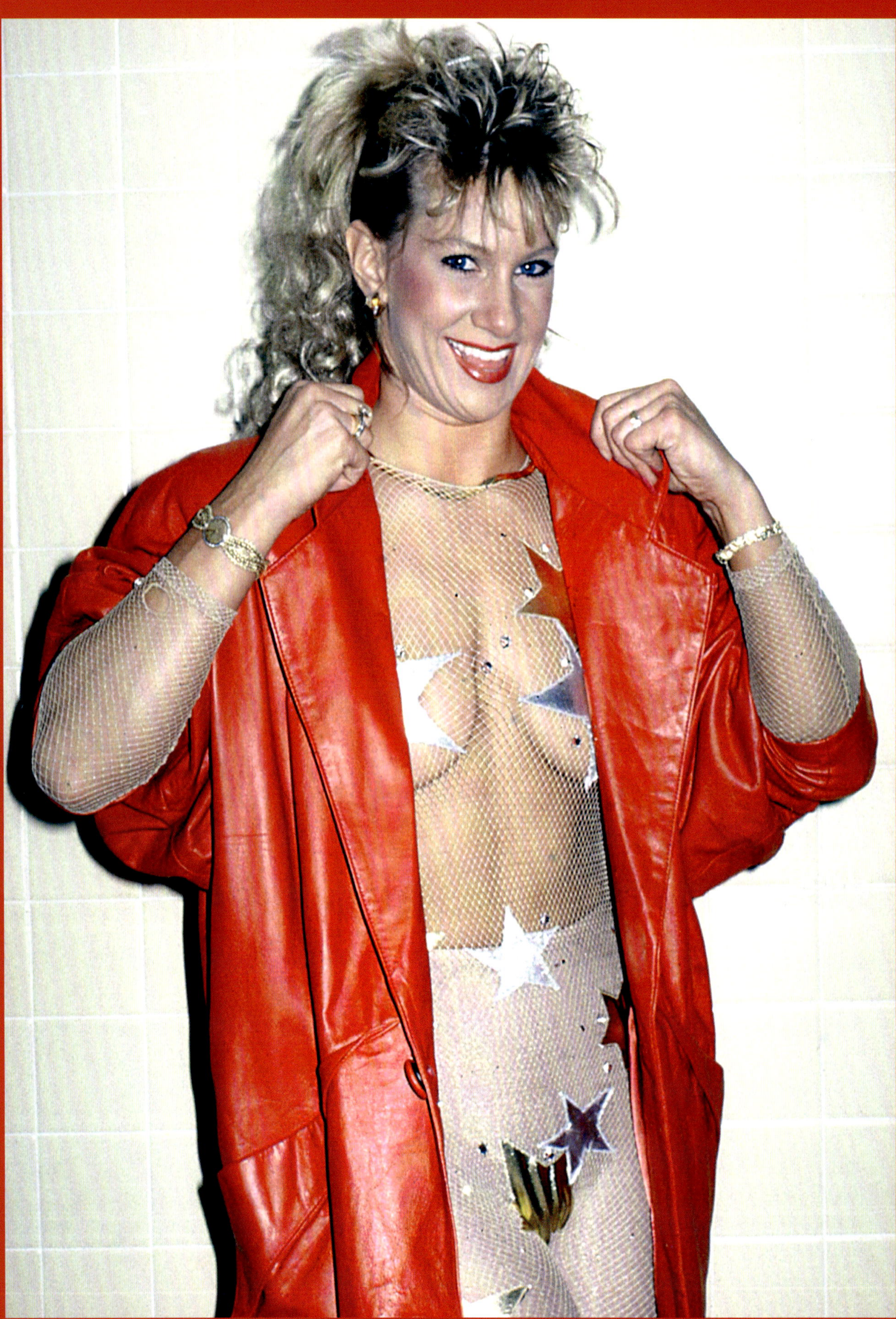

# DEBRAH MICELI
## ALUNDRA BLAYZE / MADUSA

Active 1984–2000

Three-Time WWE Women's Champion
WWE Hall of Famer

**Throughout the 1980s and '90s,** Alundra Blayze set the professional wrestling world on fire. As a pillar of the women's division and a relentless advocate for women's equality in wrestling, Blayze was a tireless champion both inside and outside the ring.

Blayze began her sporting life in gymnastics, hence the gymnastics gear she wore throughout her wrestling career. Leotards felt familiar and comfortable to her, and she used them to make a bold statement. One of Blayze's iconic looks included a spandex leotard with boy-cut shorts and a sleeveless mock turtleneck that screamed *Blayze! Blayze! Blayze!* in glittery neon letters. Another signature look included a white singlet engulfed in flames, with *BLAYZE* boldly printed front and center. "I was an athlete who was fiery, blazing the trail and on fire in the ring," said Blayze.

Also recognized worldwide by the name Madusa—meaning "Made in the USA"—Blayze frequently wrestled in two-piece American flag–themed apparel. Such patriotic gear showcased her national pride and told the story of her wrestling character.

Today, Blayze may be best remembered for showing up on WCW Monday Nitro and dropping her WWE Championship belt in a trash can on live TV, which proved to be one of the most shocking moments in wrestling history. When asked if she knew this moment would live on in wrestling infamy, Blayze said, "Oh, hell no! . . . Neither [producer and booker Eric Bischoff] or I had any idea that the Monday night would explode thereafter, making both companies probably one of their highest financial gains of all time. Which I never see a dime for, and those circle-jerking men made millions."

**"I came up with the name [Alundra Blayze], and Vince agreed. The reason why I chose that name is because it started with the letter *A* and I knew I'd be at the beginning of anything they printed. I knew if they tried to drop that name and use the name [Blayze] fully, I would still be in the front with the second name, as it started with the letter *B*. It was as easy as ABC. Alundra Blayze, champion."**

–Alundra Blayze

Alundra Blayze as WWE Women's
Champion. Photo by George Napolitano.

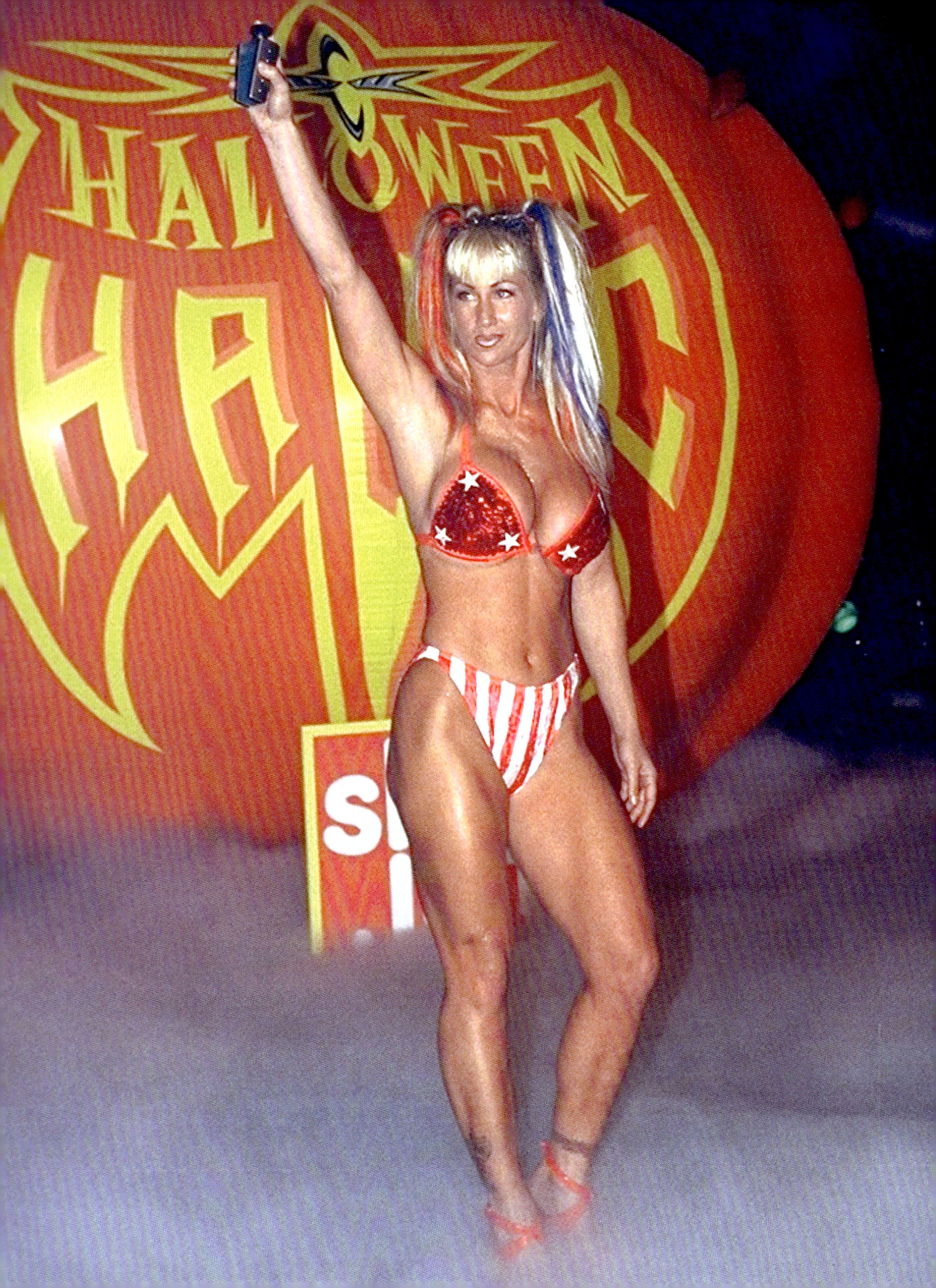

HALLOWEEN
HAVOC

Decades later, Blayze still represents women's power in a male-dominated industry, and she has never backed down from a fight she believes in. Moreover, she set the tone for future generations of female wrestlers, no matter what they're wearing. "I wanted to bring more athleticism and sexiness to our era," said Blayze. "My idea of sexiness was about being athletic, intelligent, and remaining strong in the presence of men."



OPPOSITE: Madusa at Halloween Havoc at the MGM Grand in Las Vegas, Nevada, on October 24, 1999. Photo by George Napolitano.

RIGHT: Madusa as AWA Women's Champion at Showboat Pavilion in Las Vegas, Nevada. Photo by George Napolitano.

"If you go back to all my interviews, the tone never changed! I'm proud to say that my integrity was never for sale. That's one thing that has always vouched for me . . . what I believed in as a woman in this business. Later in my career, I started to lose myself because of how women were being portrayed and marketed. I felt that I needed to change with the product to be relevant. I knew it was time for me to retire because that's not what I was about. I was what women's wrestling stood for. So, at a time, and even somewhat today, when men thought that when women spoke up, voiced their opinion, or said no, we were hard to work with, I respectfully found another way to do it. I think hitting my pinnacles so many times in a career against an industry full of men, surviving, and still being alive today to tell the story, is pretty remarkable. Not turning to drugs, drinking, or other extracurricular activities. I stood tall, lost a lot, and loved what I did, and wouldn't have changed a thing about how I believed what women deserve . . . [is] respect, time, and financial gains equal to the men."

—Alundra Blayze

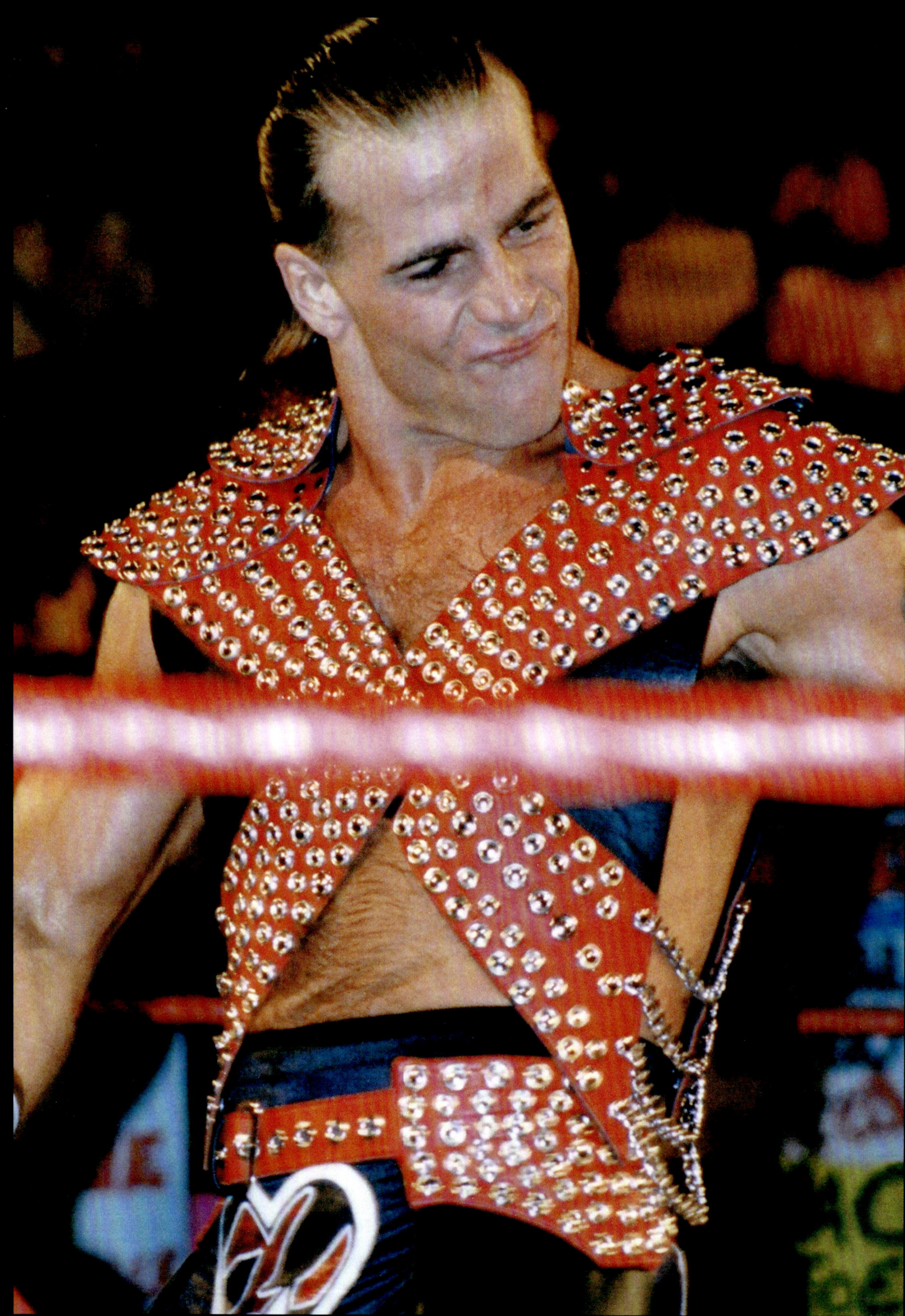

# MICHAEL SHAWN HICKENBOTTOM
## SHAWN MICHAELS

Active 1984–2010

Two-Time WWE Hall of Famer
First-Ever WWE Grand Slam Champion

**Commonly known as** The Heartbreak Kid or The Boy Toy, Shawn Michaels is easily one of the most recognizable professional wrestlers in history. With his smug attitude and expertly crafted gear, Michaels had undeniable star appeal. From the very beginning of his career, the wrestler understood that clothes were key to building a winning persona. "I remember talking to ["Macho Man" Randy] Savage, and he was always tight-lipped about who did his outfits," Michaels recalled. "He told me he had his own gear guy, and that's what gave me the idea. I didn't know if I would be able to afford it at the time, but when I started my singles career, I wanted to be the guy that didn't wear the same thing all the time. Savage always had something new, and that was something I recognized."

So Michaels found a designer from Chicago who would go on to make many of his iconic looks throughout his decades-long career. "I was introduced to Julie Youngberg, who made tights for me and Marty Jannetty as a tag team," Michaels said. "When I went singles, I was the only one she was making gear for, and I tried to keep her as my own for a very long time. Everyone was blown away by what I was wearing. Her sister Terry [Anderson] eventually started making gear for The Undertaker, and it evolved into getting them both a job with [WWE]."

Shawn Michaels at the WWE Survivor Series in Montreal, Canada, in 1997. Photo by Steve Argintaru.

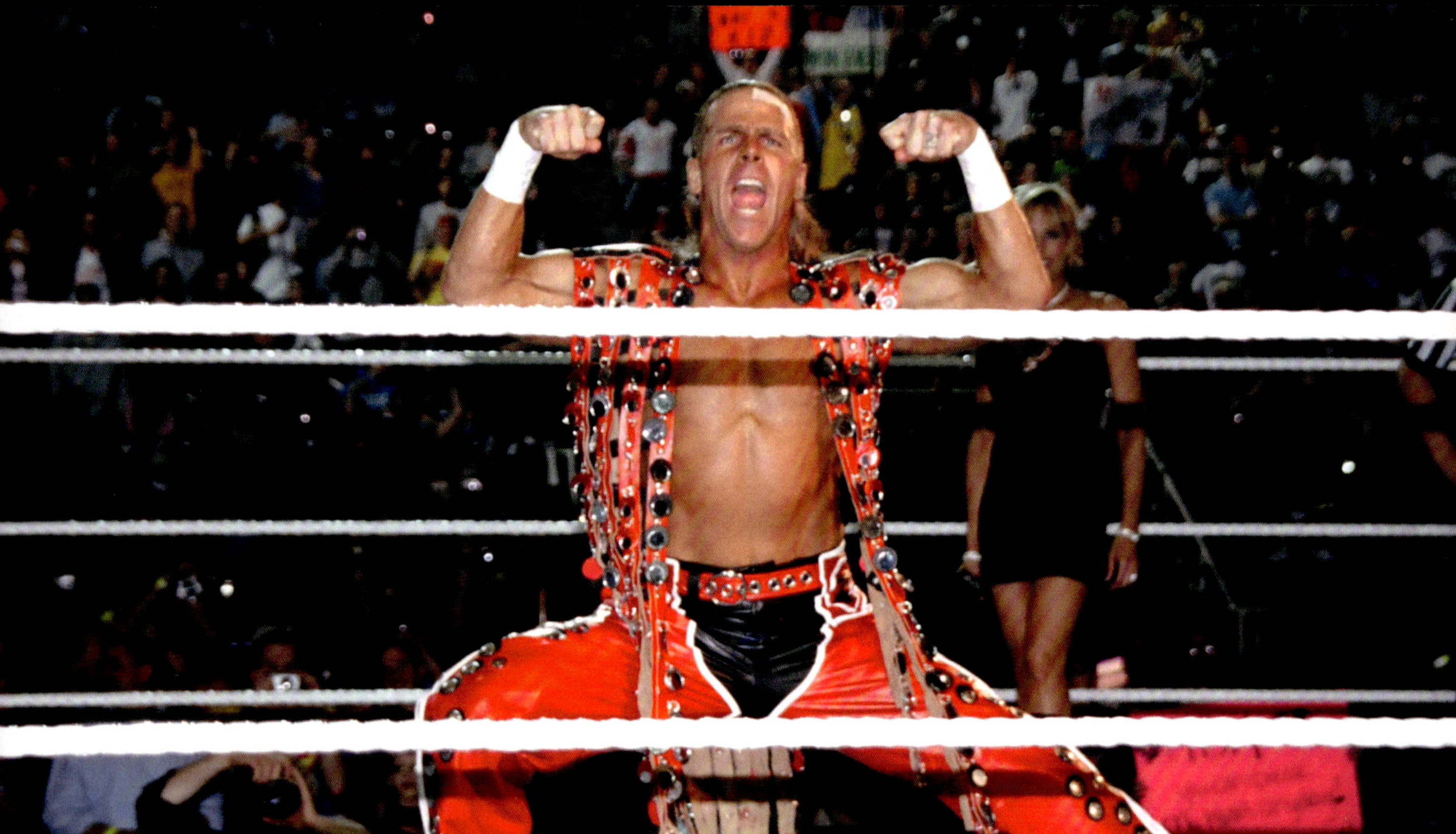

Though Michaels was inspired by the legends before him, he knew that he wanted his gear to reflect his own experiences. "Back in the late '80s, everyone was kind of using red and black," the wrestler remembered. "At the time, as The Rockers, we were just using a black-and-white tiger stripe, and it was very basic. It wasn't until the mid '90s where the colors evolved, and we evolved with them. When I became The Heartbreak Kid, I didn't want to completely lose where I came from. I kept a lot of my tiger stripes, and I wanted to try to make it a natural evolution." The tiger stripes eventually morphed into one of Shawn Michaels's trademark symbols: the broken heart. He remembers how the emblem came to life: "[WWE] wanted me to be called The Idol and it just didn't feel natural. I had these white trunks with different shapes of tiger stripes on them in different areas of the gear. Curt Hennig told me about an old song by Chris LeDoux called 'Shot Full of Love.' In this song it says, 'I used to be a heartbreak kid.' Curt then said it once [during] commentary [about me] and I just started calling myself The Heartbreak Kid. It was then that those [tiger stripes] became a broken heart."

Wearing bold leathers, fringe, and metal studs, The Boy Toy was provocative and fiery. Youngberg told us how she often created clothing that matched a mood: "I got a lot of my inspiration from movie soundtracks. I would hear a beautiful musical score and just keep playing it over and over, and that's what would stimulate my brain to come up with something. I did one look, after the *Waterworld* soundtrack, which was fully turquoise. Another I did while listening to the *Dragonheart* soundtrack, and the attire had scales made out of plastic all over it. . . . There was [also] a look I made after I watched *Braveheart*. This gear had a bunch of little metal rectangles all over it. I was nineteen and still living at home with my parents at the time. After I cut all of the pieces for the look, my dad ground them down so they weren't sharp and then drilled holes in the outfit so I could rivet them on."

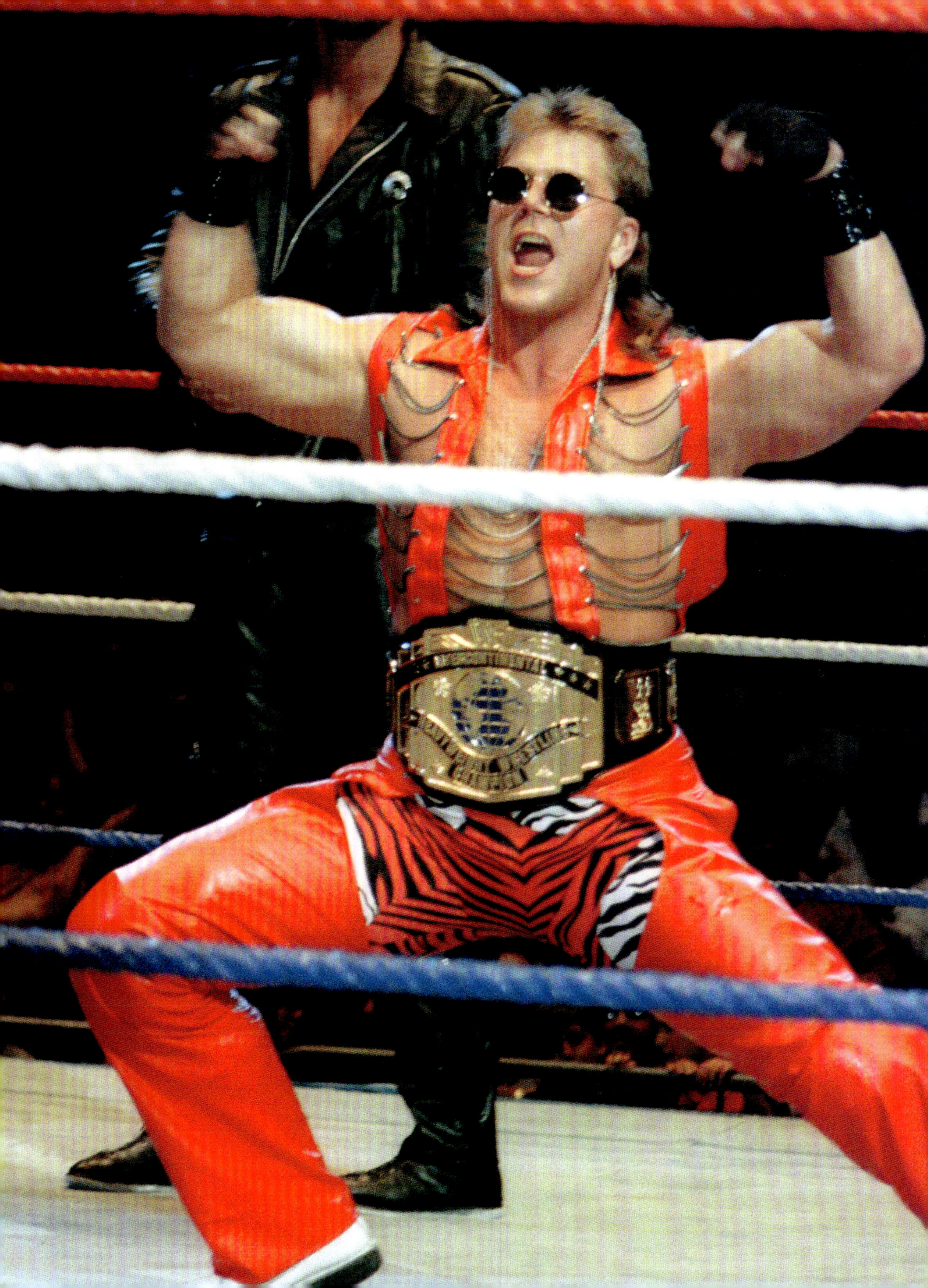

—Johnny Gargano, WWE Superstar, on following in the footsteps of his mentor and childhood hero, Shawn Michaels

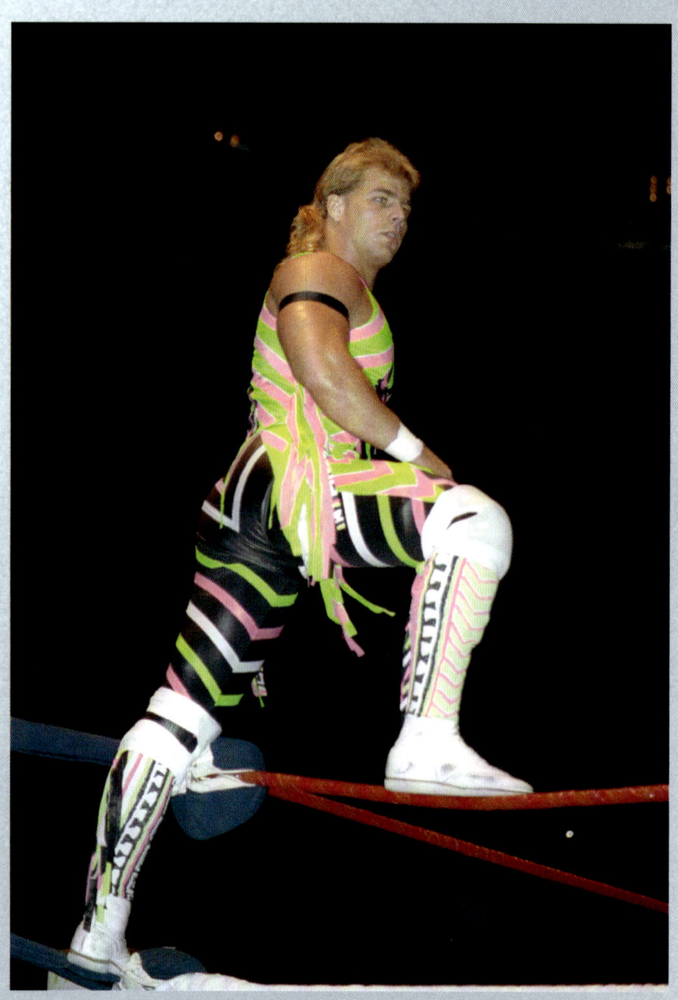

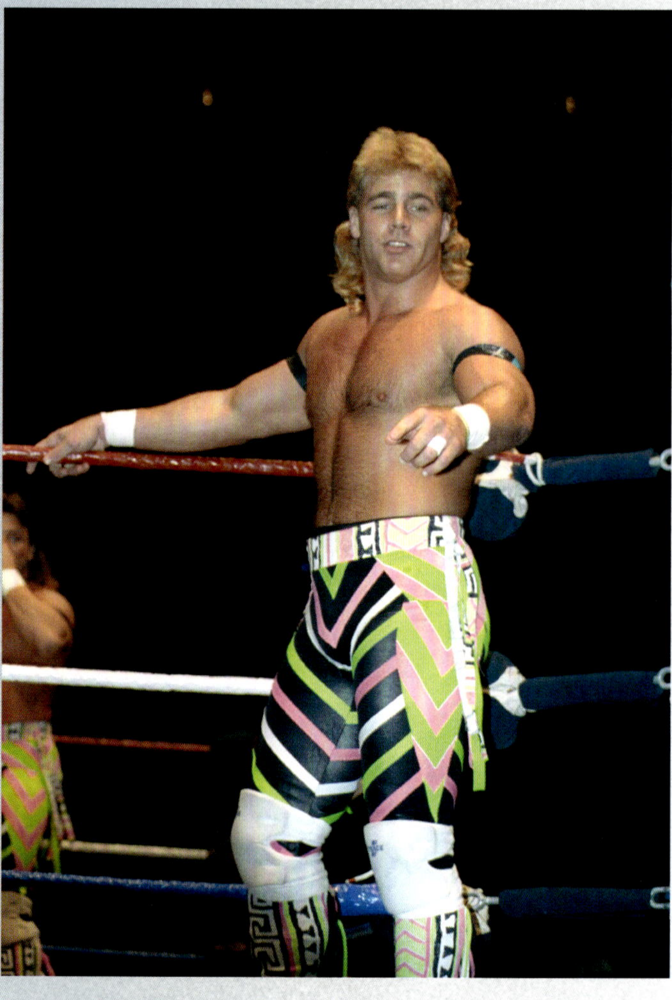

BOTH: Shawn Michaels as a member of the tag team The Rockers. Photos by Bob Mulrenin.

Shawn Michaels was also the first wrestler to incorporate glass mirrors into his attire. "It all really started when [wrestling valet] Sherri Martel would hold out a mirror for [Shawn] when he came out to the ring," said Youngberg. "He would do his little cocky dance, and my thought was to add mirrors to the outfit. Adding these pieces was a process in itself. I bought the glass from Hobby Lobby or Michaels, and I would create little casings out of leather to go around the glass. Next, I would glue them down and then add more leather and stitch around the edges so it wouldn't hurt anyone. I wouldn't want a weapon out there."

Shawn Michaels remembers this cocky little dance: "I'm a kid from Texas who was doing something he never thought he'd have the possibilities to do, at the level that he never thought he could reach. I just always loved cowboys and chaps, and so it felt like it naturally worked with the character and the gimmick, so to speak. Strangely enough, with the song and kind of doing a striptease and taking them off, it all ended up working together. I can't sing or dance a bit, but for that thirty or forty seconds I was out there, I looked like I knew what I was doing."

Even in an era known for groundbreaking matches, physical aptitude, and abundance of swagger, Shawn Michaels always managed to steal the show. Every week, he delivered fashion-forward moments that married function and form. "The most important thing about making Shawn's gear was that his look had to be durable, and he had to be able to get out of them in an instant after walking down the ramp," said Youngberg. "It was a great challenge."

Shawn Michaels's legendary career is highlighted by a night that many consider the greatest match of all time. "WrestleMania 25 is a combination of my real-life story, but that [story] sort of juxtaposed against The Undertaker, who's The Prince of Darkness," the wrestler recalled. "At that time, so many people knew of faith being a part of my life. It was [wrestling producer] Michael Hayes that thought, 'Hey, wouldn't this be a great idea if you were in all white and Taker was in all black, and we could find a way to get you to descend from the heavens and him rise from below.' From my understanding, Michael had pitched the idea to the powers that be, and they weren't a big fan of it [at first]. . . . Once they bought into it, I put on all the white and Taker had on all the black, and it's something you can clearly see. You can get it, you grasp it, it's a very simple story. Even though The Undertaker was not a villain at that time, it was sort of the underdog [Undertaker] versus the bad guy [me]. It all came together and is one of those things that you can't really call, but you just know that it all feels so incredibly right in the moment."

After impacting millions of fans over the years, Shawn Michaels credits his long career to his ability to adapt, because evolution in the wrestling world is paramount. "I think it would be challenging for people to have the twenty-five- and thirty-year careers that myself, Undertaker, and numerous others have [had] without evolution," he said. "Finding ways to seamlessly grow in a way that looks natural to the fans is what makes that [strong] connection to an audience. Our fans are much smarter and [more] sophisticated than they've ever been. They know the difference between

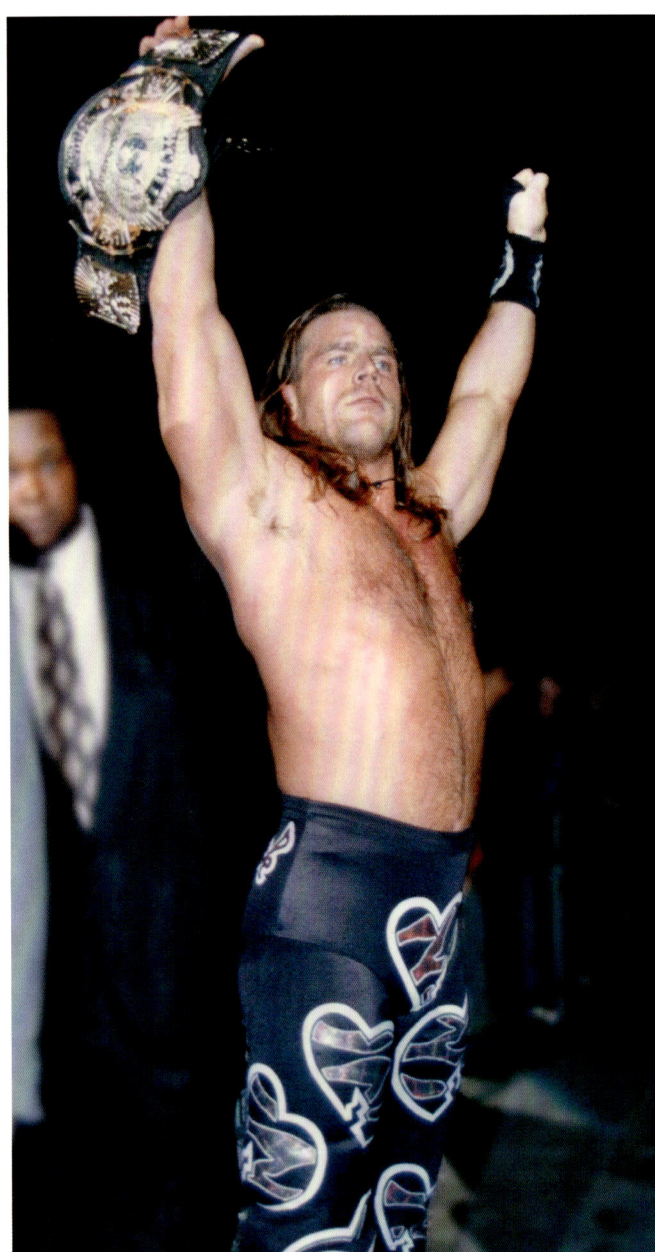

being authentic and evolving just for the sake of saying so. In my opinion, [the fans] need to really see it come from inside to have a long career in this business."

Shawn Michaels retired in 2010, but he didn't leave wrestling for good. Now the legendary wrestler shares his knowledge and experience as a senior vice president of talent development and creative at NXT, a division of WWE committed to training future generations of stars. "One of the things that happens in this line of work is that many [young wrestlers] see things that they deem to be successful. In a perfectly normal and smart way, people want to duplicate or copy what has [successfully] been done before. But sometimes without knowing it, people get into a comfort zone, a formula, and I think they get afraid to break the formula to try to build their own [brand]," said Michaels. "This is where you should be making mistakes and trying things. That is something I continue to try to do . . . get people to think about being innovative and do different things, because you never know. That's where genius and greatness is discovered. . . . This business is built on being the next big thing."

**"I would go to Ace Hardware and go shopping for Shawn's outfits. I was buying things like acorn nuts and convex washers to complete the look. One of my absolute favorite sets of Shawn's was from [WWE] Bad Blood in 1997. I used screen door material. Another [outfit] I loved was from WrestleMania 9 in Las Vegas. It basically only had sleeves, a collar, and mirrors with chains with little crosses hanging from them. That was our first jaunt using mirrors."**

—Julie Youngberg, seamstress and gear designer, on getting creative with Shawn Michaels's gear

ABOVE: Shawn Michaels as WWE World Champion at SummerSlam in Montreal, Canada, in 1997. Photo by Steve Argintaru.

OPPOSITE: Shawn Michaels as the WWE Intercontinental Champion on *RAW* at the Hammerstein Ballroom in Manhattan, New York, on February 22, 1993. Photo by Bob Mulrenin.

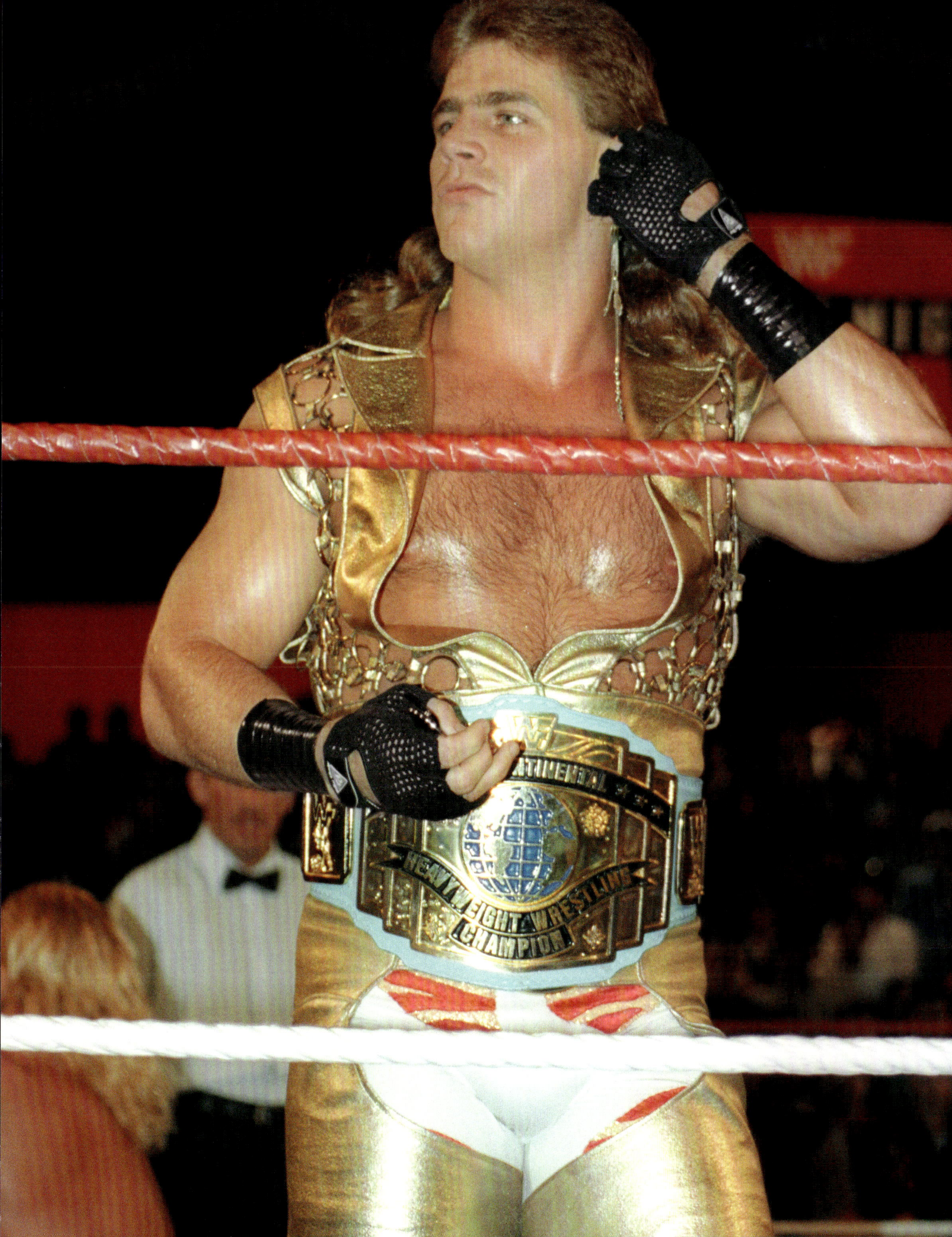

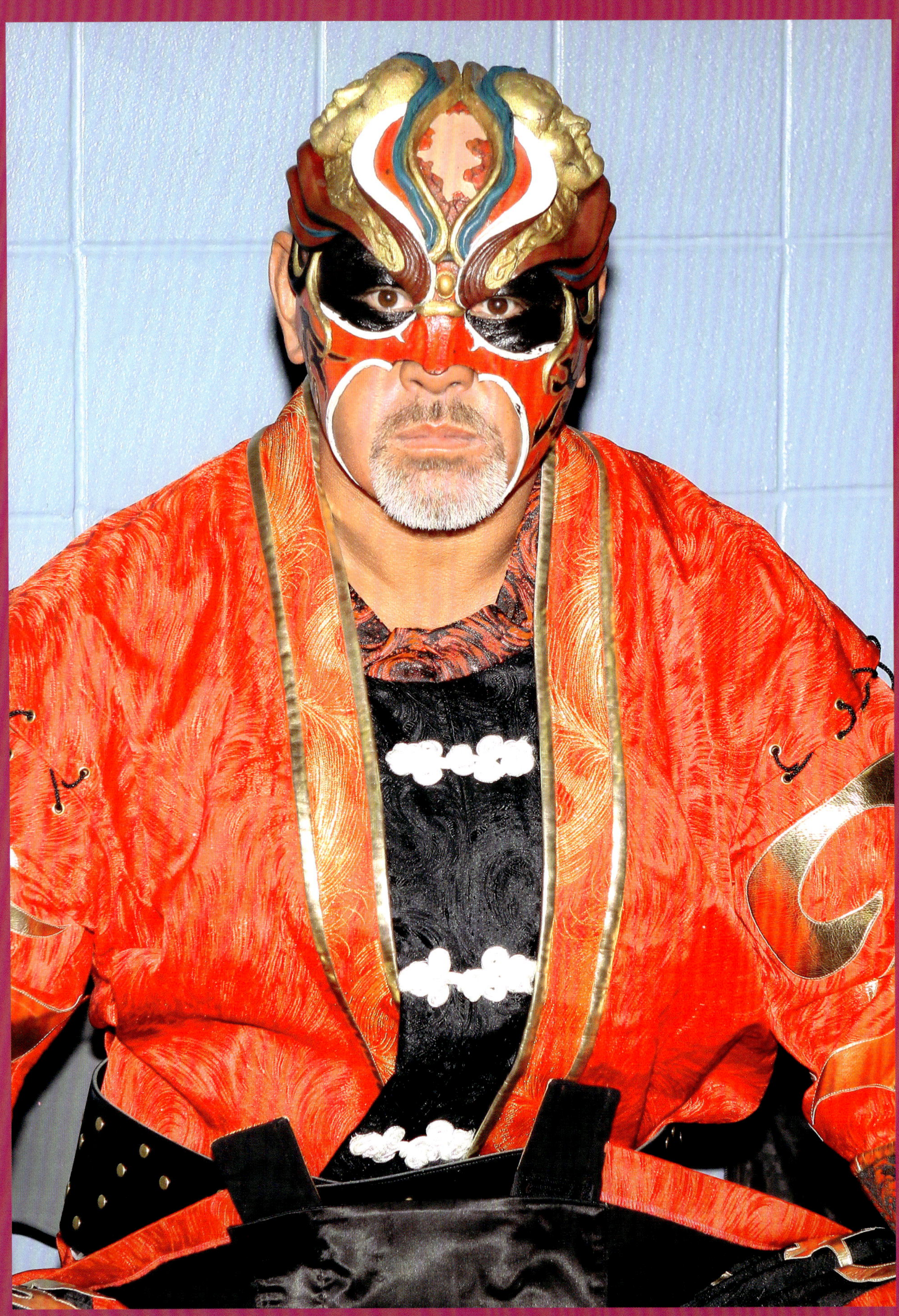

# KEIJI MUTO
## A.K.A. *THE GREAT MUTA*

Active 1984–2023

Nine-Time World Champion
WWE Hall of Famer

**Keiji Muto was** a major player in integrating Japanese wrestling styles and techniques into American culture. Better known by the name The Great Muta, Muto proved that great talent is undeniable, regardless of the language spoken. In the ring, he acted like a theatrical showman, but he wrestled like a warrior. He invented moves like the Shining Wizard that carried over into the sets of other American wrestlers, including Samoa Joe and Bryan Danielson.

Not only did he elevate what happened on the mat, The Great Muta also used his attire to create an aura of unpredictability. He typically donned a Kabuki-influenced red, black, or white satin robe embellished with kanji characters, dragons, and other embroidered symbols. His robe, which resembled the ceremonial and theatrical garments worn in Japan, blended elements of a kimono, samurai armor, and Japanese martial arts to create a fearsome identity. He wore a hachigane, or a metal forehead protector designed to reflect sword strikes, fully covering his head and face. A zukin, or a cloth hood commonly worn by ninjas to hide their identity, helped conjure mystique. With wide sleeves and a sash, called an obi, around his waist, he came to the ring ready to fight.

The Great Muta backstage. Photo by George Tahinos.

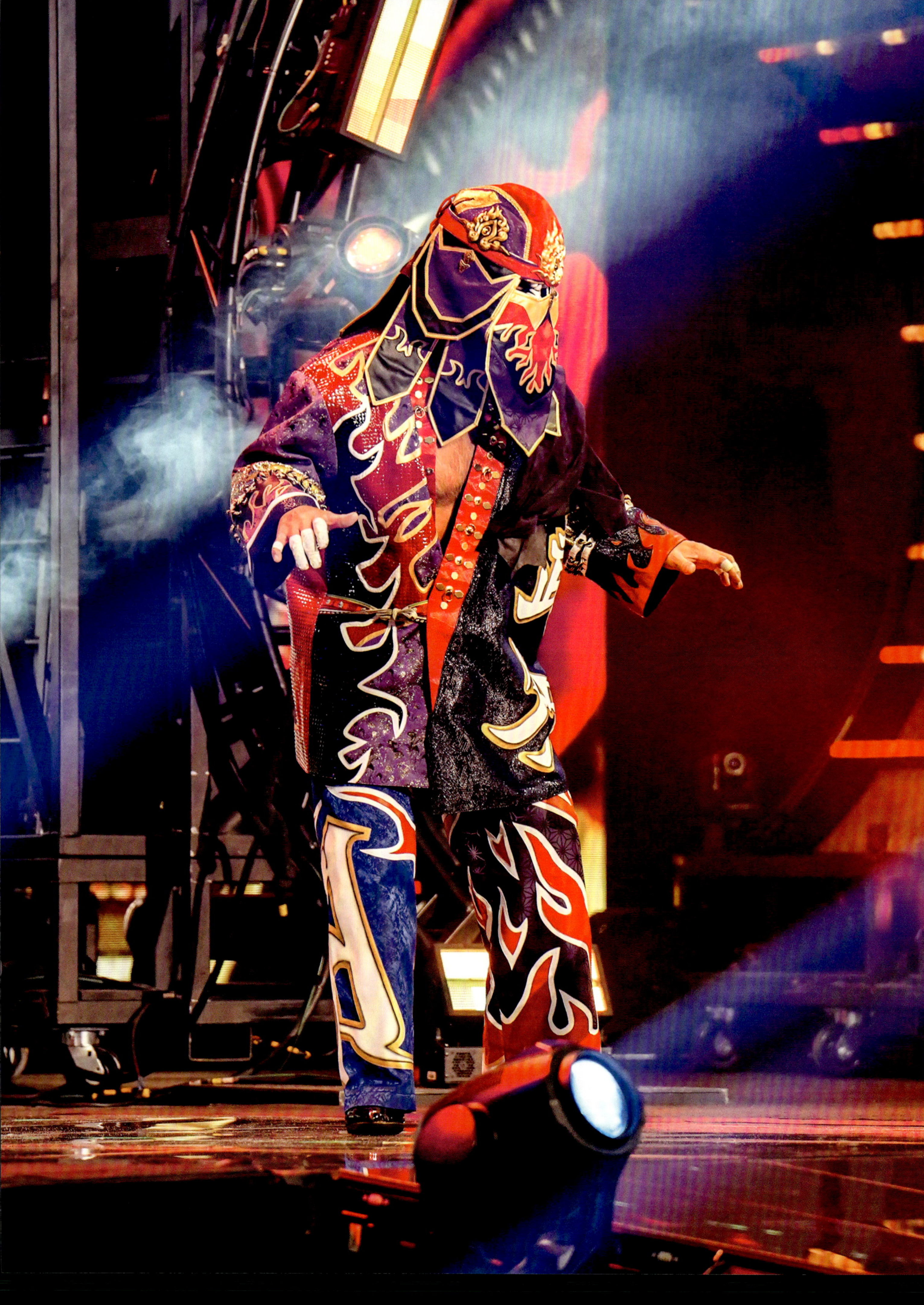

Muto complemented his attire with matching face paint under his headpiece. He used paint to express his feelings and emotions as a character, and fans enjoyed the surprise of the design. When Muto would make his entrance into an arena, he would simply transform the mood in the room and set the tone for what Great Muta fans would see. From emerald green to royal blue to cherry red, his face paint made him recognizable across countries. Incorporating everything from distinct, simple lines to symbols and splatter, his face paint was original and occasionally creepy. On some occasions, he would paint monstrous designs that felt predatory. Other times, Muto incorporated alliances into his paint. When he became a member of nWo Japan, for example, Muto expressed his pride with black-and-white face paint representing the faction's colors and his dedication to the group.

Muto thought carefully about his look and considered even the smallest details. He even matched his face paint and attire with the colored mist he spat at his opponents. Credited with popularizing the art of using colored mist in the United States as a scare tactic or a way to establish presence, Muto often used green mist, which frequently represents poison. He also used red, yellow, or black mist, depending on the level of pain he wanted to inflict, and dyed his tongue to match for even greater dramatic effect.

Today, many modern wrestling stars, such as Asuka, Shinsuke Nakamura, Aleister Black, and Rosemary, have borrowed Muto's tactic of using mist to intimidate their opponents. When he finally retired in 2023, The Great Muta had succeeded in bridging the gap between two diverse styles of wrestling, and in doing so, he became one of the sport's most legendary stars.

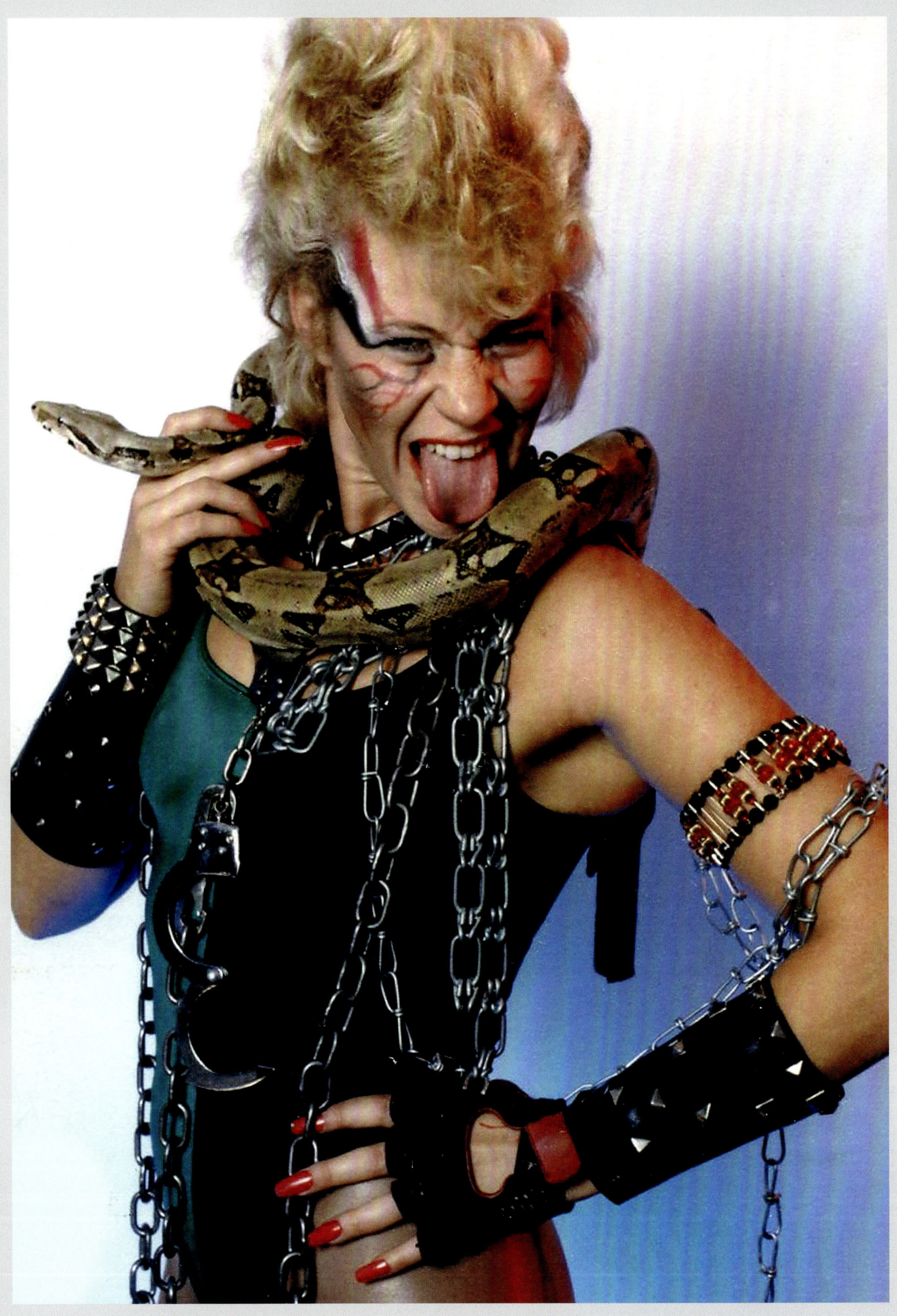

# GERTRUDE VACHON
## *LUNA VACHON*

Active 1985–2007

WWE Hall of Famer

**An angel with** a devil's spirit, Luna Vachon was captivating, unapologetically fierce, and a fearless competitor. Commanding attention no matter the room, be it a crowded arena or an intimate backstage set, Vachon brought a ferocious intensity matched only by her rock star–style outfits. Her hardcore looks were enhanced by metal studs, leather and chains, body paint, piercings, and offbeat patches shouting things like *Freak* and *Lunatic*. These eccentric details created endless intrigue as Vachon bucked convention while bringing her character to life.

Luna Vachon had a tag team partnership with fellow wrestler Tommy Dreamer, whom she accompanied to the ring for a portion of her career. Years later, he still remembers Vachon's individuality as an entertainer: "The moment the camera went on, I equated Luna to if Satan and Pamela Anderson had a baby. There's a specific promo I remember where she was behind me, and I hear her groaning like [she's in] *The Exorcist* before she came out and was revealed to the audience.

**"I used to hear some pretty amazing stories from Bam Bam Bigelow where Luna was the only woman that he was ever afraid of. Bam Bam was tough; he was a legitimate bounty hunter. He told me that there were times [when he] thought he was going to get into a fight, but Luna would have already knocked the guys out."**

–Tommy Dreamer, on Luna Vachon's reputation

Luna Vachon poses with a snake during a shoot. Photo by George Napolitano.

In ECW [Extreme Championship Wrestling], I was known as The Innovator of Violence, and together we were doing a Mickey-and-Mallory type of gimmick from *Natural Born Killers*. Luna was never afraid to beat the crap out of men and bleed alongside us. It was a different time in the '90s, and she was a massive star coming to a company that really needed it."

Luna Vachon was a massive star because of her commitment to her role; she would do anything—including covering herself in blood—to make the crowd believe in her character. "There was one time in ECW where I was bleeding and, out of nowhere, Luna took my blood and put it all over her face like it was arousing her," said Dreamer. "Because we were two people bred out of violence, she understood how to tell the story as the modern-day Bonnie and Clyde. When she showed up, fans would go insane."

There was a rarity to the way Vachon presented herself—she was everything unconventional in an era when women were glamorous and small. "Luna was unique, different, and sexy," said Dreamer. She had a raspy voice and a shaved head. She stuck out her tongue with thrasher metal intensity. She painted bolts of lightning on her face and body. She expressed herself in ways that defied the typical beauty standard—rejecting tradition and gleefully flaunting her independence.

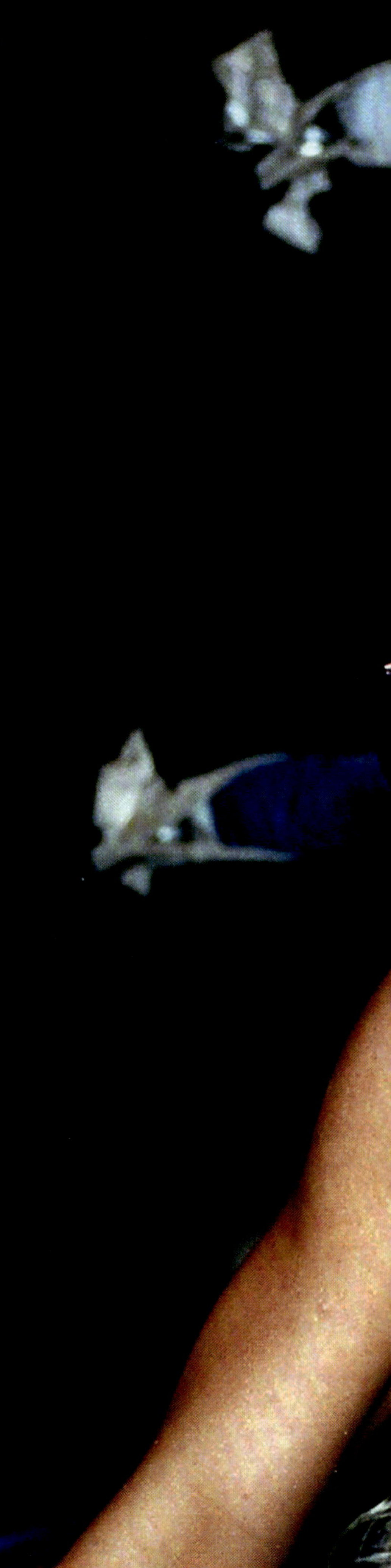

Luna Vachon interacts with the audience at a WWE event. Photo by George Napolitano.

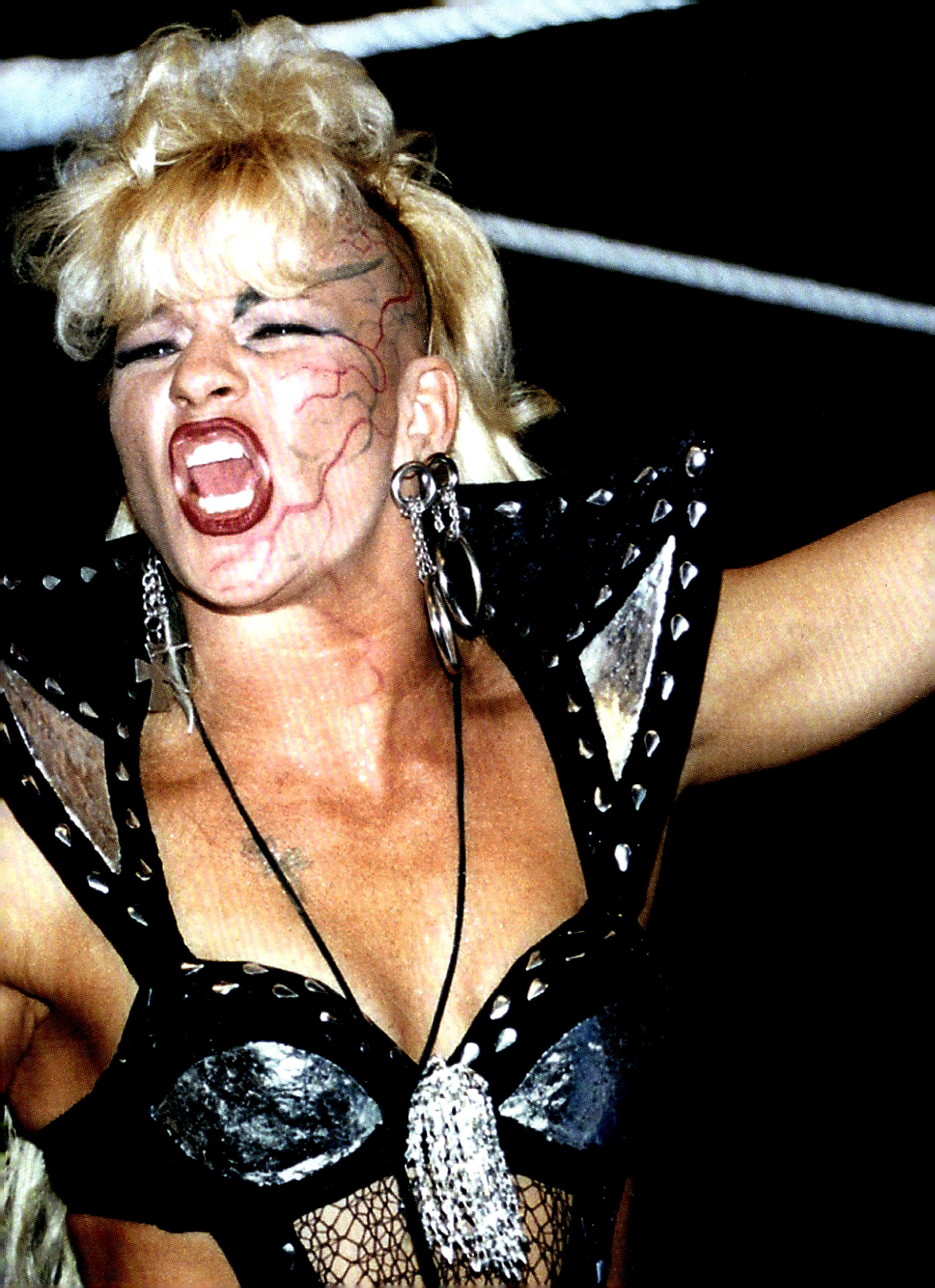

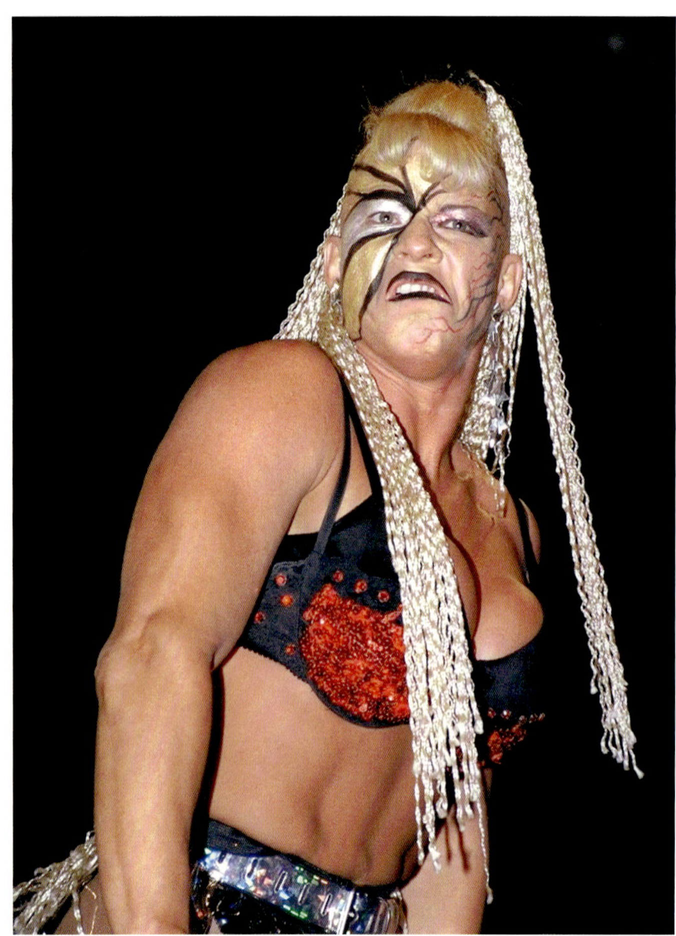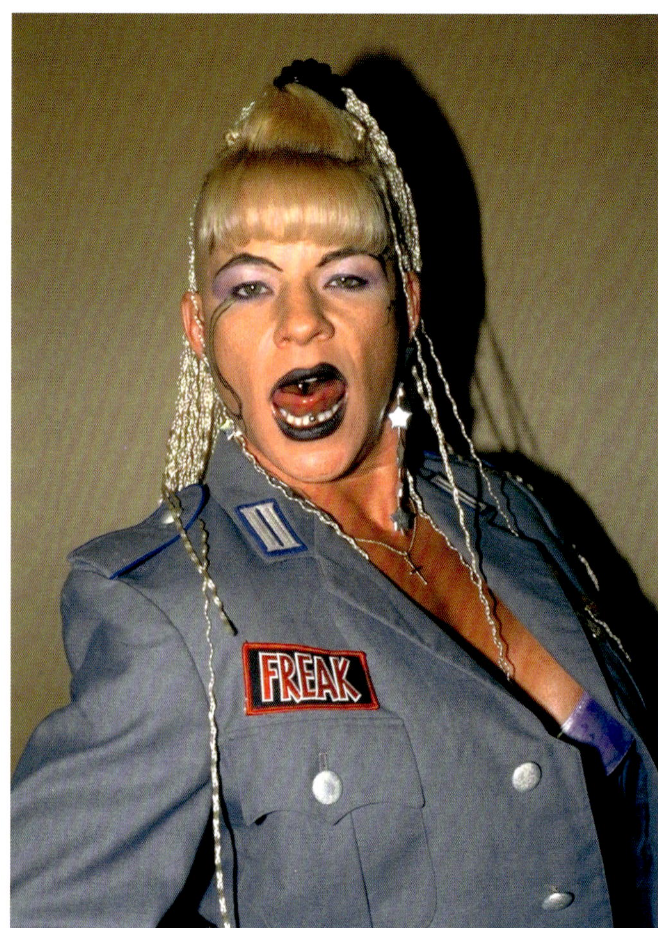

She accessorized to the nines with statement earrings, bold necklaces, chains, and thick belts. Vibrant eyebrows, bold lipsticks, and crimped hair told Vachon's story—while Vachon herself helped change the types of roles women wrestlers could play.

Given her fierce demeanor, people are often shocked to learn Luna Vachon was quite different away from the ring. Many of Vachon's colleagues remember her as someone much softer, even sweet. "She was the nicest, [most] loving person, but just had this tormented soul," said former wrestler Terry Taylor. "If you were to ever meet her, her aura was nothing like her appearance. Gertrude was kind, touchy-feely, and almost like a wounded child."

Dreamer fondly remembers Luna Vachon's softer side: "Inside the ring, she was like an uncaged animal," he said. "Outside of the ring, Luna was like the sweetest puppy dog. She was very close to me and my wife, Beulah McGillicutty, and every show, Luna would ask to do my wife's hair. Back then, we would often all share one locker room, and you would see Luna styling and combing another woman's hair. And the next second, she was cussing her out in the ring as her character."

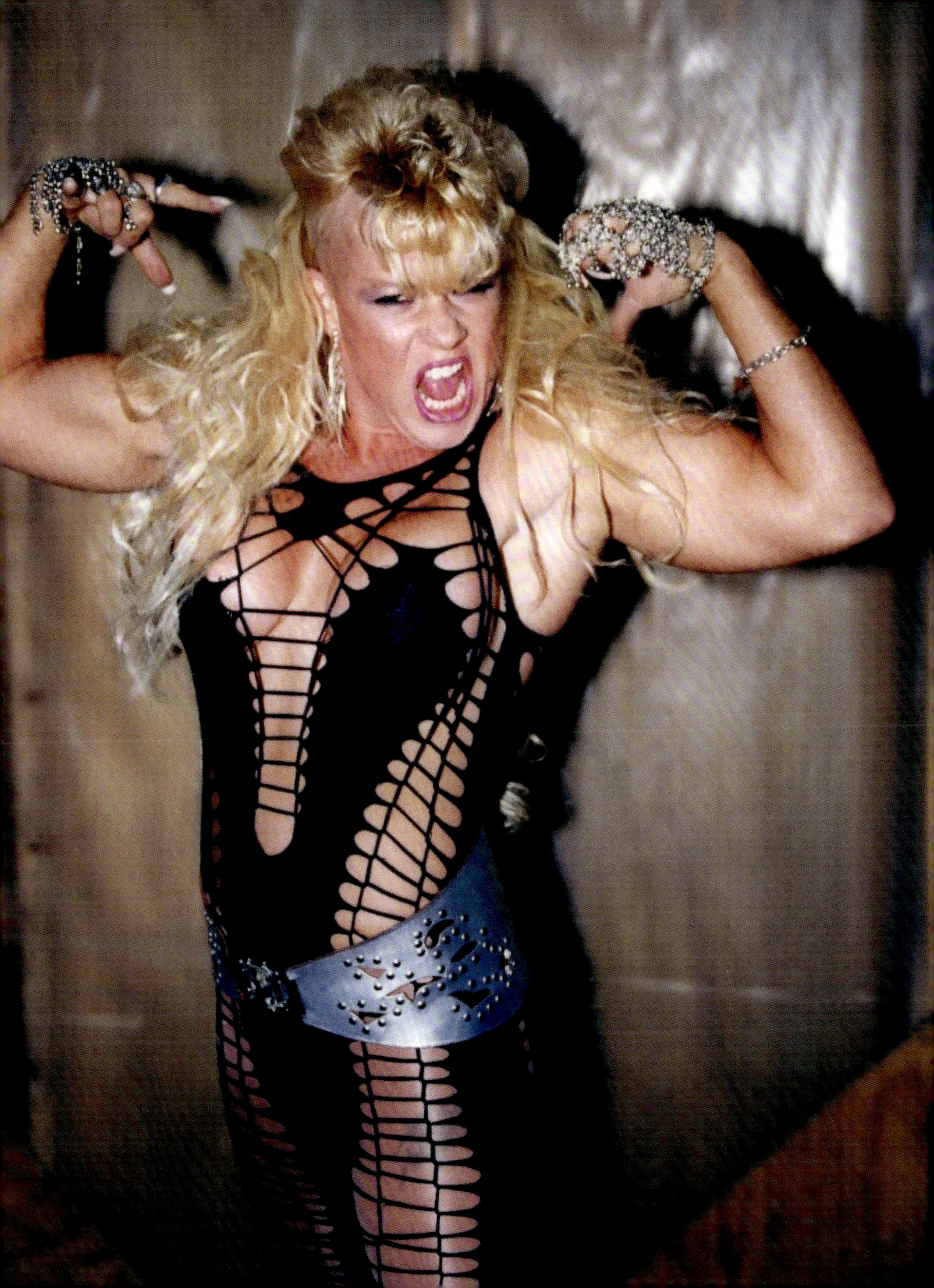

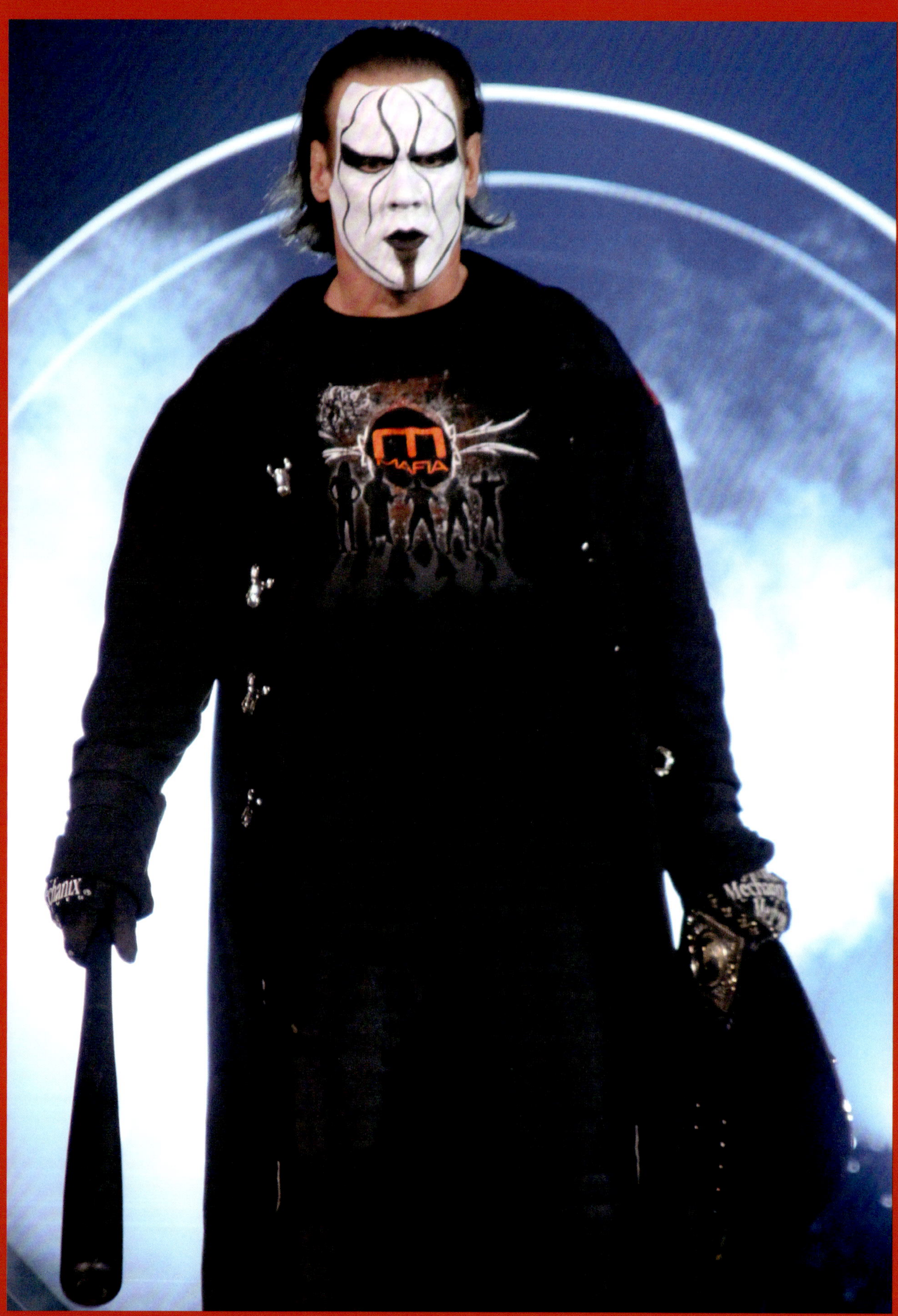
MAFIA

# STEVE BORDEN
## *STING*

Active 1985–2024

Fourteen-Time World Champion
WWE Hall of Famer

**Professional wrestling has** known lots of stars, but very few are considered the face of a franchise. Steve Borden, a.k.a Sting, remains the heart and soul of one company, WCW, that changed the industry as we know it. As a loyal soldier to World Championship Wrestling early on, Borden developed foundational skills that catapulted him throughout his career. Today, The Icon is considered one of the sport's most recognizable super-stars both for his long list of accomplishments and his evolutionary appeal.

Borden started his career as Flash, one half of The Blade Runners, a tag team duo he created with The Ultimate Warrior. Wearing simple black tights and black face paint around their eyes and mouths, The Blade Runners Flash and Warrior terrified opponents with their intimidating skill and commanding mystique. This was the beginning of the use of face paint for both of the wrestlers, and symbolized what was to come for Borden that would cement his legacy.

As he embarked on a solo career in the '80s and '90s, Borden continued using face paint—but this time to craft a very different persona. Borden donned bleached blond hair, shimmering fabrics embellished with tassels and sequins, and bold face paint in bright blues, hot pinks, and greens that shaped his Surfer persona. Around this time, fans were introduced to the scorpion emblem that would become central to Sting's iden-tity. The wrestler has never revealed the significance behind the symbol, but the history of the scorpion dates

Steve Borden as Main Event Mafia Sting for *TNA iMPACT!* Photo by George Tahinos.

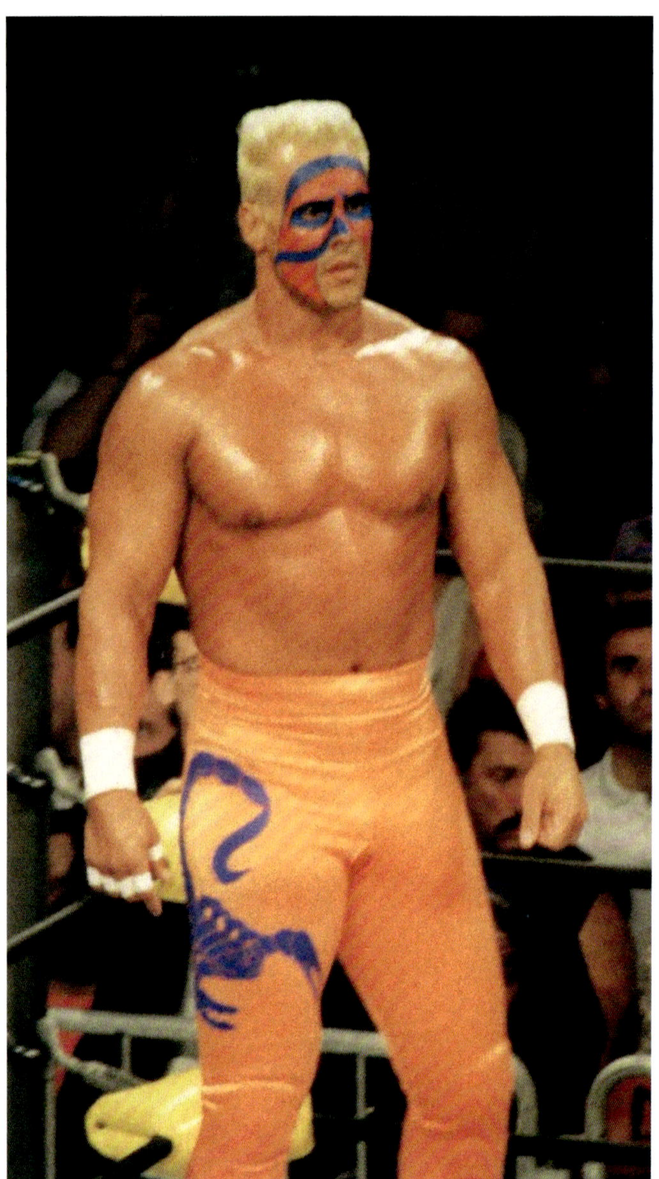

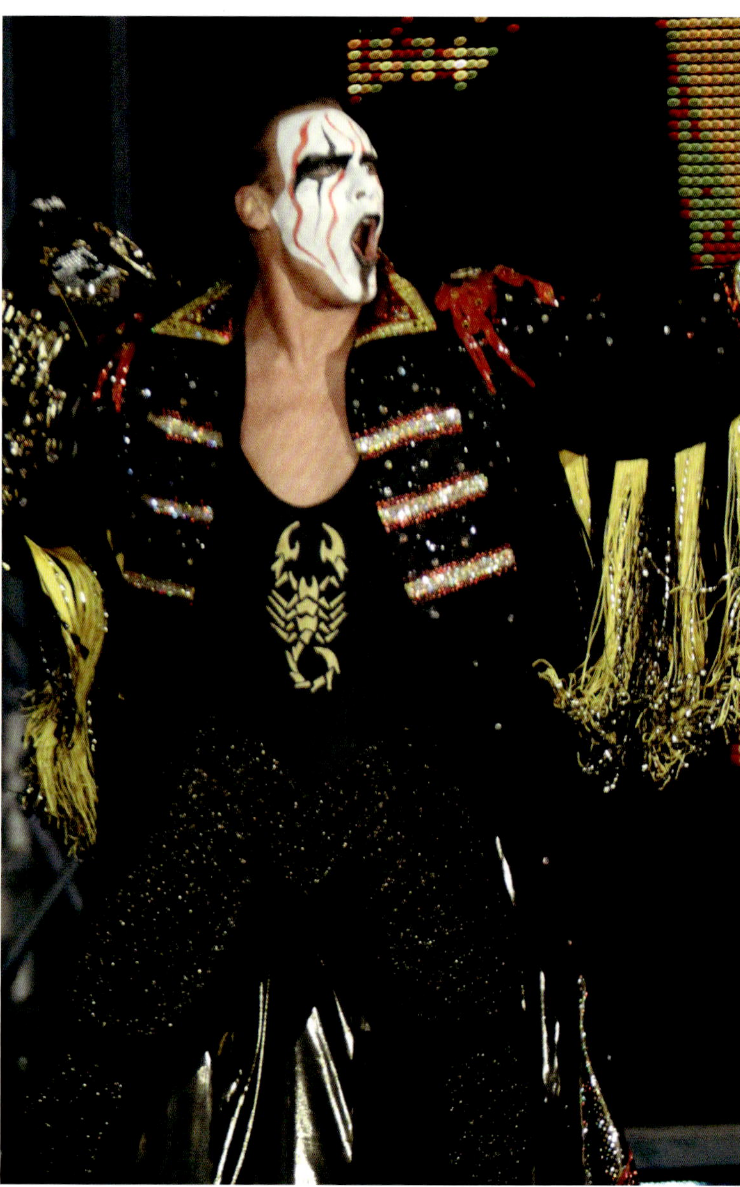

back to a WCW storyline where Sting wrestled a mystery opponent named The Black Scorpion. Perhaps adopting the logo was a way to commemorate the feud and provide a more visual angle to the story. Or maybe it represented the animal's territorial instincts and fighting style; much like Borden and his in-ring skills, a scorpion moves precisely toward its prey, and it stings when it bites.

But in 1996, Borden shocked fans by debuting a much darker persona, the one he's best known for. Inspired by the movie *The Crow*, Borden's vengeful new character wore a long black leather trench coat over a full body singlet, with his signature scorpion printed in white up the sides of his body. Along with black-and-white face paint, black gloves, long black hair, and Borden's trusty baseball bat in hand, these details reinforced his unpredictable behavior. In this era of his career, Borden went silent and let his vicious new aura do the talking. He acted edgy and mysterious and lurked in the shadows, often in the rafters and catwalks of arenas. The wrestler's mysterious actions intrigued fans, who found themselves fascinated by his chilling intrigue and sudden attacks by descending from high above, just waiting for the right moment.

Color began creeping back into Borden's attire in 1998, when he began donning

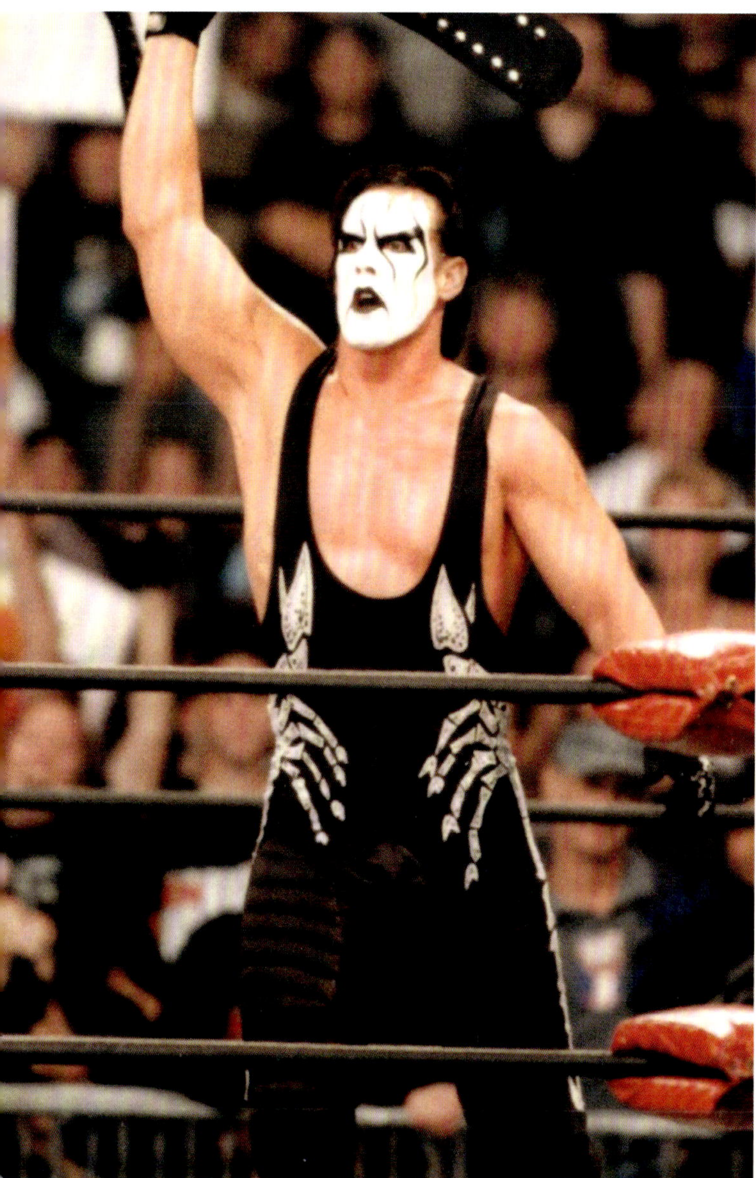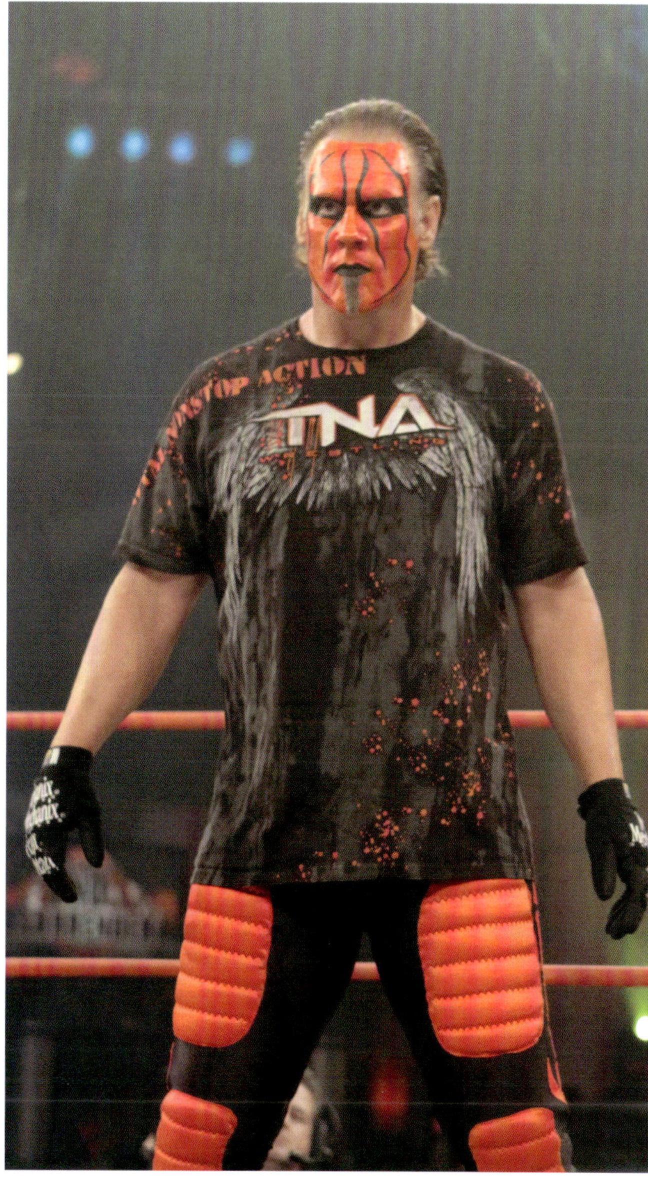



red-and-black face paint and gear upon joining nWo's
Wolfpac faction. As a member of the Total Nonstop
Action Wrestling (TNA) roster sporadically throughout
the 2000s, Borden again incorporated the color red. In
2011, Sting took the look a step further and used red hues
in his face paint to make The Crow look more like The
Joker. The red face paint offered a variation on his look
but remained only an extension of the original character.

Given Borden's forty years of dedication to the
business, it's undeniable that his final moments in All
Elite Wrestling (AEW) were impactful, as he helped
new generations of stars and closed the door in the ring.
With paint as his armor, he may have seen it all while
lurking in the shadows, but we will always celebrate his
timeless legacy in the spotlight.

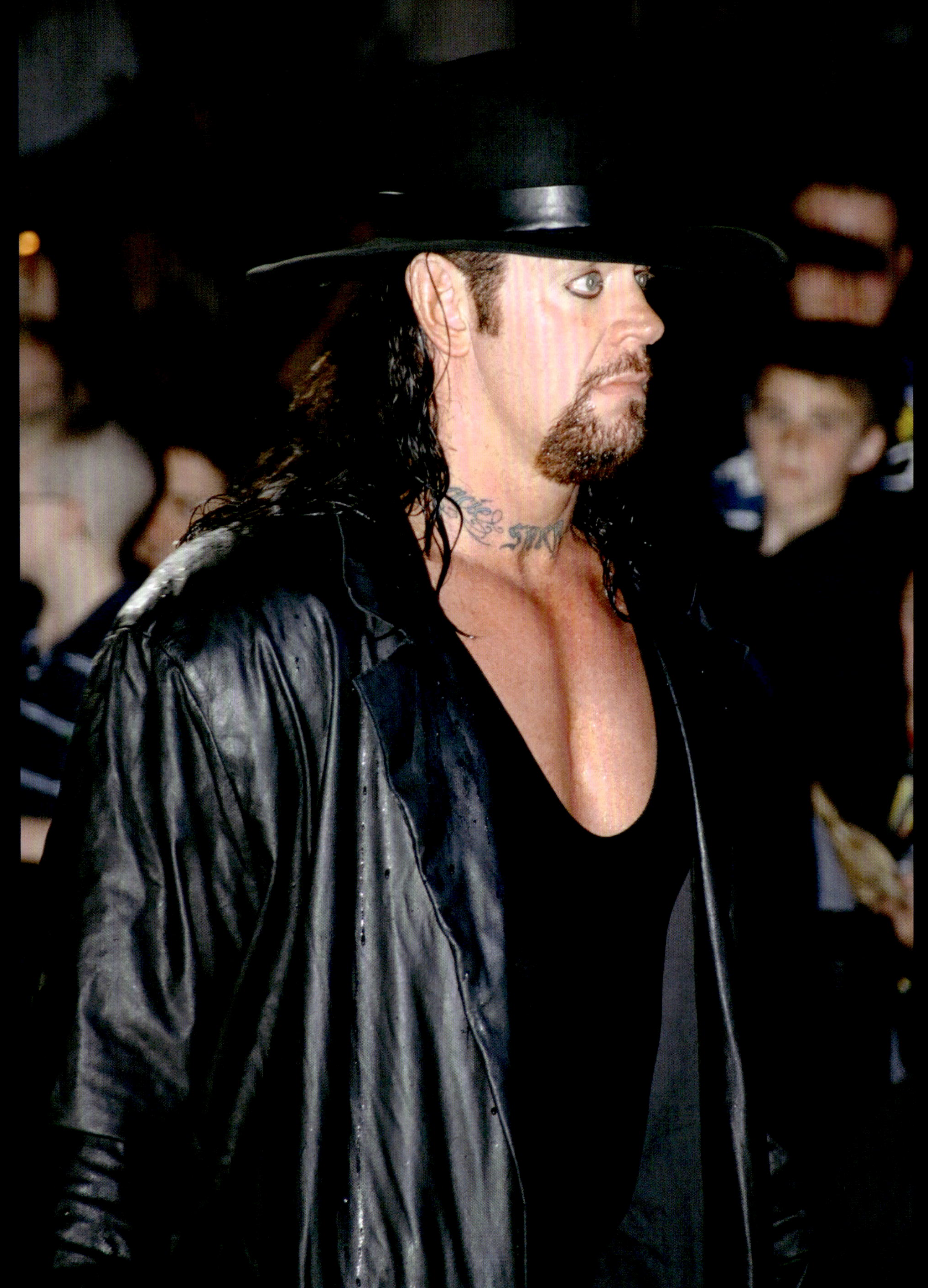

# MARK CALAWAY
## THE UNDERTAKER

Active 1990–2020

Twenty-Five (Twenty-One Consecutive) WrestleMania Victories
WWE Hall of Famer

**Some legends transcend,** and some redefine. Mark Calaway, a.k.a. The Undertaker, changed the way we view professional wrestling. Committed to never breaking character, Calaway masterfully blended realism and imagination, to the delight of the audience.

The Undertaker was intimidating and mysterious, always leaving fans in a state of suspense. With his dark, gothic clothing, The Undertaker's trademark look included a leather trench coat, wide-brimmed hat, distressed gloves, and black eyeliner. As he rolled his makeup-smudged eyes back in his head and stuck out his tongue, he almost appeared supernatural, the main character in a dark romance between performer and viewer. Even when his character was still in its early days of development, this original look cemented the imagery commonly associated with his persona. "In the beginning, everything was a chance," said Calaway, who wasn't initially sure how The Undertaker would resonate with fans. "I wasn't connected enough at that point to know whether or not it was translating and reaching the audience. At the end, it was important to hold on to the essence of the character despite it evolving to an even darker space."

Costume designer Terry Anderson created many of Calaway's most famous looks. She recalled working with Calaway as they brainstormed a look for The Phenom [one of The Undertaker's personas]: "One day, he walked up to me at TV [backstage], and he goes, 'Hey, can you make leather coats?' I said yes. And he goes, 'Can you make me a Pinhead coat? Like from the movie *Hellraiser*?' I made him his first jacket, and it was very plain. I didn't know how far I could go into it because Mark never really told me what he wanted the jacket to look like. He would give me a genre and he would say something like, 'Make it look Western, or like The Dark Lord.' As time went on, working with Mark, I would do so many different things that people normally wouldn't put in a jacket. At one point, I found some leather cording and ended up crocheting medallions for the outfit. I put them on his jacket and then embellished them with metal. I liked the creative freedom he gave me, which doesn't always happen. Often people will want this color or that, and honestly, I can't get into what I'm designing as much as if they just said, 'Hey, do what you do.' And Mark always did that with me."

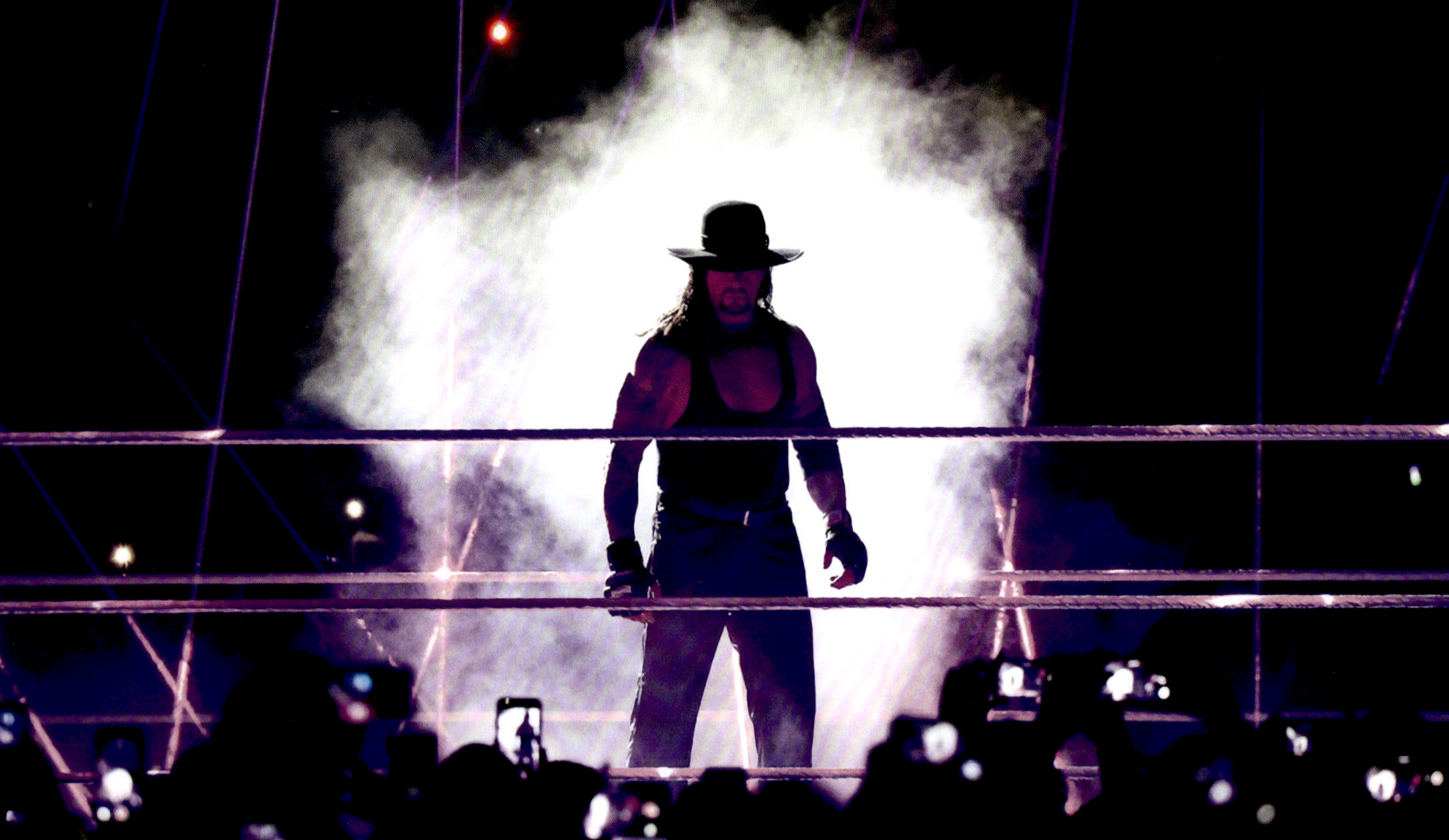

Calaway was wise to relinquish creative control to Anderson, who seemed to possess her own supernatural ability to pull fabulous looks out of thin air. "There were so many things I created on the road," said Anderson, who was always looking for ways to add texture to The Undertaker's ensembles. "If you don't add texture to something that is black on black, you're not going to see anything but a black outfit," said Anderson, who came up with the idea of weaving black leather into Calaway's perfectly sinister look at WrestleMania 29. "I came up with the idea of adding leather strips somewhere on his outfit, but it wasn't like I could run quickly to get a loom to weave on," she said. So the ever-resourceful seamstress rummaged through the trash to create what became one of her favorite Undertaker outfits. "I ended up getting a cardboard box from the garbage can at the hotel and some number two pencils from the front desk. I just started jabbing those into the cardboard box, and that box became my loom that I wove pieces on," she recalled. "A lot of the work, I made up as I went. I typically don't go into the outfit going, 'Oh, I'll do this!' It just comes to me."

Anderson also made a jacket on the road for WrestleMania Miami. "It was kind of put together the same way I made WrestleMania 29's," said Anderson, who discovered an ingenious way to dry leather strips on the road: "Normally what I do is I mold all of the leather pieces I'm using. First, I get them wet, mold them, and then throw them in the oven at a very, very low temperature so they can dry. Well, on the

**"What I wore, and every detail of it, from head to toe, was carefully crafted to bring out the darkness of The Undertaker and the demons he held within. My look told you that there was something internal about The Undertaker that you might not want to cross!"**

—Mark Calaway on bringing his character to life

road, I don't have access to an oven. So I took my sewing machine, covered up one side of it with cardboard, taped it all around, and stuck my blow dryer into the one side. I had a cookie rack that I brought from home, and I stuck it inside my machine. That's what I used to dry all these pieces that ended up being nailed onto his riveted jacket."

With every metamorphic change of Calaway's character, including his Deadman persona, The Undertaker never lost his mystique. As he modified his look throughout the years, at his core Calaway used drama to tell his story. That could mean being accompanied to the ring by his urn-toting manager, Paul Bearer, as The Western Mortician, or channeling a leather-vested, bandana-clad biker while ripping a Harley-Davidson as The American Badass. Regardless of which version of his character appeared in the ring, Calaway's entrance was always a sight to behold.

The Undertaker also created a place for fans from all walks of life to recognize what makes them one of a kind. Calling his fans the "Creatures of the Night," Calaway reached people around the world. "I realized early on that I made it OK for people to be unique, that it was OK to look different and act different," he said. "You don't have to conform to the boxes people try to create for you. You have to step outside the box and be true to who you are."

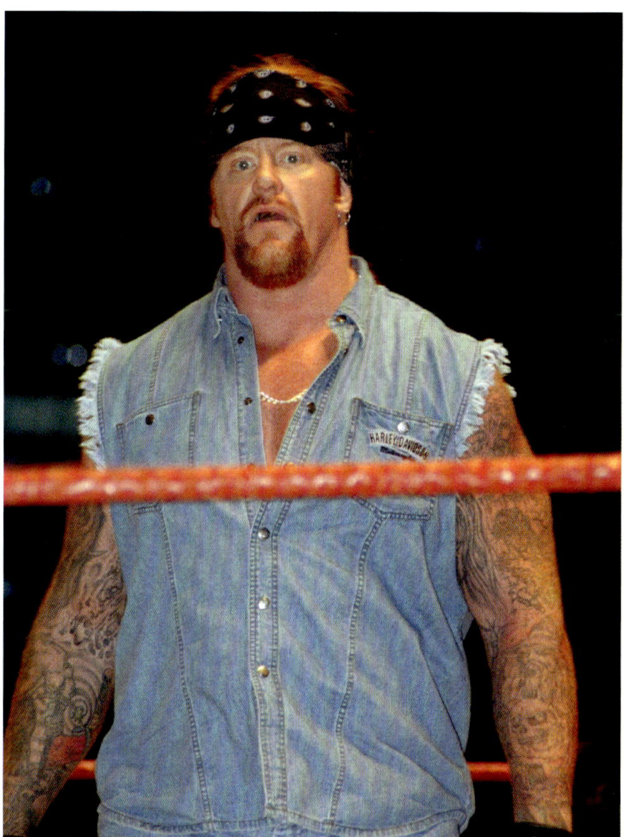

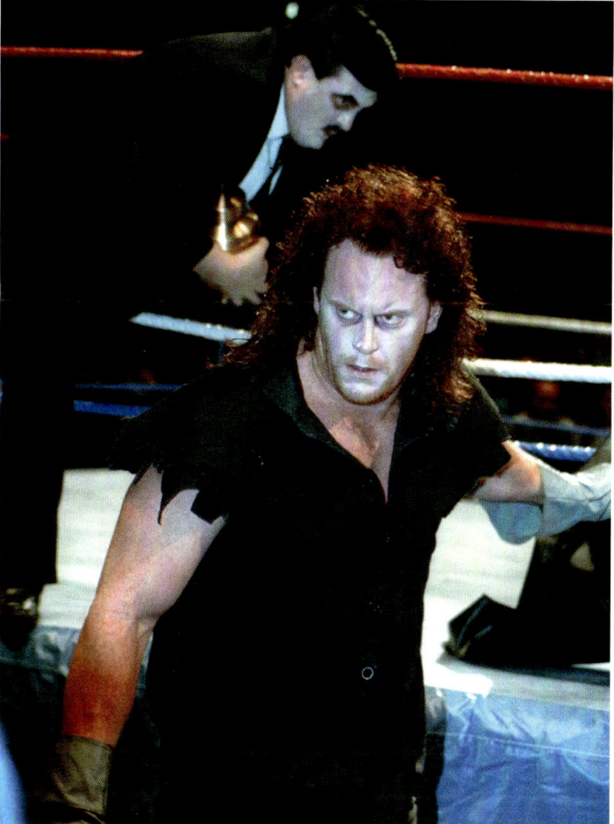

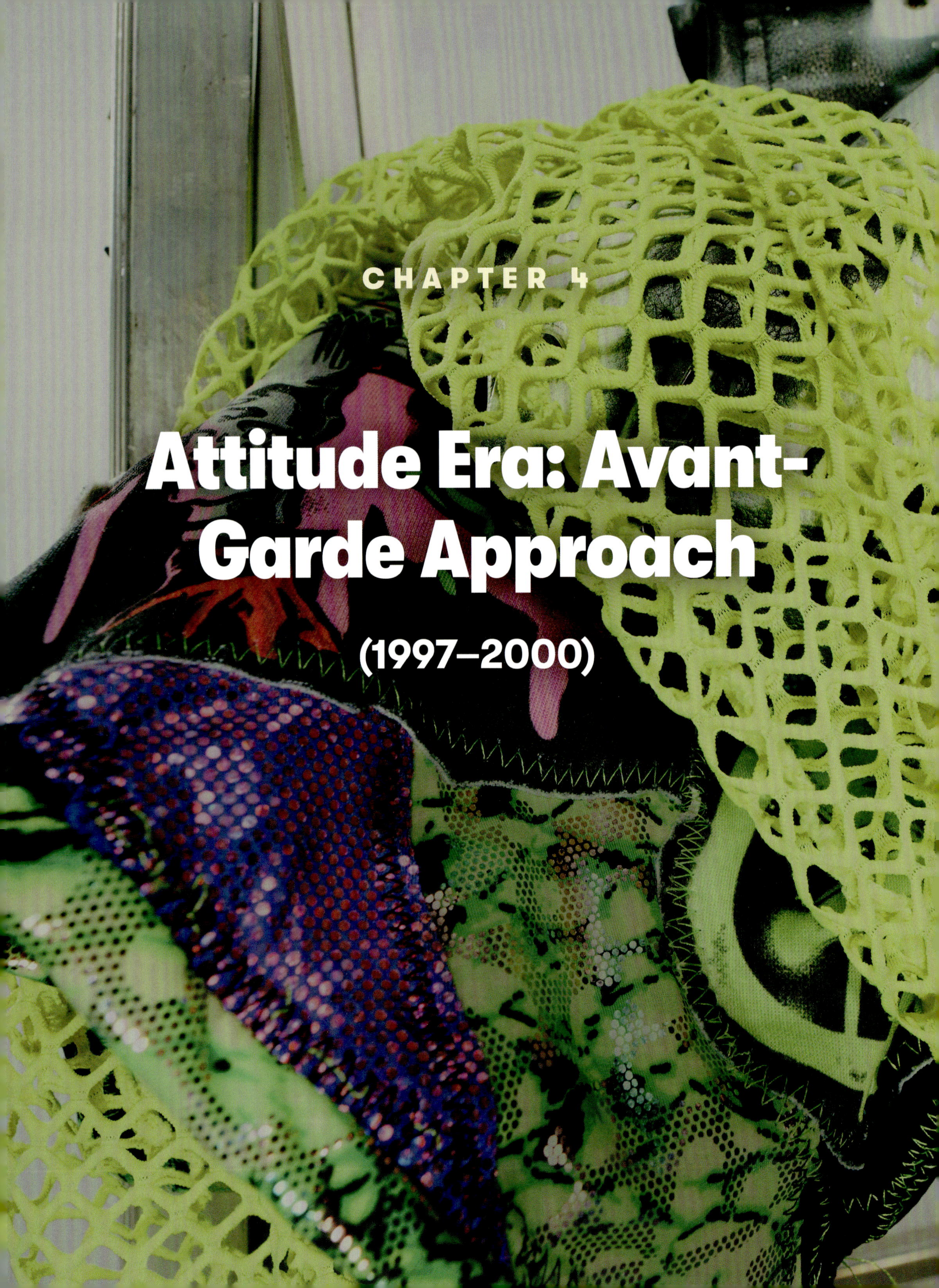



# Attitude Era: Avant-Garde Approach

## (1997–2000)

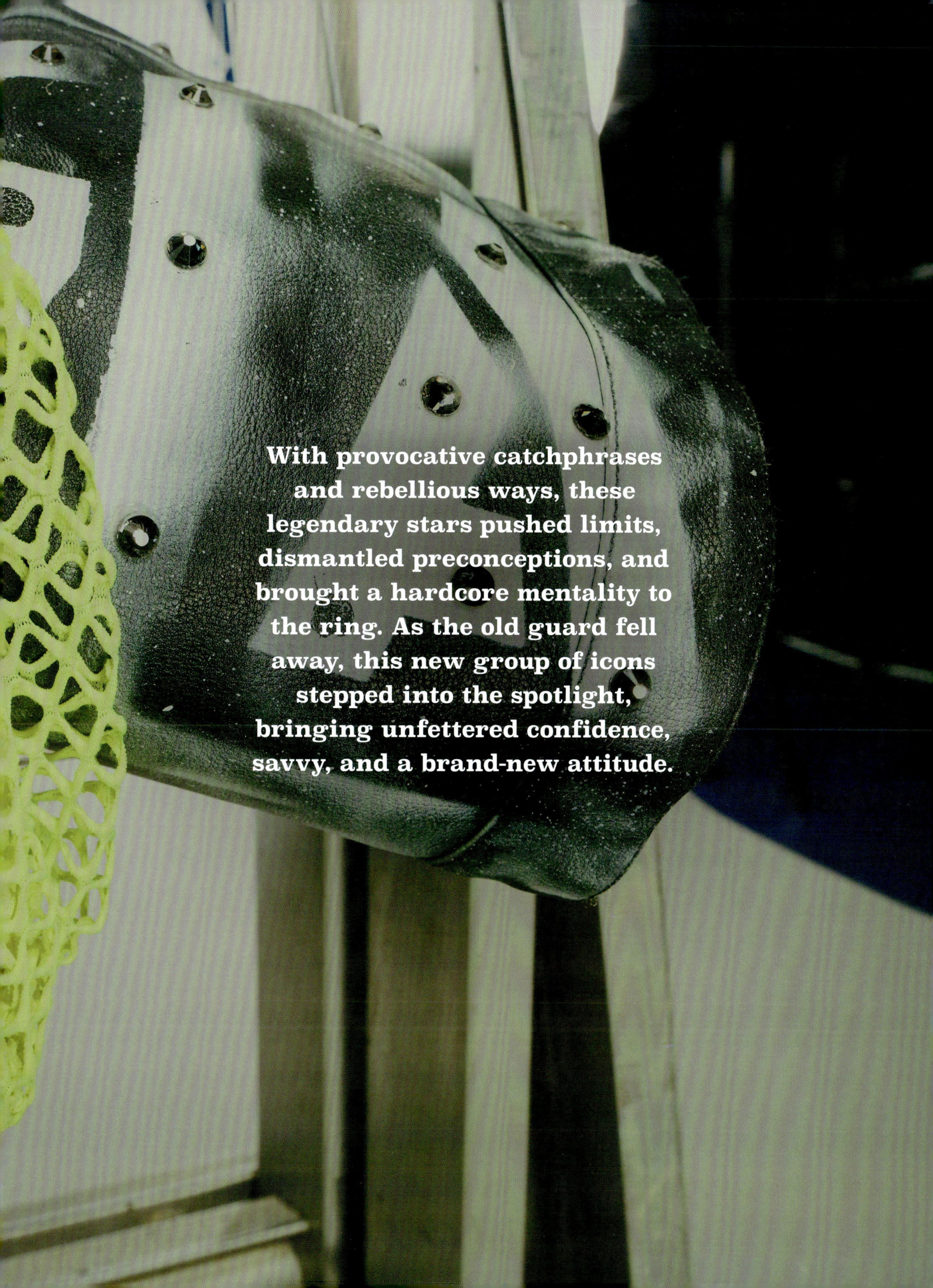

With provocative catchphrases and rebellious ways, these legendary stars pushed limits, dismantled preconceptions, and brought a hardcore mentality to the ring. As the old guard fell away, this new group of icons stepped into the spotlight, bringing unfettered confidence, savvy, and a brand-new attitude.

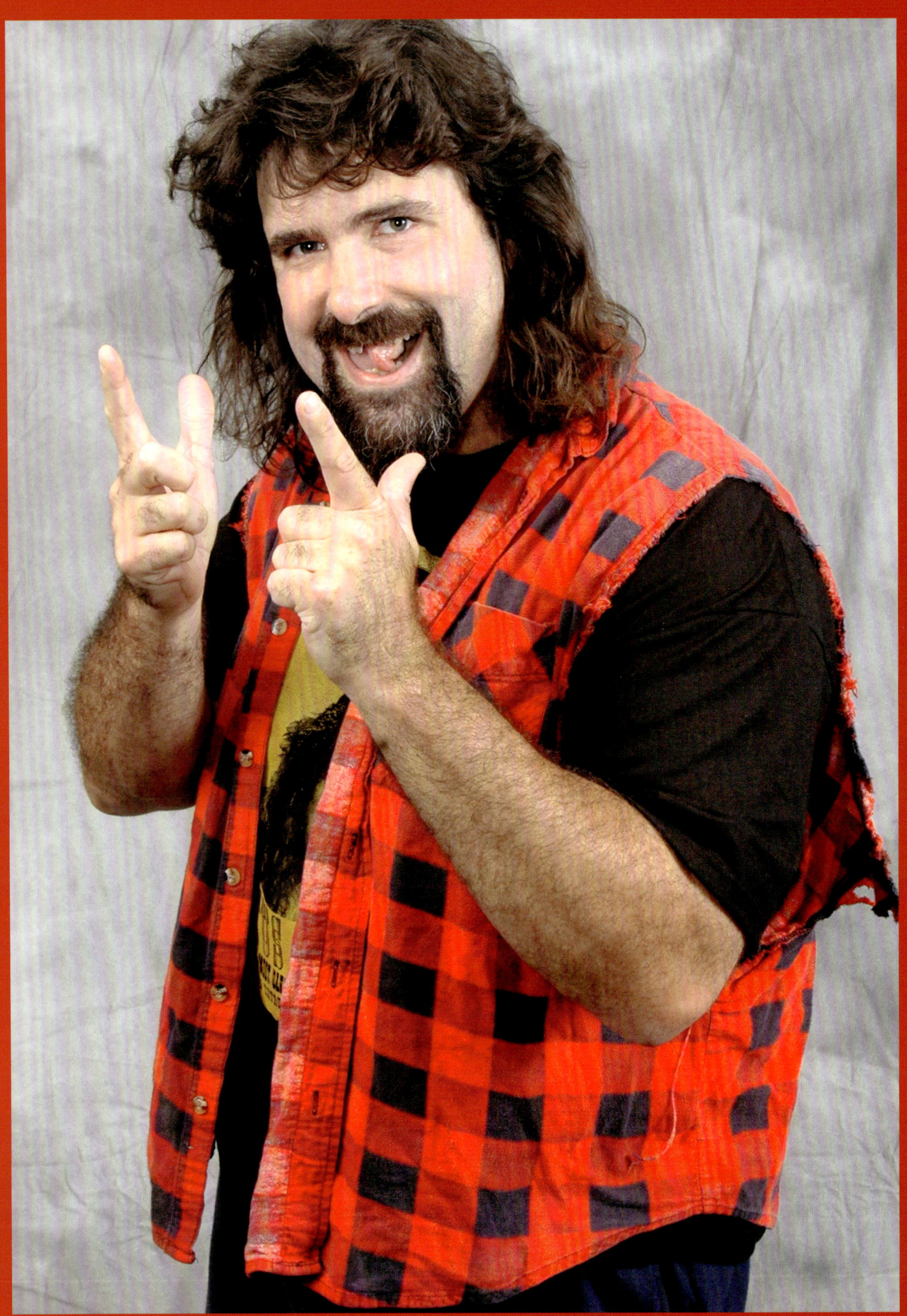

# MICHAEL FOLEY
## *MICK FOLEY*

Active 1983–2012

Three-Time WWE Champion
Deathmatch Legend

**Mick Foley was** the first professional wrestler to portray three distinct characters in quick succession, challenging the usual process of developing a single persona. Bloodthirsty lumberjack Cactus Jack, demented Mankind, and the happy-go-lucky Dude Love would become known as The Three Faces of Foley, cementing the wrestler's renown as a jack-of-all-trades in an industry simply defined by legends and heels. "I think evolving on the national stage is vital," said Foley. "You need to tweak the character before the audience realizes it needs tweaking. If they realize it before you do, it's really difficult to get back to where you were." He came to this conclusion after watching other Attitude Era wrestlers utter the same catchphrases week after week: "I would look at guys literally doing the same promos week in and week out and say to myself, my family, to some of the other people in business, 'Don't the fans need more than this?' I always thought, 'There's going to come a time when they need more, when the business isn't as red-hot.' I also thought the guys who were keeping the business afloat would be seen as the guys who couldn't draw when they were preventing a collapse. We never had a collapse, but we did see a lot of popular guys who did not evolve. I took a lot of pride in trying to see what was needed before the fans realized things needed changing."

**"You don't hit home runs in life unless you strike out a lot. Fortunately, we're not talking about strikeouts, but I had a lot of misses, too."**

—Mick Foley

Mick Foley poses for the camera in signature red-and-black flannel. Photo by George Napolitano.

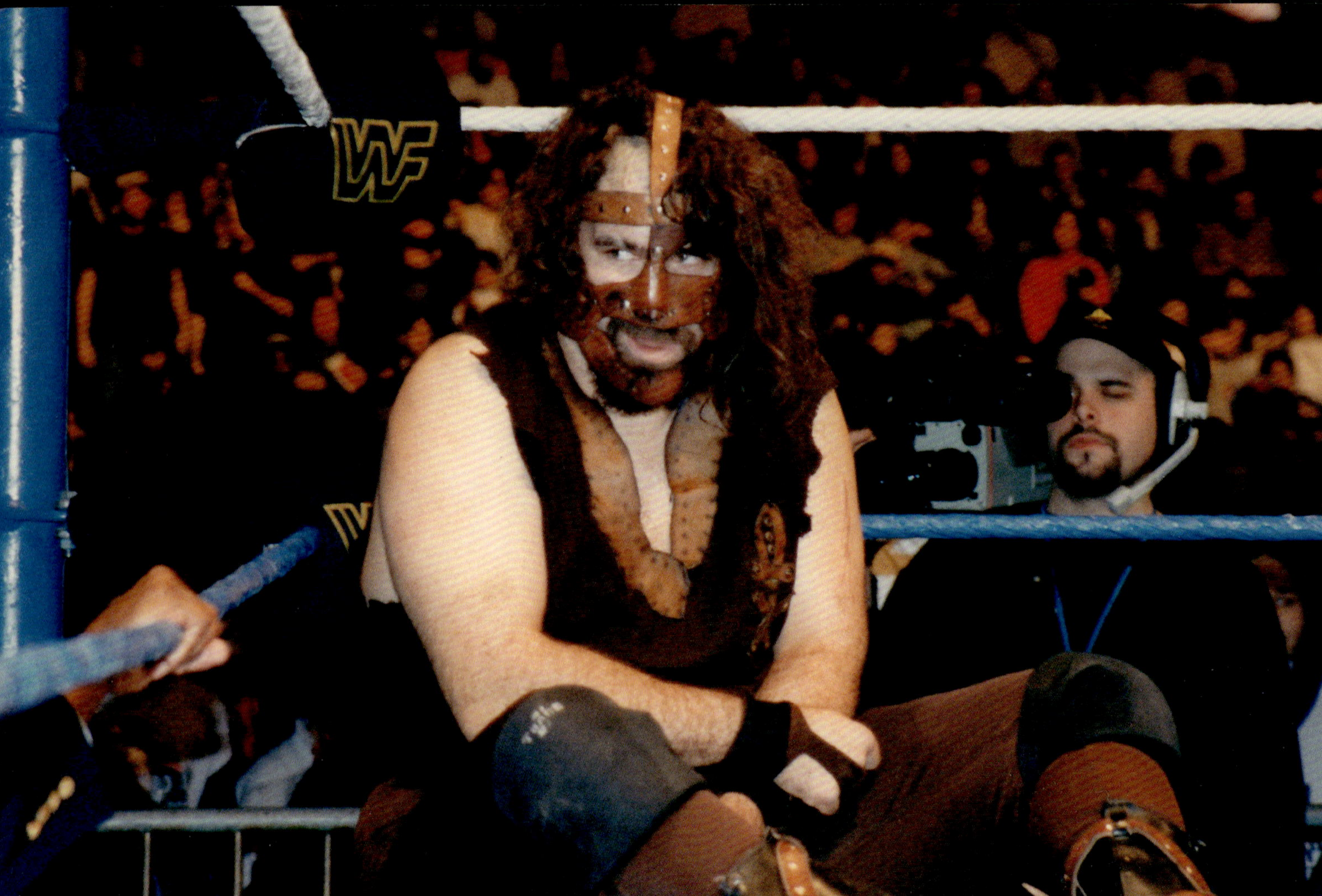

Versatility wasn't Foley's only advantage. Celebrated as one of the world's toughest wrestlers, Foley amazed fans with his strength and willingness to do whatever it took in the ring—once even going so far as Cactus Jack that he lost half his ear in a match. Foley's second character, Mankind, was even more unpredictable and violent. Mankind's unsettling mannerisms, manic behavior, and deranged masks foreshadowed the mayhem fans witnessed whenever he stepped into the ring. "When I became Mankind, I had a lot of say in the character, other than the fact that they saddled me with the color brown," Foley said. "I'm not convinced it wasn't an intentional attempt to give Mankind the worst color of all time."

But despite being burdened with the worst color in wrestling, Foley proceeded to shape Mankind into an unforgettable character. "The symbol on the bat was my idea, to combine a Celtic cross with an axe, something that nobody ever put together, so it looked ominous," the wrestler recalled. "The mask was the reason I was hired, because Mr. McMahon had liked one of the prototypes of masks made for The Undertaker. Undertaker needed a mask after fracturing his orbital bone and they didn't want him out there in just a hockey mask, so a bunch of ideas were drawn up. The Mankind mask was the prototype of one of those ideas. Originally Mankind was a very dark character because I did not want to just be [my other persona] Cactus Jack with a mask. And I would wear the mask for hours trying to get into the feel of the character."

Somehow, Mick Foley's original masks have survived years of wear and tear. According to Foley: "I wasn't able to wash the mask. No one really thought that through. I had two masks, and both of them started out as beige because they were leather. They had been painted a bit to give them an almost ancient look by the

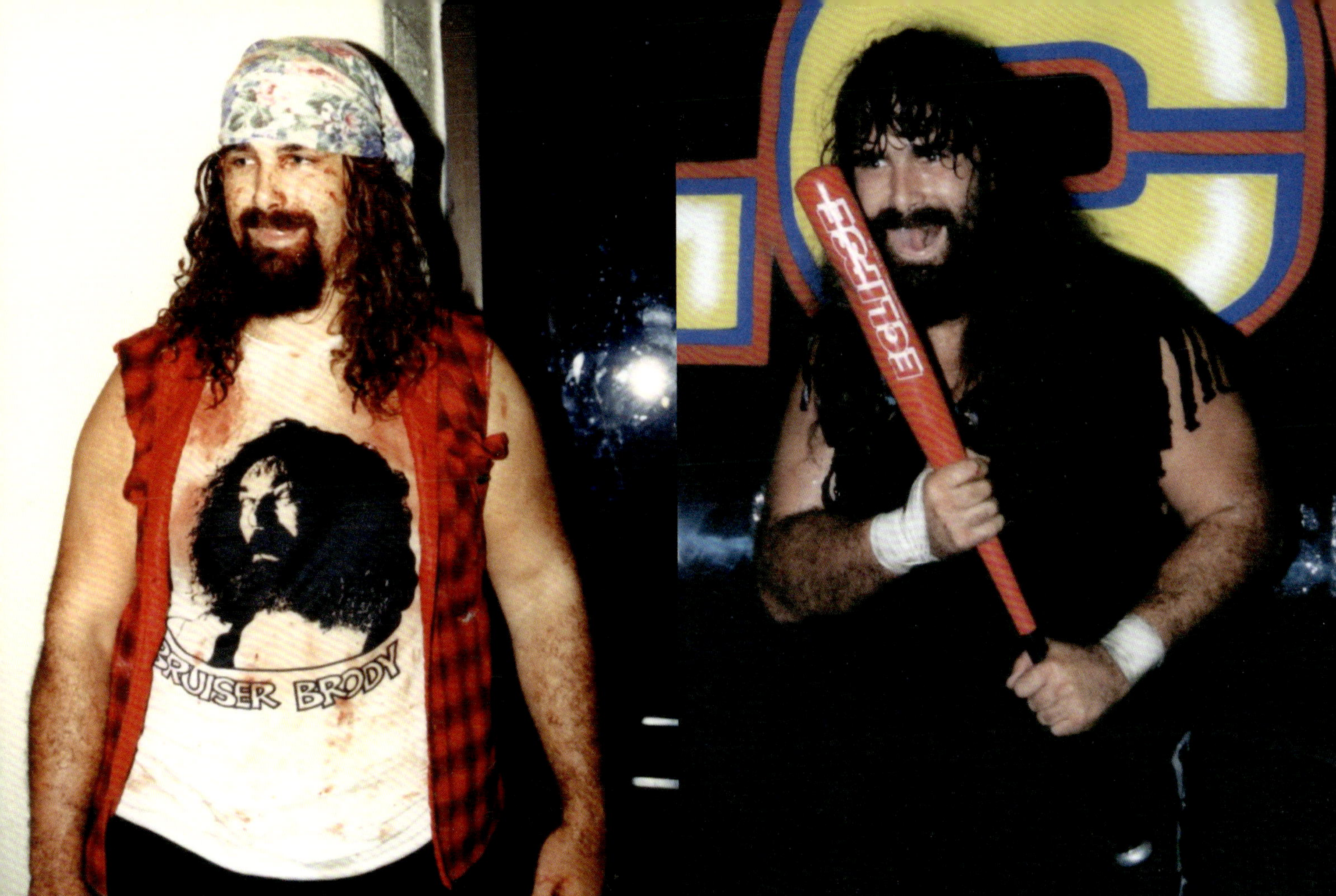



mask maker, who was really steeped in mythology. By the time I finally was presented with two new masks in 1999, those two originals were dark brown, almost black, soaked through with sweat, and were not a pleasant sensory experience. I was basically wearing the mask on top of my head. I would put Vicks VapoRub on my mustache, pull the mask down, and when I heard my music playing to go out, I would go. It smelled terrible."

Foley's Midas touch was such that he even transformed a sweat sock into a million-dollar marketing product. With Mr. Socko, Foley proved that his genius lay in his nonconformity. "I was lucky to have been at WWE at the time when we were encouraged to try different things and see what worked," said Foley. "I thought [Mr. Socko] was very average when I did it, but when ["Stone Cold"] Steve Austin thought it was funny, I thought there may be something to it. I certainly never expected that nearly twenty-seven years later, grown men would be paying me to draw faces on a sweat sock. I am fortunate that it became a big part of who I was and, to much dismay, of younger siblings across the country who grew up with socks in their mouths."

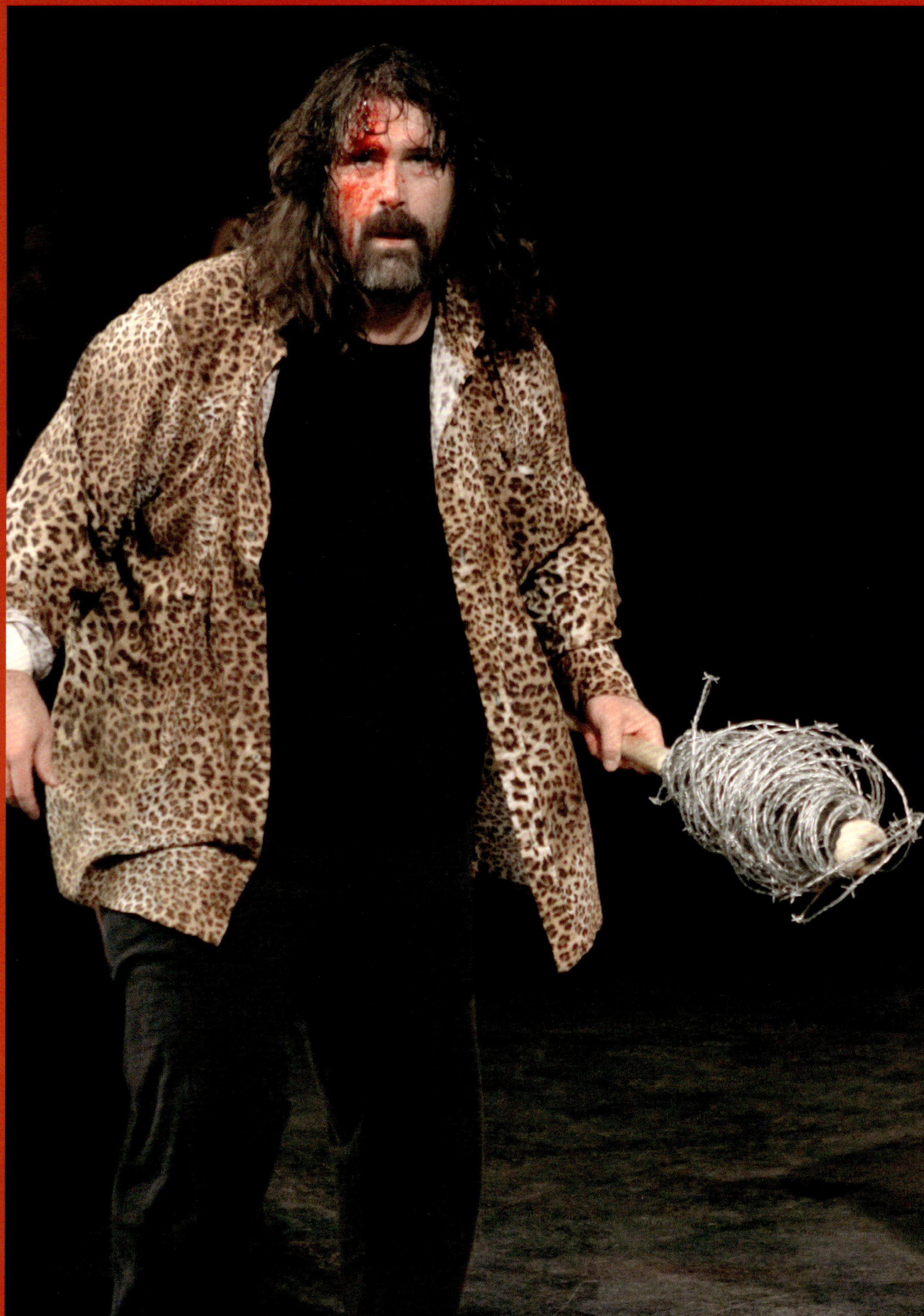

"As Cactus Jack, I started with [a] Tarzan singlet and tights and then I went with the butcher straps. I realized the more covered up I was, the better I did, and I felt more comfortable that way. I got my first flannel when I was thirteen, and I believe I still have it. It's got legitimate tears from barbed wire matches, but the first tears came when my friends and I tried to climb a fence. Maybe that was a harbinger of things to come . . . when I jumped down from the top of the fence as a kid and the barbed wire caught me and put about three or four good sizable tears in that quilted flannel and I wore it anyway. I wore the flannel for my final match of my full-time career in February 2000 against Triple H. And even though I wore a variety of different things when I was a commissioner, it was the flannel that resonated with people."

–Mick Foley

Despite his many roles, Foley's biggest accomplishment may have been proving that wrestlers don't have to look a certain way to enjoy an accomplished career. "I helped pave the way for a creative mind and a not-so-impressive physique to make an impact," Foley said. "I think more so even than the change of characters. Guys like Kevin Owens and the work that Bray Wyatt did were partly possible because guys like me helped expand the definition of what a wrestler could look like. And with that, what a top wrestler could look like. Clearly, there are guys like me out there, who are average or less, with less than average physiques, who aren't pushed as top stars, especially by WWE."

Foley retired his wrestling personas in 2012, but he continues to entertain fans as a motivational speaker, author, and wrestling ambassador. "It's too long for this book, but I learned a lesson that became pivotal to me. It's not the number of people you reach; it's the impact on the number of people you are able to reach. My youngest son, Huey, and I did a late-night Christmas Eve appearance [at a children's hospital where I was dressed as Santa]. The children were woken up to observe Santa. I was basically performing without acknowledging there was an audience. And when we got in the car, I said to my son, 'I feel like I just had a big pay-per-view match.' And he said, 'But, Dad, there are only three people there.' I said, 'It doesn't matter. It's just about creating something and creating memories.'"

Mick Foley against Motor City
Machine Guns, TNA iMPACT, April 9,
2009. Photo by George Tahinos.

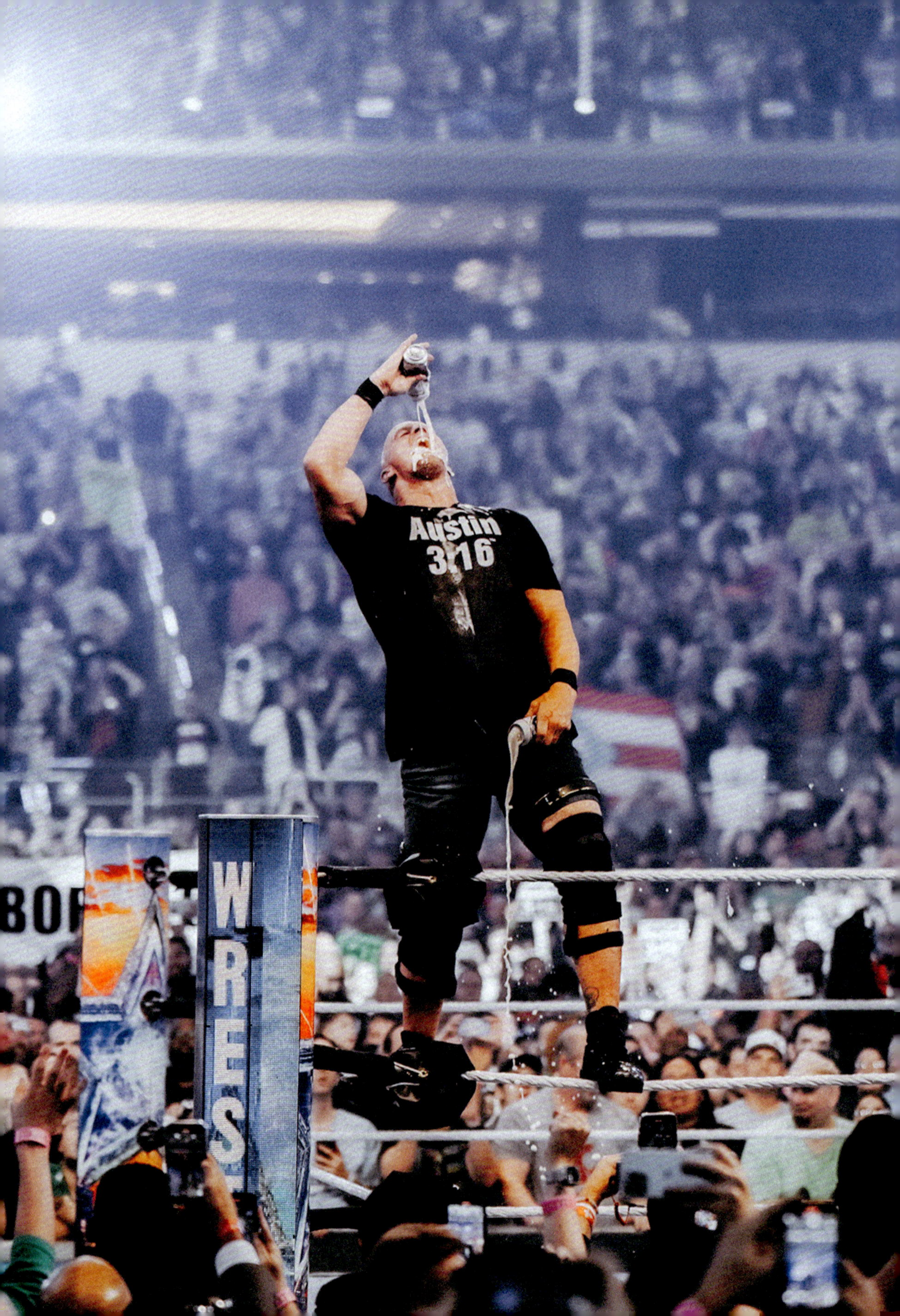

# STEVE WILLIAMS
# "STONE COLD" STEVE AUSTIN

Active 1989–2003

Six-Time WWE Champion
Three-Time Royal Rumble Winner
WWE Hall of Famer

**A rebel who** encouraged fans to stick it to their boss, Steve Austin stood up for what he believed in—and against what he didn't. He believed in raising hell and telling it straight, through not only his words but his in-ring movements and overall appearance.

Better known by his nickname "Stone Cold" Steve Austin, Austin's look was strategically bare-bones to connect with regular fans—and signal his disdain for wrestling's pomp and flashy attire. "Stone Cold" Steve Austin wore basic black trunks, a leather vest embellished with a steellike skull, and knee braces that represented his fighting spirit. His shaved head, trimmed goatee, and simple look told opponents and fans that "Stone Cold" Steve Austin meant business.

Costume designer Terry Anderson, who made Steve's legendary look, recalls the origins of the skull emblem on his vest: "His very first outfit was drawn up by [WWE]. What they gave to me, I made it and was like, 'Oh, I hate this design,' because the look just wasn't him. It looked like a biker logo on the back of his vest, with a star on the back of his trunks. I remember watching him on the monitor as he was wrestling. He comes back and he goes, 'How'd it look?' And I said,

'Steve, it looked like you shit a star.' It was just terrible. So he said, 'All right, we need to talk because I can't wear crap like this. Can you make me a vest with a skull on it?' I didn't want to do just the same appliqué or paint a skull; I wanted to do something different."

As Anderson considered ways to improve the design, she stumbled across a technique that would define "Stone Cold" Steve's in-ring style: "I started doing some research into making 3D leather pieces. Ironically, while I was doing that, I had a craft show on TV that I would just turn on for background noise. There was this lady taking glue and covering paper-bag cutouts that she made, and then she would burn the glue with a candle. When she finished burning the glue, she would take her finger and wipe off all the soot and it looked like metal. So, I'm like, 'Oh my god, if I could do that on the leather, that would be great.'"

Anderson began experimenting with different ways to achieve a similar burnished look. "I ended up buying so many different kinds of glue," the designer said. "The kind of glue that she was using in the demonstration did not work on the leather because it was water soluble. Athletes get wet with sweat, water, rain, etc., so that couldn't work.

"Stone Cold" Steve Austin at
WrestleMania 38 in Dallas, Texas.
Photo by Chris Horrell.

I tried waterproof glues, but the waterproof glues wouldn't burn correctly to give me that metal finish." Anderson finally found a glue that was water soluble when wet but became waterproof after it dried. "It worked out perfect! I would literally cover the back of the piece of leather with Elmer's glue and stick it on a cookie sheet. I would then hold it upside down over a candle and just move it back and forth. My shoulders would kill me because it took me about a day of just nothing but burning pieces until they looked burned enough. I'd leave them to sit another day to fully dry all the way through, and then I would rub the soot off. I would have waxy, grimy, dirty nails that took forever to go away. Anytime I traveled, it looked like I was digging a garden."

Fortunately, Anderson's hard work paid off. Not only did Steve love his new look, but his iconic vests would provide the perfect vehicles for his signature catchphrases. Now when he stepped in the ring, he wore leather vests emblazoned with slogans like *S.O.B.* and *100% Whoop Ass*. Soon Steve was rocking vests emblazoned with his signature skull and *Austin 3:16*. When Austin and Anderson transferred Austin's new catchphrase to a T-shirt in 1997, it became the bestselling wrestling T-shirt of all time.

The Austin 3:16 T-shirt was a basic black T-shirt with simple white letters. It felt irreverent and cool. In an era when wrestling was about pushing the envelope, this controversial design raised eyebrows among more traditional folk. But Austin never backed down on the design, leading fans to respect him even more. The Austin 3:16 T-shirt ultimately played a massive part in "Stone Cold" Steve's overall success, becoming an excellent example of how the right threads play a critical role in crafting a wrestler's persona.

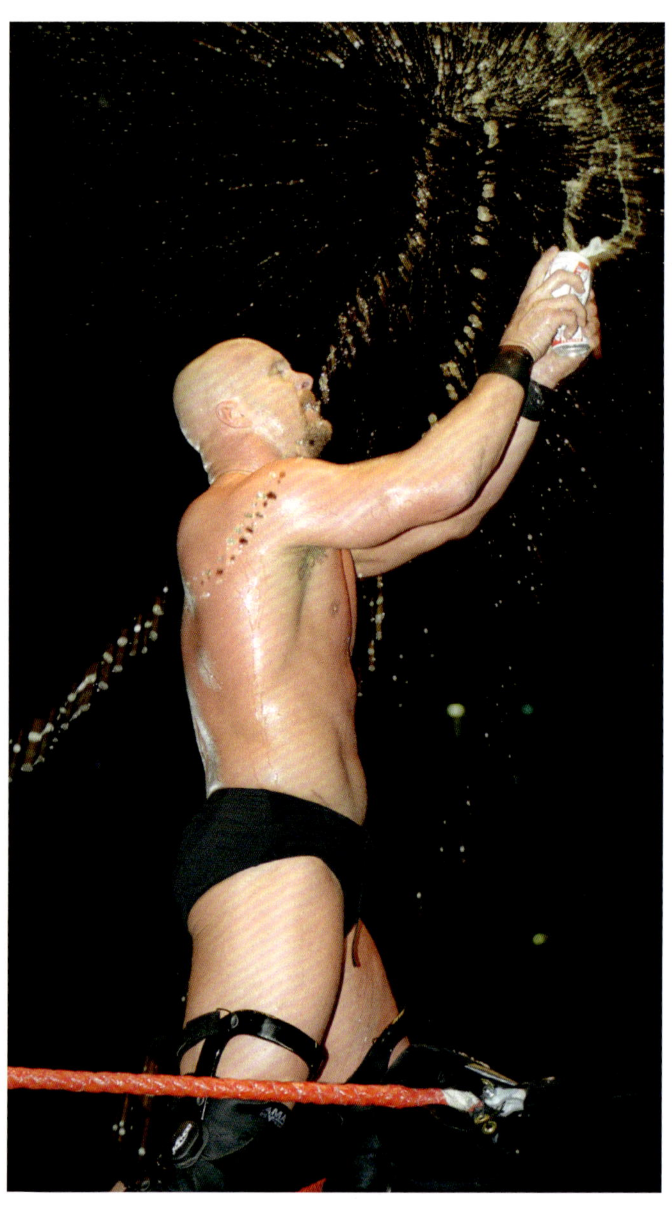

ABOVE: **Steve Austin at WWE live event in New York at Madison Square Garden. Photo by George Tahinos.**

OPPOSITE: **Steve Austin doing his signature pose. Photo by George Tahinos.**

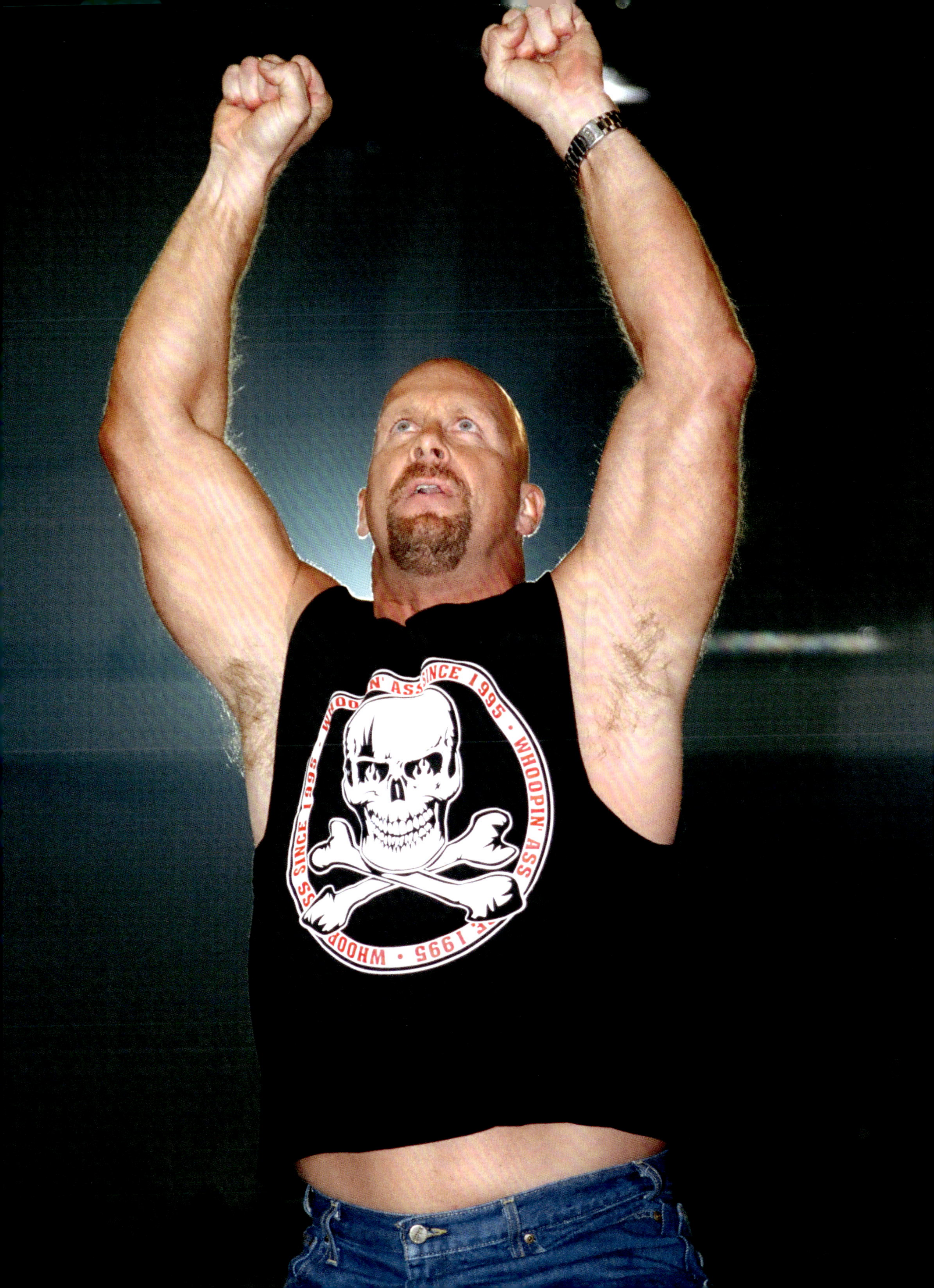
WHOOPIN' ASS SINCE 1995 • WHOOPIN' ASS
WHOOP ASS SINCE 1995

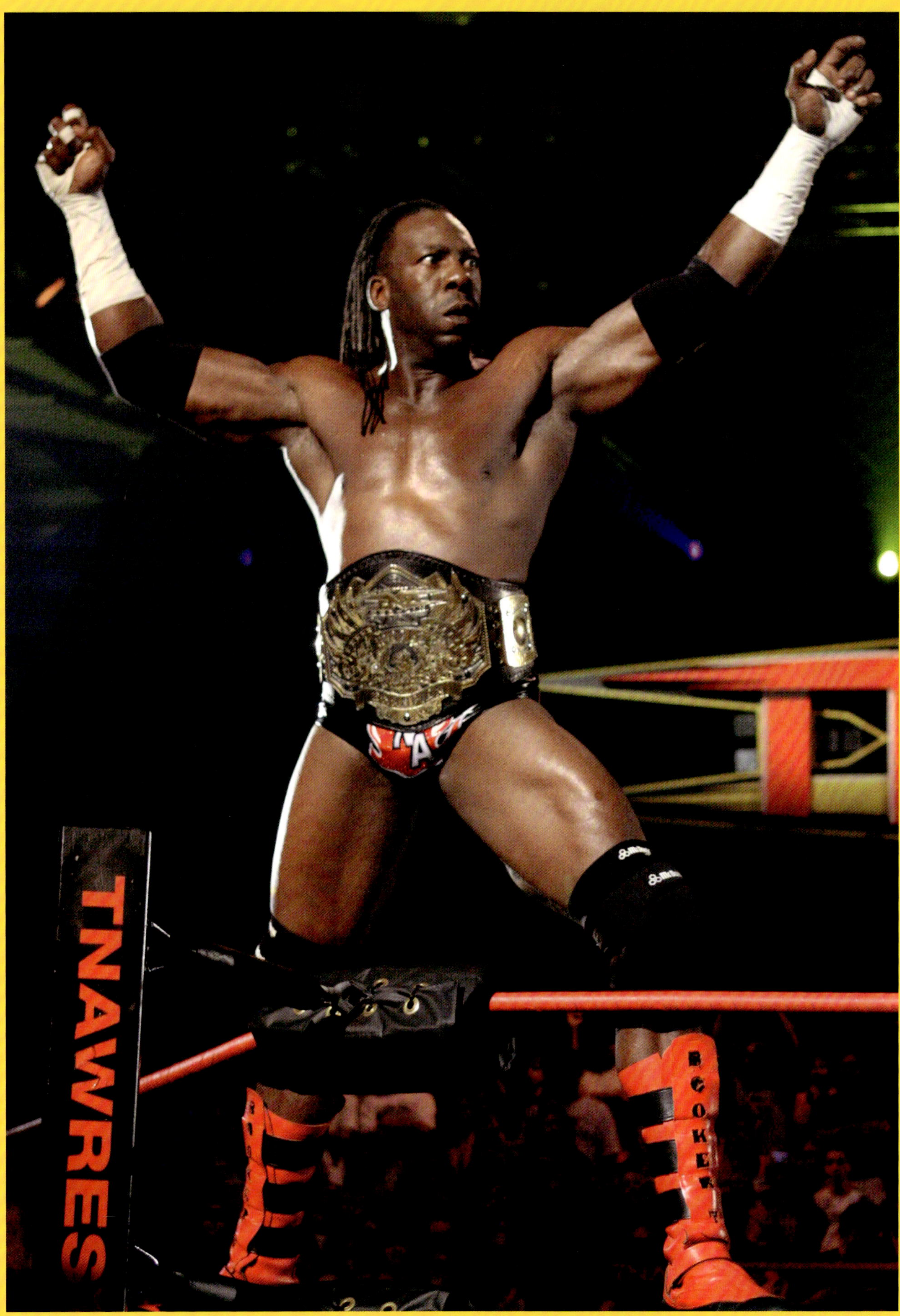

TNAWRES

# BOOKER T. HUFFMAN JR.
## *BOOKER T*

Active 1989–2023

Six-Time World Champion
WWE Hall of Famer

**Involved in some** of wrestling's most memorable moments, Booker T. Huffman Jr. was as unfiltered and unapologetic as it gets. Better known as his character, Booker T, the champion wrestler has always believed in the power of presentation. From his early days of tag team wrestling to a successful solo run, Huffman has prioritized being visually distinct throughout every phase of his career: "Your look has to be on point. That is one thing I always focused on, sometimes more so than my in-ring work. I always had different-color boots, tights, shorts. If you're not focusing on your appearance, how you stand out, how you cover your weakness, you're definitely not thinking properly in this business."

Early in Huffman's career, Booker T and his brother, Lash (better known as Stevie Ray), created The Harlem Heat, a bold tag team duo known for its attitude and intensity. The brothers debuted in wrestling gear emblazoned with red-and-yellow flames. Huffman took us back to those early days: "We were trying to figure out what to wear as far as the flames in Harlem Heat. We didn't have a lot of money kicking off our careers, so I went to this country store called Boot Barn and saw these T-shirts from a country musical act named Brooks & Dunn. The shirts had flames on them, and I took those shirts and went and had them tailored for us, and we made the sleeves the hat."

Booker T as the first-ever Legends Champion donning the old TNA World Championship. Photo by George Tahinos.

As The Harlem Heat became more popular, the Huffman brothers decided to upgrade their look. Now they wore one-piece spandex jumpsuits that accentuated their physiques and seemed held together with single metal rings on their bare chests. "I asked a lady that used to design costumes for 'ladies of night' to make an outfit for my brother and me," said Huffman, whose edgy new look was completed with matching arm cuffs, sunglasses, and traditional kufis. "This look was what she came up with, and what was really cool about it was that the little circle in the middle actually came off a vacuum cleaner. We needed something to make the straps connect and that's what she found to incorporate, and it worked."

Booker T reinvented himself again in 2001 as he jumped from WCW to WWE. Huffman knew he had to evolve to find success at the new company. "I always say you have to make it in the locker room before you make it in the ring," he said. "When I left WCW, I left everything behind, including my short hair. I wanted to totally reinvent myself, not to fit in with the crowd but to be different than what I was before."

When Huffman won the King of the Ring tournament in 2006, fans saw a new character begin to take shape. King Booker was regal with a playful twist. As King Booker, Huffman wore a red crushed-velvet robe accented with animal-print fur and carried a scepter. King Booker pulled his locs up over a luxe crown detailed with colorful jewels. Huffman's hair became central to King Booker's identity, making him instantly recognizable as a celebrity figure.

As Huffman sank into the character, his royal vision became a reality. "I don't think anyone thought that King Booker was going to be special. At least no more than any of the other kings," said Huffman. "But I thought in my mind, 'I want to be remembered as the greatest king to ever do it,' and it was a great year. The red robe and crown are somewhere in props still. My black robe with lion heads on the side was actually made by one of my students [at Reality of Wrestling, formerly known as Pro Wrestling Alliance]. He wanted me to have a gladiator-type robe, so he built it for me."

With each phase of his career, Huffman continued to grow into a global phenomenon. In 2020, Bad Bunny showed his support of the WWE Hall of Famer with a hit song, "Booker T," and invited Huffman to star in the video. "GI Bro was my first character I ever played, and then I ended up bringing it to the big screen," the wrestler recalled. "For Bad Bunny to write a song about me and then want me to actually be that GI Bro character [for the video] was really cool. I asked him, like, 'Man, what do you want me to wear? A nice suit?' It was his choice for the GI Bro look. He was directing, producing, and everything else, and that video turned out pretty cool. It just let me know that all the characters that I played over the years have hit someone. That's what's cool about the journey of my career."

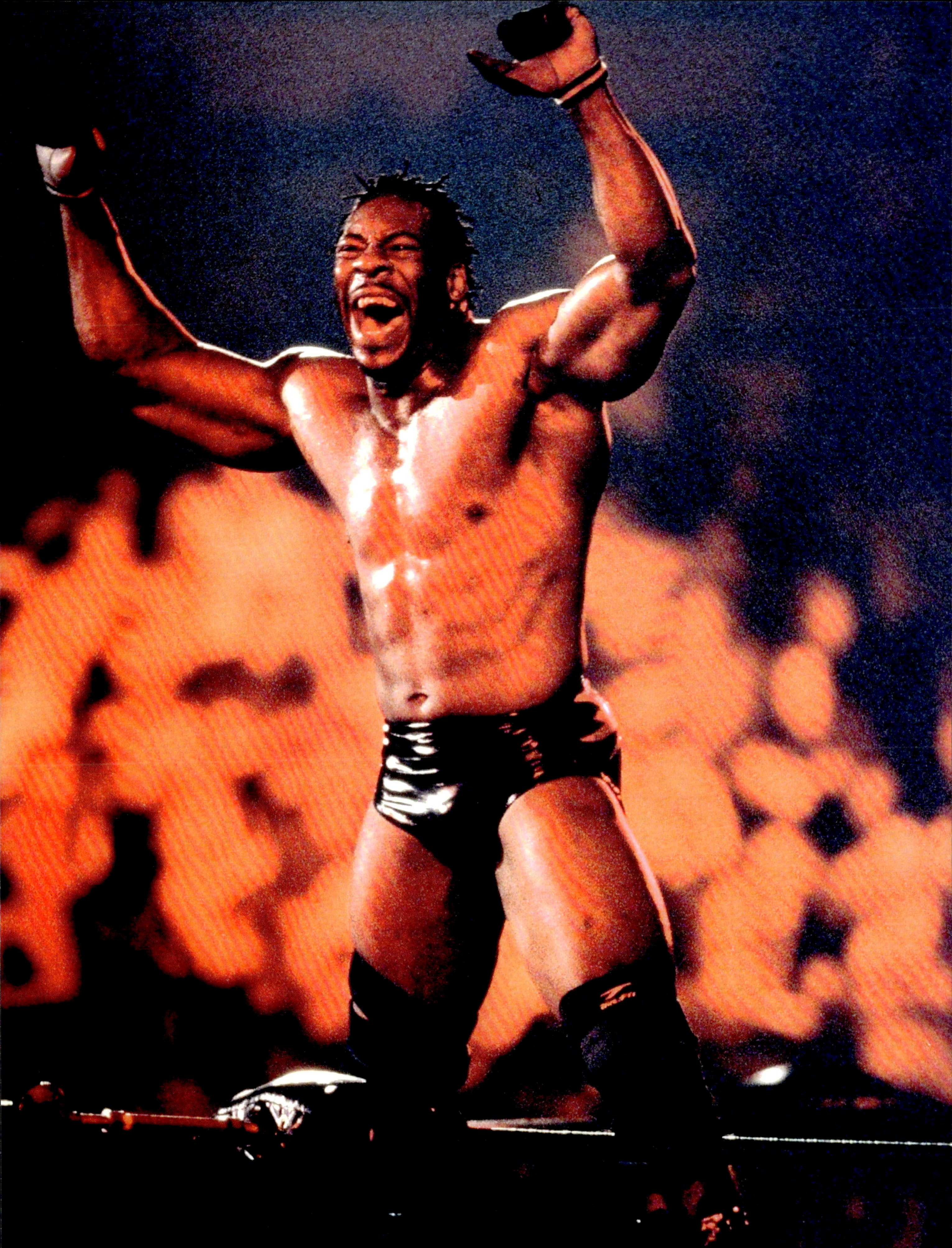

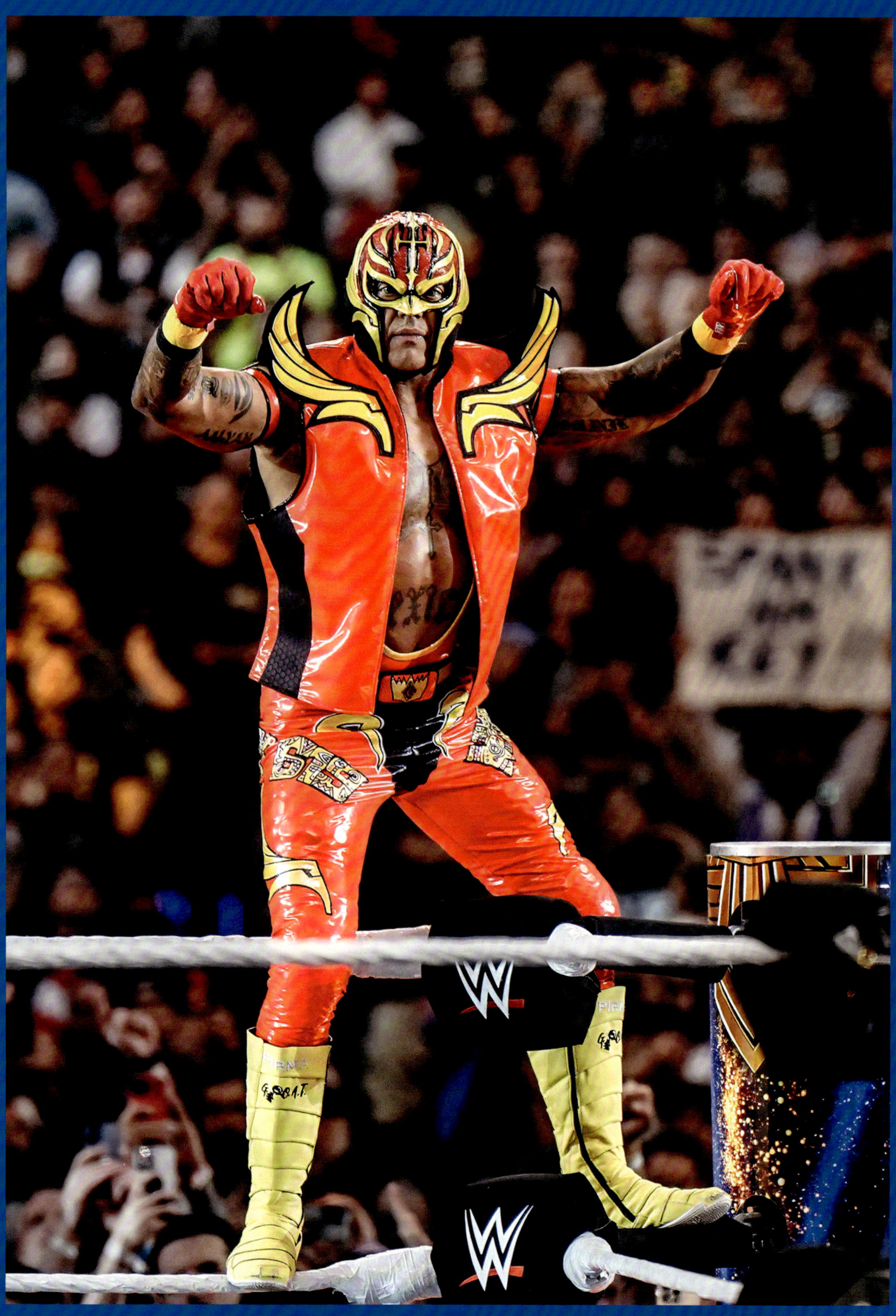

# ÓSCAR GUTIÉRREZ
## *REY MYSTERIO*

Active 1989–present

WWE Grand Slam Champion

**After four decades** of wrestling, Rey Mysterio has become a household name. Known for his acrobatic style and high-flying moves, the Mexican wrestler is equally famed for the colorful masks he wears in the ring. But for Rey Mysterio, whose real name is Óscar Gutiérrez, the masks are more than just a colorful persona. They're an important way to honor his Mexican heritage and the luchadores who came before him. "El Santo was a legendary wrestler who created the aura of the mask," said Gutiérrez. "He transcended not just from a wrestling ring but from Hollywood. In my eyes, that's when the mask became iconic and a part of our culture."

Gutiérrez adopted his signature look after watching his uncle and namesake, Rey Misterio Sr., don a Mexican wrestling mask before entering the ring. "Growing up as a kid, I watched my uncle dress as a normal civilian until we were three minutes from the arena parking lot," he said, remembering how his uncle would don a mask before greeting the fans gathered outside the arena. "I remember there would be people surrounding the car asking for pictures and autographs. In Mexico, you walk through the crowd and that's a fan's opportunity to approach you as a superstar. That legacy is something I have to carry on until I stop doing what I love, which is lucha libre."

Preserving tradition has been paramount for Gutiérrez throughout his career. Most of Gutiérrez's masks are made of brightly colored fabrics with some form of a cross covering his forehead. This classic look has become a type of armor under the bright lights. But on special occasions, Rey Mysterio adds even more symbolism and flair to his usual style. Case in point: For WrestleMania 22, Gutiérrez stepped into the ring wearing a mask adorned with a spectacular plumage of hawk feathers, which symbolize power in Mexican culture. "That night was a representation of my ancestors, the Aztecs," he said. "It was a headpiece that we call 'El Caballero,' which was representative of a hawk with obvious feathers. I had a chest piece, wrist and knee pieces, and had the look made in Mexico as a way of embodying my people, what I believe in, the history of Mexico, and the fighting warrior spirit that Mexicans have."

Of course, Rey Mysterio's singular style wouldn't be the same without Hayashi Masahiro, a Japanese designer with whom Gutiérrez has found a wonderfully symbiotic partnership. Hayashi, whose creative vision aligns with Gutiérrez's vision and goals, has made hundreds of masks and sets of gear to tell Rey Mysterio's story over the years. "The first set [of gear] I made for him was in 1996," said Hayashi.

Rey Mysterio against son Dominick Mysterio at WrestleMania 39 in Los Angeles, California. Photo by Kimberly Morrell.

"It was a silver metallic spandex outfit with rainbow colors. That set is one of the most important to me because the silver mask changed my destiny. Being able to be with him as he became famous and successful all over the world is treasure that is more precious than anything else. Even now when he wears a mask, I am his number one fan. We are now dear friends who share the same values and hope to make more history."

Each mask holds a special place in Gutiérrez's heart. "I've lost count of exactly how many masks I have [worn] over the years, but I would say four hundred to five hundred total. With each set of gear, I typically get two different masks: one that is open in the back and one that is closed. I also have my interview and TV appearance masks that are a little bit more fly and have bling to them. I'll wear an outfit and then put it away for a while, and then something will pop onto my radar as a flashback from TV, and I'll bring it back out." Making these masks is a labor of love for Hayashi. "I still have all his WCW masks," the designer said. "He wanted to change the colors of the mask every week, and it takes me three to five hours per mask. We've used a variety of fabrics over the years. Denim; his old Louis Vuitton, Gucci, and Etro bags; and many more."

Gutiérrez is so respected in the industry that other wrestlers have begun to mimic his trademark style. Over the years, wrestlers such as Seth Rollins, Santos Escobar, and Adam Copeland have all paid homage to Rey Mysterio's signature look. Other ensembles, including the masked bodysuit Gutiérrez wore for Halloween Havoc 1997, became instant fan favorites. "Never in a million years did I think that outfit would transcend the way that it did," Gutiérrez said. "That night was a very special night because I was supposed to lose my mask. And funny enough, that was the first outfit I ever wore where the mask was attached to the turtleneck and the bodysuit. So I couldn't just take off my mask—the whole piece would have to come off. It was a unique piece."

The groundbreaking look was inspired by *The Phantom*, whose protagonist wears a purple bodysuit. "I remember speaking to Hayashi, my costume designer, and I said, 'Well, maybe we do *The Phantom*, and we make it a Rey Mysterio version.' The *Phantom* movie had just come out, and I believe at the time it wasn't a big hit, but I just loved that character." Hayashi also incorporated tributes to one of Gutiérrez's wrestling heroes and the birth of his son. "One of my all-time favorite wrestlers—Santos Escobar's father, who wrestles as El Fantasma in Mexico—his outfit is purple with white and black; it was really cool," the wrestler remembered. "For Halloween Havoc, Hayashi airbrushed everything on the chest, even on the back, which is something that a lot of people don't know unless you point it out.

Rey Mysterio at Royal Rumble in 2025.
Photo by Kimberly Morrell.

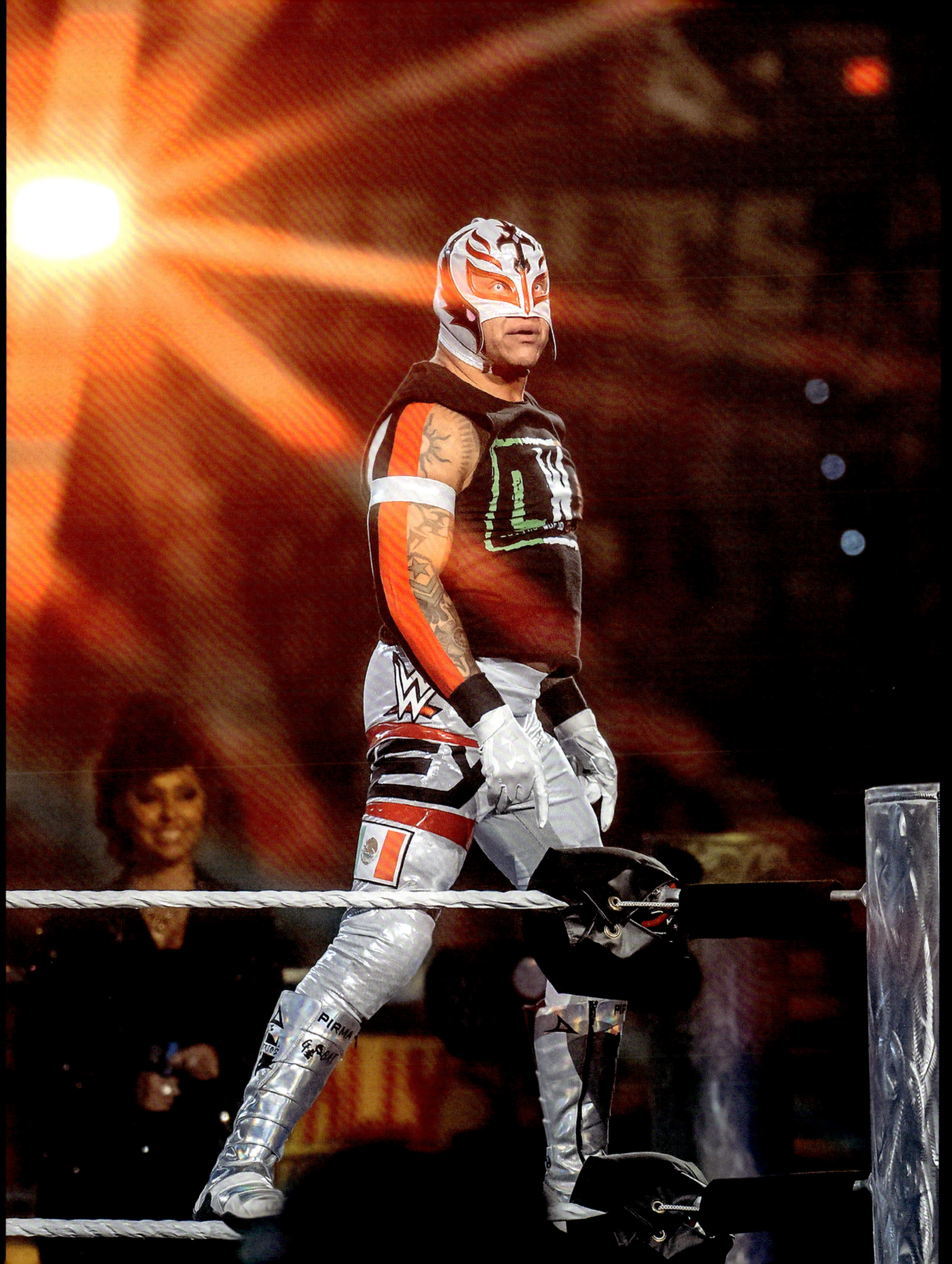

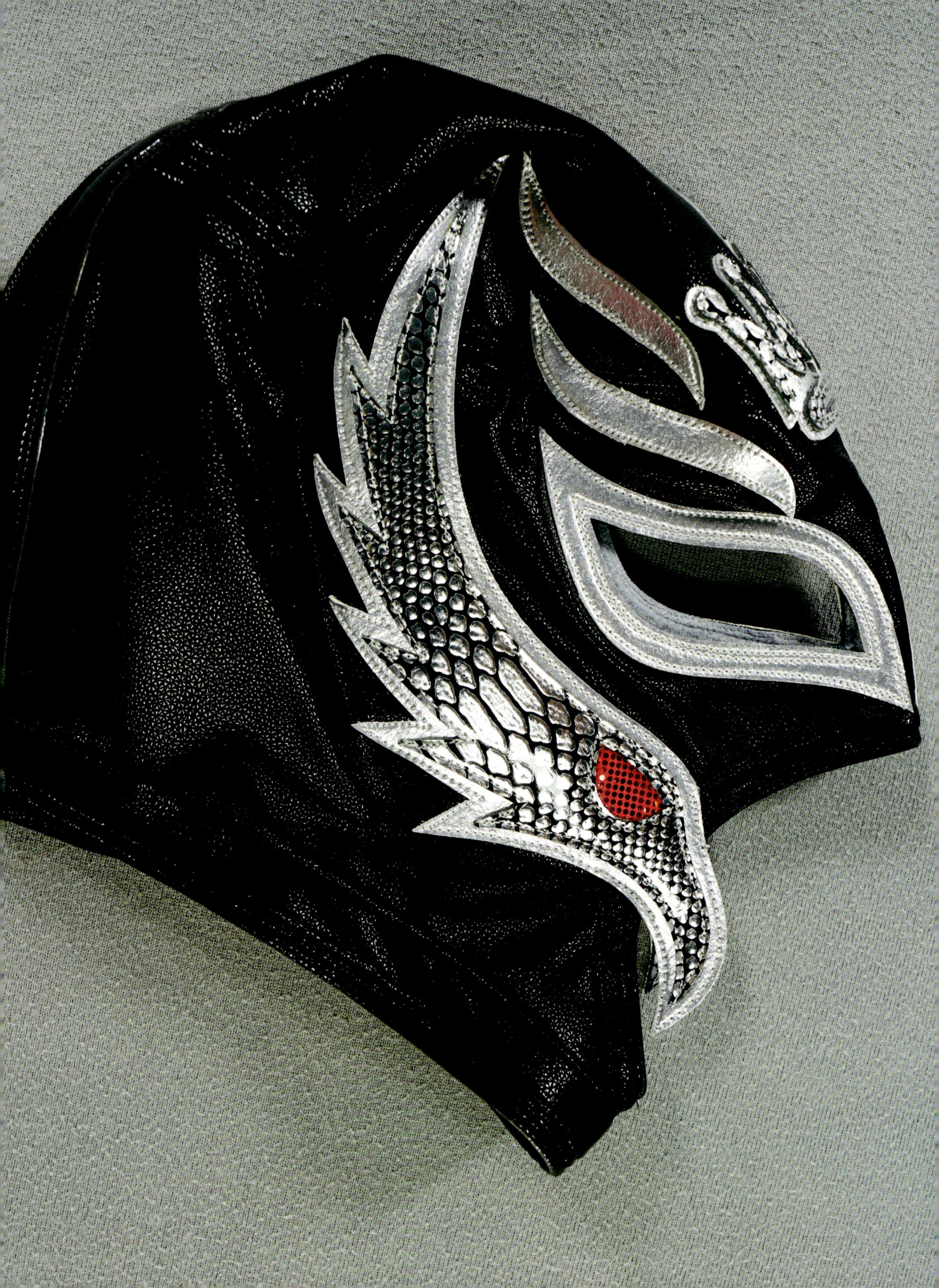

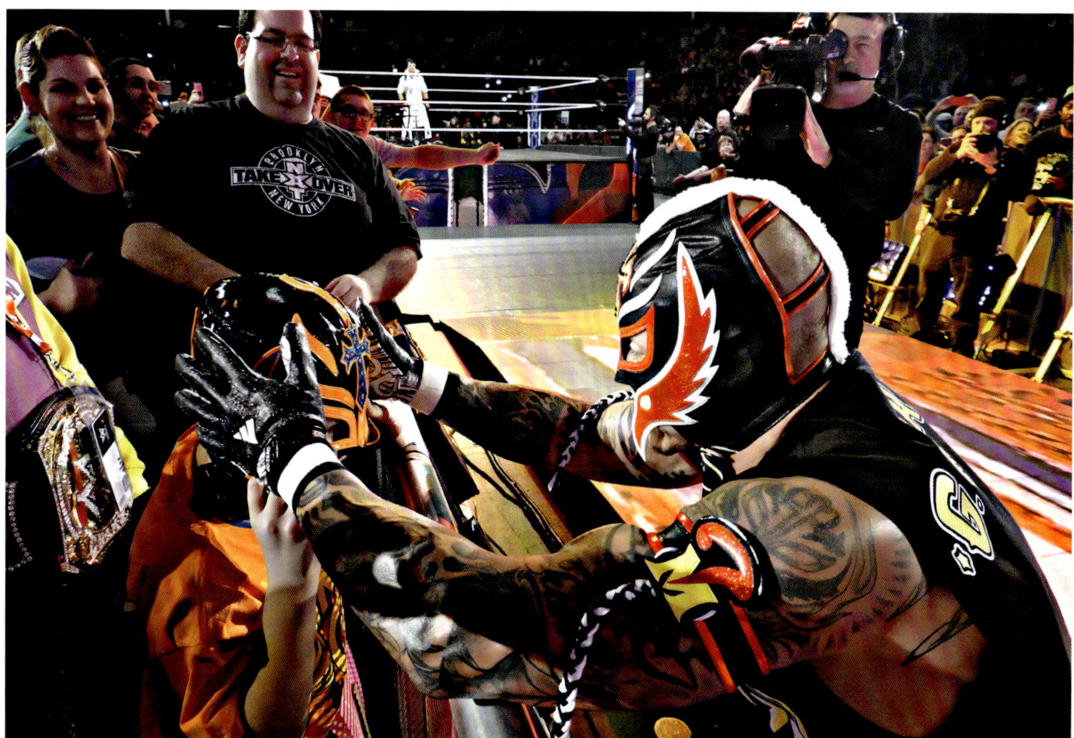

He made some designs along my shoulder blades on each side. But on one of them, if you look closely, it says *Dominik*. That was the year [my son] Dominik was born, in April of 1997."

One of their biggest challenges was finding the designer a copy of *The Phantom*, which wasn't showing in Japan. "At that time, there was no Skype or FaceTime," Hayashi recalled. "Our international call charged every second. Unfortunately, the *Phantom* movie was not coming to the Japan theaters, so I didn't know about the movie. I found pictures from movie magazines and made the designs in my brain. I never draw pictures on paper. I tried to collaborate Rey's question mark with Phantom's black line designs. When I decided to write *Dominik* on the back side, I believe

nobody found that meaning. . . . I think it's one of my best."

Over the years, Gutiérrez has learned to slow down and let his brand quietly evolve: "When you're younger, you get very excited and intense when you step up into the ring, and you want to do a million things. I've learned over the years that it's not necessary to put everything out on the table at once. Instead, it's important to feed your audience with little bits and pieces to up your brand, build your style and your name. That's hard for someone [who is] breaking into the business that's young because you just want to be noticed and be seen. Over the years I've learned how to slow down and not really feed everyone at once."



OPPOSITE: Iconic Rey Mysterio mask. Photo by Basil Mahmud.

TOP: Rey Mysterio with a young fan at WWE SmackDown in Newark, New Jersey, in 2018. Photo by Kimberly Morrell.

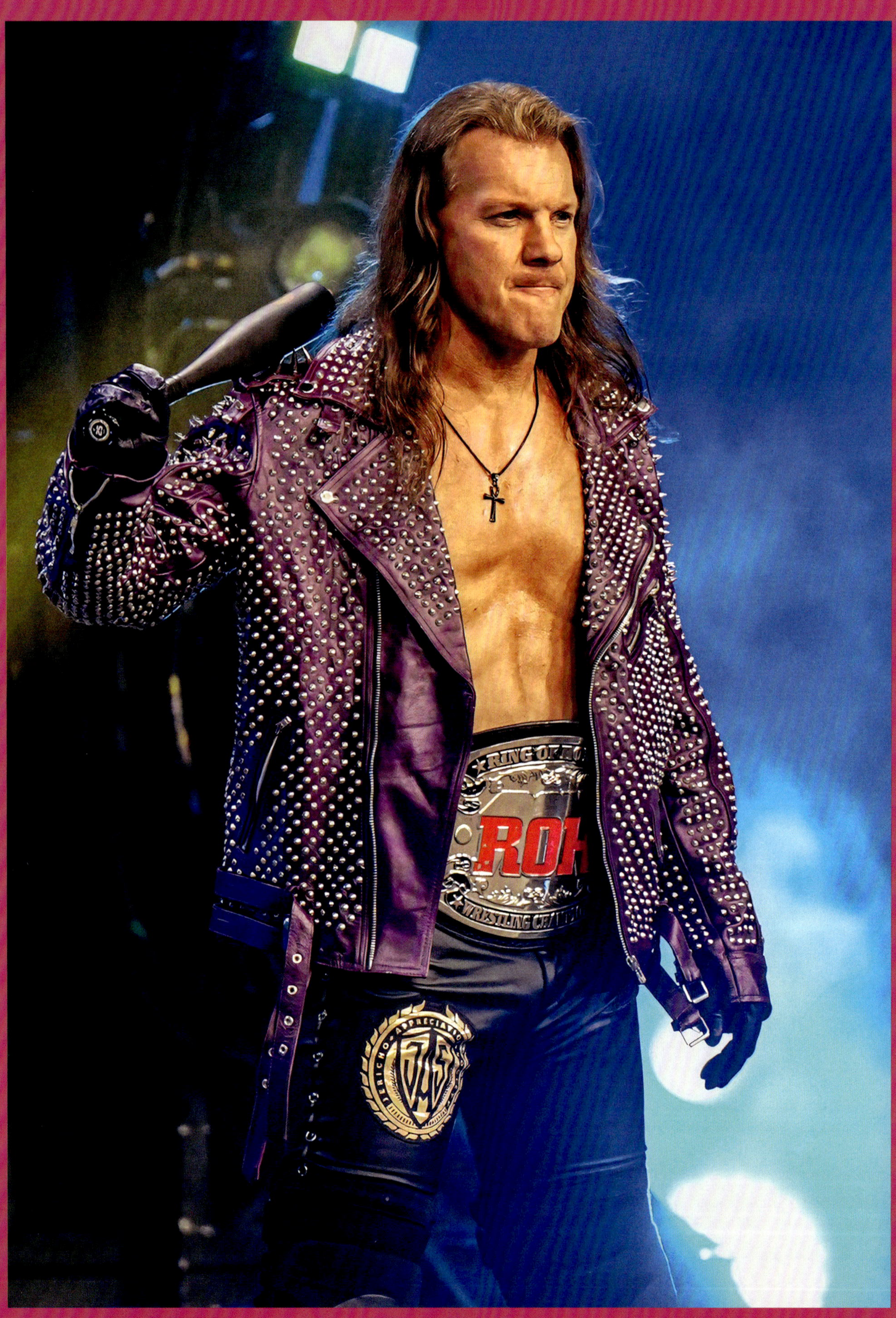

# CHRISTOPHER IRVINE
## CHRIS JERICHO

Active 1990–present

First Undisputed World Champion in WWE history

**Chris Jericho reinvented** the wheel time and time again, becoming one of the most evolutionary wrestlers of all time. With a talent for breaking the mold and keeping opponents and fans on their toes, Jericho flaunts rotating looks that always feel fresh and transformative. Decades after he first stepped into the ring, Jericho's penchant for change has become his signature look.

The wrestler's metamorphic style began early in his career. "I realized early on, if I had different-colored tights or different hair, different facial hair, they would make a new action figure for every look," Jericho said. "While some guys had two or three [looks] for the year, I had like ten or fifteen because I was constantly changing. I remember the late, great [wrestler and producer] Pat Patterson, who was very much a mentor of mine, [going], 'You look different every week.' That's the idea, and that's still something that I keep in mind to this day. Sometimes I overlap the personas, but mostly I wait until one is feeling just a little bit stale, maybe a month or two before that, and then it's time to make a switch. It's all kind of instinct at this point."

Jericho credits many of his ideas to an iconic rock star: "My biggest influence in showbiz for this exact idea is David Bowie. I always appreciated the fact that Bowie changed his look and his sound, and you never knew what was coming next. I've always had that mindset, and I know when it's time to evolve and completely switch over to something else. It becomes part of being a professional, knowing how to read the room. I think it's very important to do that, especially in wrestling, because you're on TV fifty-two weeks a year, sometimes twice a week.

Chris Jericho defends the ROH Championship at AEW Dynamite in Philadelphia, Pennsylvania, on September 28, 2022. Photo by Kimberly Morrell.

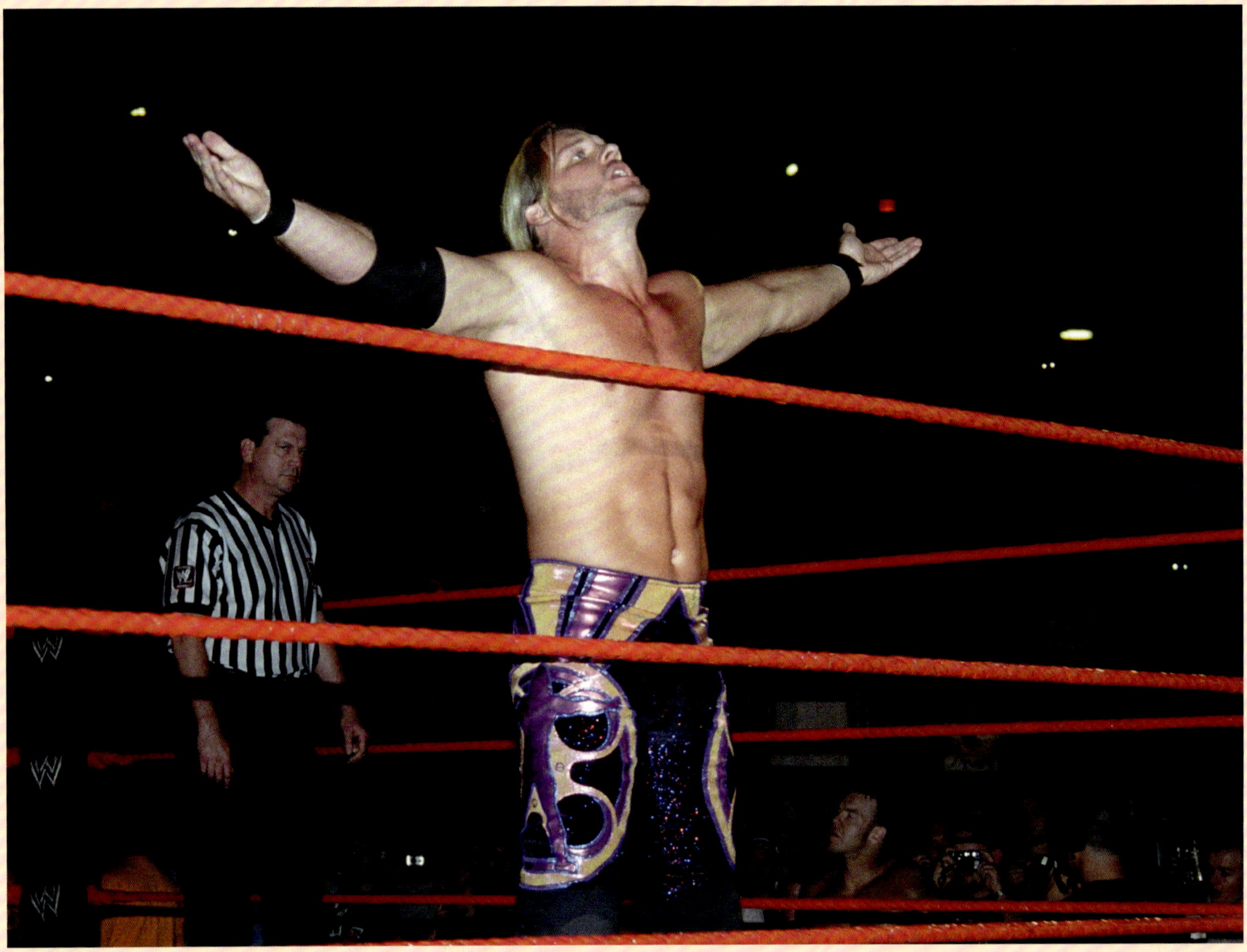

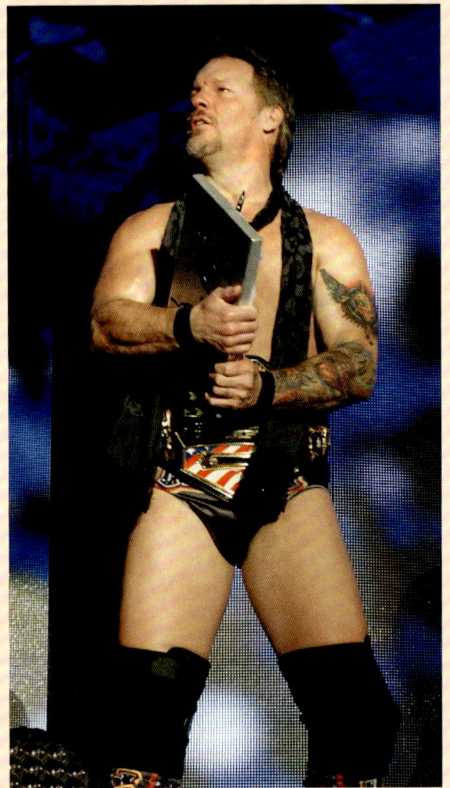

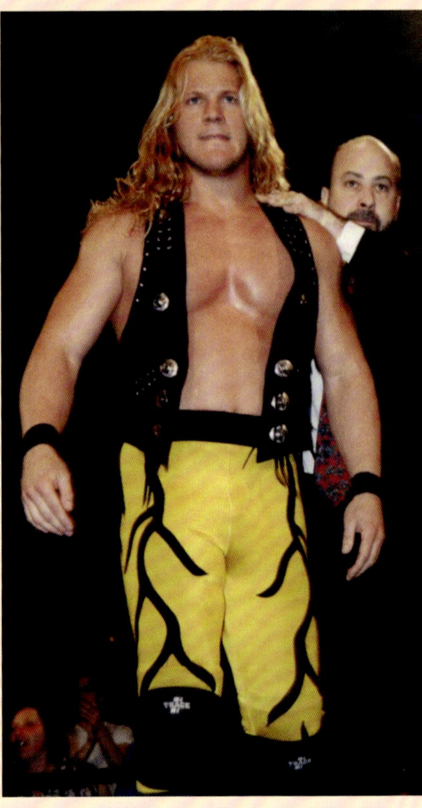

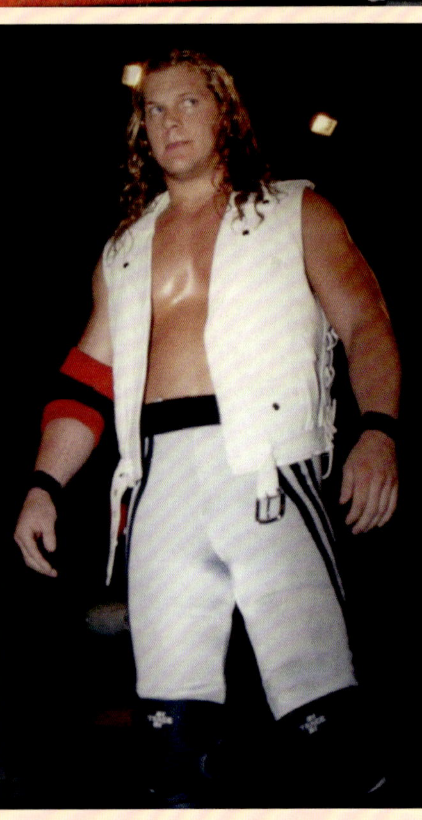

If you're on *SmackDown* or *Dynamite* and *Collision* or whatever it may be, that's a hundred times a year people see you. It can't be the same for a long period of time, where all of a sudden it becomes a nostalgia act, and I never wanted to be nostalgia."

Many of Jericho's personas and outfits have gone down in wrestling history. One particularly flashy jacket is even on display at the Hard Rock Cafe in Tampa. This memorable coat defined Jericho's shining turn as Y2J, a turn-of-the-century character inspired by Y2K: "I had a designer that I was working with that had worked with David Lee Roth and Justin Bieber. I found this certain design of stressed leather and I saw that he had done a piece for Alicia Keys that had some blinking lights on it, and I was like, 'Can you do that, but with like a thousand lights?' We made four [jackets], and they would break all the time. If you were to unzip the back of the jacket, it was like taking a giant bowl of spaghetti and throwing it against the wall. There were so many lights, and if one wire breaks, a whole string of lights goes down."

One of the only downsides to such distinct gear is that everyone wants to try on Jericho's outfits, sometimes with disastrous effects. "There was a time at WrestleMania where I worked CM Punk. I had a brand-new jacket and I found out after that [wrestlers] Christian and Tyrus or another one of the guys were messing around and putting it on backstage," said Jericho, who still recalls the decades-old incident. "That thing was not meant to be put on and taken off. So I go up there for my match and I hit the lights, and one half is blinking, and the other half is not. If you look back, I'm actually walking into the ring like Count Dracula, to one side, because one side wasn't working. We're live, and what are you gonna do? That would happen all the time because even though these are great pieces, they are meant to be put on a mannequin, not do what I do and travel with them."

Regardless, the Y2J jacket was such a hit that fans began emulating Jericho's illuminated style: "Those jackets were very popular, and people in the crowd would make copies of them. As a matter of fact, one time in Australia, mine didn't work, but I saw a guy in the crowd had one. I had our security go and borrow his jacket so I could wear it for the entrance. He had a four-hundred-dollar jacket, and mine cost me fifteen thousand dollars. Today my jacket is in the Hard Rock in Tampa, eternally plugged in so it always works."

To Jericho, styling is a form of storytelling. "Nine times out of ten, my looks are intentionally thought out," said the wrestler, who has worn everything from long hair and tights to short hair and scarves. The only goal is to stand out from the crowd: "In 2008, the reason I wore the suit and talked quietly was because maybe only one or two were wearing a suit at the time. No one was wearing a suit and talking quietly. Everyone was yelling and shouting. It seemed like the right way for me to do things. I always think, 'What's the opposite of what everyone else is doing?' And that's what I'll do. This is show business. If you want to make it, especially to any certain length of time, you have to do things differently and change it up."

TOP: Chris Jericho as Y2J. Photo by George Tahinos.

BOTTOM LEFT: Chris Jericho during The List of Jerichos era in WWE. Photo by Kimberly Morrell.

BOTTOM MIDDLE: Chris Jericho as The Lionheart in ECW. Photo by George Tahinos.

BOTTOM RIGHT: Chris Jericho in ECW. Photo by George Tahinos.

Jericho left WWE in 2017 and began wrestling in Japan, where he gave life to yet another character, with a very different direction. Wearing a spiky black jacket, long blond hair, and sinister face paint, Jericho's new character was delightfully evil. "As The Painmaker, I could be a little crazier in New Japan [Pro-Wrestling], and I was bigger than a lot of the guys there," said Jericho, who embraced his new persona. "I was going through a real Bruiser Brody phase where he would just go in the crowd and throw around referees and the rookies who watched the matches. I could just be a little bit more nuts and different as a character."

The Painmaker was much darker than Jericho's previous personas—after all, this character was inspired by a serial killer. "That's actually when I stopped wearing tights," said Jericho. "I thought, 'What would a serial killer look like if he became a wrestler?' I had never worn face paint before. Somebody had drawn some sort of a picture where I was wearing a Jack the Ripper top hat and I remember showing Guido, who was the booker of New Japan, this idea, and I said, 'We have to bring that hat.' I had just seen a Clockwork Orange [House of Fun] match or something with Alice Cooper, and I thought, 'What if there's some kind of makeup that I do that's nothing elaborate but just some lines on my face like I'm kind of crazy with lipstick that always kind of went to the side?' It wasn't supposed to be like a Sting or a Road Warrior [look]. It was so primitive and archaic, but I really liked it. I was working with [Japanese wrestler Kazuchika] Okada, who was The Rainmaker and where it all started. I called myself The Painmaker. . . . The whole thing became something different, like an alter ego."

With decades of character transformation under his championship belts, Chris Jericho knows there will never be another wrestler quite like him. "I'm not going to compare myself to Metallica or The Stones or somebody like that, but when those bands are done, you'll never have another band like them. I don't think there'll ever be another wrestler like Chris Jericho as far as how my career arc has gone."

Chris Jericho at AEW Dynamite in Albany, New York, in 2022. Photo by Kimberly Morrell.

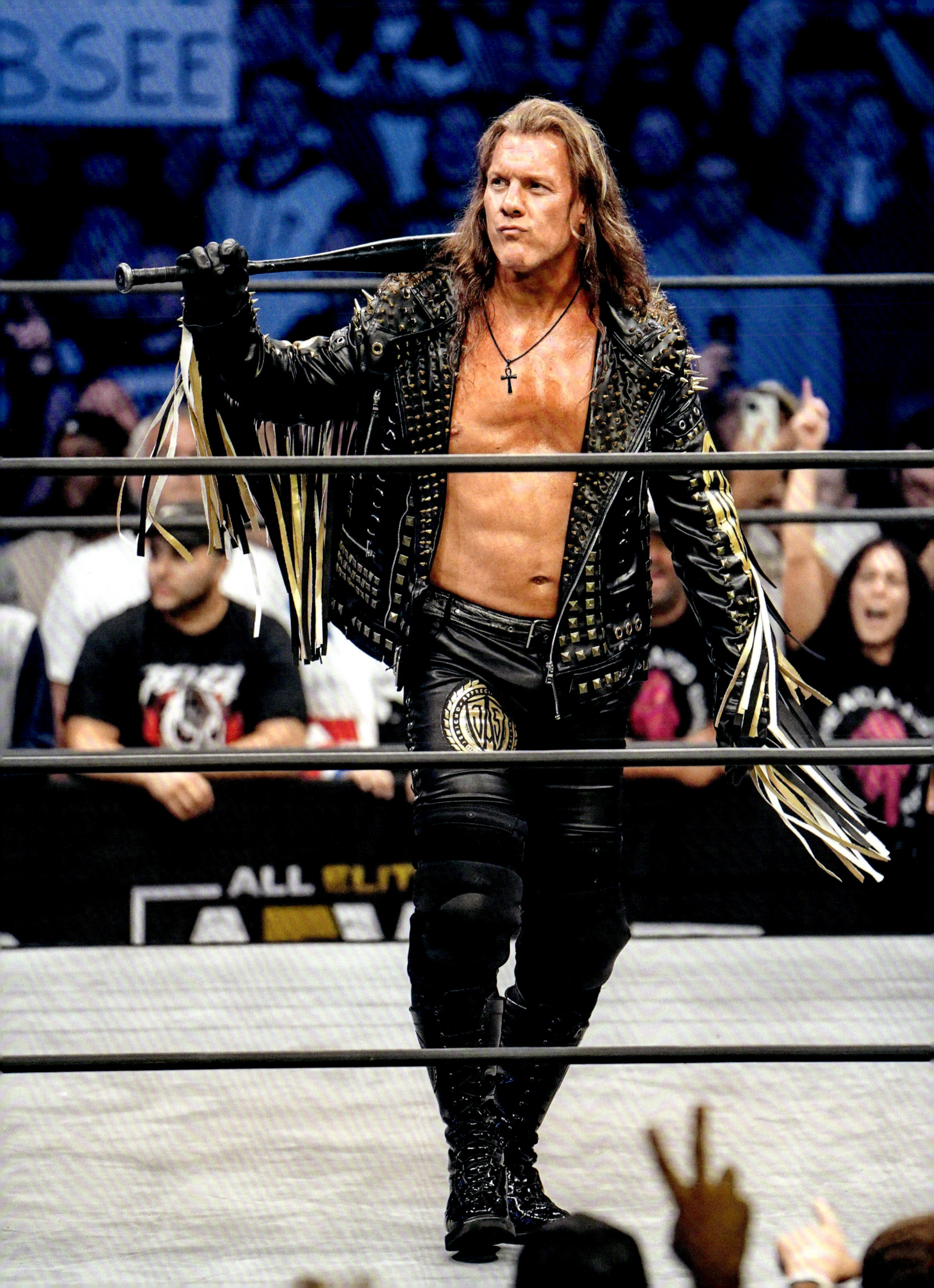

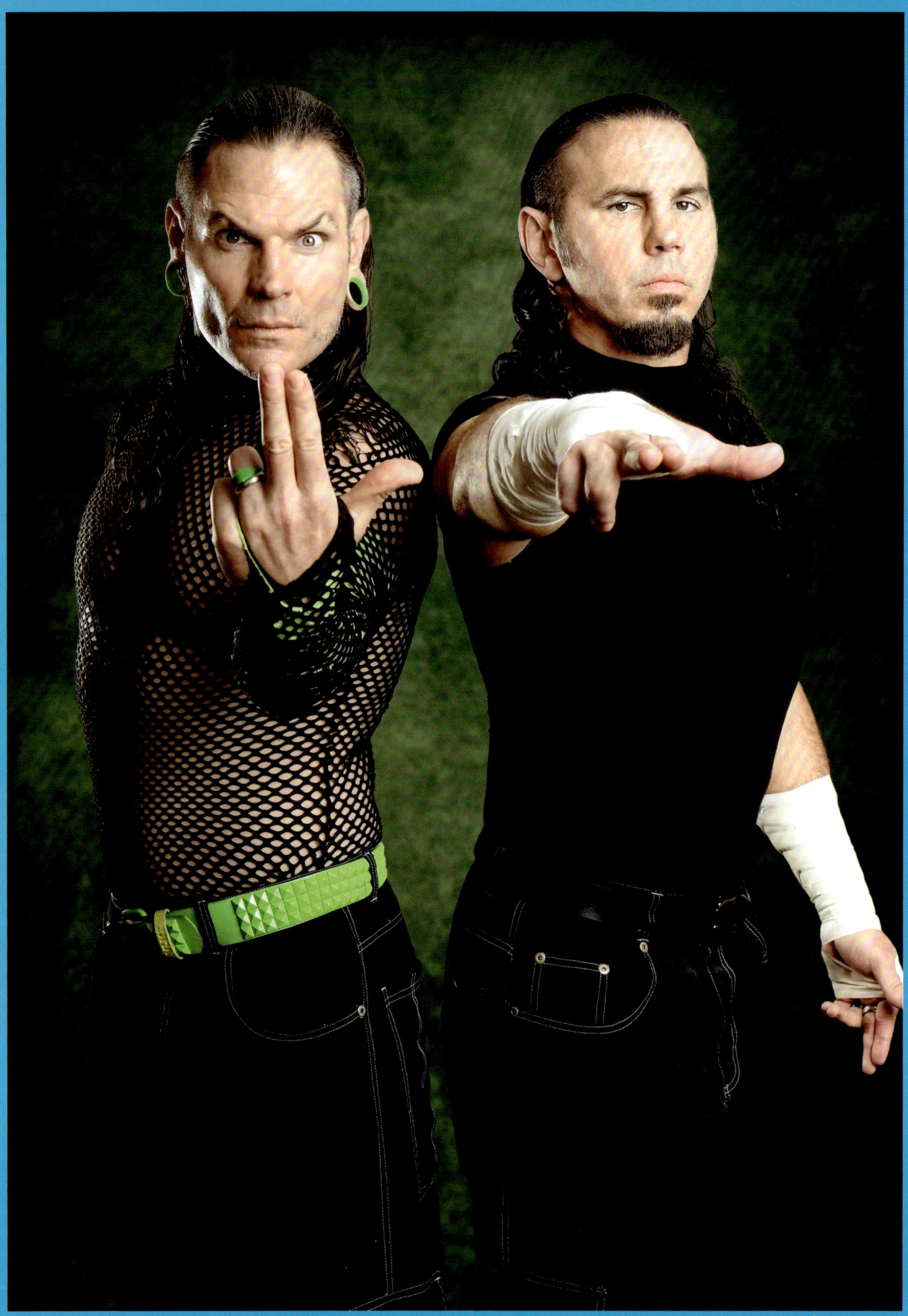

# MATT AND JEFF HARDY
## THE HARDYS



Active 1992–present

Pioneers of the TLC Match
Thirteen-Time World Tag Team Champions

**Brothers Matt and Jeff Hardy** were more than just a formidable tag team duo—they also wowed fans with their synchronized moves and undeniable cool factor. Known as The Hardys or WWE's The Hardy Boyz, the brothers popularized the concept of a TLC match, where wrestlers wield tables, ladders, and chairs to best their opponents in the ring. Along with their athleticism, the brothers brought a fresh look to the ring with dyed hair, punk style, and a '90s grunge aesthetic. Soon, tight-fitting mesh shirts, ripped arm sleeves, and baggy oversized pants had become The Hardys' signature aesthetic. Today, you can still see both men wearing similar looks in the ring.

According to Matt, their grungy look only came together during a last-minute trip to the mall: "We debuted earlier than expected in WWE with [wrestler and former manager] Michael Hayes, which led to us rushing on a new look. Michael had suggested something similar to The Freebirds—tight jeans, cowboy boots, and big belt buckles. Jeff and I asked to update the look so it was a little more modern. We stumbled upon Gadzooks in a local mall and chose to go with black Kikwear pants, which later became our iconic look. The employee helping us that day recommended the tight shirts and said it was a trendy look. Upon deliberation, Jeff and I dug the look and felt we could move and wrestle in it just fine. We then asked Michael if he was cool with it. [Michael] "P.S." Hayes greenlit it and then looked at the Gadzooks employee and said, 'Y'all got my size?' He was without a doubt a team player."

In 2000, The Hardys teamed up with Amy Dumas, also known as WWE Superstar Lita, to form Team Xtreme, embracing their personal style. "Team Xtreme was the most authentic version of us because we literally wore things we liked and thought were cool," said Matt. "It's still unbelievable to see how many fans come to our signings dressed like us."

Matt and Jeff Hardy. Photo courtesy of Matt Hardy.

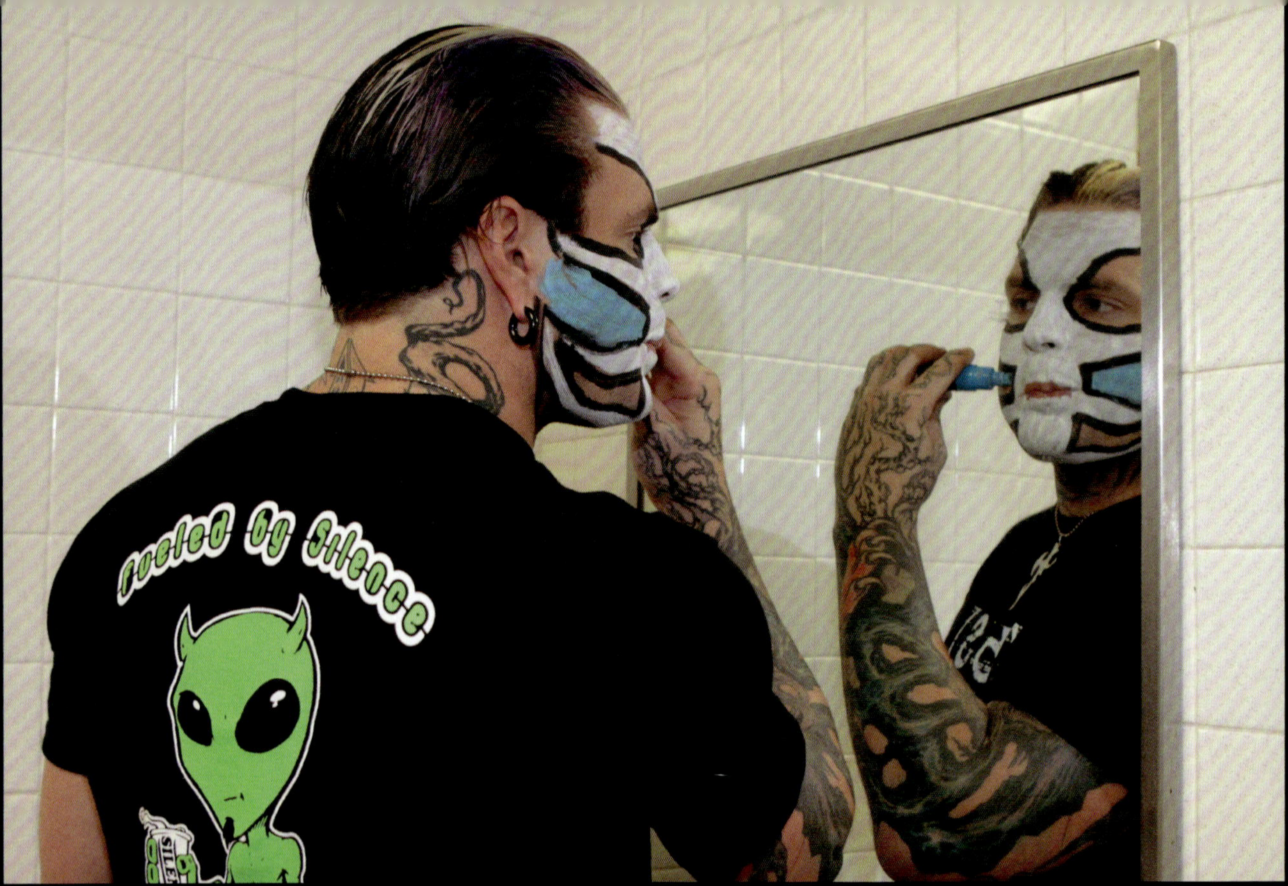

fueled by silence

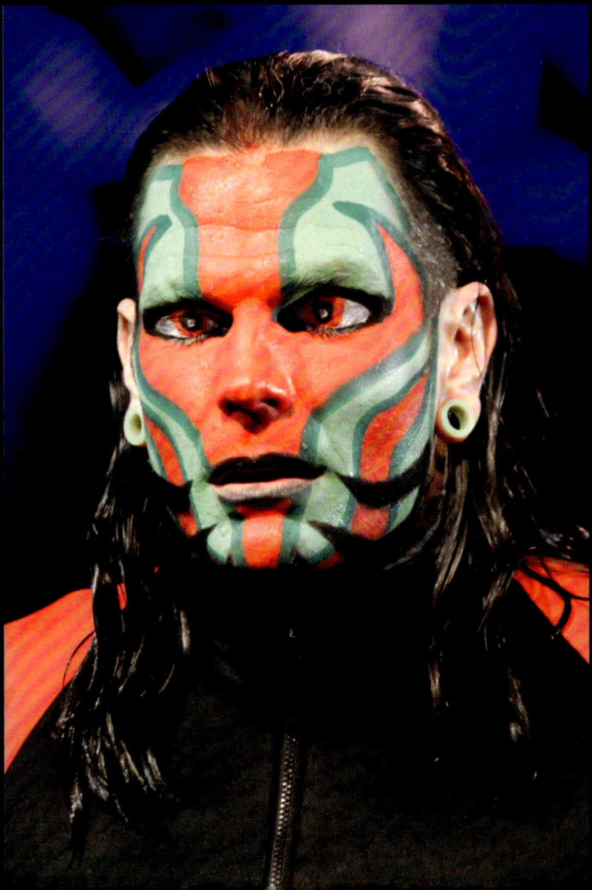

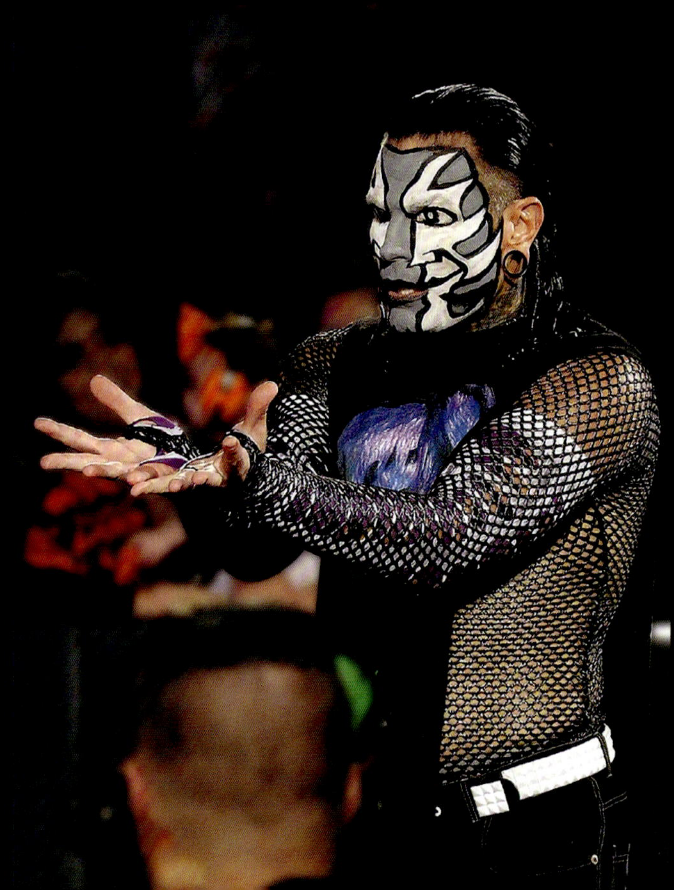

After Team Xtreme disbanded, the brothers embarked on successful solo careers and created their own unique styles. The younger Hardy brother, Jeff, found inspiration in those who came before. Known as the highflyer on the team, he embraced daring, unpredictable looks championed by wrestlers of previous generations. "If it wasn't for Sting, The Ultimate Warrior, and the Road Warriors, I wouldn't have become who I am in the ring today," said Jeff, whose bold gear, piercings, and face paint elevated his daring new persona. "I feel like my face paint is on a completely different, authentic, and enigmatic level. The ring is my canvas and so is my face. I normally start with two colors in mind, and then I imagine what my alien skin [face paint] will look like. Once I start painting, the image usually always changes. Seventy-five percent of the time I end up loving how it looks. It's never the same and it's all very abstract . . . because my brain is abstract."

Jeff also uses masks to channel various alter egos and personas. "[My alter ego] Willow is the god of my imagination," said Jeff. "The mask I wore [as Willow] was inspired by Jushin 'Thunder' Liger. His coat and umbrella coordinated extremely well with the mask. When Willow spoke, I never worried about making sense humanly. It was always cool to feel that freedom. Back in the early days, I needed to be a good guy and bad guy. Willow became my alter ego and my brother's ultimate rival, which meant I was pulling double duty a lot then. I see Willow resurfacing at some point in TNA [Total Nonstop Action Wrestling]. His prior surface was only scratched, and his taste in fashion has changed."

**"The Final Deletion was breakthrough material. It means a lot knowing what we created was so special. There was never really a goal for me. I just enjoy the process of change. I've had a spin-off of The Final Deletion in my head for quite a while called The Final Recovery. Maybe the future holds it."**

–Jeff Hardy

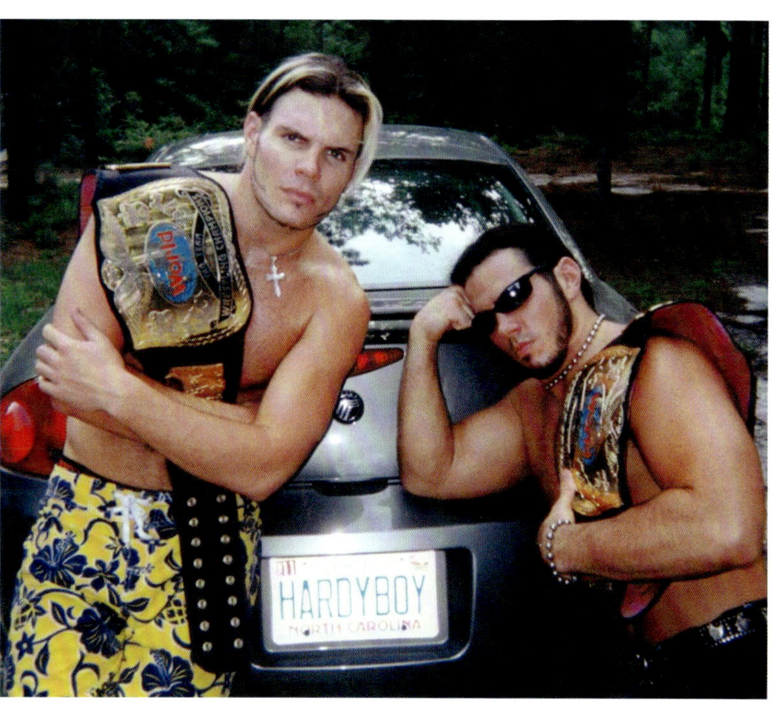



OPPOSITE, TOP: **Jeff Hardy applies his face paint backstage. Photo by George Tahinos.**

OPPOSITE, BOTTOM LEFT: **Jeff Hardy at TNA event. Photo by George Tahinos.**

OPPOSITE, BOTTOM RIGHT: **Jeff Hardy at WWE Hell in a Cell 2018. Photo by Kimberly Morrell.**

RIGHT: **Early days of The Hardys. Photo courtesy of Matt Hardy.**

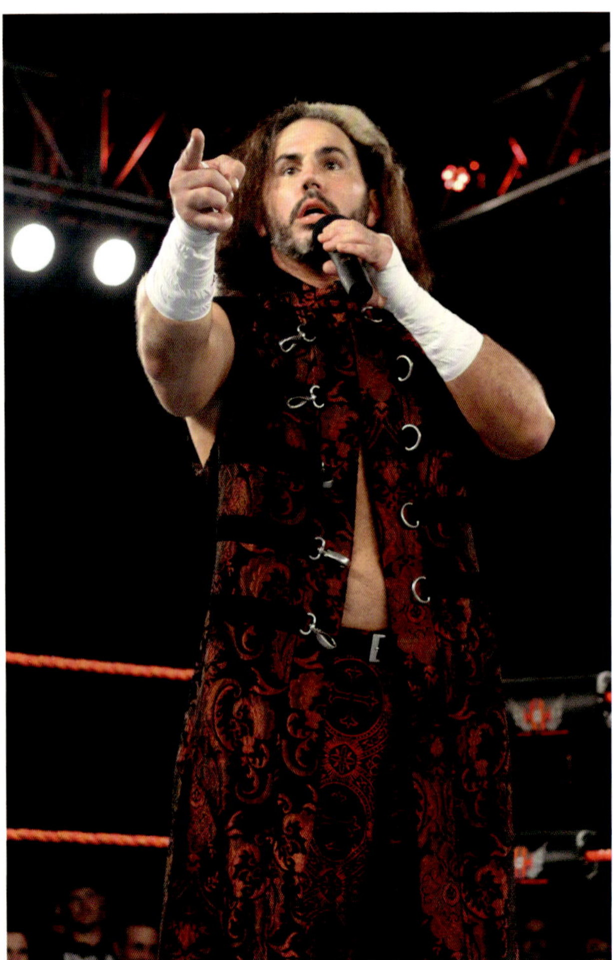

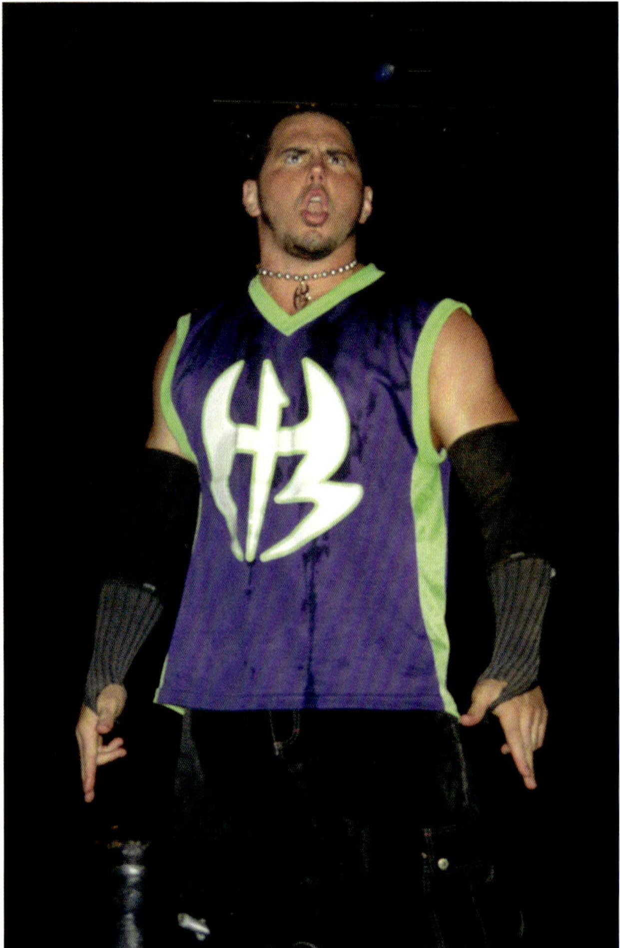

Meanwhile, Matt—the brawler of the group— began wearing gothic, alternative gear with a slightly villainous flair. In 2016, The Hardys changed the landscape of sports entertainment television by executing the first-ever cinematic match in professional wrestling history, The Final Deletion, accented by Matt evolving into the theatrical Broken Matt. "I wanted Broken Matt Hardy to be as different as possible," said Matt. "I wanted him to look different, speak differently, and act differently. I had been saving some of the initial Broken Matt robes for a while, awaiting a new evolution of my wrestling persona. I tried my best to give Broken Matt an archaic look, as [if] the character's essence (or soul) was something I had been cognizant of for two thousand years. I'm obviously not immortal, but I developed the idea that I could possibly become aware of what bodies my soul has been in, thus making my *essence* immortal. I got some help about clothing ideas from some of the vampires on *True Blood*. It was my wife's idea to do my hair like Sweeney Todd, and it fit perfectly. The most important thing about Broken Matt was to look and appear different from regular Matt Hardy."

Today, the Hardys remain two of the most dedicated and artistic wrestlers in the business, and both brothers connect solidly with their supporters. "I've started calling our fan base the 'dieHARDYS' as they're so loyal," said Matt. "It's strange—in many ways it's normalized to us because we see it so often, but it always puts smiles on our faces when people cosplay and dress like us."

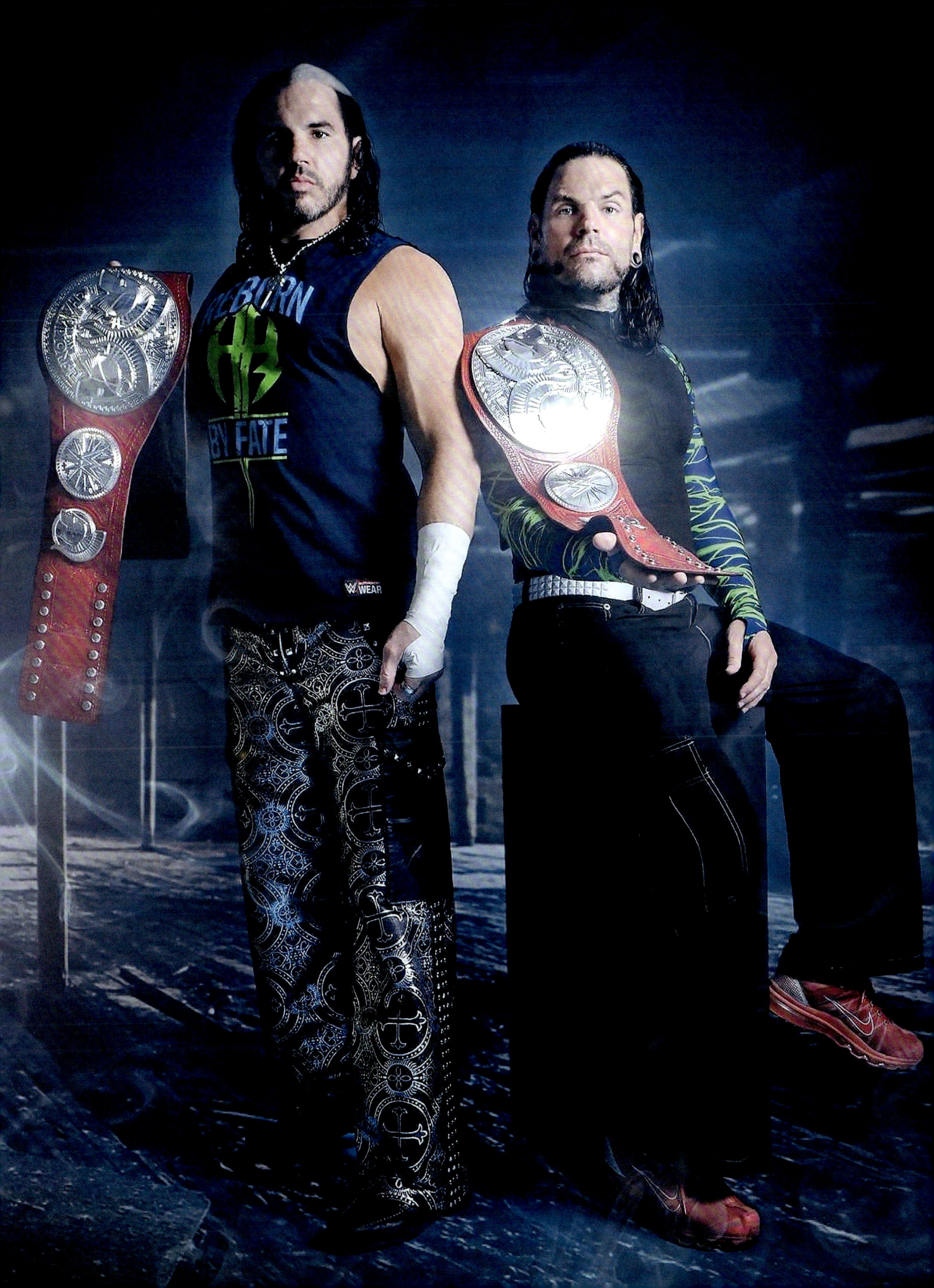

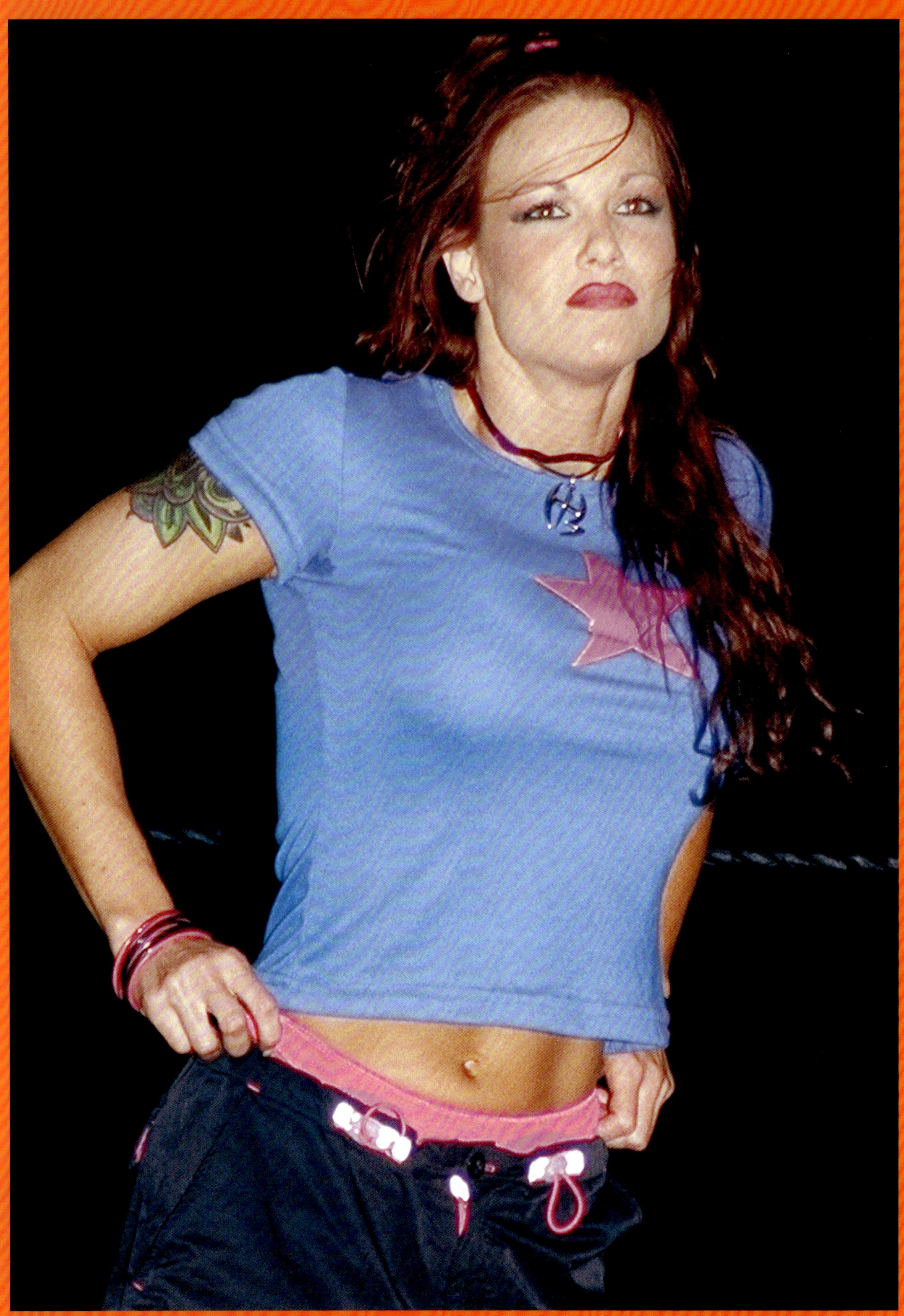

# AMY DUMAS
## WWE'S LITA

Active 1999–2006

Four-Time WWE Women's Champion
WWE Hall of Famer

**Known around the world** as WWE Superstar Lita, Amy Dumas was famous for her unapologetic attitude. Cutting her teeth in the punk rock / hardcore scene in Fort Lauderdale, Florida, this trailblazer defied gender expectations from an early age. "I grew up doing judo, skateboarding—all things that were primarily male-dominated hobbies," said Dumas, who always considered herself a tomboy. "I never even really put on makeup before being in wrestling. There was part of me that wanted to be considered one of the boys but also wanted to feel feminine and be myself. So my look was a little street cred mixed with a little bit of internal femininity as well." Dumas's independent style showed through her attire, which was sexy and cool but far less revealing than what most female wrestlers were wearing. Cropped tanks and baby tees provided a fitting yet flexible look, allowing her to move swiftly in the ring. Mesh details not only made her attire breathable but also left it looking edgy and raw. Low-ride jeans and baggy cargo pants held up with studded belts teased what would become her signature look—a thong peeking out above her panty line. "The thong out of the pants was just a way for me to accessorize and kind of meld femininity with being a tomboy," said Dumas. "Starting my career with [wrestler] Papi Chulo [Essa Ríos], we got all of our gear made down in Mexico. The look ended up being pretty prevalent in Latina culture as well."

Lita in signature look for a WWE
event. Photo by George Napolitano.

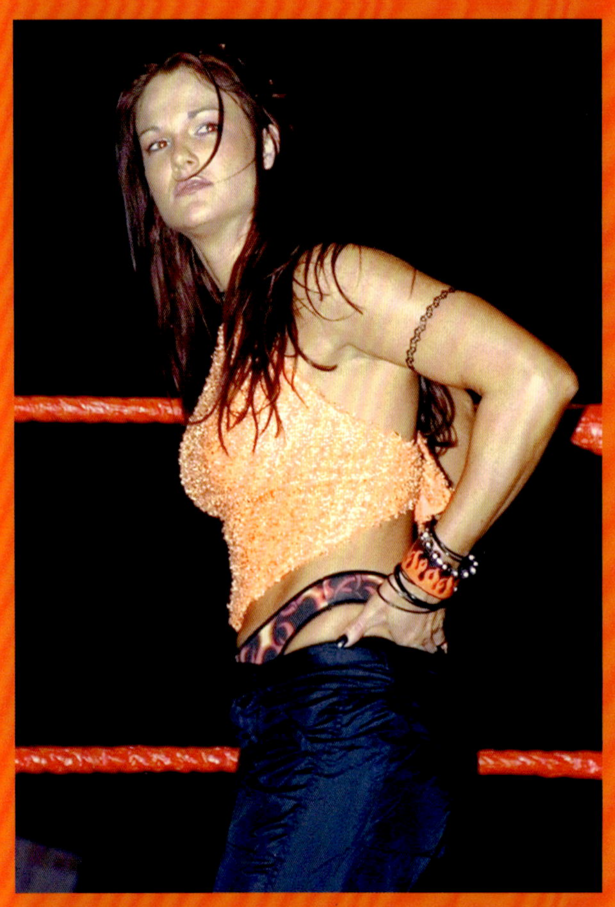

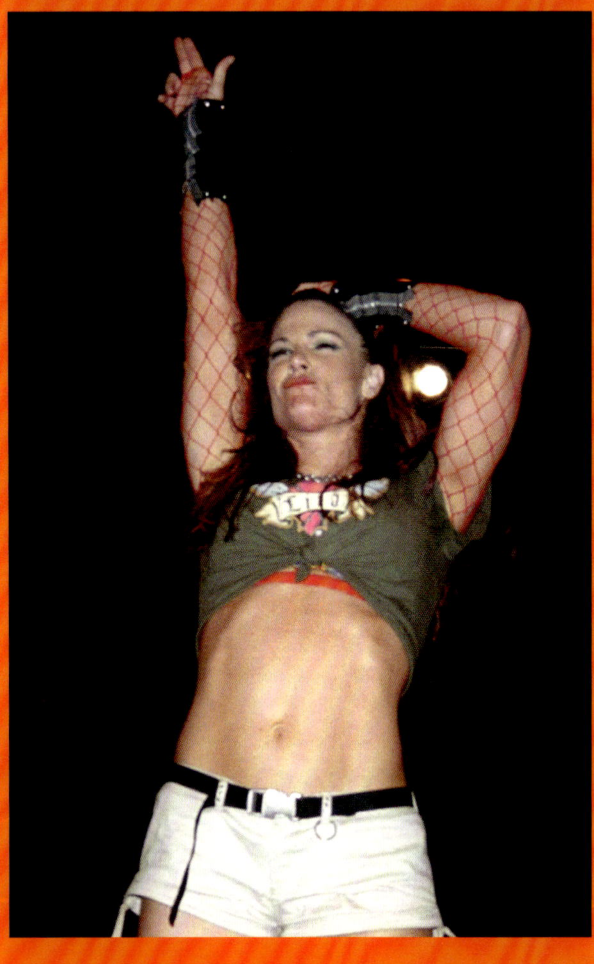

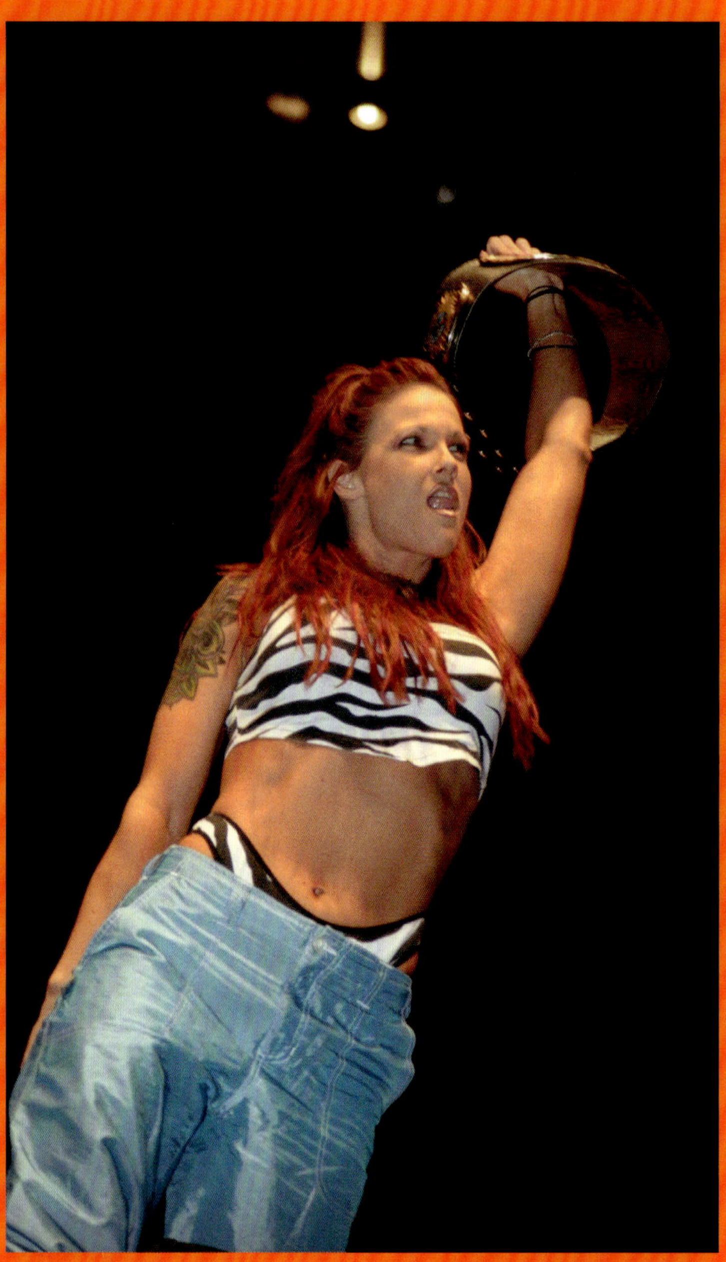

Dumas's fiery style also extended past her clothing. "I had been dyeing my hair red prior to getting hired with WWE, and I did think, 'I guess I'm going [to] have to dye my hair blond now because that's what I see out there on the roster,'" said Dumas, who was delighted to learn she could keep the distinct hue: "I remember Terry Taylor was doing some of the work in talent relations at the time, and he just very offhandedly said to me, 'We'll send you some paperwork, and I don't know if I already told you but you can probably keep your hair red.' When he said that, it just really landed in a way where I was like, 'Oh, I don't have to change my hair, nobody's telling me that you have to look a certain way!' I think from there I just leaned in to it and did more of a really bright red. I did intentionally look at the landscape of the locker room and was like, 'OK, nobody has this look. Everyone either has blond hair or brown hair, and I'm going to lean in to who I am.'"

But while Dumas leaned in to her looks in the ring, she remained intentional about how she was viewed offstage. "It's funny. I see backstage pictures of me all the time. I would always wear like a sweatshirt or a hoodie over my clothes until I went out there, and it was [a] conscious [decision]. I would like to think we're an evolved species; I'm not going to put my boobs in your face while I'm trying to have a conversation or whatever, but I wanted to be treated as much as I could like one of the guys and that was very conscious in the way I carried myself."

Above all, Dumas's relatable style made her a crowd favorite. "Having women or men come up to me saying 'You seem like you could be my friend' was always such a big compliment to me because what we had seen prior on TV was just this unattainable look," she said. "We had either seen the most beautiful bikini model, this extreme oddity, or this Ninth Wonder of the World, and I was more like your everyday person. I liked feeling like I made somebody who considered themselves average think that they could be like a standout with just a little bit of creativity."

TOP LEFT: Lita sporting her iconic low-rise pants with visible thong detail. Photo by George Napolitano.

RIGHT: Lita as WWE Women's Champion. Photo by George Tahinos.

BOTTOM LEFT: Lita in signature mesh shirt and cargo pants. Photo by George Tahinos.

# JOANIE LAURER
## CHYNA

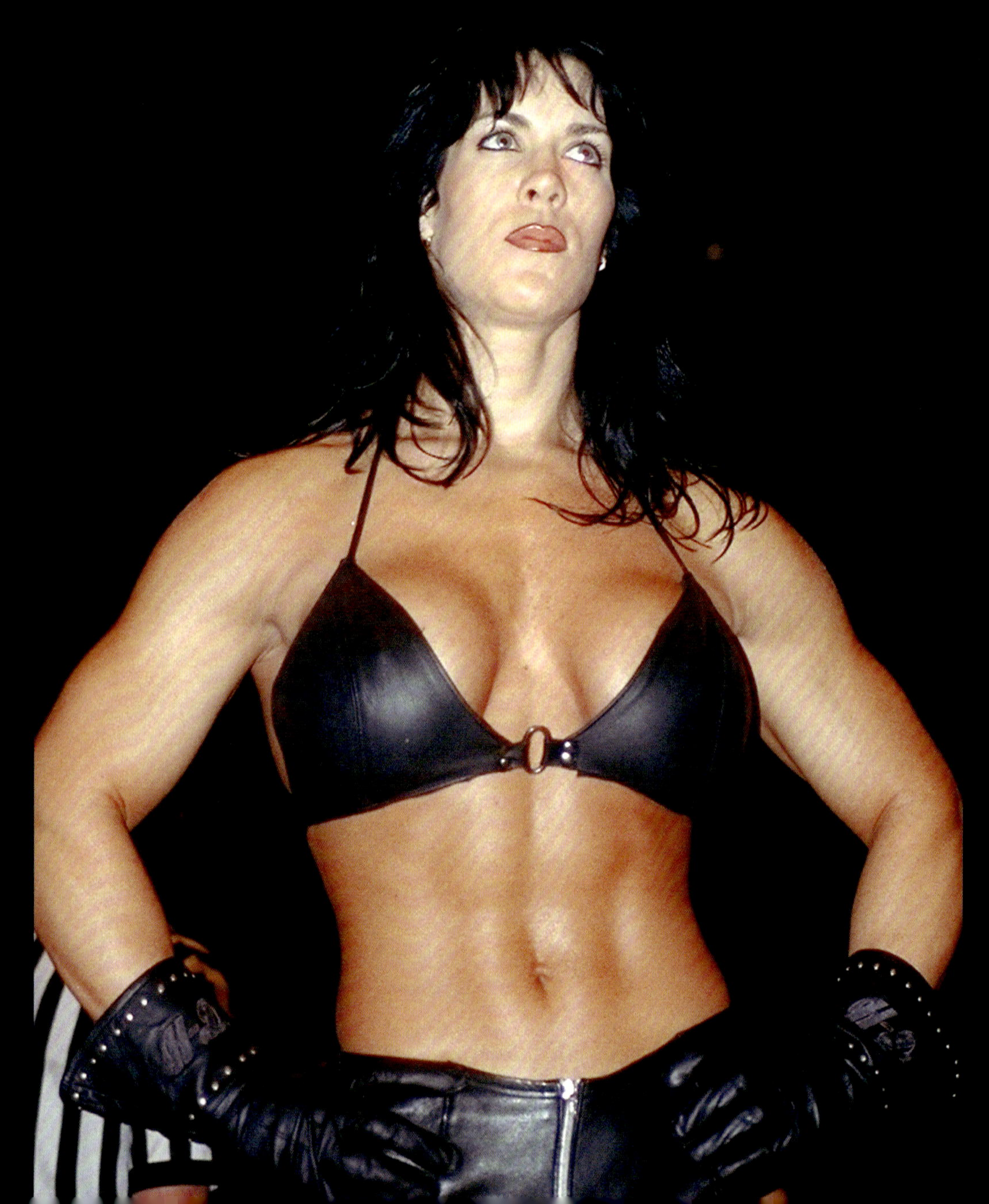

Described in wrestling circles as The Ninth Wonder of the World, Chyna was never timid about her appearance. Instead, she embraced her larger build by flaunting her muscles and accentuating her features with gear crafted to fit her body shape.

Laurer was never afraid to show a little skin, expertly blending femininity with grit. Chyna was usually seen wearing a black leather two-piece top with boy-cut shorts embellished with grommets and metal studs, which enhanced her no-nonsense persona. Chunky belts, straps, and chains only added to her hardcore, rock star–style.

Julie Youngberg, who made several looks for Laurer, recounts her inspiration: "She always had a lot of ideas. Typically, she would show me something that was skimpy, sparkly, and had studs. The goal with her was to completely cover the outfit in bling so it looked metal. When she would wear gloves, it was because she thought they looked badass with the look. I remember one time she brought me photos of Tina Turner from *Mad Max*, and we created a look off that."

Towering over most of the locker room, Laurer proved she could hang with the toughest of men. A crucial member of D-Generation X, a tag team of (otherwise male) Gen X wrestlers, she found her place in the dynamic perfectly, channeling her stoic persona as the muscle and stability of the group. Chyna was also the first female to take part in the WWE's men's Royal Rumble match, showing the world that women can thrive in a male-dominated world when given the opportunity.

OPPOSITE: **Chyna in signature leather outfit. Photo by George Napolitano.**

RIGHT: **Chyna early in her career. Photo by George Napolitano.**

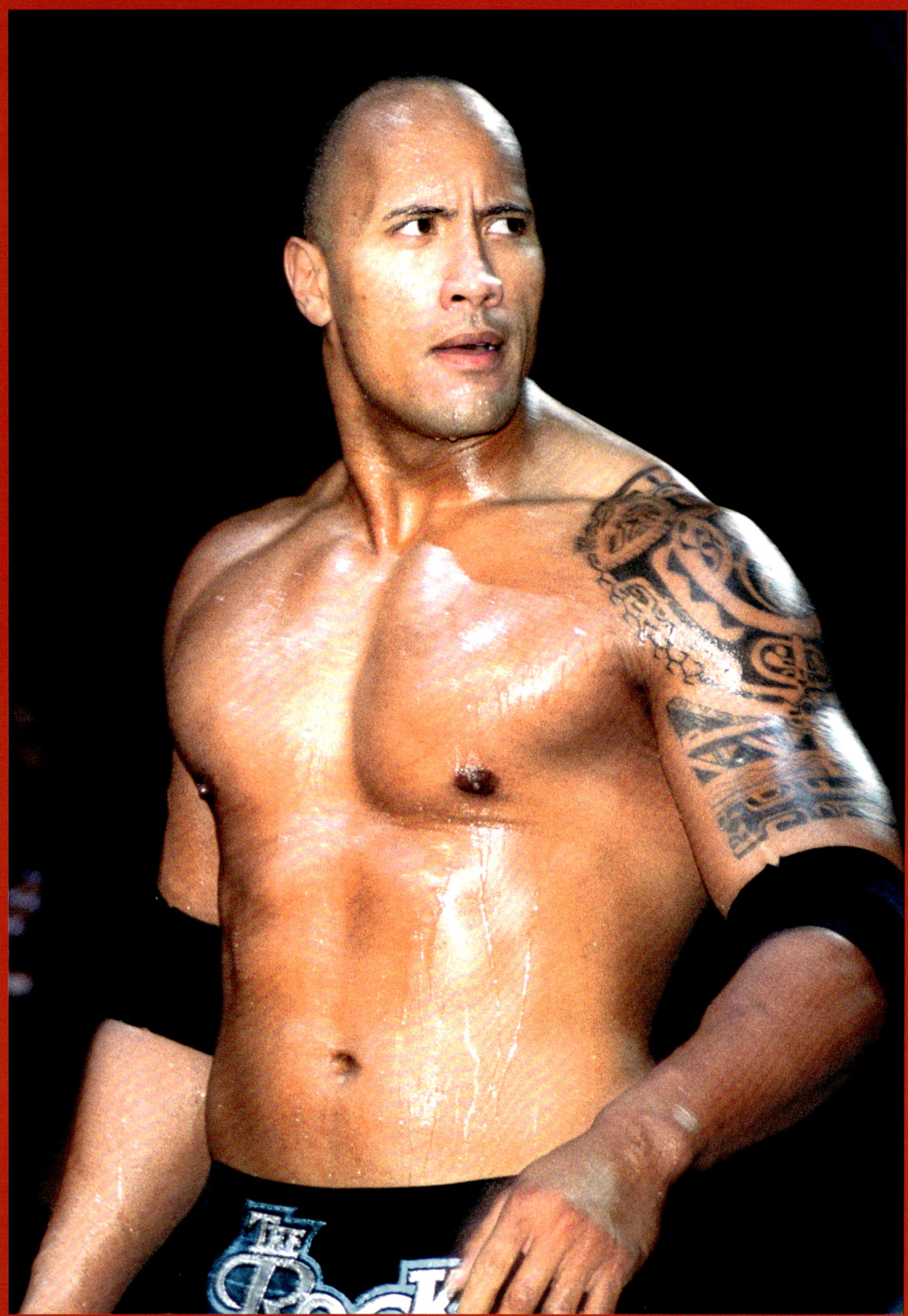
The Rock

# DWAYNE "THE ROCK" JOHNSON

Active 1996–present

Ten-Time WWE World Champion

**It's no secret** that Dwayne "The Rock" Johnson is a global phenomenon. But before becoming one of the biggest celebrities in Hollywood, he was a young athlete—and his roots lie in wrestling.

When Johnson debuted in 1996, his attire leaned into tribal symbolism with fringe and tassels, an homage to his Samoan identity. Back then, he was known as Rocky Maivia or The Blue Chipper, but fans weren't buying it. Soon after, Johnson joined Nation of Domination and found success with simple black trunks, gold chains, and a cocky attitude. Looking back on it now, this simplicity may have reminded fans of *the* iconic fit—Johnson's throwback 1994 photo with the raised eyebrow, flattop haircut, black turtleneck, fanny pack, and Cuban chain. Around this time, he began branding himself with the new name—The Rock—and bull logo that remain universally known today.

Terry Anderson, who has worked alongside Johnson throughout his wrestling career, recalled how this conscious shift in his attire changed everything: "When he was first brought in, they had a company do his outfits through a creative service department. I don't remember the first time he ever walked over to me to ask me to make his gear, but I took over almost immediately after that first one, because he hated it so much and got such terrible feedback. It was a round chest piece, and it had long black-and-tan fringe that hung from it."

Dwayne "The Rock" Johnson. Photo by George Tahinos.

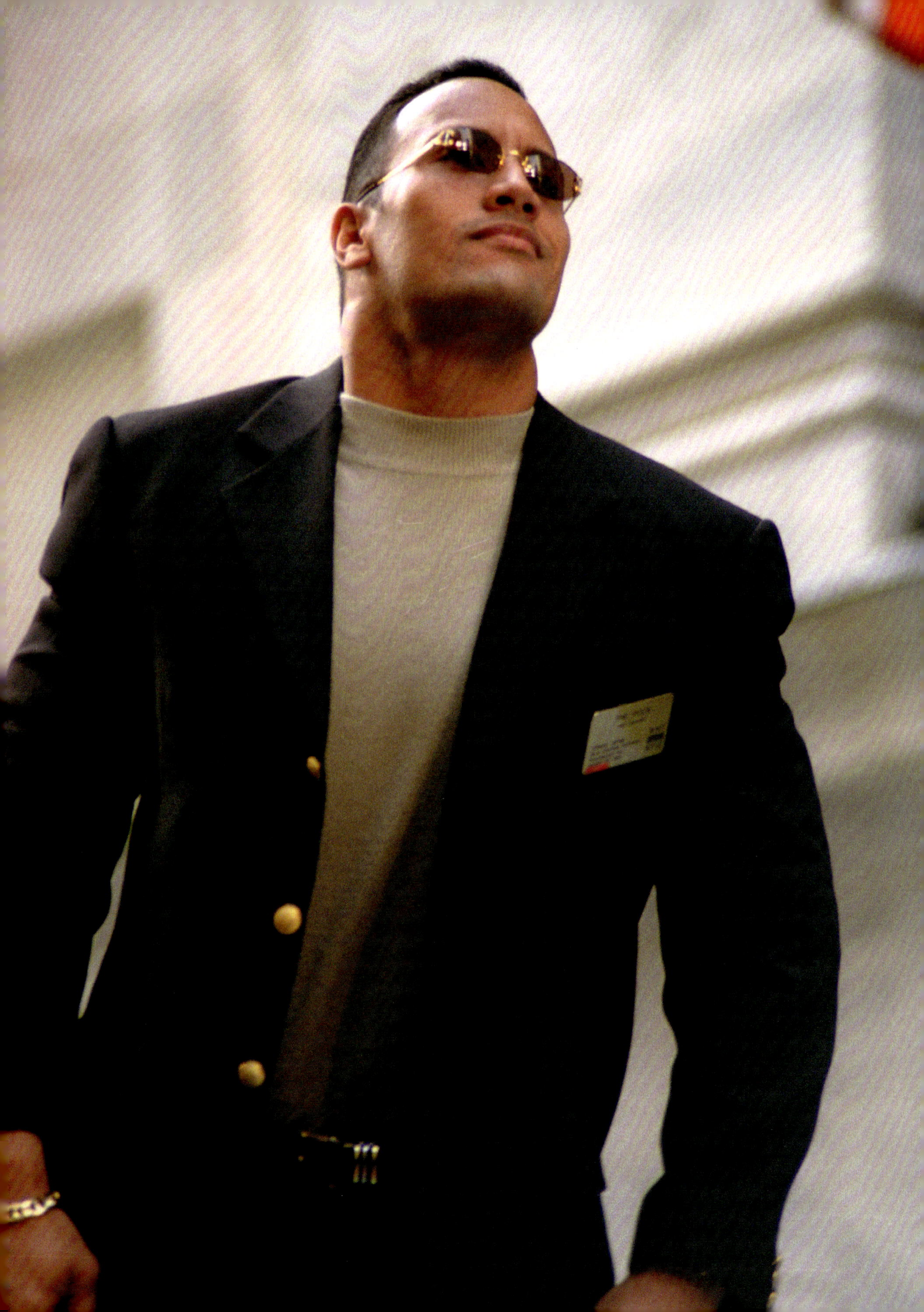

The pair got to work crafting The Rock's new look, which incorporated everything from Johnson's nickname to his signature to his tattoos. According to Anderson: "The first couple [outfits] I made for him were based off of designs that creative services had sent me. One day, he was like, 'Hey, can you take my signature and put that on my trunks?' He signed *The Rock*, and then I blew that up really large to put on his trunks. Next, he wanted his bull tattoo on the back, so I did that. Eventually, we moved to a standard 3D-shaped *The Rock* on the front, but I always put the bull on the back." From the beginning, Johnson took an active role in the creative process. "He would always give me the colors, but Dwayne is very particular," she said. "I remember when I would give him the trunks, he would turn them inside out and he would inspect everything. A couple times, he pointed out that my sewing machine skipped a stitch. From that point on, I knew his stuff had to be perfect."

During the 2000s, Johnson's clothing evolved in keeping with his new persona. The Rock portrayed unrivaled confidence in his new era, wearing designer jackets, Rolex watches, and luxe shoes, painting a picture of wealth, superiority, and total dominance. Taking influence from high fashion, Johnson now wore Versace-inspired attire. In 2024, Johnson delighted fans by donning a custom Versace-inspired tuxedo that showed off his tattooed physique at WrestleMania 40.

The seamster behind that iconic suit, David Alan, remembers how the look came to life. "I got a call about thirty days before WrestleMania," said Alan, recalling how WWE producers asked if he'd like to be involved. "They asked if I wanted to do a big project for WrestleMania, and initially I had turned it down." But after learning that he'd be dressing The Rock, Alan immediately reconsidered: "On the phone, they're like, 'Well, if we tell you who the talent is, maybe that will change your mind.' They mentioned it was going to be for The Rock, and of course it was an opportunity that I wanted to jump at, but I also knew that my reputation was on the line."

Dwayne "The Rock" Johnson buttoned up for a WWE event. Photo by George Tahinos.

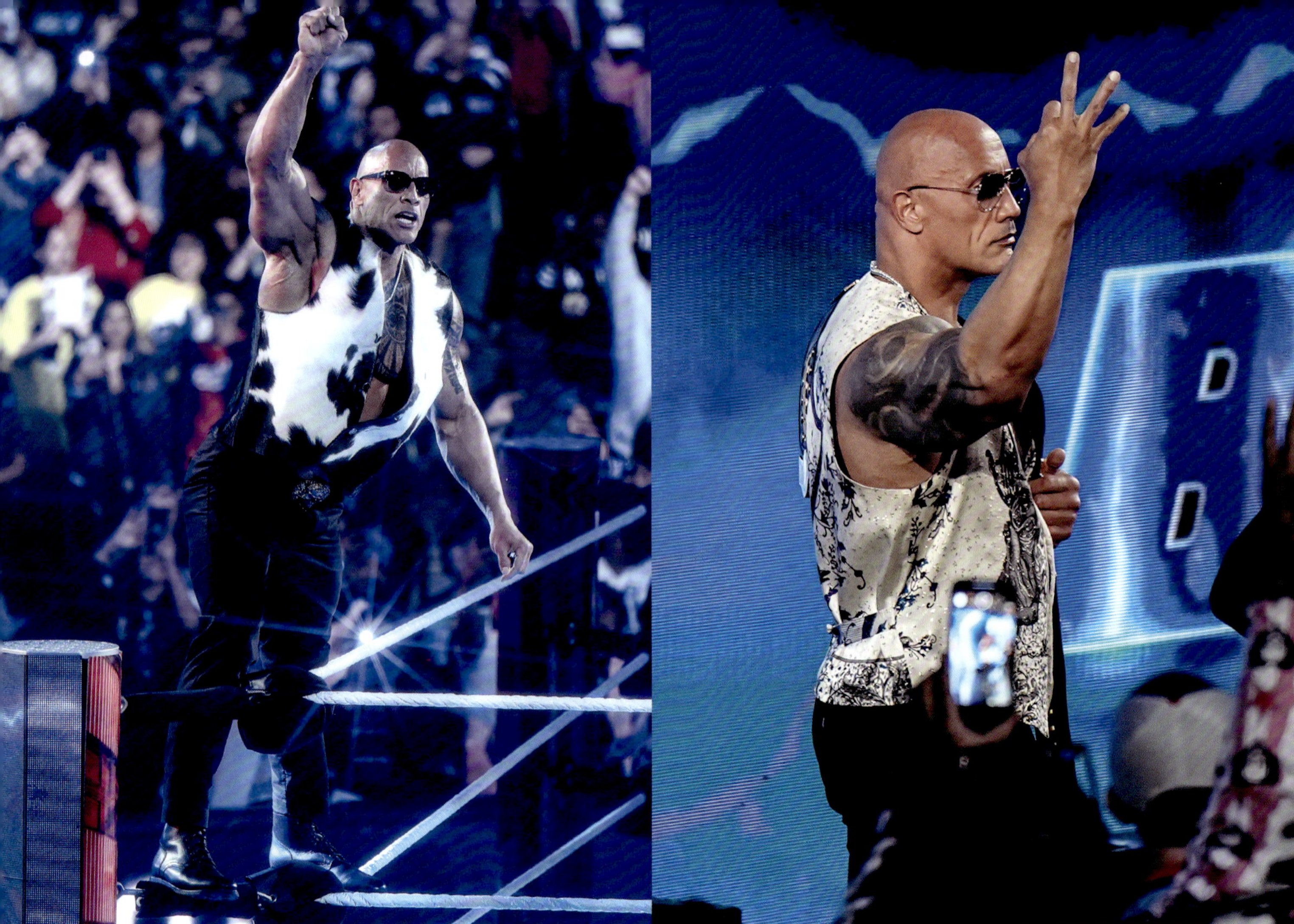

Alan got to work designing an outfit worthy of one of the WWE's biggest stars. "My team put together some ideas from watching him in character. We really dove into things. I noticed he was wearing a ton of Versace-style clothing and he's a big fan of Elvis," said Alan, whose final look folded elements from both Versace and Johnson's tattoos into a white custom suit that could have been worn by The King. "There was a *Friday Night SmackDown* in Dallas in March of [that] year, and I met with him at his trailer. We had a pitch deck that we showed him, and we got him measured," said Alan, who was about to witness The Rock's commitment to crafting a winning persona. "Midweek, they wanted to make some revisions and changes to [the suit], making sure certain features and attributes of his body were showcased through the garment. It was pretty incredible to see the magnitude of what he and his team look at and how important every little detail actually is."

But when the garment arrived about three days before WrestleMania, the team realized they had a problem. "The file that we designed and sent to our manufacturer, they downgraded the quality of the file, and the garment arrived and was completely pixelated," said Alan. "So, I got about four thousand gems, and I hand glued the crystals all over the garment to make sure the pixelation was gone." Not only did Alan's last-minute fix disguise the mistake, but it added even more bling to the final ensemble: "With the bright lights of WrestleMania and the chaos, the blunder that we ended up having actually enhanced it drastically."

After collaborating with The Rock for WrestleMania 40, Alan had even greater

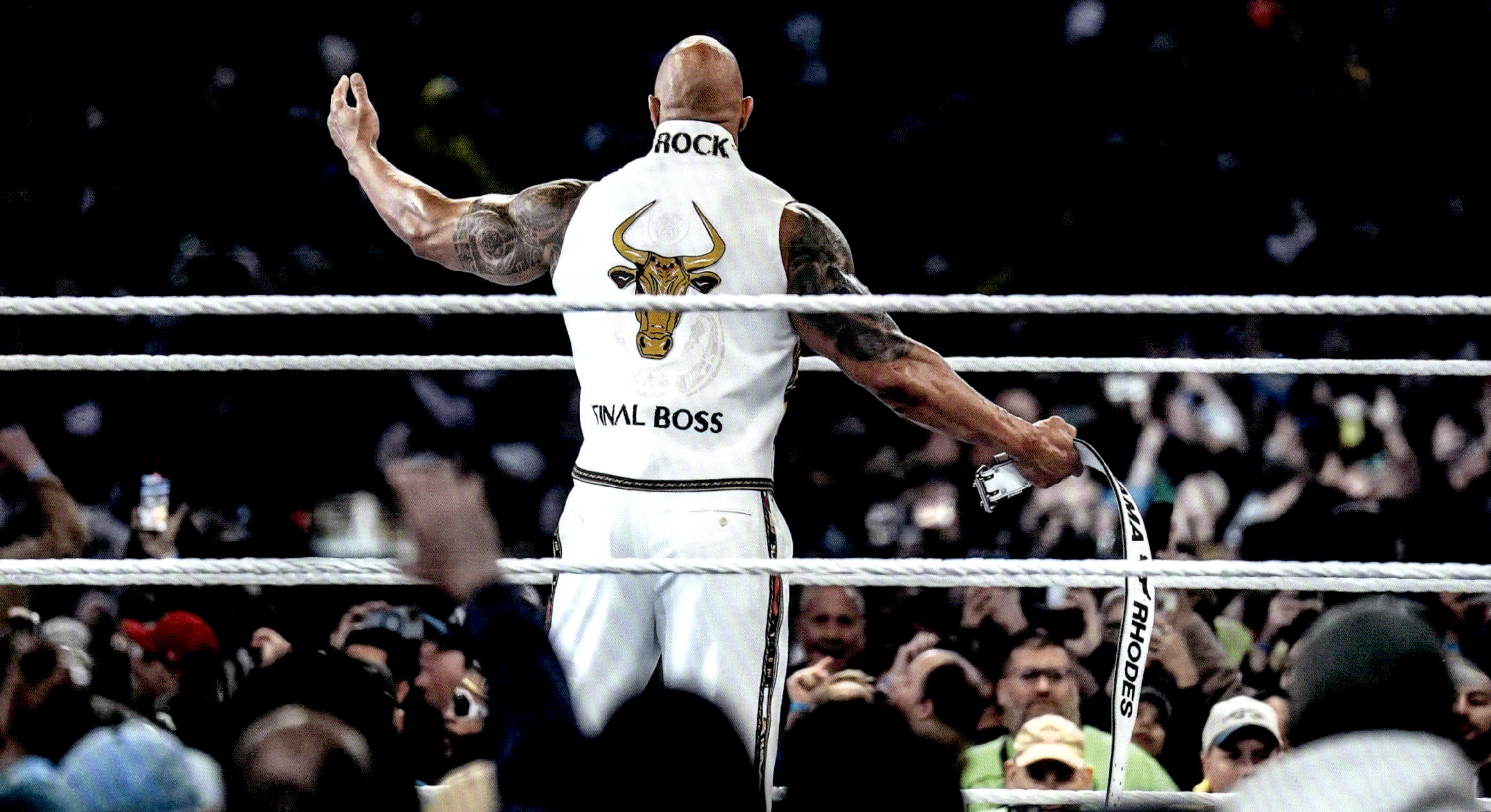



From left to right:

The Rock at WWE RAW in Brooklyn, New York, in 2024. Photo by Kimberly Morrell.

The Rock at WWE Bad Blood in 2024. Photo by Kimberly Morrell.

The Rock at WrestleMania 40 in Philadelphia, Pennsylvania. Photo by Kimberly Morrell.

respect for the WWE star. "Presentation to me is one of the most powerful and important things that a lot of people, more men, really lack or don't see the appreciation or value in," said Alan, who believes Johnson's success stems in part from his commitment to his character. "The Rock's career has flourished and grown to be one of the biggest [and most] recognizable names in the entire world. It was pretty surreal watching everything unfold."

Today, The Rock remains sleek and sharp, and continues to electrify fans worldwide. That's because Johnson knows how to leverage the spotlight and make each moment feel like a red-carpet event. Whether he's in the newest hit movie, delivering The Rock Bottom, or entertaining millions of people with his charisma . . . we will always be able to smell what The Rock is cooking.

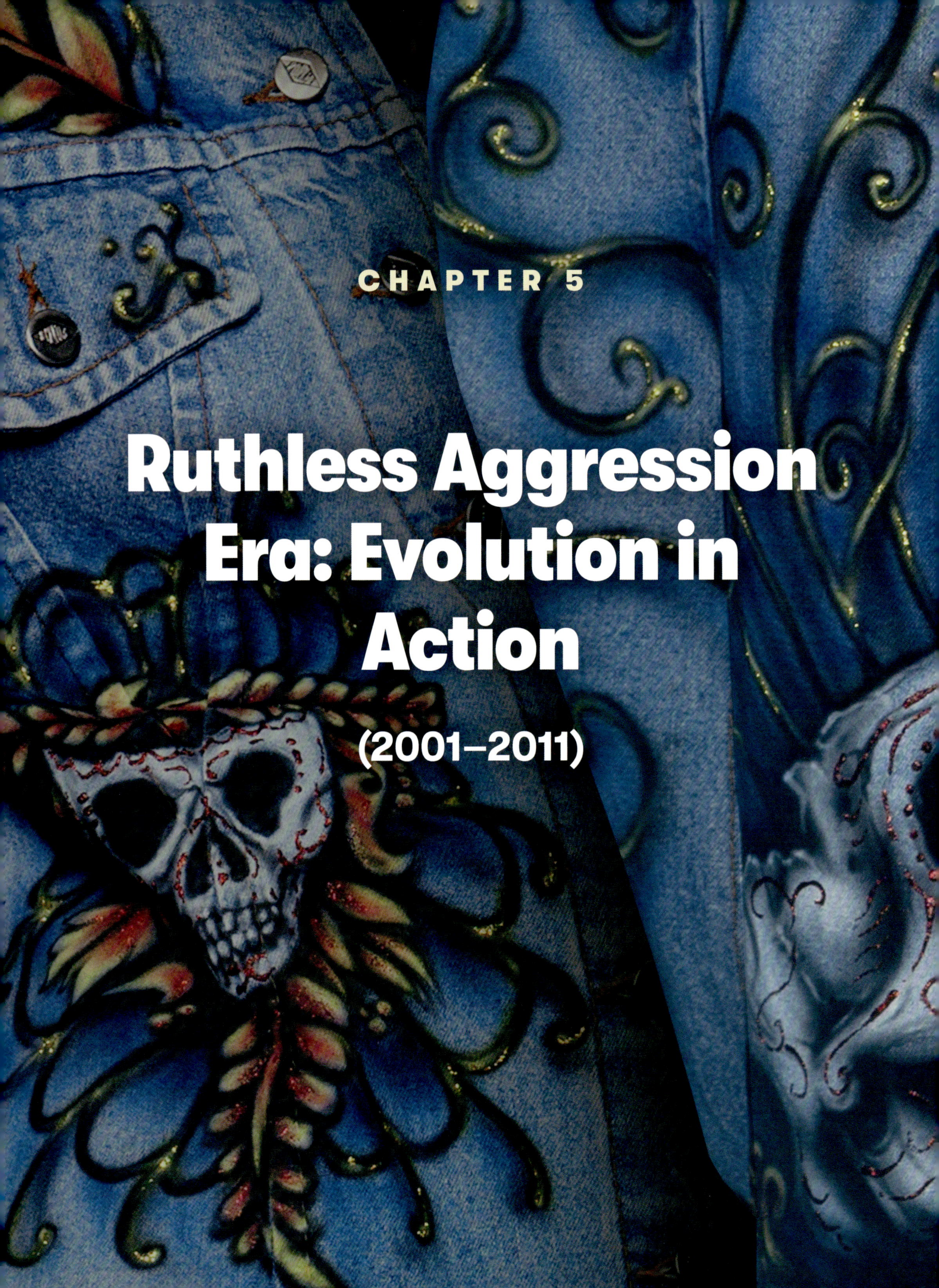

CHAPTER 5
Ruthless Aggression Era: Evolution in Action
(2001–2011)

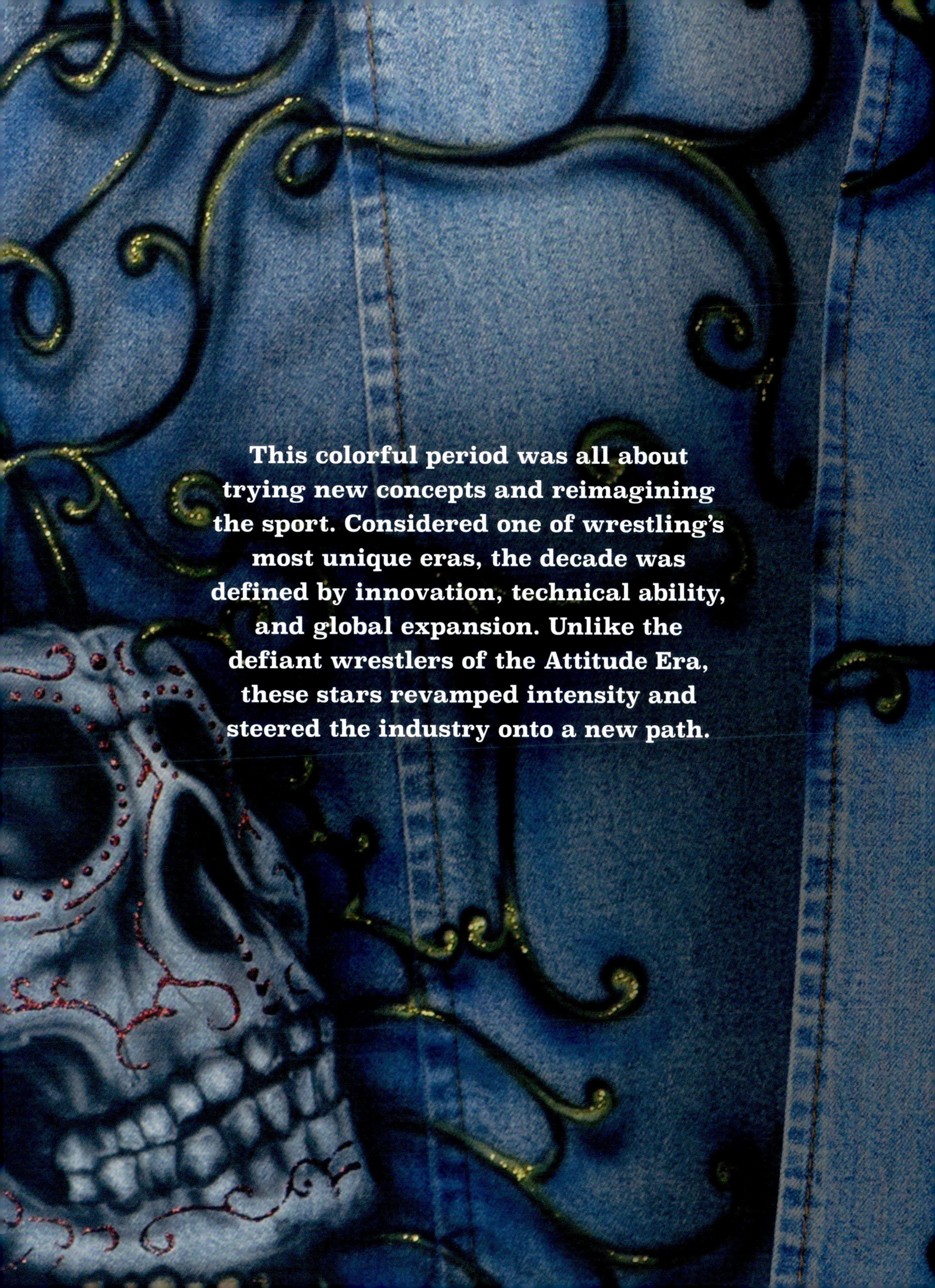

This colorful period was all about trying new concepts and reimagining the sport. Considered one of wrestling's most unique eras, the decade was defined by innovation, technical ability, and global expansion. Unlike the defiant wrestlers of the Attitude Era, these stars revamped intensity and steered the industry onto a new path.

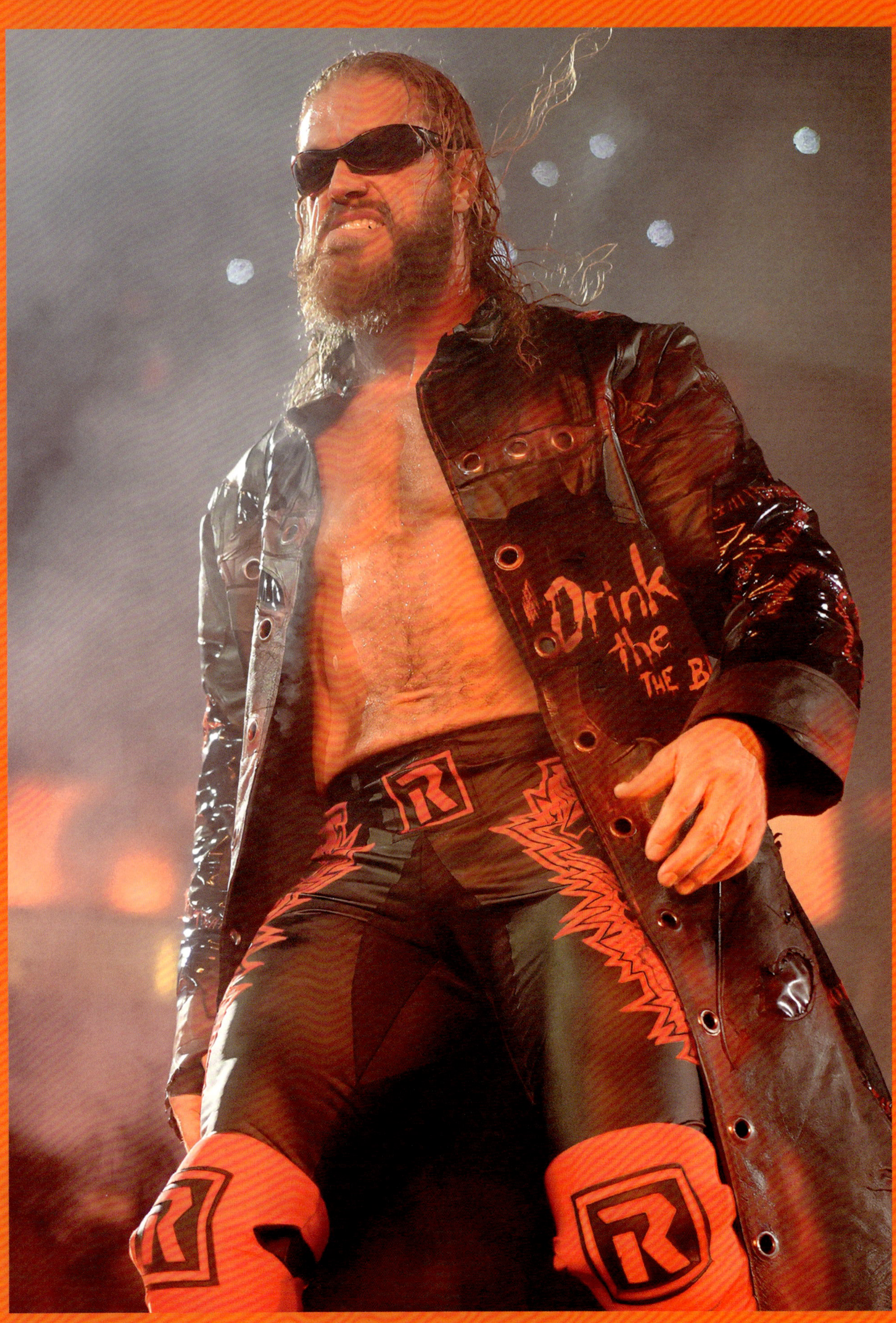
Drink
the
THE B

# ADAM COPELAND
## *WWE'S EDGE / AEW'S COPE*

Active 1992–present

Eleven-Time World Champion
WWE Hall of Famer

**As much as** you may think you do, do you actually know him? Considered one of professional wrestling's most remarkable athletes, Adam Copeland commands respect because of his accomplishments, talent, and ability to push through trials and tribulations—and, of course, his edge. Even after a career-altering injury left him sidelined for a decade, Copeland remains one of the sport's most fascinating (and fashionable) stars.

Though best known for his time as WWE Superstar Edge, Copeland has inhabited many personas over the years. He started his career wrestling beside Gangrel and Christian Cage in a wrestling faction known as The Brood. Inspired by a clan of vampires, the mysterious gang wore gothic attire, silver choker necklaces, and wraparound sunglasses—with rock star confidence. But while his partners donned ruffled vampire shirts, Copeland sported a long leather or polyester jacket to separate himself from the pack. "It was a choice I decided to make so I wasn't pirate shirt guy number two," said Copeland, referring to the *Seinfeld* episode where Jerry reluctantly wears a puffy shirt on TV. "I just thought three dudes in puffy shirts might not be the visual I was looking for. Not that there's anything wrong with that. OK, I'll quit the *Seinfeld* references now."

Years later, trademark jackets are still a part of Edge's persona. "I had done the T-shirt to the ring thing, but to me it just looks lazy," said Copeland. "We're supposed to look like superheroes. At least the way I always envisioned it. And that's part of what drew me to wrestling in the first place. Superheroes come to life."

Edge at WWE SummerSlam in 2021.
Photo by Kimberly Morrell.

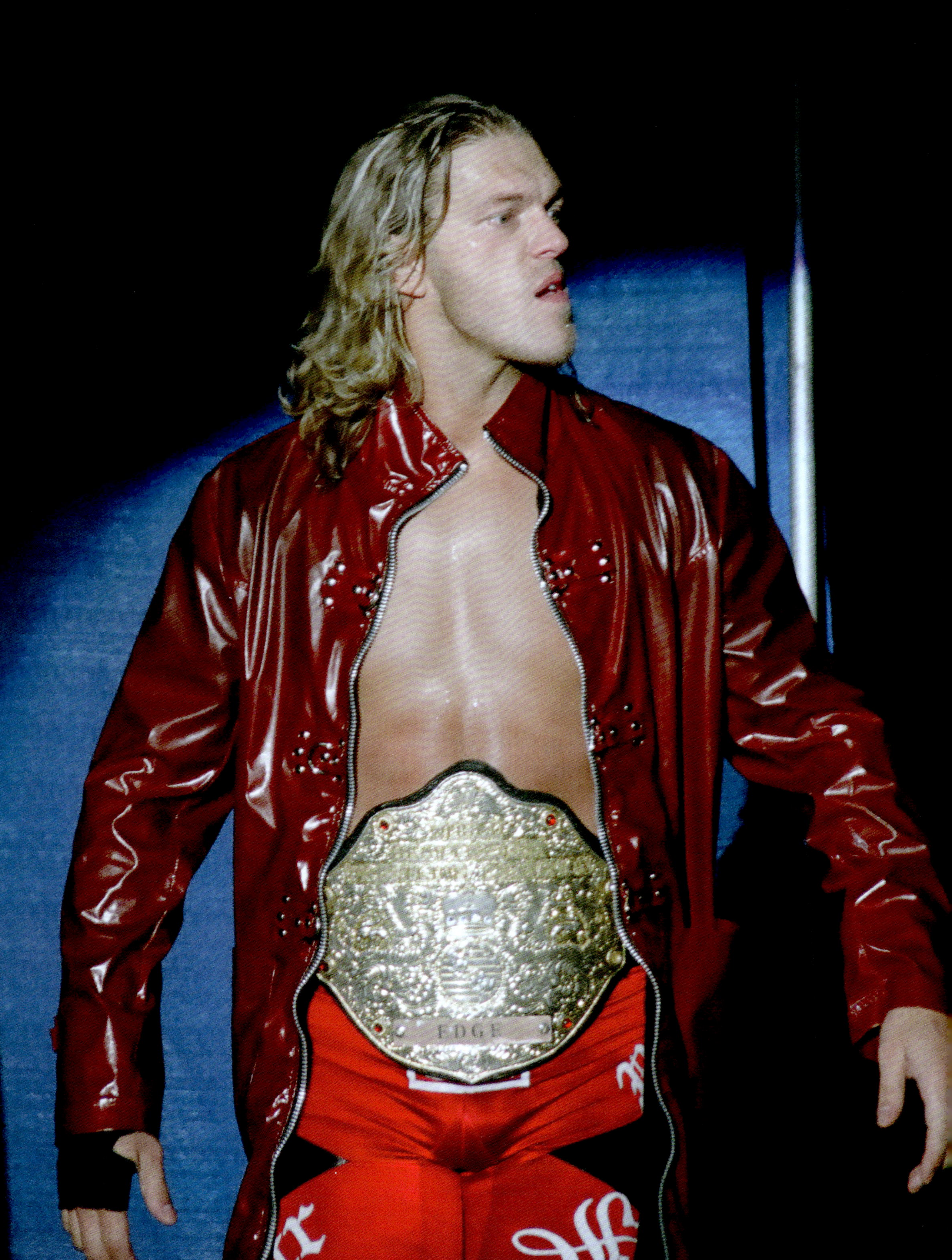

Copeland reserved one of his most memorable looks for WrestleMania 39, where Edge's fiery entrance revealed him wearing a demonic mask and winged jacket. It was an appropriately showstopping entrance for a steel cage match between two long-standing rivals. "With that match being Hell in a Cell, the culmination of a yearlong feud where The Judgment Day [faction] kicked me out of the group I created and then attacked my wife," said Copeland, who unleashed the most sinister version of his character—Brood Edge—for the occasion. "The more evil incarnations of our characters, Demon [Finn Bálor] versus Brood, it felt like the culmination of all of that. It felt like it was the perfect opportunity to really have some fun creating. I had a mental picture and got to work. Luckily, I work with the absolutely, ridiculously amazing Sylvia Jensen at Wornstar, and no matter the insane task I lay at her feet, she picks it up and scores a touchdown. 'Hey, Sylvia, how about some devil wings made from leather that I can control with my hands?' I found the mask in Poland. I have no idea why it exists, but I thought it would look crazy under the lights with all the pyro and Slayer blasting behind me. A lot of people in creative positions didn't think it was a good idea. I disagreed. It's Mania, ya gotta go big. It also ended up being my last Mania. My first WrestleMania appearance was with The Brood. It felt very full circle."

Throughout the years, Copeland's looks and motivations have been inspired by his favorite bands and movies: "Music has always been my muse on the road. Early Edge was based around Nine Inch Nails. The Brood was Lost Boys. Edge and Christian [Copeland's former tag team duo] was inspired by obnoxious Bill

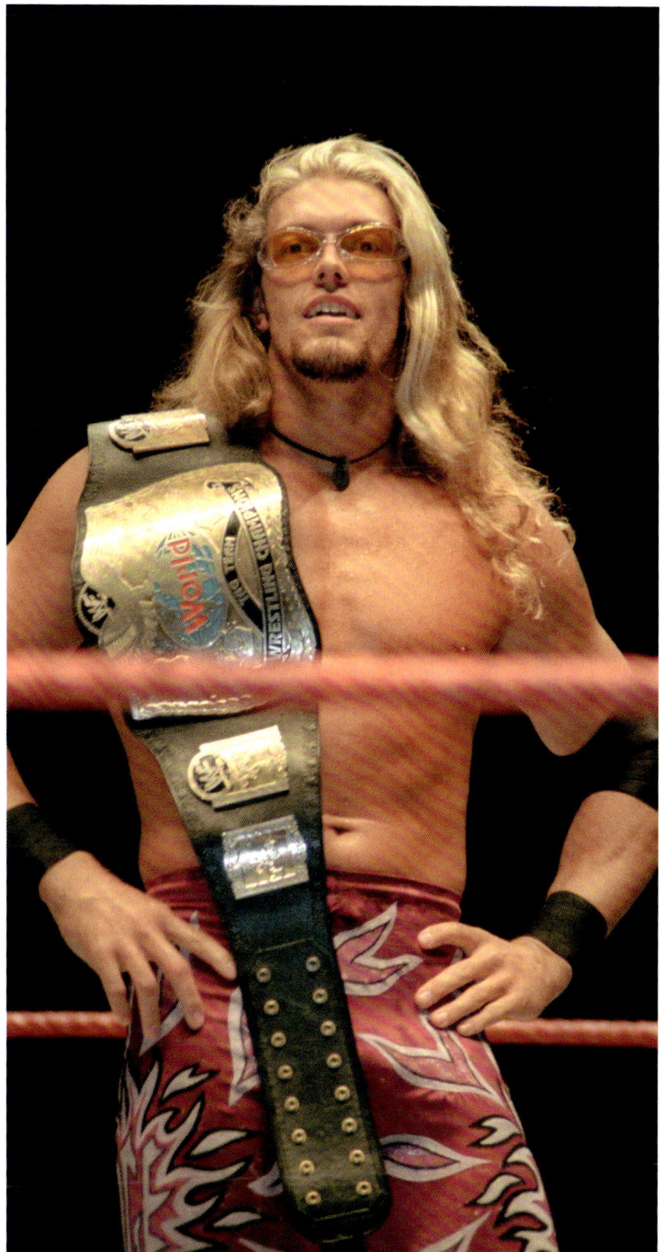

and Ted from the movie [*Bill & Ted's*] *Excellent Adventure*. Rated-R Superstar was based around the idea of *Appetite for Destruction*–era Guns N' Roses, before the piano ballads and churchyard guitar solos. My character now is more of a Kurt Russell in *Death Proof* vibe. All of the aforementioned characters have a definite fringe quality. Unintentionally intentional?"

But there's one particular band that inspired Copeland's signature emblem, which he has since worked into countless jackets, tights,

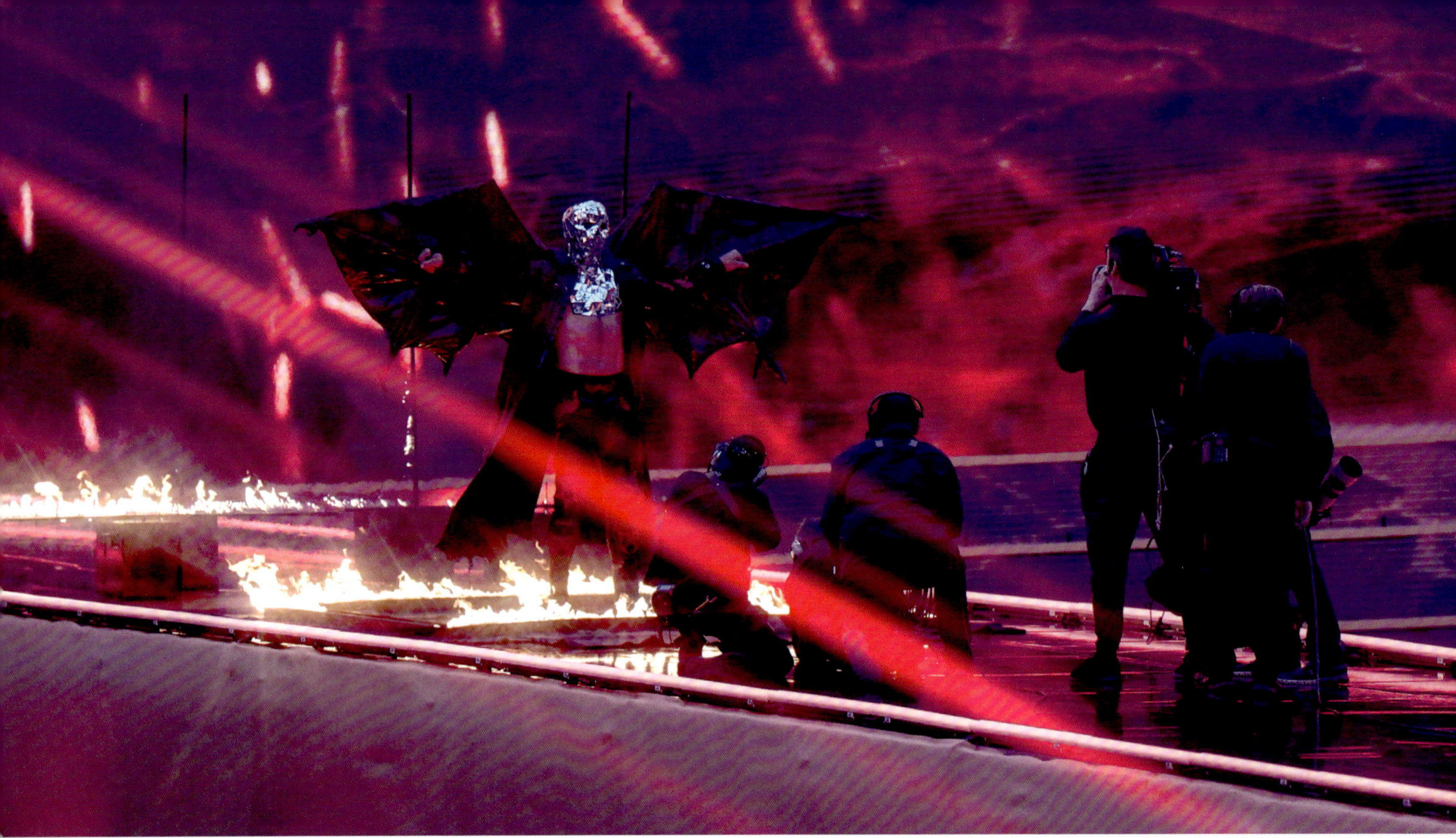

Adam Copeland as WWE Superstar Edge at WrestleMania 39 in Los Angeles, California. Photo by Kimberly Morrell.

**"I had just turned heel after a few years as a babyface. I was sent some T-shirt designs with the polling for how they tested. The last on that list was a Rated-R Superstar T-shirt. I said, 'That's the shirt, and that's the name.' Literally everyone disagreed, but I knew it was money because it rolled off the tongue so easily and I saw the marketing potential. So I just started signing everything *Rated-R Superstar* and began calling myself that during promos. I wanted to be the one to make the choice to bring something to life that I had to inhabit."**

—Adam Copeland on becoming The Rated-R Superstar

tattoos, and kick pads. "I've always had an eye for stars," said Copeland, who blames Paul Stanley, the lead singer of KISS, for his long-standing obsession. "I don't know, there is just something very appealing to me about the star, and I generally try to work it into every design somewhere."

And while Copeland—or AEW Superstar Cope, as he's currently known—hasn't even retired, his impact is already felt among the next generation. AEW Superstar Swerve Strickland credits Copeland for inspiring his own wrestling gear, which features large tribal faces embroidered on the side of his tights—inspired by the iconic imagery Copeland frequently displays on his gear. For Copeland, that's humbling. "I know what effect other talents' gear—and the creativity that went into [it]—had on me," said Copeland, who was inspired by wrestlers before him but never imagined he'd have the same impact on a new generation: "But it's very complimentary and warms the cockles of my obsidian heart to think others with the same mindset were paying attention."

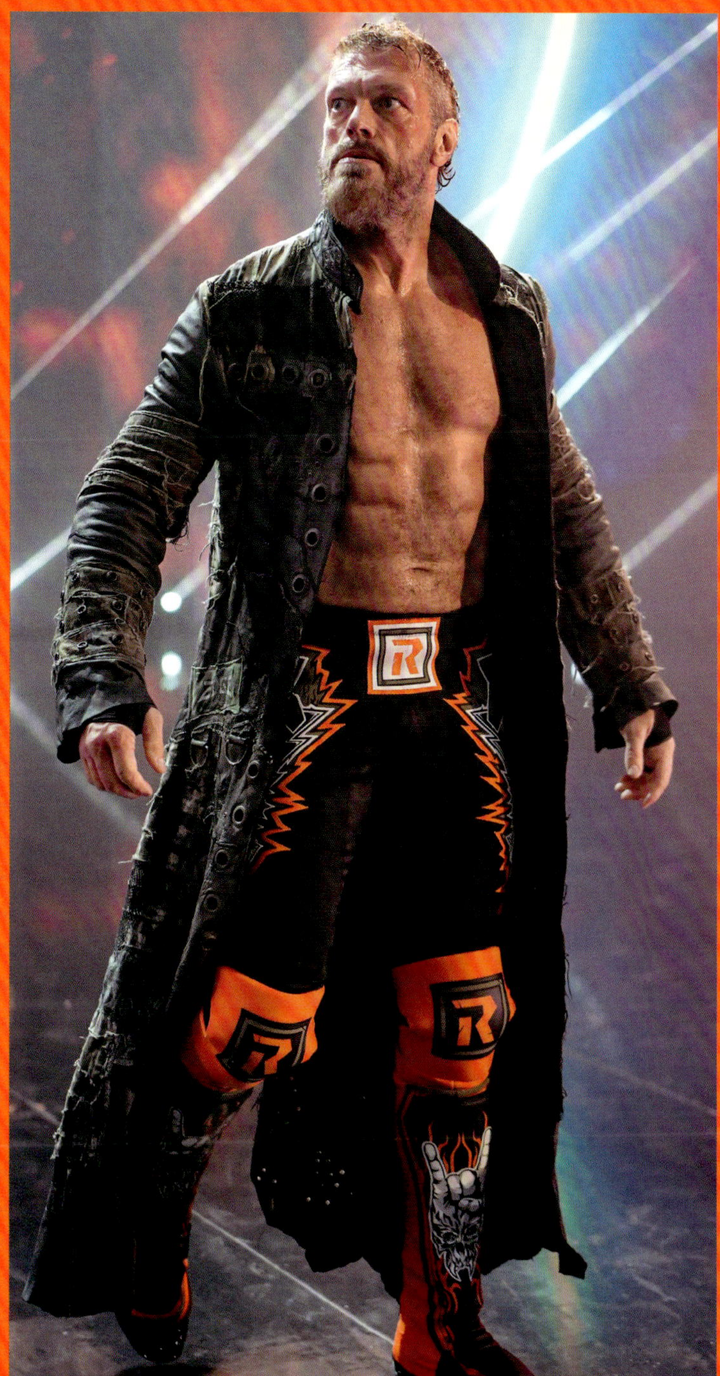

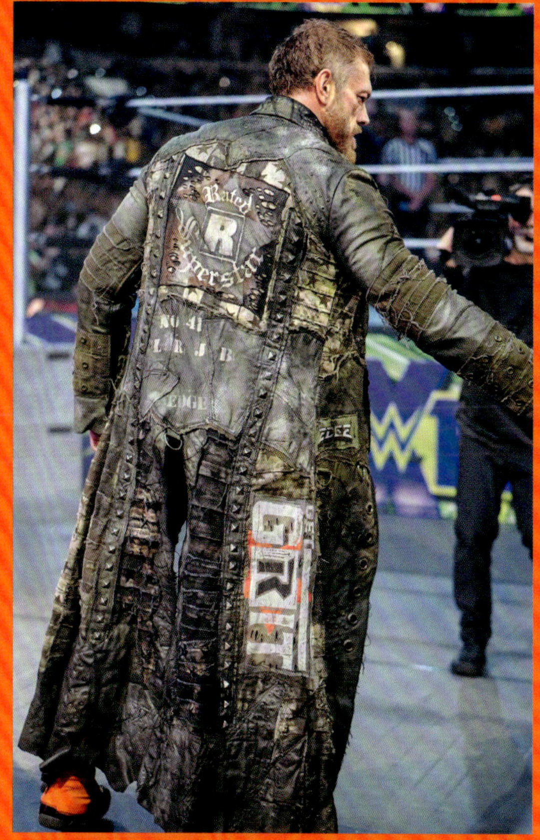

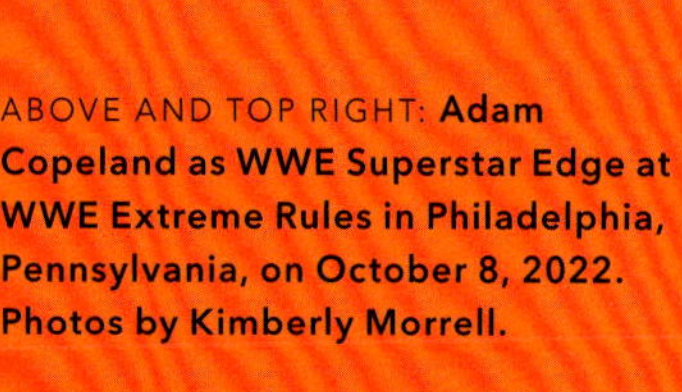

ABOVE AND TOP RIGHT: **Adam Copeland as WWE Superstar Edge at WWE Extreme Rules in Philadelphia, Pennsylvania, on October 8, 2022. Photos by Kimberly Morrell.**

RIGHT: **Adam Copeland as WWE Superstar Edge at WrestleMania 37 in Tampa, Florida, in 2021. Photo by Kimberly Morrell.**

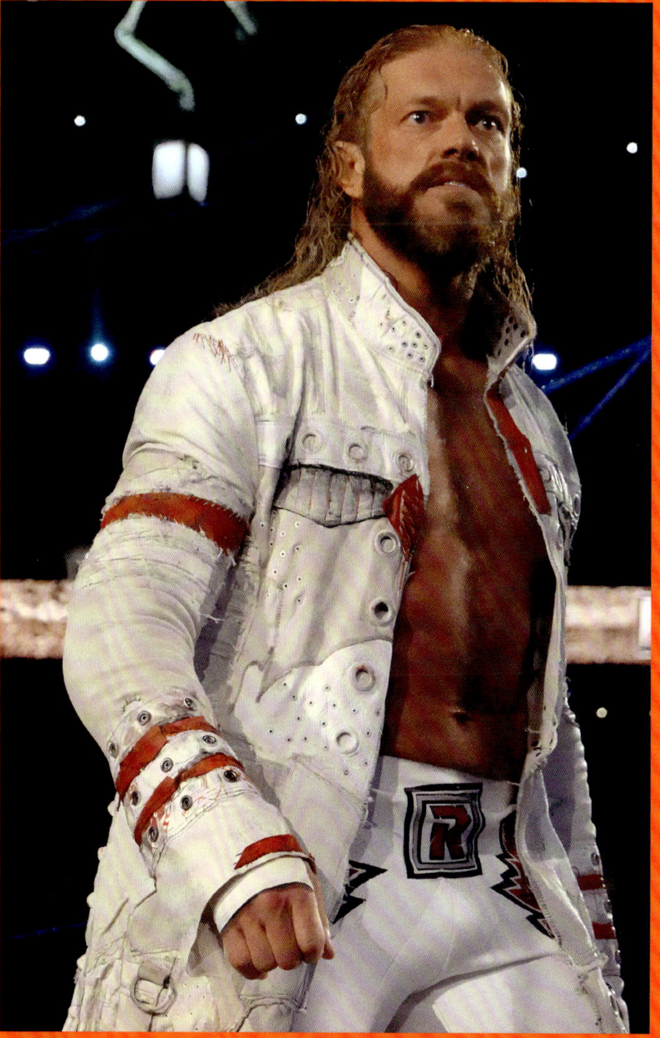

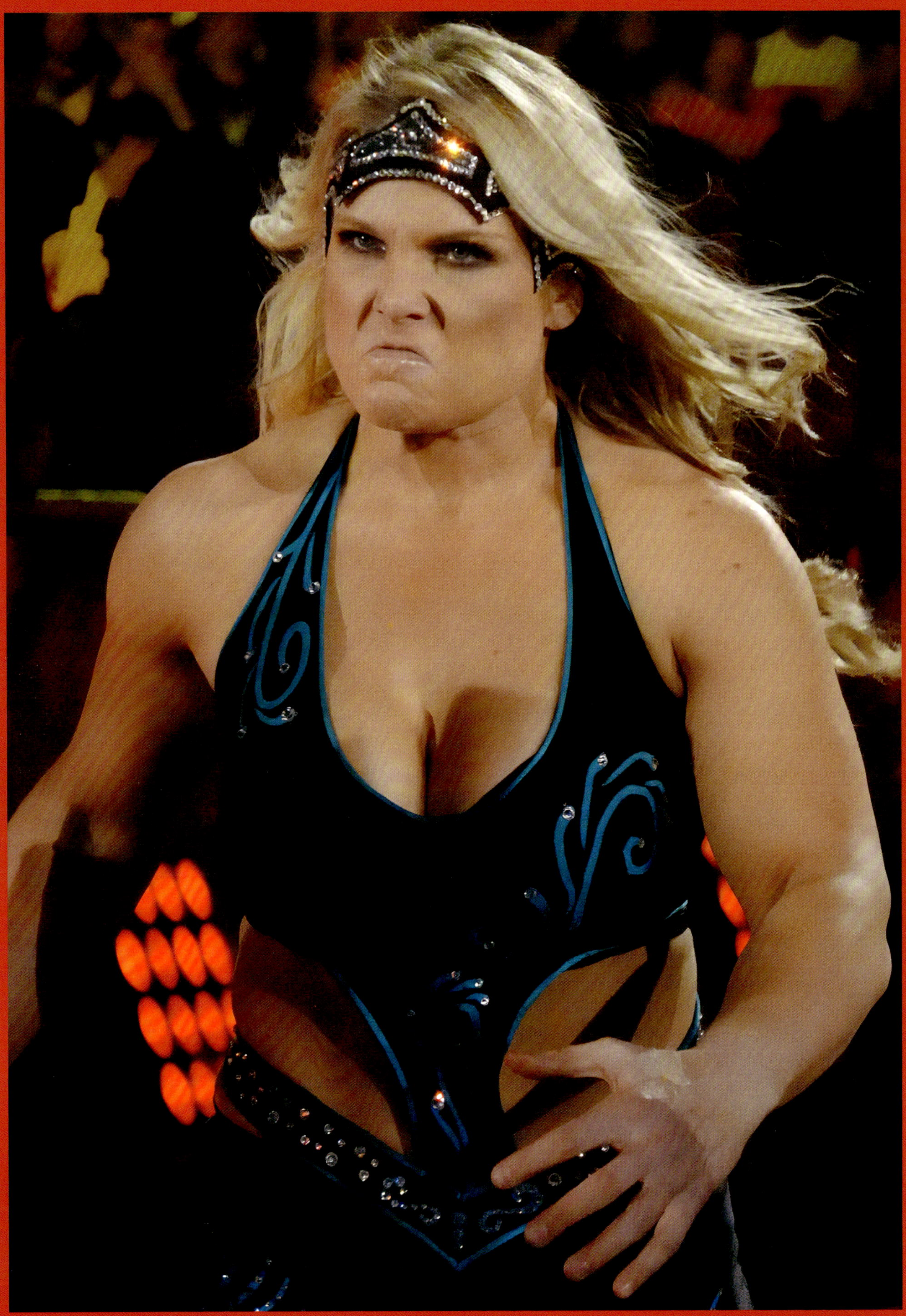

# BETH COPELAND
## WWE'S BETH PHOENIX

Active 2001–2012

Three-Time WWE Women's Champion
WWE Hall of Famer

**A champion wrestler** who dominated the ring for over a decade, a phoenix with feathers of gold, Beth Copeland opened new doors for women in the industry. Globally known by her WWE ring name, Beth Phoenix, Copeland challenged conventions each time she stepped into the ring. She was less about edge and shock factor than her counterparts. Copeland donned superhero attire to portray confidence and strength. Throughout her career, Copeland remained a tireless champion for women's wrestling and—like the legendary bird who rose up from the ashes—reimagined the types of roles women wrestlers could play.

From the beginning, Copeland was looking for ways to set herself apart from other athletes: "Girls weren't using monikers at the time, and that's why I specifically wanted a moniker to stand out, so I chose The Glamazon. Girls also weren't really wearing superhero-style costumes, so I chose something with a Wonder Woman or a She-Ra headband because our TV time was so limited. There were a lot of blonds, a lot of tan blonds, and women were only getting a minute or two of TV time. So I was like, 'What's memorable?' And for me, it was the headband. I thought, 'You may not remember my name, and you might have only seen me a second, but you'd be like, "Oh, that's the girl that wears the headband."' So, while the other girls would—even in backstage segments, if you paid attention—I didn't wear a lot of street clothes. I usually wore my gear even for backstage segments, even if I didn't have a match, specifically to brand myself heavily as 'That's the girl with the headband.'"

**"I was in the women's locker and I'm trying to do my own hair, and [wrestler] Candice Michelle goes, 'Let's do something . . . let's make your hair bigger!' She did a quick hairstyle for me, which was like this mohawk-meets-lion's-mane hairstyle. It was the match that started my career essentially because of just the way it was built, and I looked like a killer. I saw pictures of myself afterward in the whole look and I was like, 'Oh my god, I've made it.' I didn't win the title that night, but it was like this huge moment for me where I was like, 'Oh, I did it!' I'm looking at photos of myself and seeing what I used to see as a little kid watching the TV screen."**

—Beth Copeland on her first pay-per-view match against Michelle McCool at the 2007 WWE Women's Championship

WWE Superstar Beth Phoenix at WWE Royal Rumble at Minute Maid Park in Houston, Texas, on January 20, 2020. Photo by Kimberly Morrell.

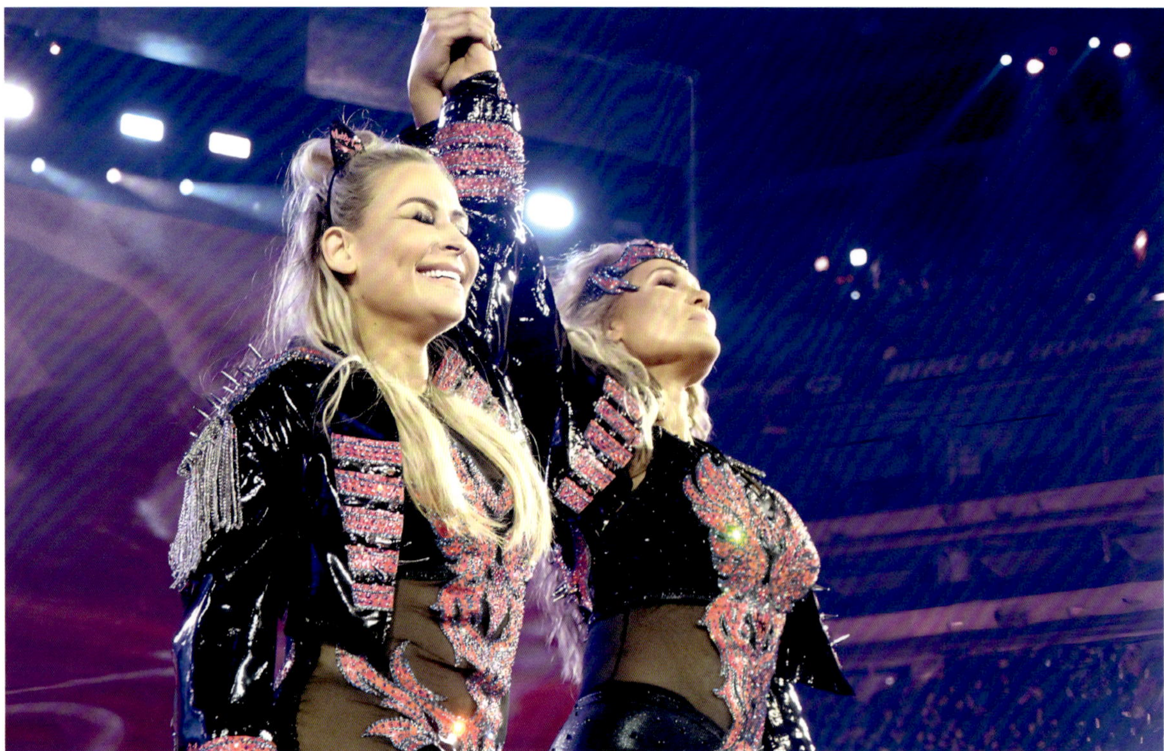

But her empowered style, as Copeland quickly learned, wasn't always in fashion: "At the time, I knew my choice wasn't popular. What was popular was dressing really sexy. Girls were wearing a lot of Victoria's Secret–style trendy, cute, sexy clothes. And me, standing there in my gear, it looked a little weird at times. I remember backstage people mentioning to me, 'You really should sex it up.' But I had a very specific thing in mind to brand myself. It wasn't because I was lazy, and it wasn't because I didn't want to wear cute clothes. It was because I really, specifically wanted to be remembered for that look."

Undeterred, Copeland remained intent on changing the narrative surrounding what women should look like in the ring. She found power in her comfortable attire and set herself apart from her fellow stars with boot-cut pants and spandex one-pieces. "My in-ring style was more so a power wrestler, which involved picking people up and hoisting them. It required a lot of physical strength," said Copeland, who chose gear to both flatter her build and withstand exertion. "My thought was that I was going to be photographed a lot and put in slow motion for my physique. Being a thicker girl, I felt that the most flattering look for me was to wear a one-piece," she said. "I still wanted to show off and highlight the positives and downplay areas that I maybe wasn't in love with. The cut of the gear was the most important thing for me, and the boot-cut idea was to give my legs as much length as possible because I just wanted to look tall, statuesque, and powerful. I wanted to give that illusion of being bigger than everybody else. The gear was spandex because I was going to be squatting and it had to be forgiving. It was important that it was well put together to ensure there were no wardrobe malfunctions with all this physical work."

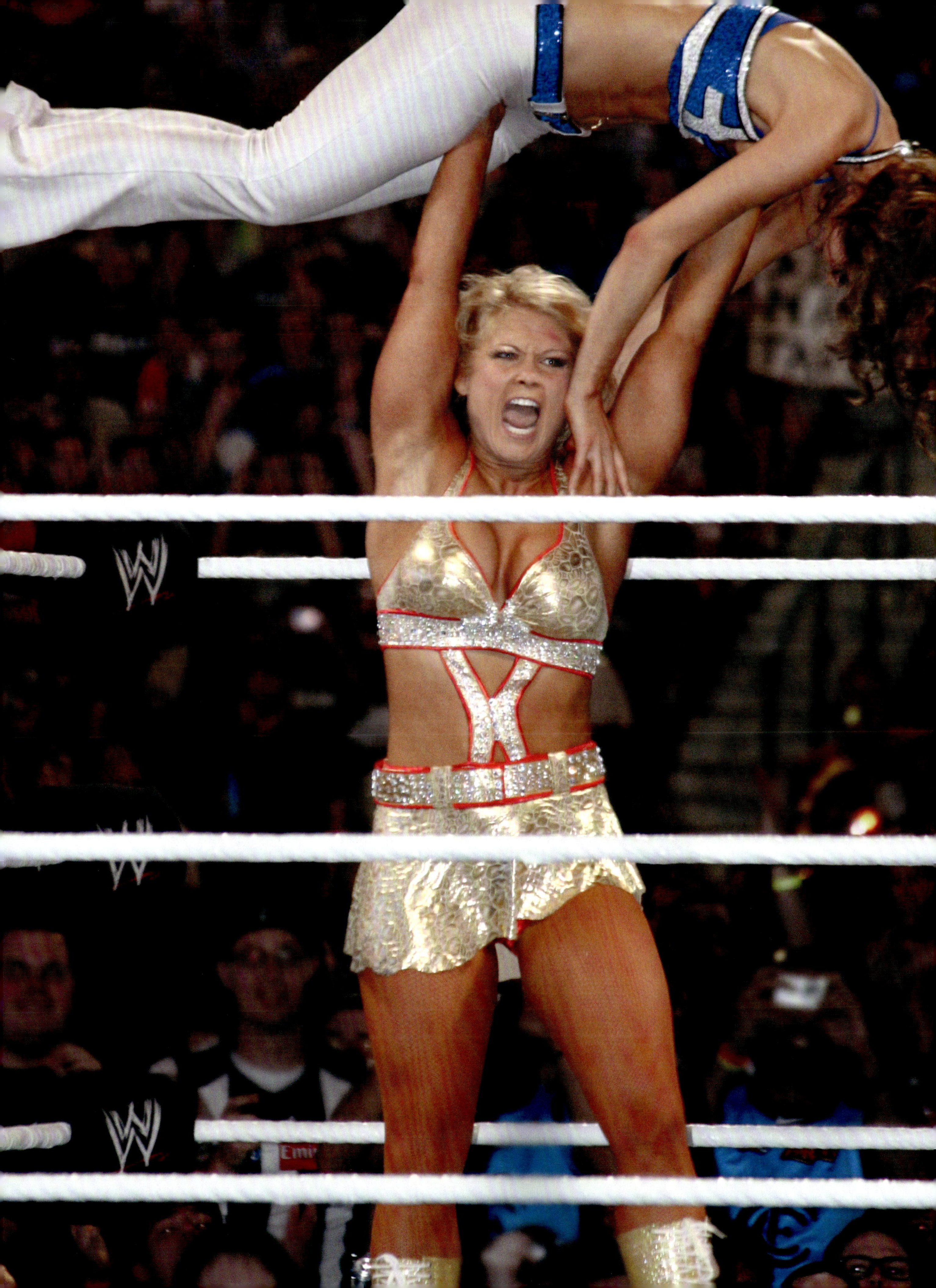

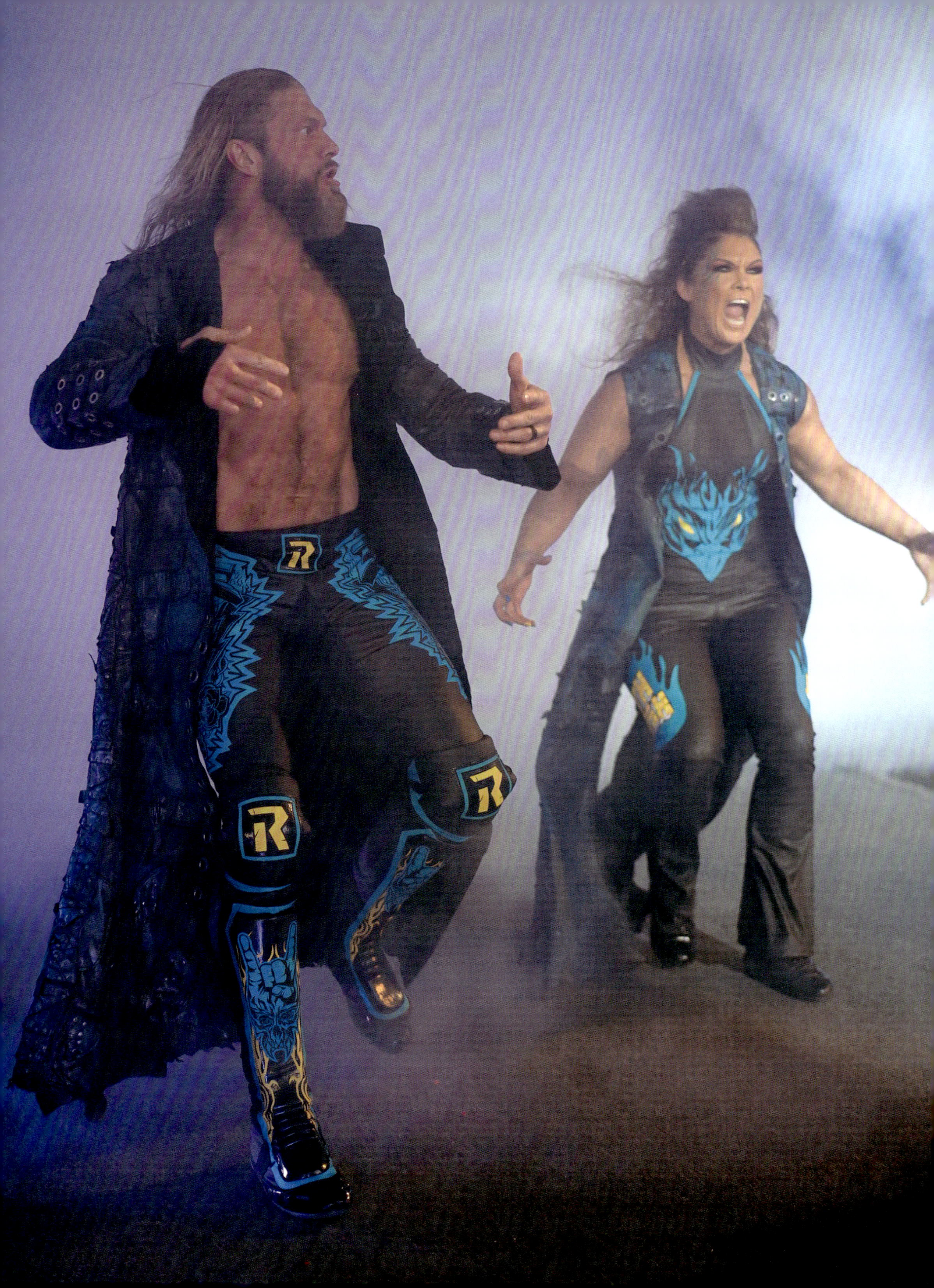

Today, Copeland is respected not only for her legacy as a three-time WWE Women's Champion but also for proving beauty and brawn aren't mutually exclusive. "I definitely wasn't the first to have these ideals of women's wrestling," said Copeland, who was inspired by the powerful women before her: "I looked to women like Chyna or [Japanese wrestling legend and WWE Hall of Famer] Bull Nakano. I saw Bull's matches with Alundra Blayze . . . and when I saw Bull Nakano on *Monday Night RAW*, I just was blown away by how these women wrestled. They wrestled like the men; they were so physical, and they told a story like a men's match. They weren't just a manager on the side kicking her shoes off and scratching someone's back—it was a real wrestling match. I knew the potential, and those women existed, even though we didn't really get to see a whole lot of that style of woman wrestler up to that point."

Copeland showed that superstars possess an undeniable presence, an indelible staying power that influences generations of fans and athletes to come, much like the way she was influenced by Bull. "It really boils down to what is unforgettable," said Copeland. "A lot happens in front [of] a crowd in a two-hour show. So for me, it's 'What's going to be the one thing, the visual, that they hang on to that makes me someone they can't forget?'"

Beth Phoenix with husband Edge at WWE Royal Rumble in 2022. Photo by Kimberly Morrell.

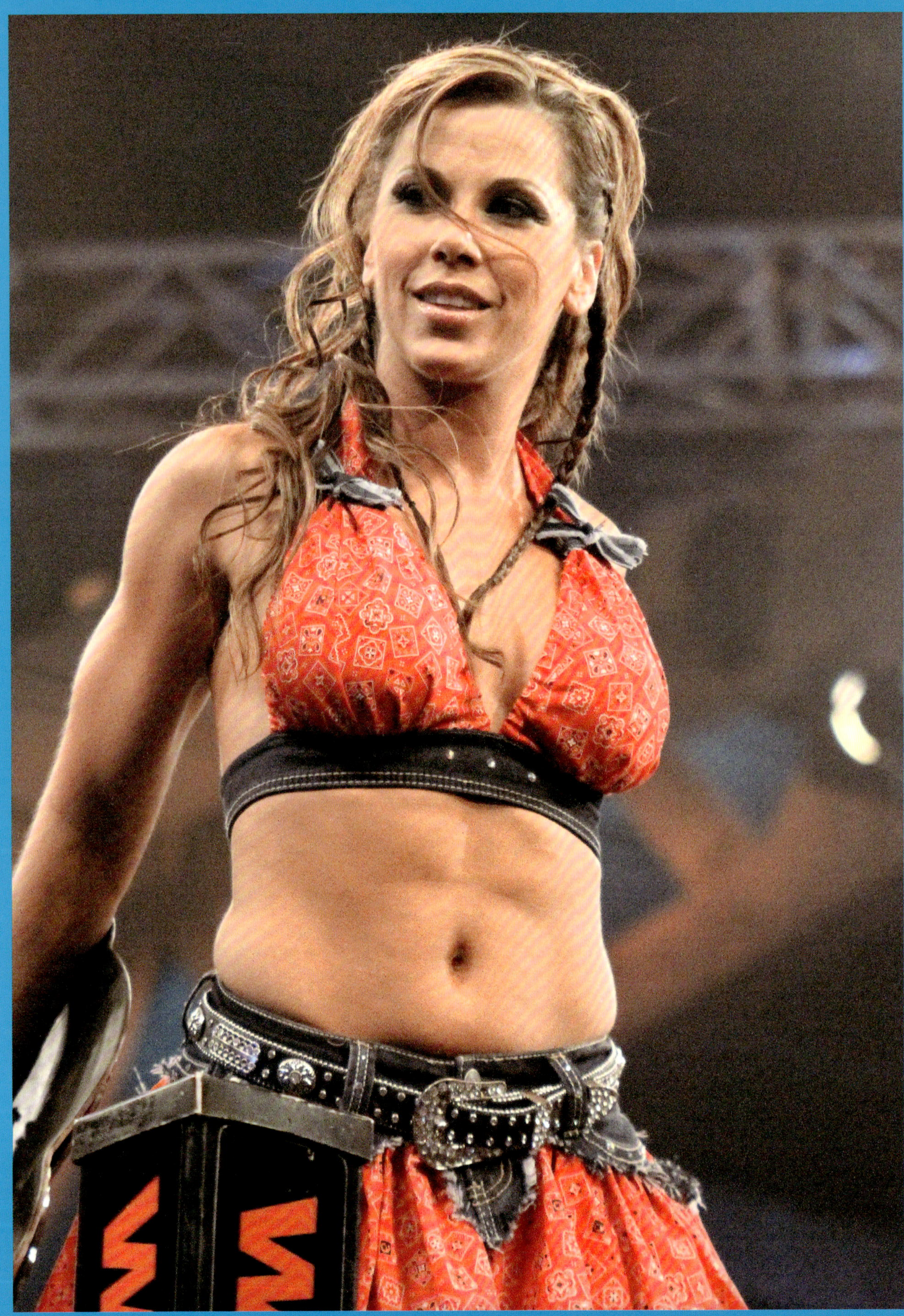

# MICKIE JAMES

Active 1999–2023

Eleven-Time Women's World Champion
WWE Hall of Famer

**As the first woman** to hold the WWE Women's Championship, WWE Divas Championship, *and* TNA Knockouts Championship, Mickie James understood the charisma and grit required to succeed in professional wrestling. The perfect mix of Western edge and powerful grace, James always pushed the limits, both in terms of athleticism and presentation. Wearing everything from low-rise, studded spandex pants to cowgirl couture with fringe, she never followed a script.

James's journey to stardom was rooted in independent wrestling, where she spent her early years making her own gear. "In OVW [Ohio Valley Wrestling], I made my own wrestling gear because I couldn't afford to have someone make them," she recalled. "The bell-bottoms I wore, I was just trying to make it work, stitching them together." As she made her way through the ranks, James tapped into her own creativity: "Everyone was trying to break out of the system and get to TV, so I thought, 'What can I do to be different?' I noticed that everyone was wearing short shorts and kneepads, and it felt very vanilla and cookie-cutter. I started doing a Punky Brewster character where I got colored contacts, and I put colored streaks in my hair. I started wearing skirts instead."

Not long after, James created the persona of a superfan obsessed with [wrestler] Trish Stratus. This move put James on the map—such a character was so different from anything fans had seen before.

Mickie James for *TNA iMPACT!* at Hardcore Justice PPV in 2011. Photo by George Tahinos.

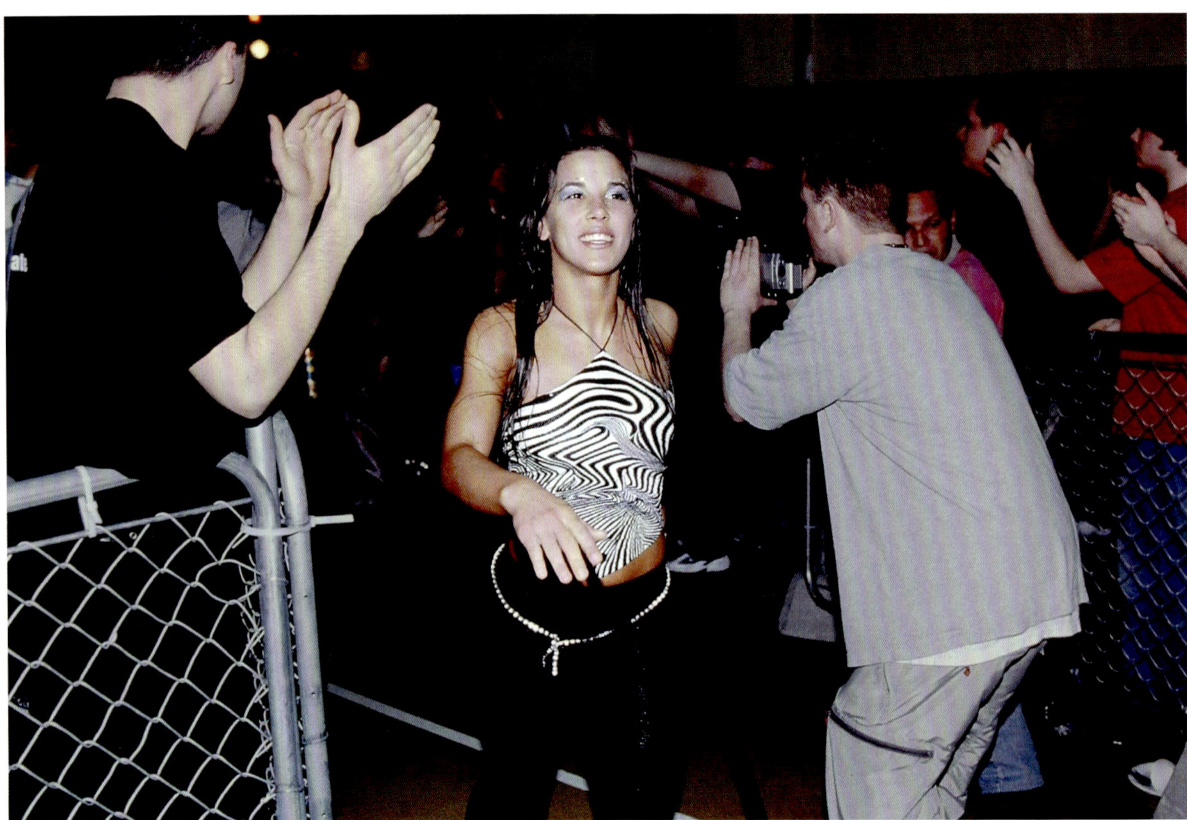

When James finally wrestled Stratus at WrestleMania, the crowd felt the superfan's star power. "When I was the superfan, I had to study Trish and watch her move because we don't move the same," said James, who thoroughly researched her new role: "I thought, 'What would a twenty-one-year-old kid wear?' In my mind, a fan wouldn't have wrestling gear. She may know how to do a few wrestling moves but wouldn't know where to buy gear. I wore Converse and pretty much everything was Baby Phat because that was the trend at the time. I had these Baby Phat snow boots that I wore, and I bought them in every color because they worked. When I found something that worked, I bought all of them. I had so many skirts and belts. The belts I wore were actually scarves that you could put your arms

through. I remember at one point I dyed my hair blond, and just when I had finally gotten it to the right shade of blond, I was told I could dye it back to its natural color. What I came up with was my version of merging the Punky Brewster character that was super happy to the boppy fan, and I think my look matched who I was in that character."

With every evolution of her career, James used a method for character development she learned early on from fellow wrestler Dawn Marie. "I would write out who [the character] was, where she's from, her backstory, her parents, relationships, music, and then get down to the little details like favorite pizza and food she eats," she said. "This helped me *become* her rather than try to play a character for a role."

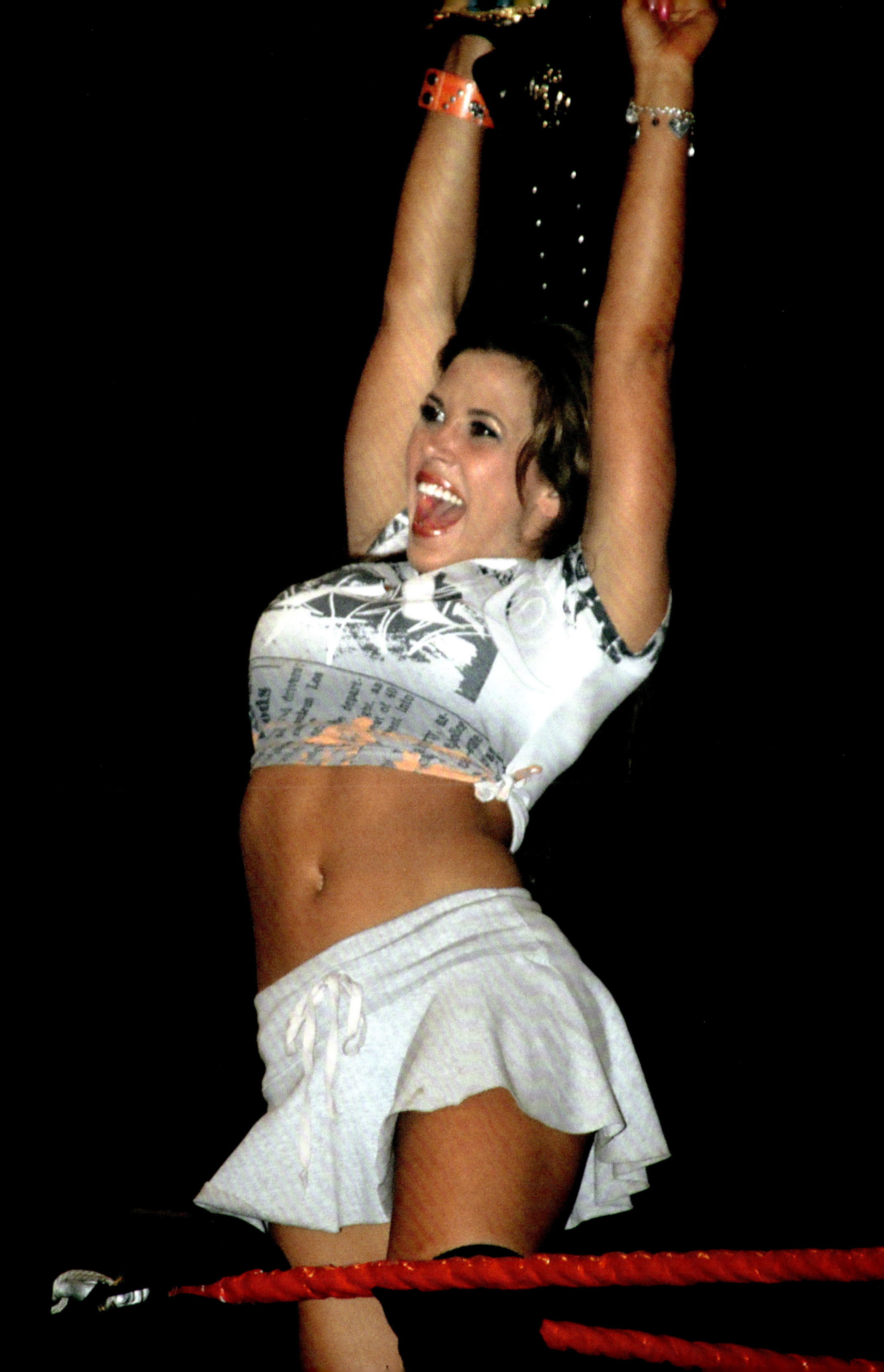

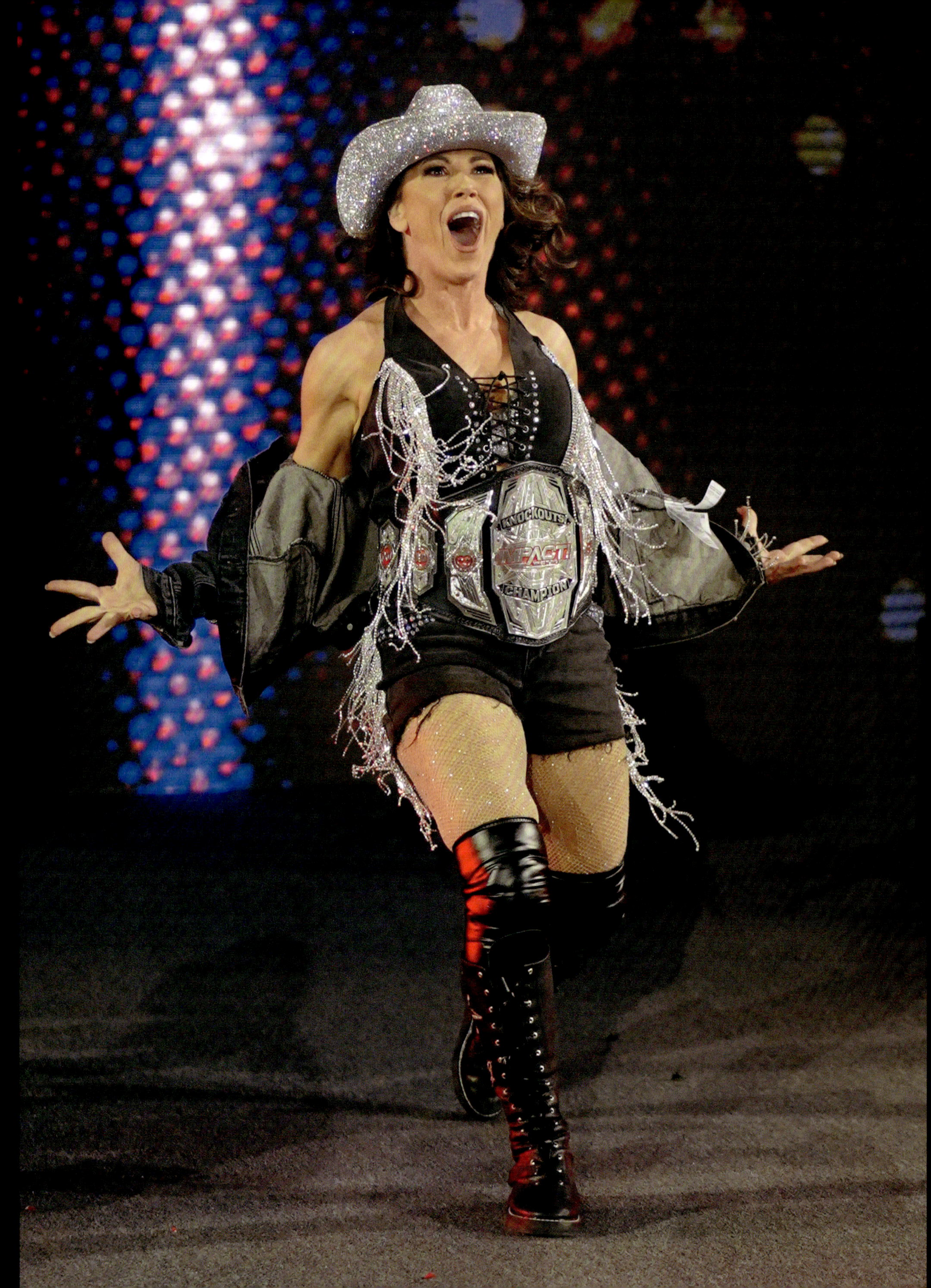

After years of experience and multiple WWE championships under her belt, in 2009 James developed her most honest persona yet. "Dixie Carter and Kurt Angle called me to come to TNA," said James, whose "Hardcore Country" Mickie James was loosely based on her rural childhood: "I didn't have to write my bio this time because I knew who I was. I went back to my bell-bottom pants like I had originally done on the indies. I grew up on a horse farm, rode four-wheelers, had to throw barrels of hay, and have my dad's working hands, so it felt authentic. I had just put out my country music album and Dixie Carter worked with [singer-songwriter] Tanya Tucker, so she was well-versed in the industry. I wanted to show everyone that it doesn't matter what you go through or where you come from—you can be whatever you want to be. They say the best characters are themselves with the volume turned up to eleven, and I felt like I had regained my confidence, and it revamped my entire career."

Dressed in denim with fringe and faux leather prints, James proudly embraced her role as a rhinestone cowgirl. Sometimes, she carried a guitar and sang her own tunes as a Southern rock star. "Hardcore Country" Mickie James quickly became one of the brightest shining stars on the TNA Knockouts roster. "I was able to be a whole different me," she said. "The Knockouts were killing it at the time and fans were talking about The Divas [WWE] versus The Knockouts [TNA] for the first time. Going from lingerie matches, pillow fights, and water fights, I got to main event and do steel cage matches. This was the type of wrestling I grew up on. I am a wrestling fan, and I wanted to be a wrestling superstar."

Mickie James as the TNA Knockouts World Champion at WWE Royal Rumble in 2022. Photo by Kimberly Morrell.

# MICHELLE CALAWAY
## MICHELLE McCOOL

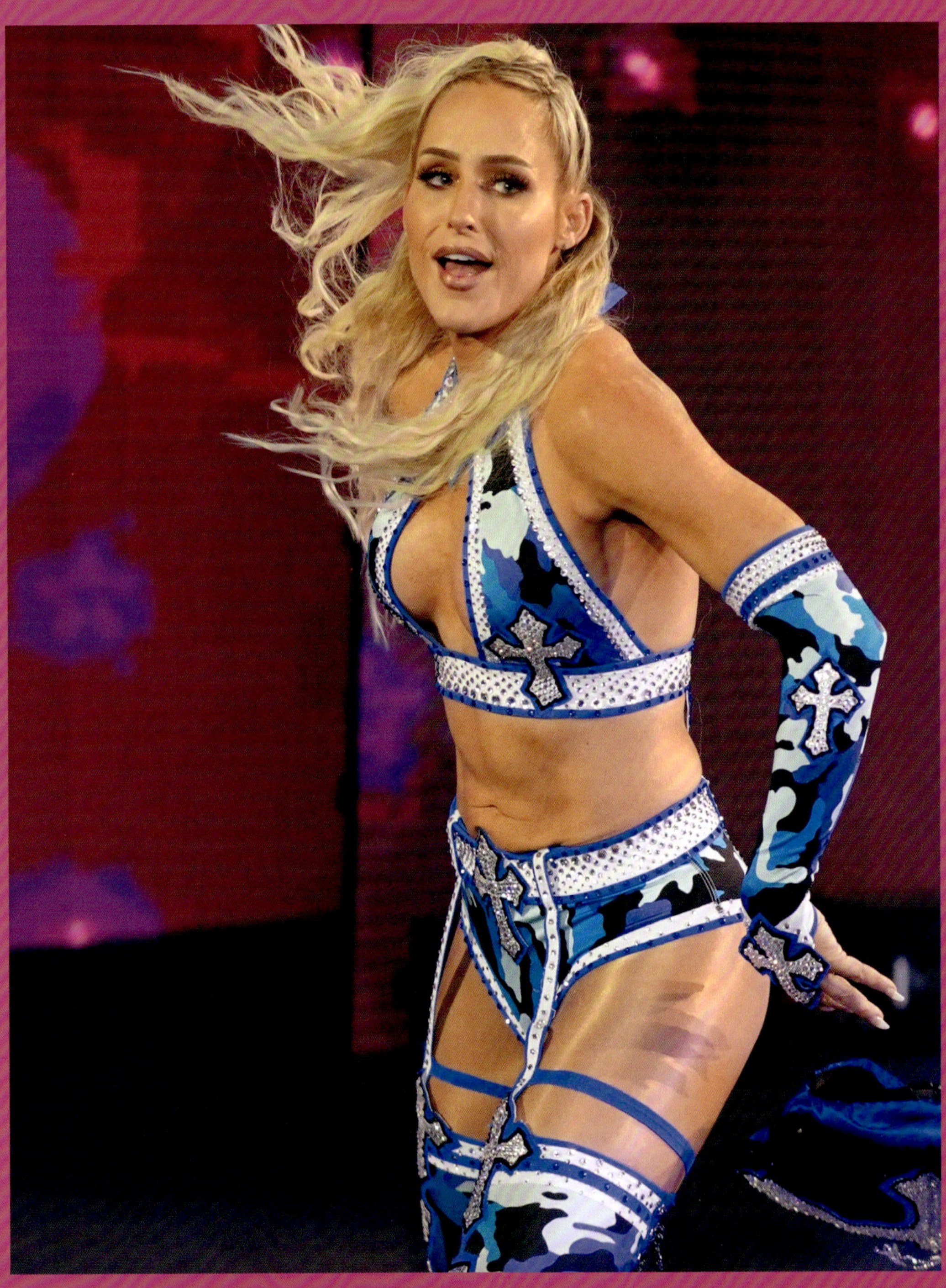

Active 2005–2011

Inaugural and Two-Time WWE Divas Champion
WWE Hall of Famer

Michelle McCool at Royal Rumble in St. Louis, Missouri, in 2022. Photo by Kimberly Morrell.

 career and brought to life a presentation that blended functionality, authenticity, and star power. As the inaugural WWE Divas Champion who held both the WWE Divas Championship and WWE Women's Championship, her undeniable skill was matched only by her memorable attire.

McCool wore two-piece ensembles that fused athleticism and fashion. Showcasing her glamour and grit, her sleek ensembles complemented her tall frame. Embellished with metallic accents and camouflage details, McCool's edgy, confident looks made a powerful statement, just like her personality. But despite her fashionable gear, McCool insists authenticity was the most important thing she ever wore in the ring. "I've always found that being unapologetically authentic to who I am, and where I came from, is critical for me," said McCool. "I am most comfortable in my baggy pants (preferably camo), Ugg boots, and no makeup. I'm not dressing for anyone but myself regardless. When I feel confident in who I am and what I'm wearing, it exudes through 'Michelle McCool' in the ring and [in] real life."

For McCool, being authentic meant folding her faith into her attire. Throughout her career, the wrestler made crosses the centerpiece of her signature style, incorporating them into everything from kick pad covers to arm sleeves. "I've always been rooted in my faith," said McCool. "The crosses told my story without me having to tell it myself, and I always wanted to make sure my faith was on display somewhere." The religious iconography also became a way to connect with her fans. "I've had many people come up to me throughout the years expressing how much it meant to them to wear a cross," said McCool. "It feels good to know that this little ol' small-town girl made an impact on their life by not being afraid to hide something so sacred."

After building a successful solo wrestling career, McCool partnered with [fellow wrestler and tag team partner] Layla in 2009 to create LayCool, a highly regarded chapter in her story. Dazzling in rhinestone, glitz, and matching looks, the exhuberant duo even coined a new catchphrase, "flawless," to help capture the spotlight. "In our era, we had to think way outside of the box," said McCool. "We were given such limited time with such little direction, and we constantly thought about ways to leave people with more questions than answers in hopes that it would result in screen time the following week. Ultimately, we needed the audience to care."

It was clear that the two worked well as a team, and they found ways to reinvent the wheel. "LayCool was so obnoxious and self-absorbed that our characters believed everything revolved around them," McCool said with a laugh. "We LOVED us! We won as a team and lost as a team! We thought we could do anything we wanted, which brought us to the idea of splitting the belt. Technically the match was a handicap match. I remember being backstage and we were joking that we both *technically* won the match because it was 'LayCool versus Beth Phoenix.' While Lay technically made the cover, LayCool won. Like it often did, the idea hit us at the same time. Not thinking it would actually get approved, we ran it by creative, and to our surprise, they said, 'Why wouldn't LayCool do something like that?' It was hilarious to us . . . and in our era, we often had to entertain ourselves, so we rolled with it!"

More than a decade after she retired, McCool is rightly proud of her contribution to women's wrestling, especially during the Divas Era lasting from 2008 to 2016. "The Divas Era is one that seems to be often forgotten," said McCool. "Garnering the simple respect of the fans was tough. I'm proud of what we did. I'm proud of the Divas title that everyone deemed 'the butterfly belt.' I'm proud of how hard I worked and how much I was able to accomplish during my time with WWE, and I know how hard I fought week in and week out. The fact that I am recognized in playing just a small part of paving the way for the girls today is one of my greatest blessings. The pivot has been real."

# NIKKI AND BRIE GARCIA
## THE BELLA TWINS

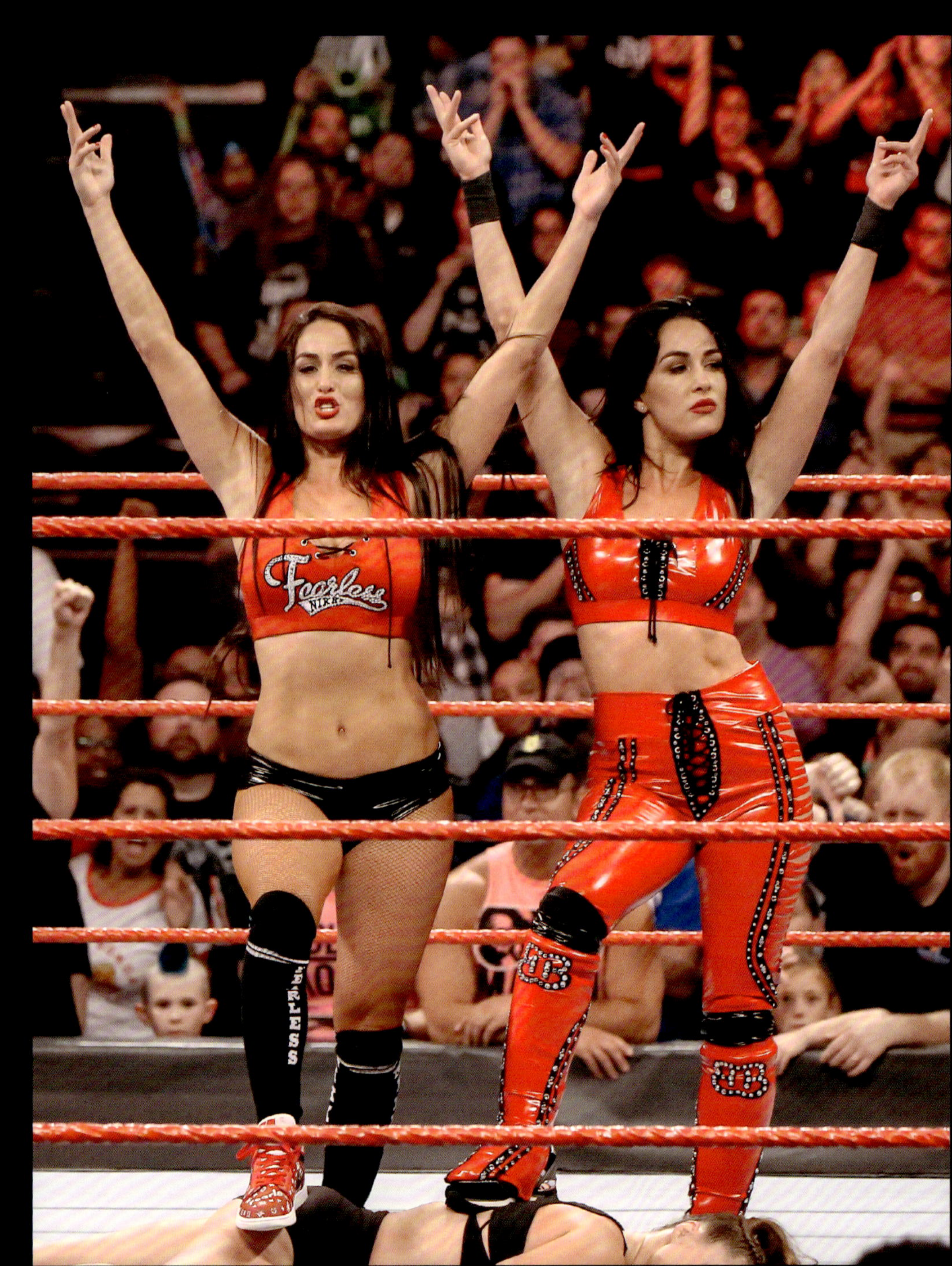

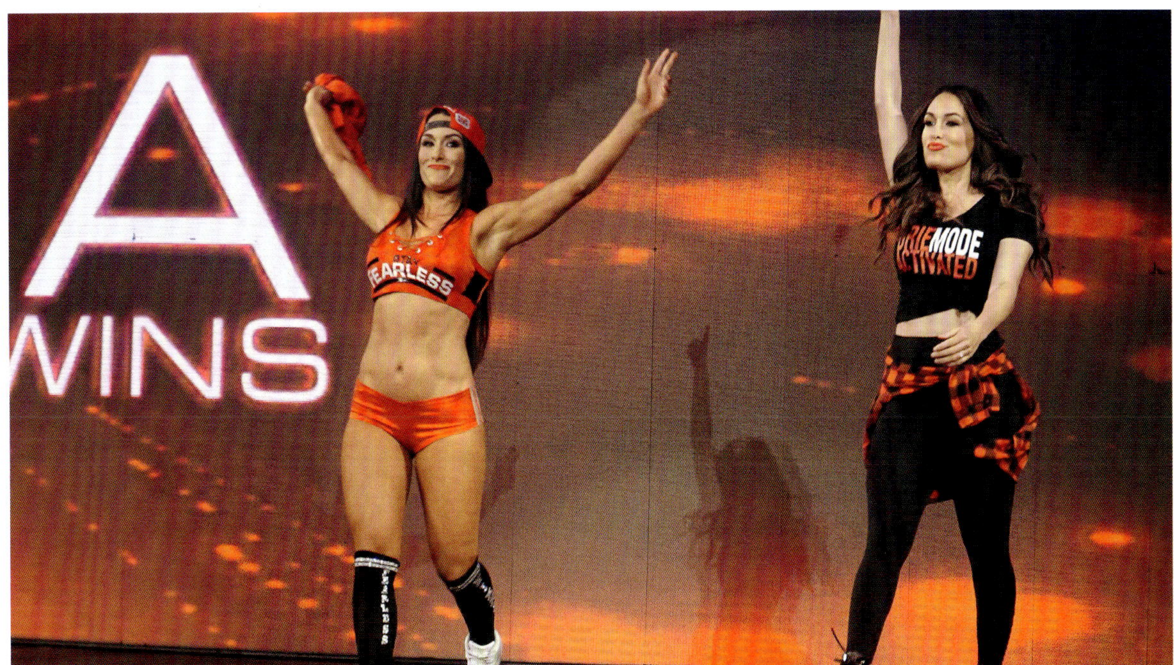


**Wearing snapback hats,** ripped pants, and cropped sports jerseys, Nikki and Brie Garcia were sporty and chic at the same time. Known around the world by their WWE ring name, The Bella Twins, the real-life twins inspired girls around the globe to flaunt what makes them beautiful and unique. Years after their retirement, The Bella Twins' fearless approach still defines their identities. As Nikki put it: "We were never trying to be anyone else but us."

The Twins knew that when you look good, you feel good, and drew inspiration for in-ring looks from their own personal styles. Taking inspiration from childhood sports, Nikki wore cropped jerseys and thigh-high athletic socks reminiscent of her early days on the field. She enhanced her look with shimmering fabrics, two-pieces, rhinestones, and bold makeup to create a glam style.

"When I started to think of [my persona] Fearless Nikki, all I could think of was my soccer days, so that was when I thought, 'I'm going to make a jersey sexy,'" said Nikki, who was known as Nikki Bella in the ring. "I was always number two in soccer, so that's why I wore zero two. My look was who I was before wrestling."

Meanwhile, Brie (a.k.a. Brie Bella) adopted a grungy rocker persona inspired by '90s style and music she listened to as a teen. For Brie, a red-and-black flannel tied around her waist became the trademark look. "Nikki was always a sexy tomboy, but I was very much a punk-rock, grungy girl growing up, so I wanted to go back to the '90s," said Brie, whose persona was largely inspired by Gwen Stefani. "I thought, 'How cool to have wrestling gear that looks torn up the way I would wear pants back in middle school,'" added Brie, who wore cropped tanks and baby tees with *Brie Mode* emblazoned across her chest. In later years, the flannel came to represent a softer, more natural side of herself. "From the reality show [*Total Divas*], [my husband and fellow wrestler] Bryan [Danielson] and I showed that we were more nature-driven and hippie," said Brie. "The flannel kind of represented the woodsy, grungy side that I loved."

But whether they wore jersey or flannel, both sisters shared an affinity for the color red. Red became part of their wrestling identity. "Red made us the most confident," said Nikki. "We would put on a red lip, and we just owned it as a woman. It's our Wonder Woman color. Like in Superman when you put on that cape, red was our cape."

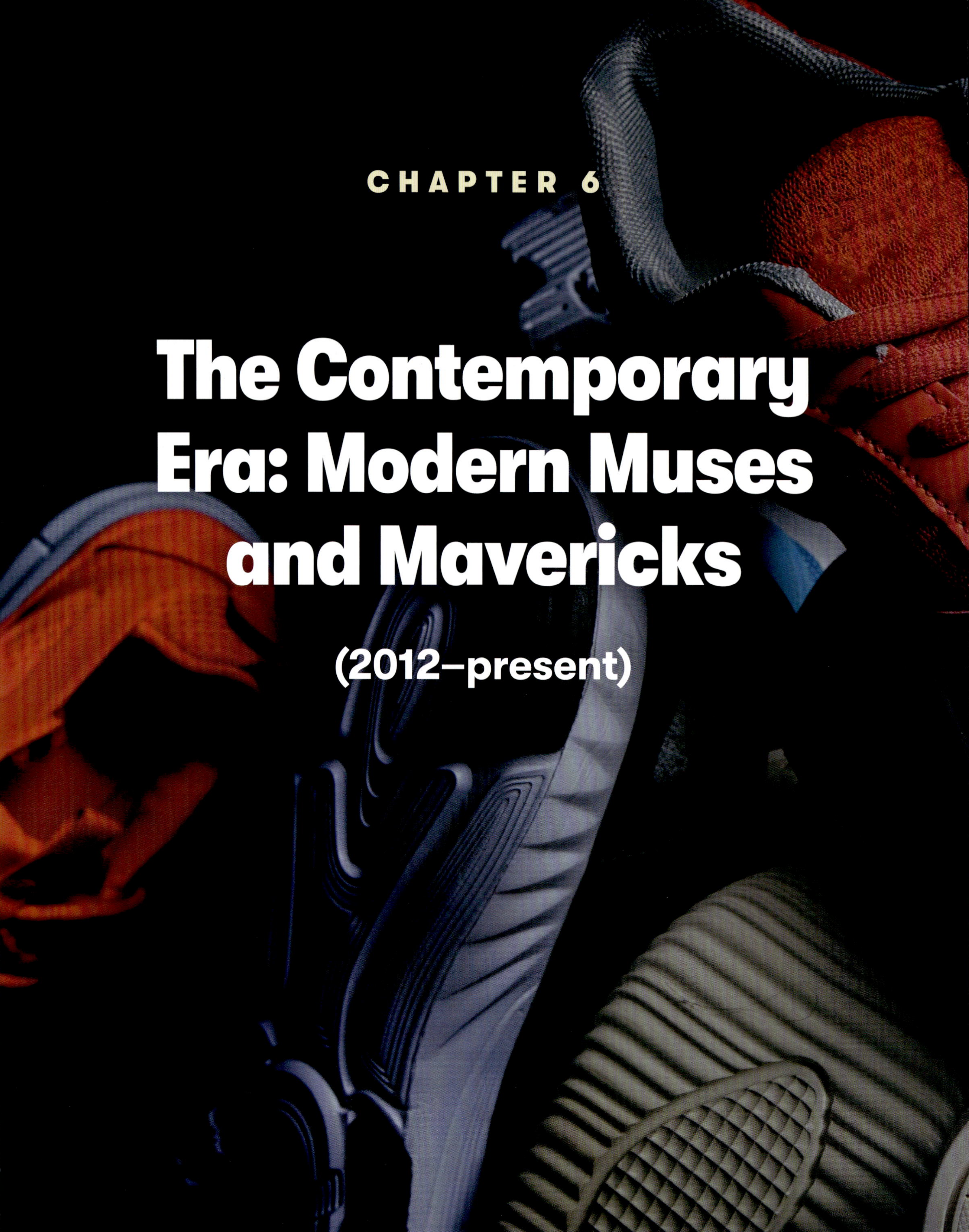


# The Contemporary Era: Modern Muses and Mavericks

## (2012–present)

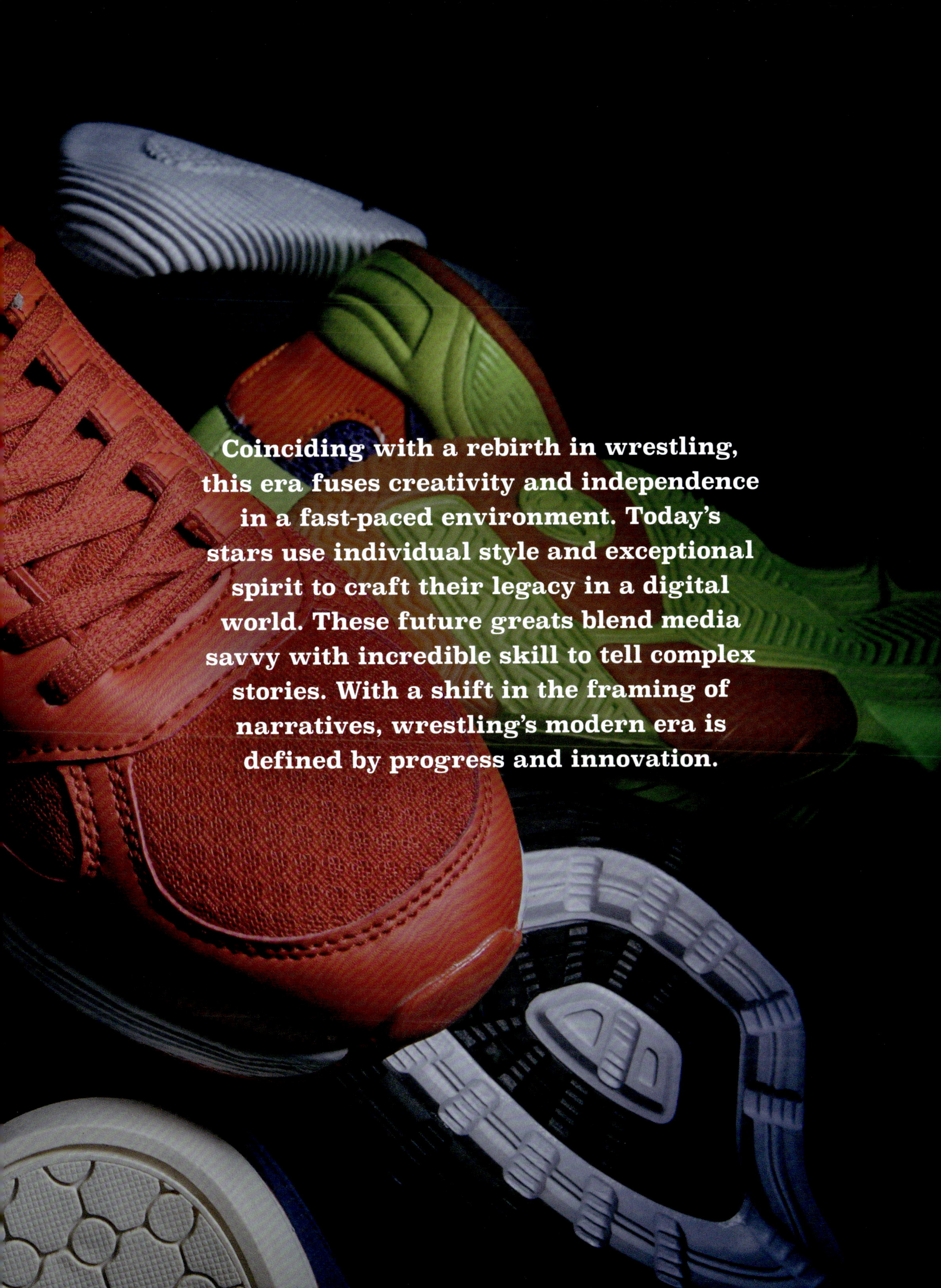

Coinciding with a rebirth in wrestling, this era fuses creativity and independence in a fast-paced environment. Today's stars use individual style and exceptional spirit to craft their legacy in a digital world. These future greats blend media savvy with incredible skill to tell complex stories. With a shift in the framing of narratives, wrestling's modern era is defined by progress and innovation.

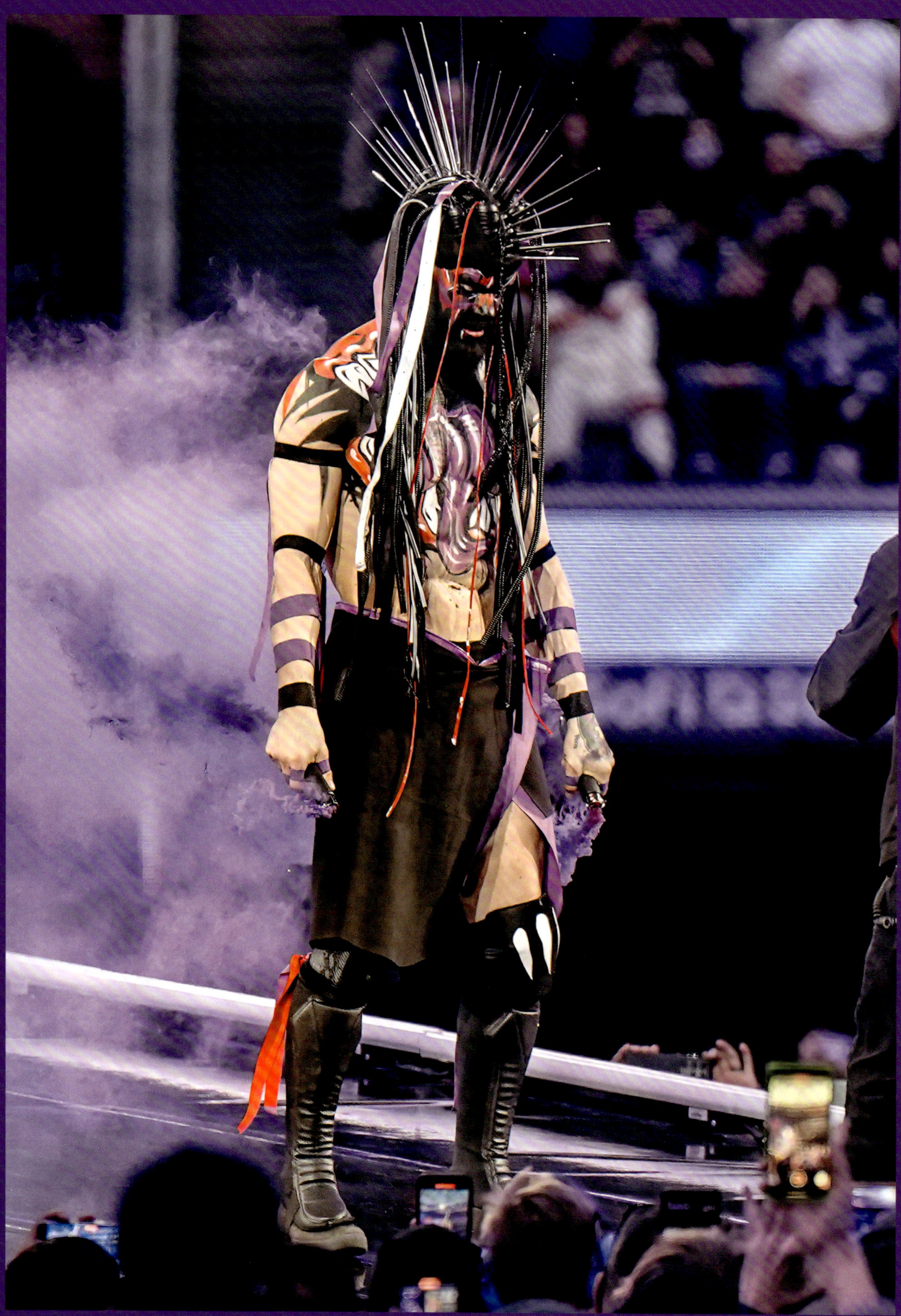

# FERGAL DEVITT
## WWE'S FINN BÁLOR

Active 2000–present

First-Ever WWE Universal Champion

**Fergal Devitt—best known** as WWE Superstar Finn Bálor—isn't just an accomplished athlete but a champion at using attire to feed a narrative. As a young star in Japan, Devitt was known as Prince Devitt and wore a light-up jacket to introduce The Real RocknRolla, giving fans a first look at what would become an impactful career. But in those early days, tech wasn't always on his side. "The jacket didn't always work," said Devitt. "The lights were operated by a remote control I kept in my pocket. I would have to take the remote out and point it at a receiver placed at the bottom of the zipper. However, the remote was a perfect rectangle with six rows of four buttons. In the dark, I couldn't tell if it was the top or bottom of the remote. After a couple of mishaps, I simply put some tape on the back of the remote so I could feel which end was which."

Devitt first earned renown as a founding member of The Bullet Club, a wrestling faction that debuted in New Japan Pro-Wrestling. Wearing black-and-white T-shirts with a memorable skull logo, The Bullet Club became this generation's nWo. Their reach was so strong that even fans who didn't watch New Japan Pro-Wrestling could recognize The Bullet Club's iconic logo and hand gesture.

After making the jump from New Japan to the WWE, Devitt began using abstract body paint to tell his story. "The original idea behind the paint was born out of a recent heel turn and a feeling I had to take away everything visually that the fans associated with me," said Devitt, who channeled his dark turn into a brand-new character: Demon. "I wanted to switch from a clean-cut babyface to a dark, evil heel, and my first concept was to

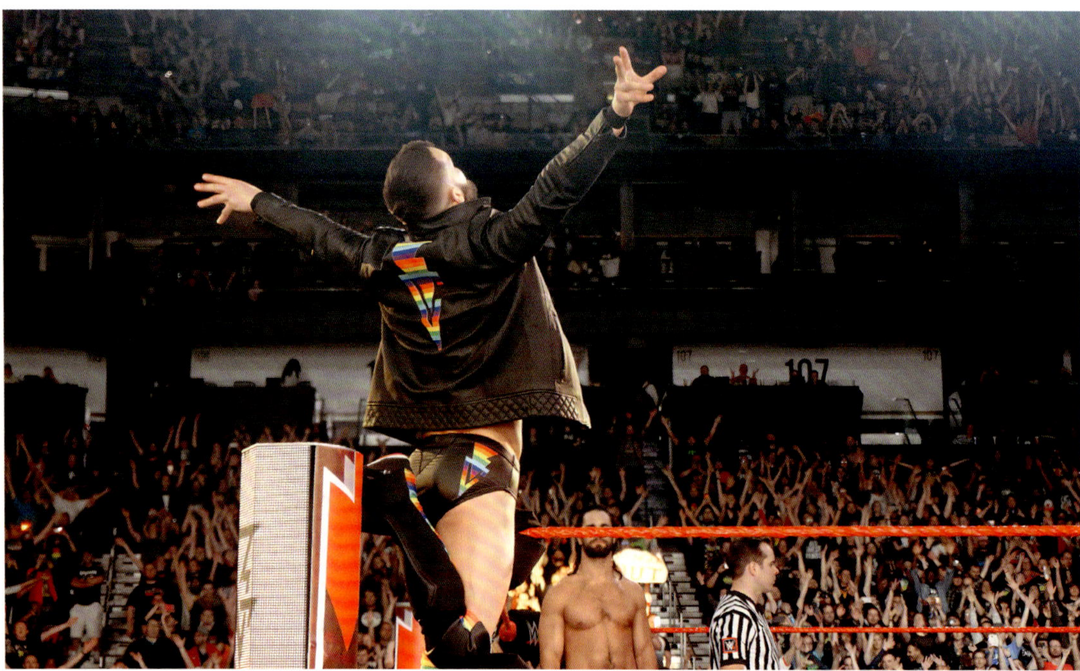

paint myself entirely black from head to toe so I would look like a shadow of my opponent on the ring. The shadow concept developed in an early version of the current Demon paint. Every version is a little or sometimes a lot different. And I don't really know how it's going to be finished when we start. It's a process where sometimes one brushstroke will inspire the next."

Today's Demon has many variations, and they're all just as impactful. But it requires several hours to create Devitt's signature character. "SummerSlam 2016, we didn't have much time to create the look, so we had to make do with three hours. Generally, I like to allow close to five hours to make the whole look come to life," said Devitt. "All of the looks are special for different reasons. I really like the Jack the Ripper version in London, England, but that was mostly down to the camera and lighting men because of how cool the entrance looked. I feel the most recent versions of The Demon we have done are really pushing the limits on what we can do with some paint on skin."

For Devitt, with every big moment comes the opportunity to influence change. At WrestleMania 34, Devitt became one of the first voices in professional wrestling to champion LGBTQ rights and inclusion. When he took this opportunity to use his leverage and speak out on inclusion, it was made clear that The Bálor Club is for everyone. During his entrance, Bálor was accompanied by members of the New Orleans LGTBQ community wearing Bálor shirts in pride flag colorways. "It was very important to me," said Devitt. "I had so many friends in and out of the business that were a part of the LGBTQ community, yet not only was there no representation of this on our show, it was almost a taboo topic in our industry. I hoped that maybe a small gesture could trigger some change going forward. I think sometimes, so many ideas come over the table that some get tossed aside or simply forgotten. I had pitched this idea [of supporting LGBTQ rights] to a couple of people, but I must give a lot of credit to Stephanie McMahon. Once word of the idea got to her, it was all systems go!"

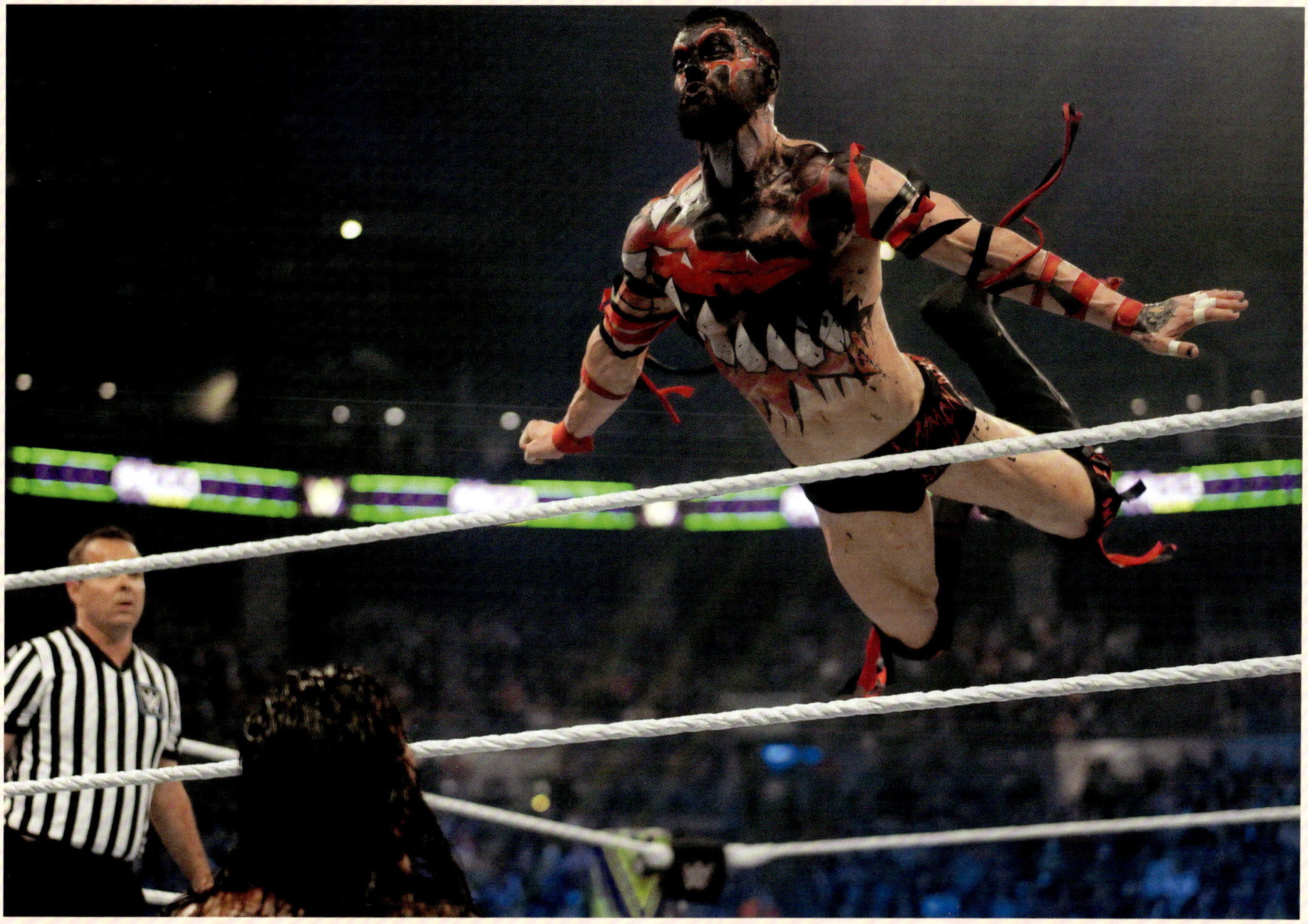

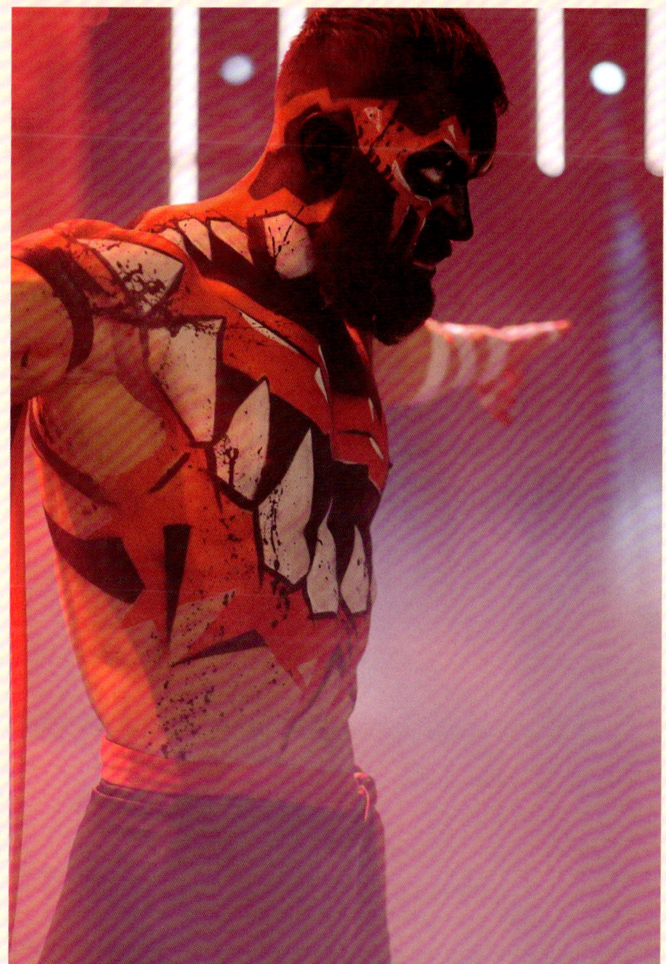
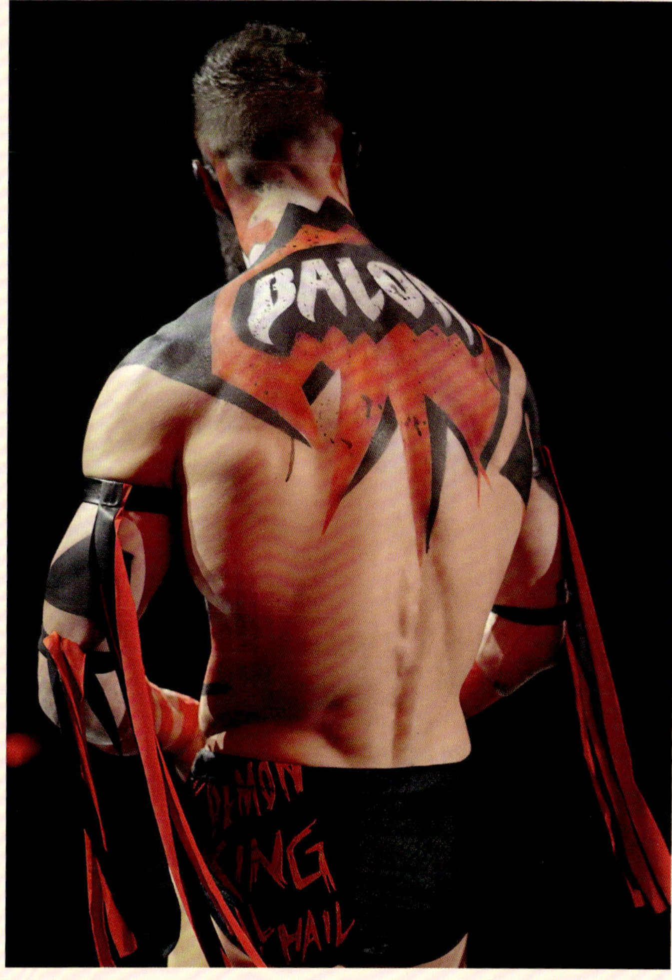

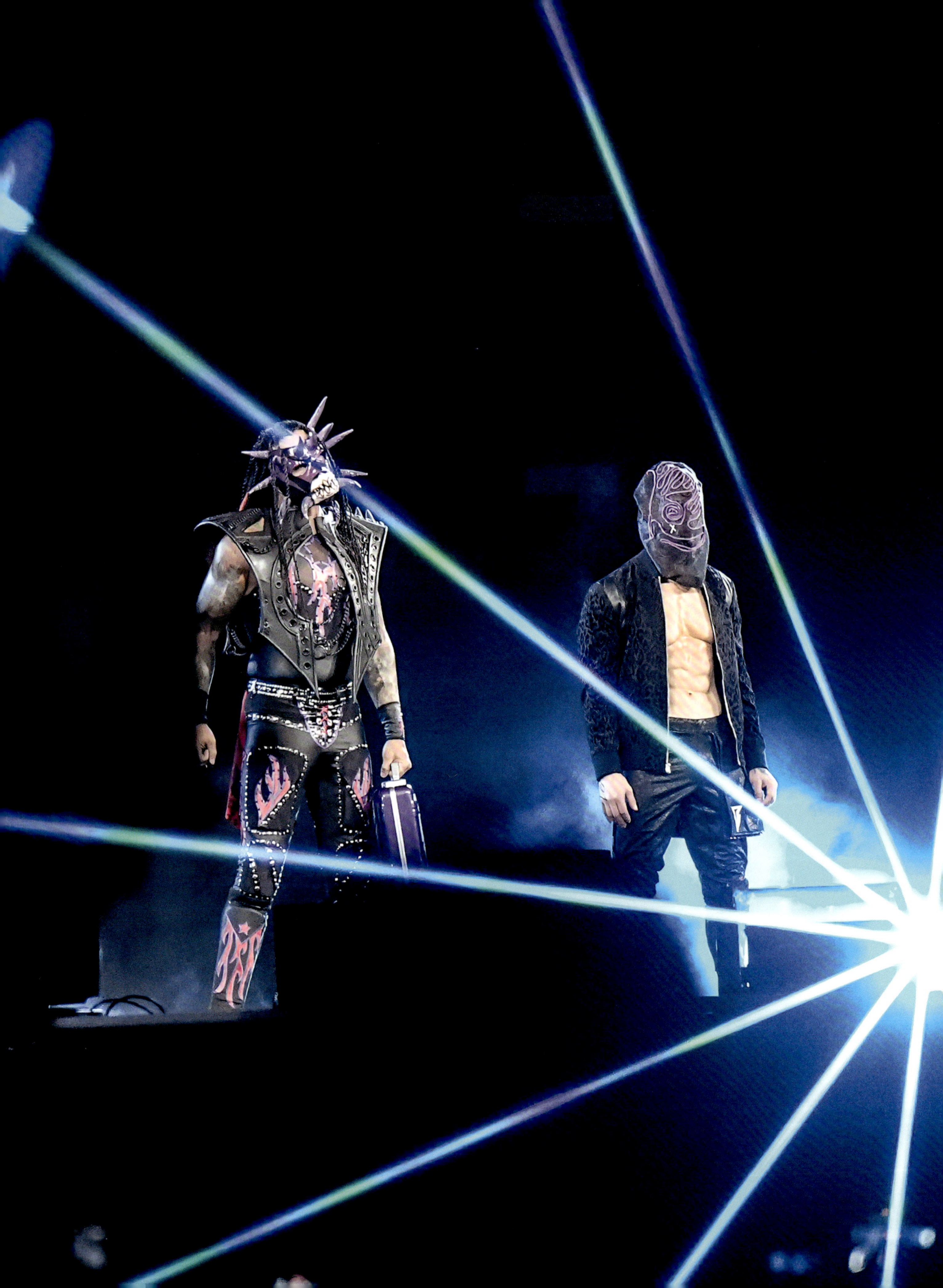

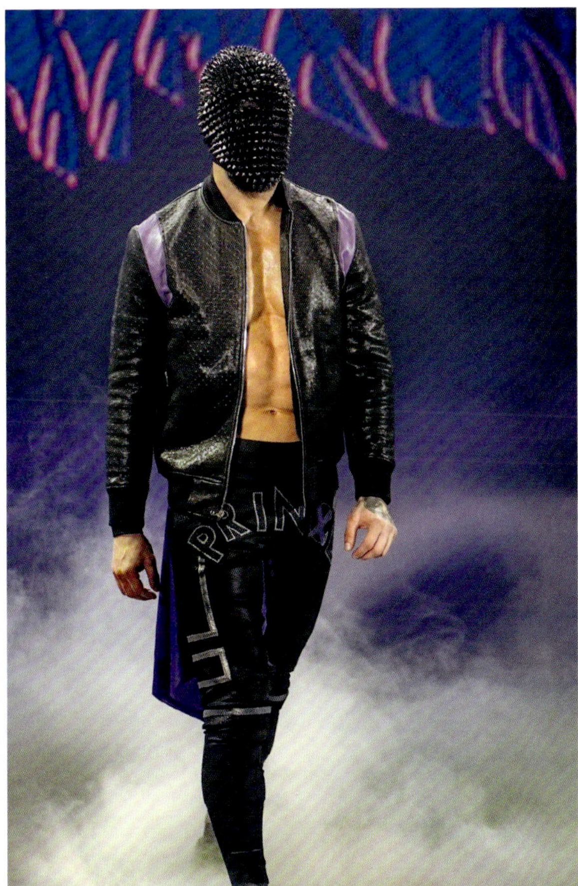

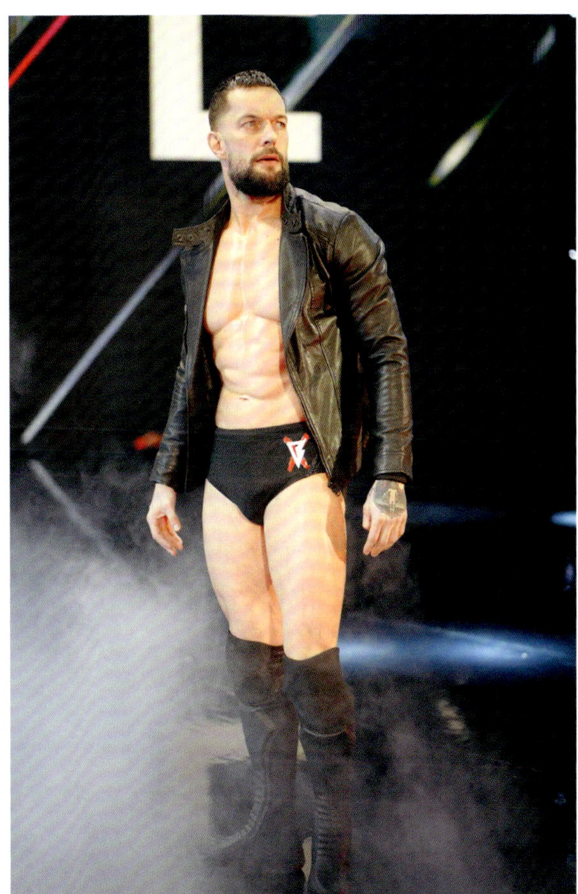

In 2022, Devitt debuted another new look when he joined The Judgment Day. This new role inspired Devitt to swap out his signature trunks for long black tights while finding new ways to differentiate himself from other members. "It's quite interesting because we all have our own very different looks, but I think we've been able to tie it all together with some common elements," said Devitt. "My traditional short trunks had become somewhat of a uniform that represented one version of a character. I switched to a looser-fitting version of long tights, and the way they feel and flow is by far my favorite yet. We've added some crazy fabrics and textures to the tights and jackets. Some things you have to see up close to appreciate the craftsmanship."

Bálor sets himself apart from the rest of the WWE's Judgment Day squad by often wearing a dramatic mask and bandanas. As much as things change, there is one clothing staple that has stayed in Devitt's wardrobe over the years. "I have had an affinity for the bandana since I was fifteen years old listening to Tupac," said Devitt. "The bandana certainly triggers something in me, and just when I think that phase is over, it finds its way back to me."

# TYSON SMITH
## *KENNY OMEGA*

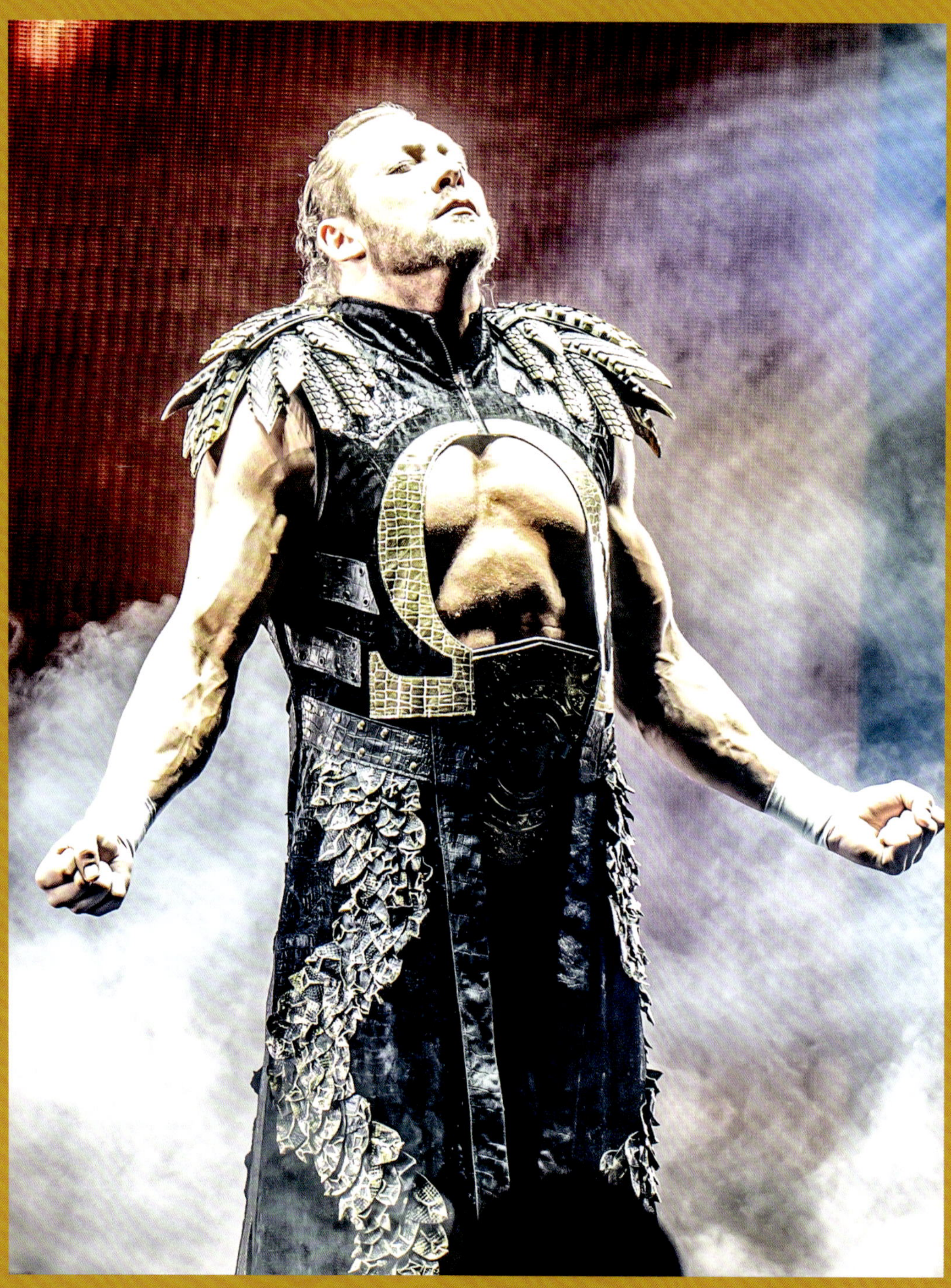

Active 2000-present

IWGP Heavyweight Champion

**Every look tells** a new chapter in the story of Kenny Omega. Each character connects with fans and immerses them in his otherwordly vision. Omega spent part of his career in Japan, where he honed his style and skills, and fans often see Omega blend anime elements with video game styles to put on a show. During big moments, Omega doesn't hold back. His clothing feels like art—regardless of the character he's playing, Omega's tights are never just made out of spandex. His cutting-edge clothes always incorporate meaningful elements that invite fans to delve deeper into the story.

Many of Omega's looks seamlessly blend pop culture, science fiction, and professional wrestling. Throughout his career, multiple monikers have been established that define his chapters, but one that stands out is The Cleaner. When the name was born, Omega had just made his move to Japan. He could be found wearing sleek sunglasses and trench coats with sharp lapels that represented his early antihero cyberpunk character. From the costume, fans could tell the character was cold, mysterious, and utterly efficient. He claimed he was in Japan to clean up the Junior Heavyweight division. As the vision came to life, the character became even more vicious and ominous. The Cleaner went hand in hand with his already established presence as a primary member of The Bullet Club, known for their cool factor and the leather jackets that they wore.

One memorable look occurred at Wrestle Kingdom 12, where Omega showed up to wrestle his rival Chris Jericho in a futuristic headdress inspired by the video game series *Destiny*. Wearing what looked like an Egyptian headpiece and carrying a weapon from the game, Omega appeared as the warrior hero Osiris, and his look immediately told fans, and his opponent, that he was ready for battle. The following year, at the height of his career at New Japan Pro-Wrestling, Omega debuted what is widely considered one of his best looks yet at Wrestle Kingdom 13. Inspired by Sephiroth, the villain from *Final Fantasy VII*, Omega stepped into the arena wearing a one-armed metallic suit of armor. On the side with a sleeve, a single wing made of white feathers represented a fallen angel— creating a powerful depiction of his character in that chapter.

Later in his career, Omega began calling himself The Belt Collector, a reference to holding multiple championships all over the world in various promotions, including AEW and TNA. With gold around his waist, to no surprise, Omega wore elaborately printed tights to the ring to accompany his champion appeal. His gear has continued to feel like armor, and with looks that never disappoint, he's proved over and over that he is worthy of the hype. And with that we say . . . goodbye and goodnight . . . BANG!

Kenny Omega at AEW Dynasty 2025.
Photo by Kimberly Morrell.

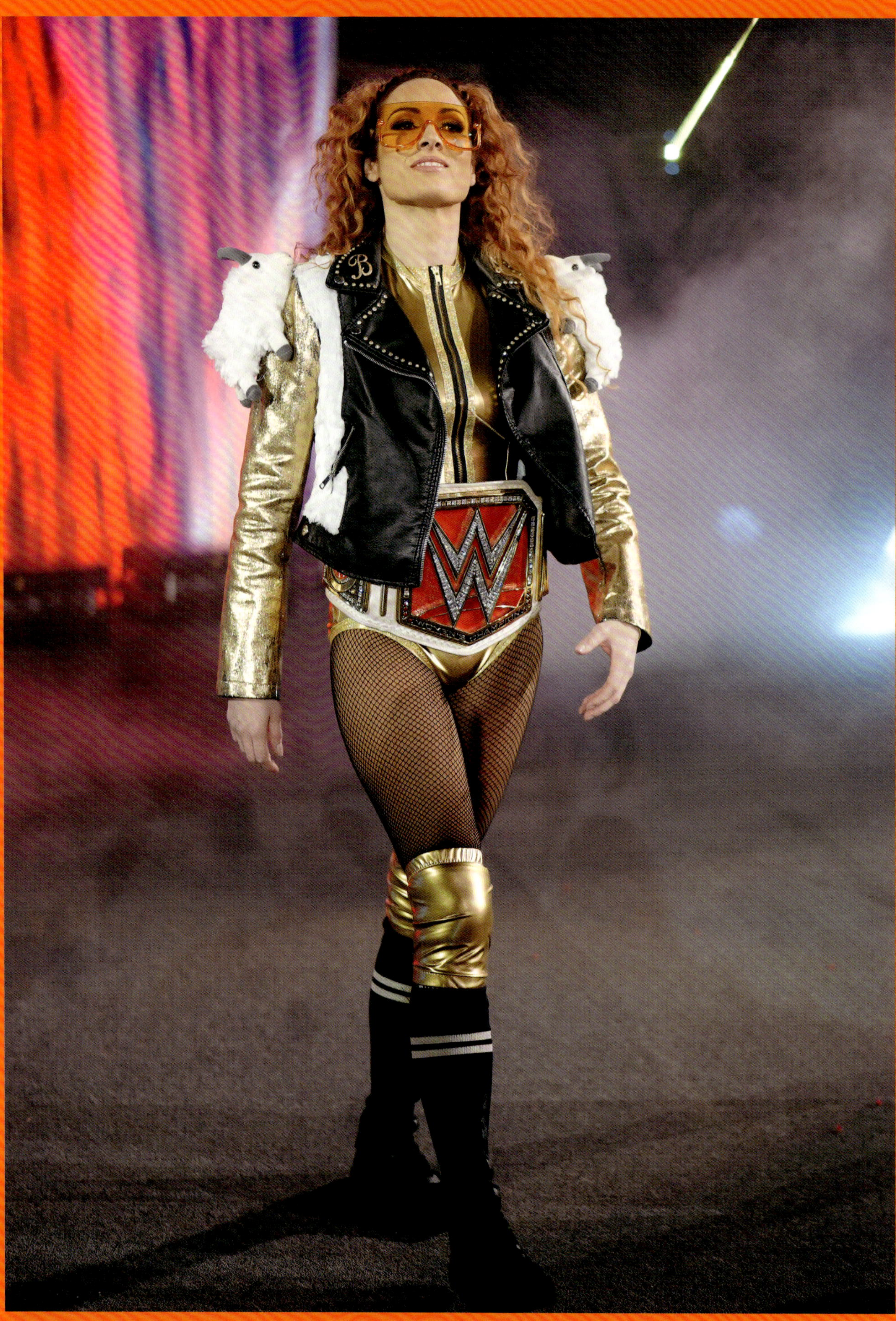

# REBECCA QUIN
## WWE'S BECKY LYNCH

Active 2002–present

First Woman to Main Event WrestleMania
Six-Time WWE Women's Champion

**Rebecca Quin, otherwise known** as WWE Superstar Becky Lynch, isn't your average girl . . . she's The Man. But The Man is just one of Quin's many personas, which range from flamboyant Big Time Becks to sassy Rebecca Knox to the steampunk Lass Kicker. With each new era of Quin's wrestling career, fans have been treated to a fresh character, a bold vision, and a brand-new look. Quin's take-no-crap, punk-rock mentality also led to her memorable role as one of The Four Horsewomen, alongside Bayley, Charlotte Flair, and Sasha Banks.

"It's all an extension of who I am . . . and then multiplied by a million," said Quin of her diverse personas. "We are all different people in different situations based on how comfortable we are, who we're with, or what mood we're in. Rebecca Knox was a bit Big Time Becks–ish—outlandish, cocky, mouthy. And I can be that at times. I would say Big Time Becks was the most fun I've ever had, particularly wardrobe-wise. There was such freedom there. I could really express myself through my clothes, and I loved that. The Man was more straight to the point; no fanciness needed, tell it as it is. And most of the time, I'm not one for fanciness or fuss, so having a uniform almost with the plain black pants, T-shirt, trainers/boots, and a leather jacket took the thought out of things. Lass Kicker was steampunk style, which I loved and adapted for a short period of time. The quirkiness of the character matched the quirks I have as a human. And then I was a ball of excited energy. Which was also true to form because I just made it to WWE and was never more hyped than to have made it to the place I loved, doing the thing I loved."

"Big Time Becks" Becky Lynch as the RAW Women's Champion at Royal Rumble 2022. Photo by Kimberly Morrell.

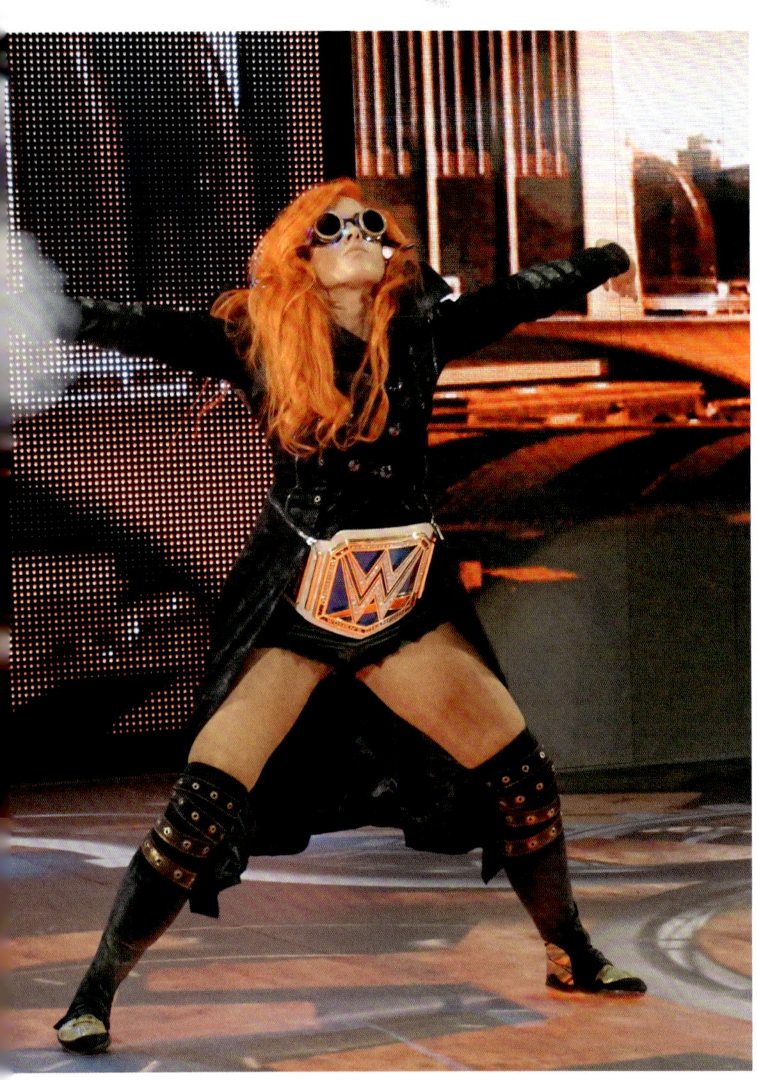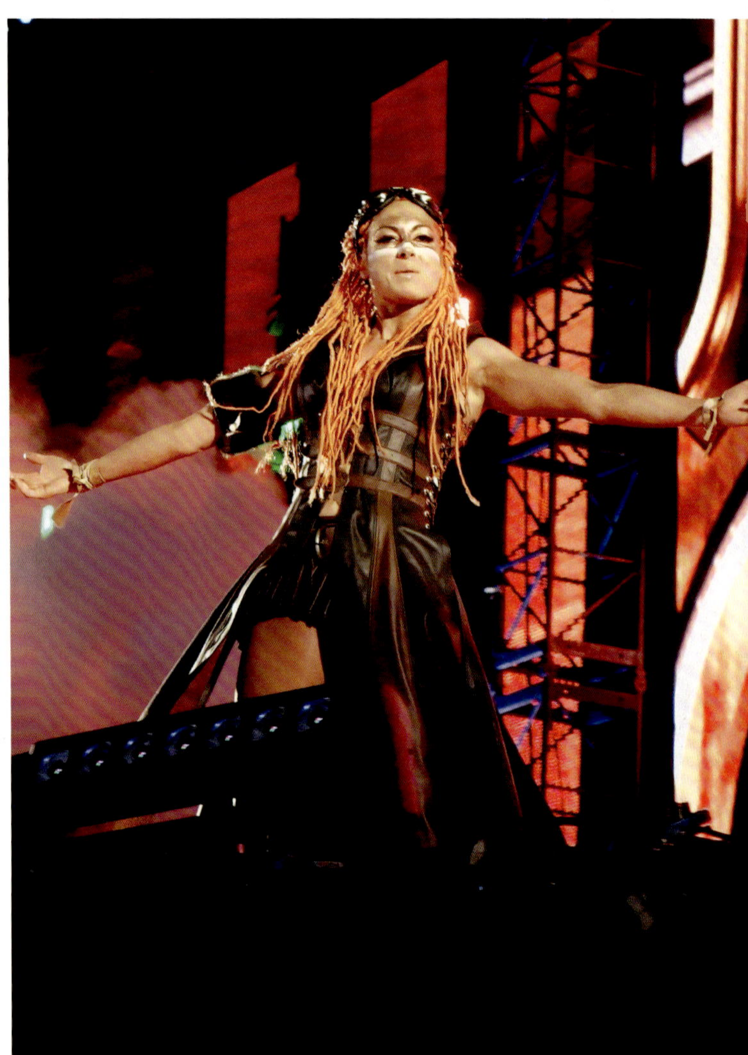

Regardless of her persona, Quin's fiery red hair and fashionable gear give her an edge as a performer. Jolene Jilnicki, who has worked closely with Quin to create some of her most elaborate outfits to date, described the wrestler's creative process. "Rebecca is one of my favorite people to work with because she can pull off some wild looks and has some great ideas," said Jilnicki. "She knows how she wants to feel for the event, and I get to use my creativity to give her the look she wants to get across." A recent example of their collaboration occurred in the run-up to a major wrestling event in Saudi Arabia. "The set for WWE King and Queen [of the Ring] in Saudi Arabia was intense," said Jilnicki, who worked closely with Quin to create a show-worthy look. "I asked Rebecca what her inspiration was, and she said, 'Whatever makes you think of "the end."' A tuxedo made me think of a grand finale, but it was hard to figure out how to do it without looking like a costume. It took a couple iterations, but I was thrilled it didn't come across looking too much like 'gear.'"

TOP LEFT: Becky Lynch as SmackDown Women's Champion. Photo by Kimberly Morrell.

TOP RIGHT: Becky Lynch at WrestleMania 33 in Orlando, Florida. Photo by Kimberly Morrell.

OPPOSITE: Becky Lynch defending the WWE RAW Women's Championship against Bianca Belair at WrestleMania 38 in Dallas, Texas. Photo by Kimberly Morrell.

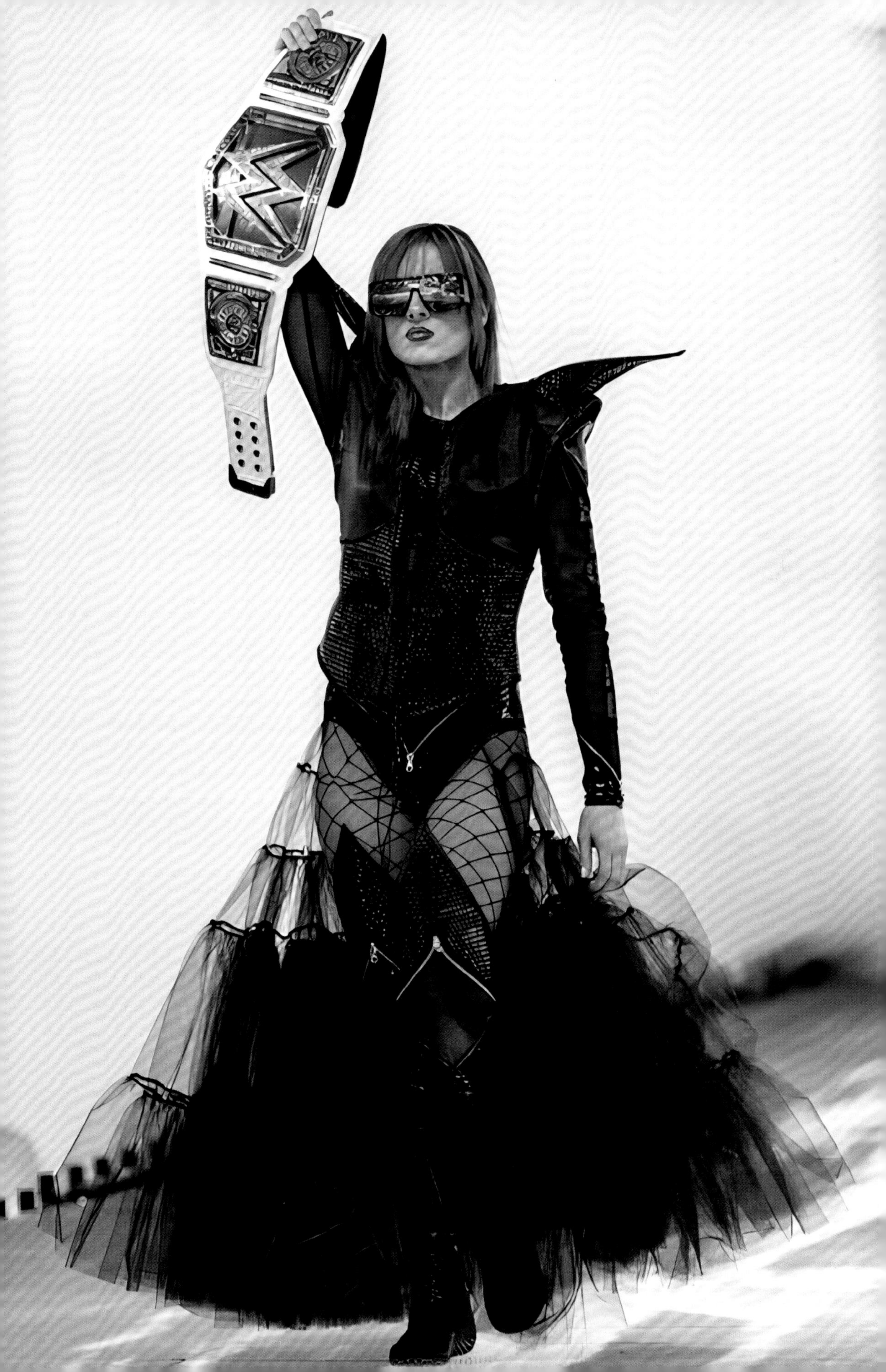

**"If someone compliments me or likes the look, that's all nice and well, but it's not why I'm wearing it. I just wear what I like, what I think is cool or comfortable, or what will make me smile 'cause it's silly. Poor Troi [Quin's stylist] has a hard time getting me in a pair of stilettos because I just don't feel like myself in them. And if you don't feel like your outfit is an extension of you and your vibe, then it's not going to work. Fashion should be an expression of yourself. It's fun that way."**

–Rebecca Quin

But despite her growing closet of unique creations, there's one particularly inspired look that remains Quin's favorite fit of all time. "My favorite match and outfit was at WrestleMania 38 in Dallas, Texas, when I faced Bianca Belair for the title," said Quin, who stunned the crowd in a sleek ensemble composed of a fitted black jacket with asymmetrical shoulder pads, a long tulle skirt, thigh-high boots, and futuristic sunglasses. "I absolutely believe how I looked helped with the match." She completed her look with bold makeup and a new hairstyle: "Bianca had just cut my hair, and I debuted a whole new style that I designed with Jolene. I remember walking the halls before the match feeling so damn cool. Thanks to the great designing of Jolene and the amazing makeup and hair talents of Megaen and Jackie on the WWE makeup team, the night was a perfect culmination."

As the years have progressed, fans have watched Quin wear louder, more vibrant outfits to the ring, especially during her Big Time Becks era in 2021 and 2022. Two years later, as a newly acclaimed *New York Times* bestselling author, she donned an elaborate getup embellished with actual text from her bestselling memoir at The Grandest Stage of Them All in Philadelphia. "I always think, 'How would you dress your favorite pop star?' And that's how I dress the wrestler," said Troi Anthoni, the stylist who helps bring Quin's visions to life. "If there would be anybody to compare her look to, it would be Lady Gaga, because we were really going out there on the looks. We're in a time where we kind of opened up a new world of 'This is how the new wrestler dresses.' It's a new wave, and to have Becky and [her husband, WWE Superstar] Seth [Rollins] be the blueprint of it all is awesome."

Becky Lynch at WrestleMania 40 in Philadelphia, Pennsylvania. Photo by Kimberly Morrell.

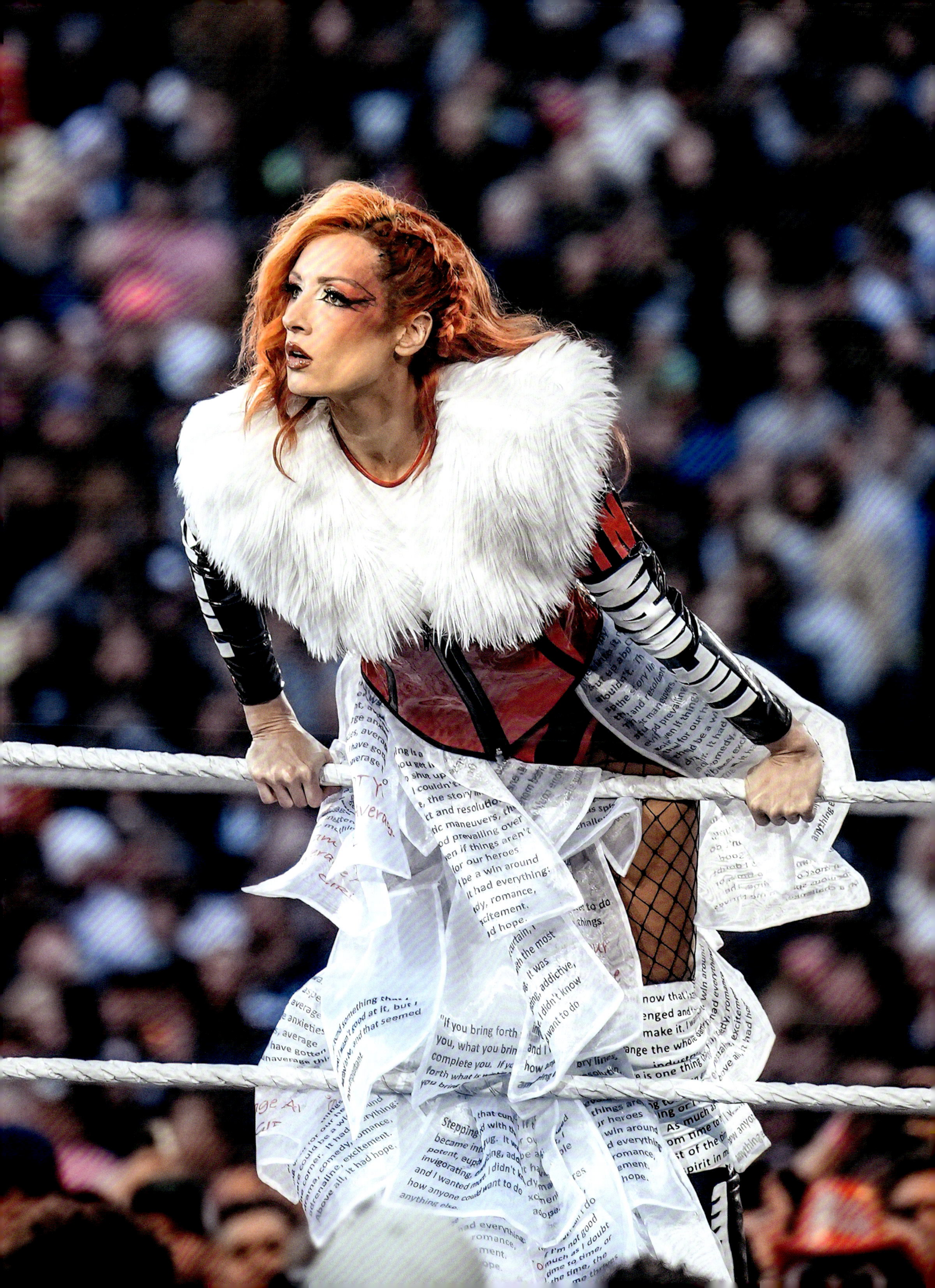

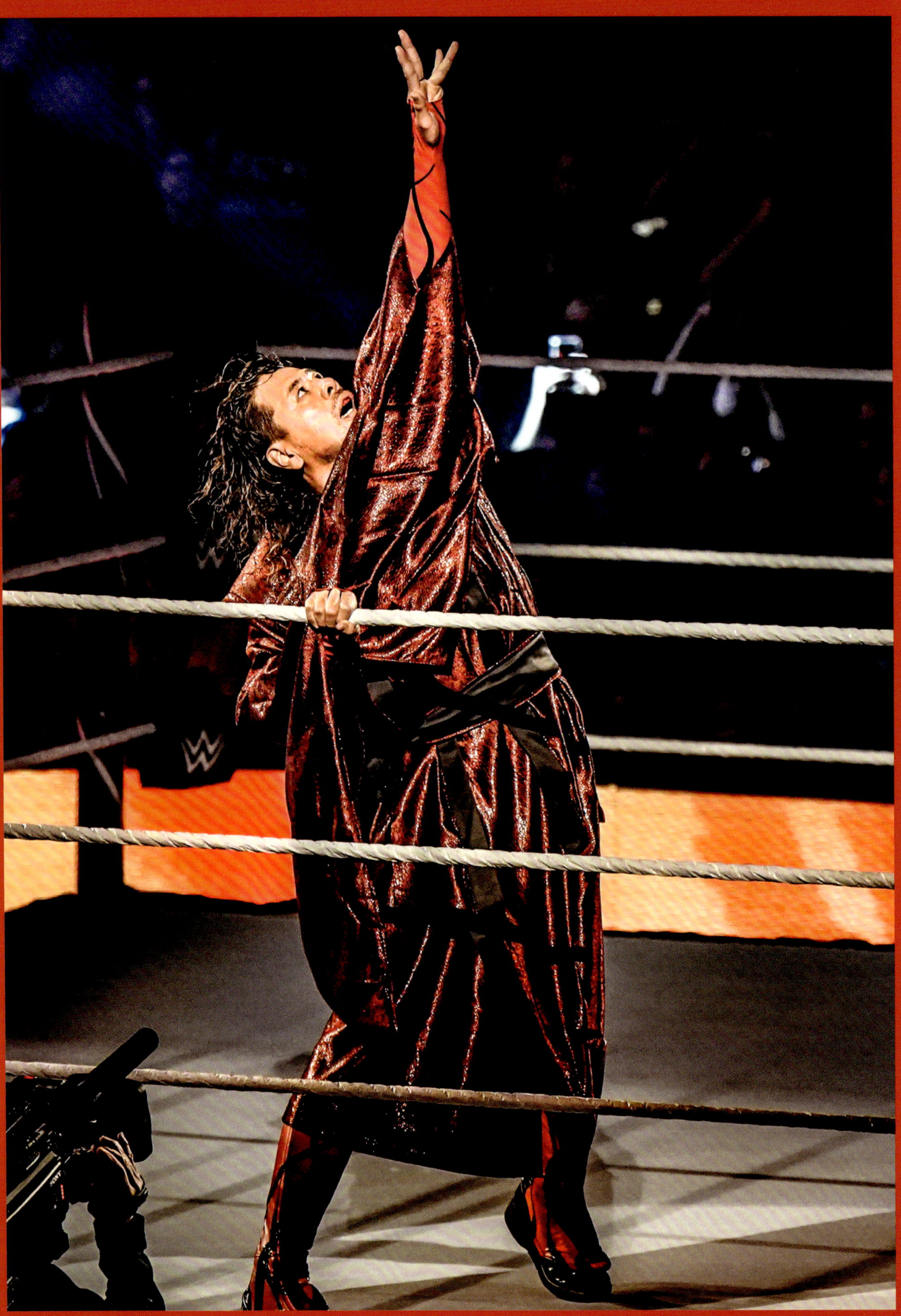

# SHINSUKE NAKAMURA

Active 2002–present

First Japanese Wrestler to Win WWE Royal Rumble
Three-Time IWGP Heavyweight Champion

**Known for his swiftness,** skill, and theatrical appeal, Shinsuke Nakamura is the perfect mix of wrestler and rock star. Whether watching live at a show or through a television screen, fans can't take their eyes off him. In turn, the intuitive athlete uses the audience as inspiration. "When I stand in the ring, I'm not just fighting; I'm putting my emotions into my wrestling through technique," Nakamura said. "The energy I give off and the fans' support and reactions are, to me, the ultimate form of communication."

Frequently called The King of Strong Style, the hard-hitting wrestler wears one-piece outfits with asymmetrical lines and monochromatic colors, usually in deep red, black, and metallic hues. "I'm always looking for something different from everyone else," said Nakamura. "I started wearing jumpsuits to use color and image on a larger scale. I also drew inspiration from David Bowie's stage costumes. Unlike many Japanese wrestlers, I avoided incorporating Japanese culture and design too easily, as I felt it would reinforce stereotypes." But that changed on January 1, 2023, when Nakamura had a final singles match with the legendary Japanese wrestler Great Muta at a traditional martial arts venue in Japan. "This experience brought a major shift in me," said Nakamura, who felt strongly connected to both his heritage and his opponent: "I became more aware of Japanese spirit, and I felt Great Muta's soul and essence within me. Now, I feel comfortable incorporating Japanese designs into my costume."

Shinsuke Nakamura against Seth Rollins at WWE Fastlane in Indianapolis, Indiana, in 2023. Photo by Kimberly Morrell.

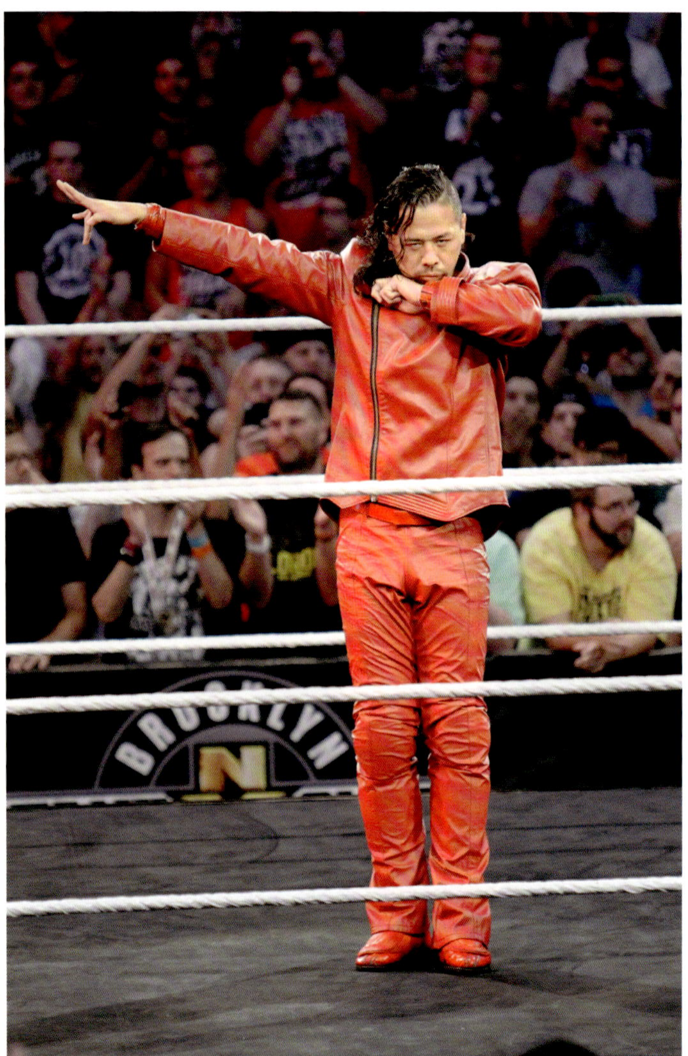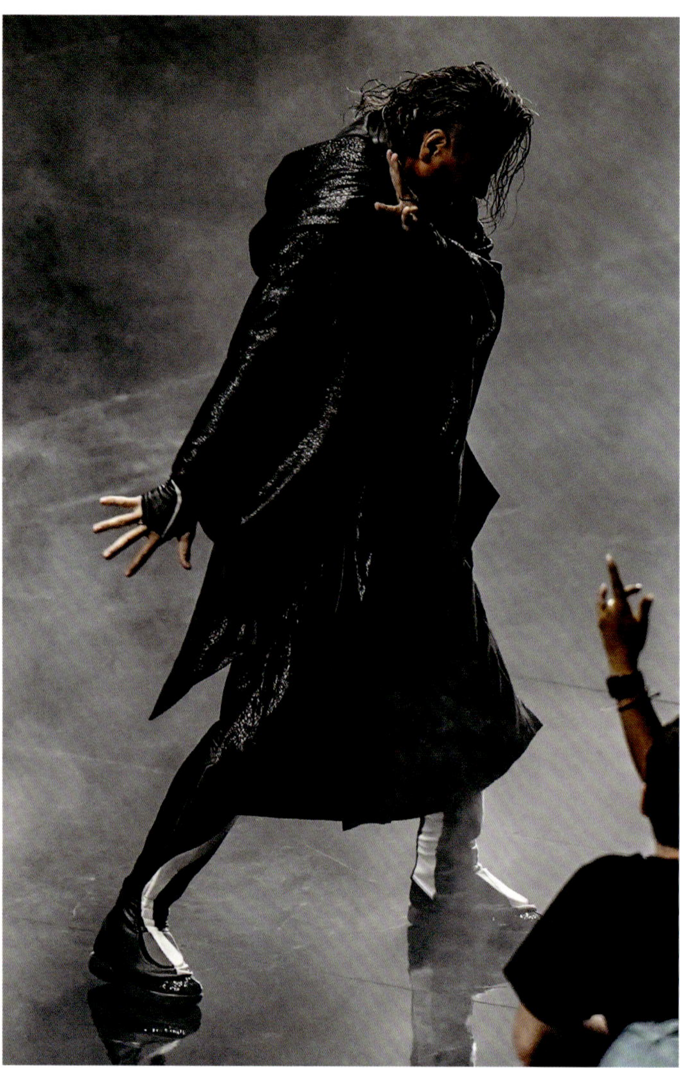

To Nakamura, the wrestler's wardrobe is much more than just gear to be worn in the ring: "My attire affects my mentality—it lifts my spirits. Jackets and capes are more than just costumes. They are part of my character, a way to signal that the fight begins the moment I enter. I choose them with the intent to create a powerful impact so that fans feel something's about to happen." For Nakamura, clothes aren't just a means of self-expression but also a declaration. "As an expression of myself, these items are essential for showing my commitment and worldview in the ring," he said. "I think my strength and unique movements can be expressed with just my body, down to the fingertips. If my music and performance make viewers feel something special, that's all I need. Of course, I make sure my appearance reflects who I am, but in the end, everything combines to create who I am. That's Shinsuke Nakamura's style."

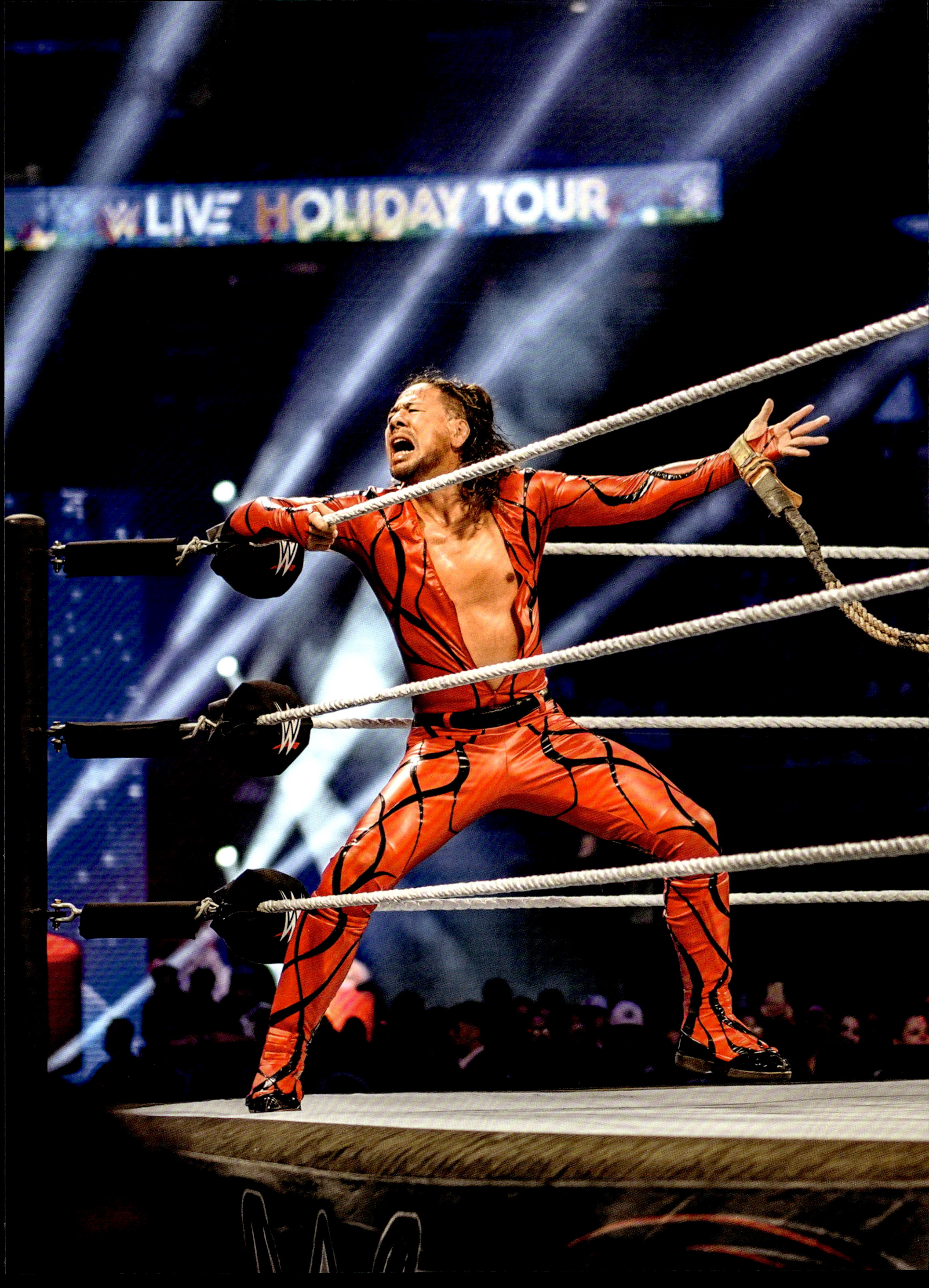

WWE LIVE HOLIDAY TOUR

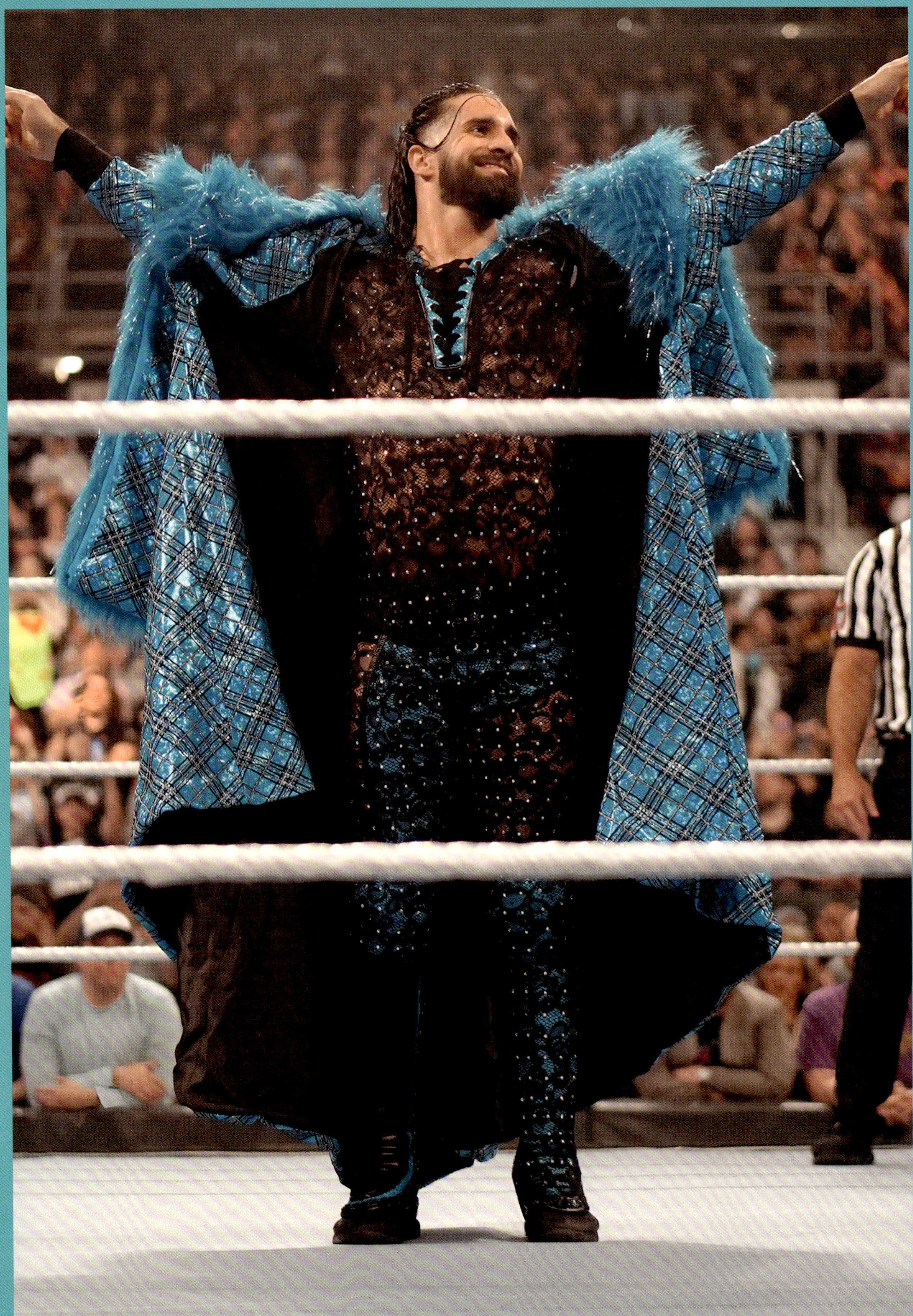

# COLBY LOPEZ
## WWE'S SETH ROLLINS

Active 2005–present

WWE Grand Slam Champion

**Colby Lopez—a.k.a. Seth Rollins—**isn't lying when he calls himself a revolutionary and a true visionary. Lopez burns it down night after night with his talent, swagger, and unlimited star power. But Lopez's rule-breaking bravado isn't just an act. "One thing I've always been good at in my life is not caring what others think," said Lopez. "I never wanted to be someone that followed the trends. I always want to be the one that bucked the trends, did something different, and stood out on their own—whether that was through a look, movement, or doing something that others weren't doing at the time. You go through phases in your life where you second-guess yourself and you become less confident, and then something happens, clicks, and you start to find yourself again. But for me, there's always been that underlying confidence inside myself to kind of not play by the rules and not do things the way they're supposed to be done."

For Lopez, it all dates back to his founding role in The Shield, a paramilitary wrestling faction whose members wore black operational gear. Despite the simple look, Lopez found ways to differentiate himself from the pack: "My role in the group in the early days was to kind of be the highflyer. I was the fighter pilot, right? Roman [Reigns] was the tank, and [Dean] Ambrose was the crazy general that was in the infantry. I was more of a paratrooper coming out of the sky, so I wanted something lighter, softer, sleeker, and more aerial than what the other guys were wearing. When I was thinking about tactical looks, like 'What does that look like for me?,' I needed to be stealthy and fast. That's where the small vest came in, the spandex underneath, the gloves, and the whole thing. It just felt like that look fit the role that I played in the group."

Seth Rollins at WWE Backlash in 2024.
Photo by Kimberly Morrell.

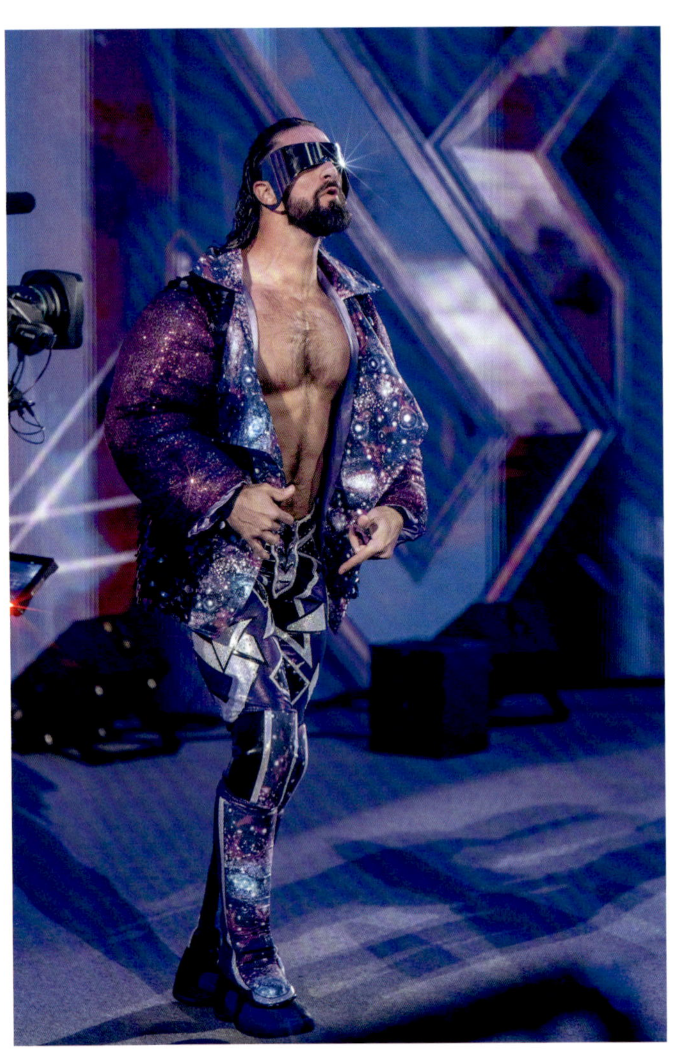
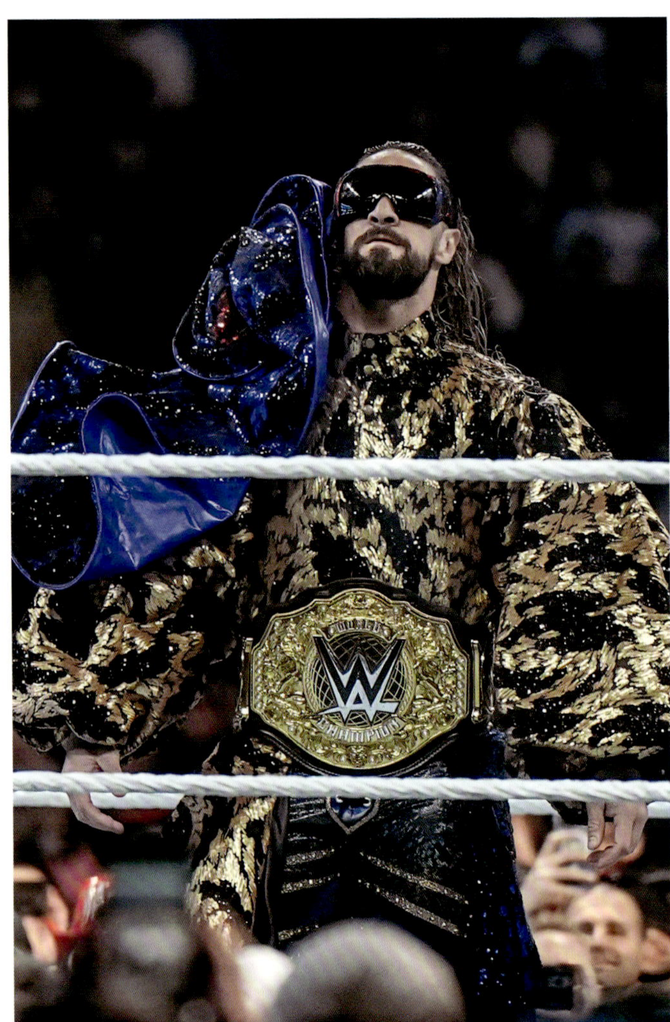

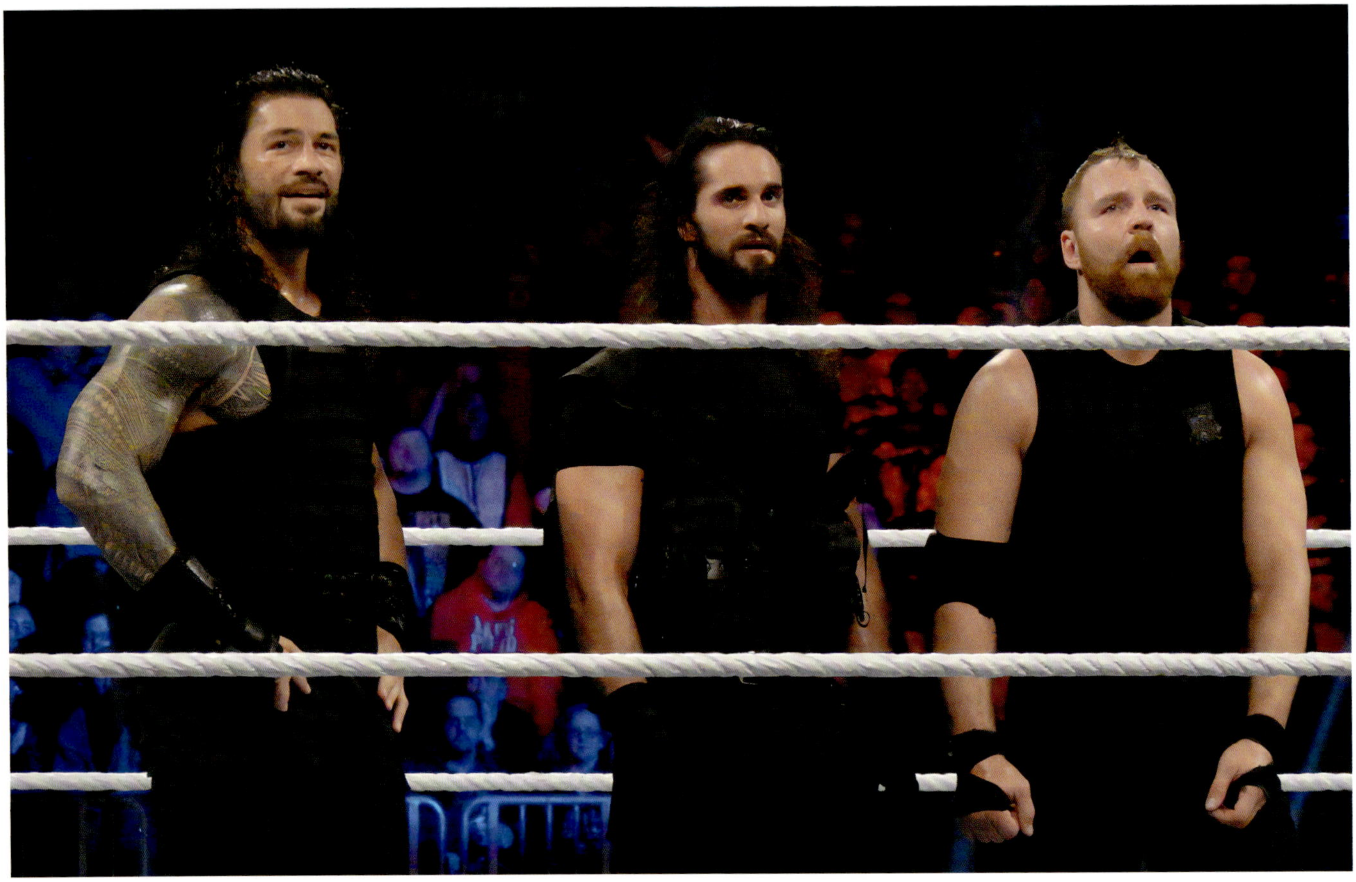

The Shield is still considered one of the most iconic factions in WWE history. Some have credited Lopez with being the mastermind, or The Architect, of The Shield. In 2022, Lopez even dusted off his old tactical gear for Royal Rumble—and seemed to succeed in throwing his opponent (and former Shield teammate) off his game: "A look that was so important and vital to the moment and is still talked about even a few years later was Royal Rumble 2022. It was the year I wrestled [fellow Shield member] Roman Reigns for the WWE Universal Championship, and it was the first time that I had worn The Shield gear in a long time," said Lopez. "Nobody saw it coming or had any idea that it was going to happen. The tactical look itself is such an iconic look and something that myself, Roman, and Ambrose cultivated a decade in advance. Bringing it back always makes people feel a certain way. I'm getting a little bit of goose bumps just talking about it. That moment, the fashion, and being in the ring with Roman, the subversion of the expectations of what people were used to seeing versus what they saw there. It was very much a very special night, where everything kind of came together in one moment."

TOP LEFT: Seth Rollins for WWE RAW at Madison Square Garden in Manhattan, New York, on March 10, 2025. Photo by Kimberly Morrell.

TOP RIGHT: Seth Rollins at WrestleMania 40 in Philadelphia, Pennsylvania. Photo by Kimberly Morrell.

BOTTOM: Seth Rollins as part of The Shield. Photo by Kimberly Morrell.

Over the years, Lopez has transformed into a style icon by blending the worlds of fashion and professional wrestling. Lopez has pushed boundaries throughout his career, especially when it comes to his attire, which has revolutionized wrestling gear to such a degree that he's considered a fashion architect. In funky sunglasses, long fur coats, and daring haute couture, Lopez has helped bring celebrity fashions into the ring. "We are introducing the fashion world to the wrestling audience," said Troi Anthoni, the personal stylist behind Lopez's dramatic looks. "People often want to know, 'Why is Seth wearing this?' 'Why is he wearing that?' We look at MGK and Jared Leto for inspiration but do our own thing."

Along with Anthoni, Rollins collaborates with seamster Sarath Ton to create attention-grabbing attire. "I'm kind of a bigger-picture person when it comes to concepts; I'm not good at the details," said Lopez. "They're good at the details, and we make a really good team in that way. I'm able to have a perfect understanding of the character, where I want it to go, how it exists in a bubble or outside of a bubble, and they're good at making sure the details line up. Colors, patterns, stitching, shoes, and glasses are the details they look at. I can't imagine the details; I can imagine the concepts, and then they help me kind of put them all into place."

But Lopez's flamboyant style also wouldn't be possible without the fans who meet him halfway. He has spearheaded a progressive mentality for this generation and continues to forge the future. "WrestleMania 40 in Los Angeles was a special night for me," said Lopez. "I wore a very loud outfit with a bright pink [two-piece] and red jacket that had a train. It was so out there and over-the-top. If I had worn that outfit on a whim at any point four or five years earlier, I would have been laughed off the stage and not taken seriously. It was such a moment; everybody was on board singing my song, and it felt like a quintessential Seth Rollins moment."

**"The looks always start with a germ of an idea. It always starts with what's different or what can I do that's far enough off the line that it's going to grab someone's attention. Then I'll see a vibe. At first, I was hesitant about pushing the envelope with the fashion and gear game, and the more I did it, the more comfortable I got in that skin and the easier it was for me to take risks. I hope that if I fail, I fail forward."**

—Colby Lopez

WWE Superstar Seth Rollins at WWE Money in the Bank in Toronto, Canada, on July 6, 2024. Photo by Kimberly Morrell.

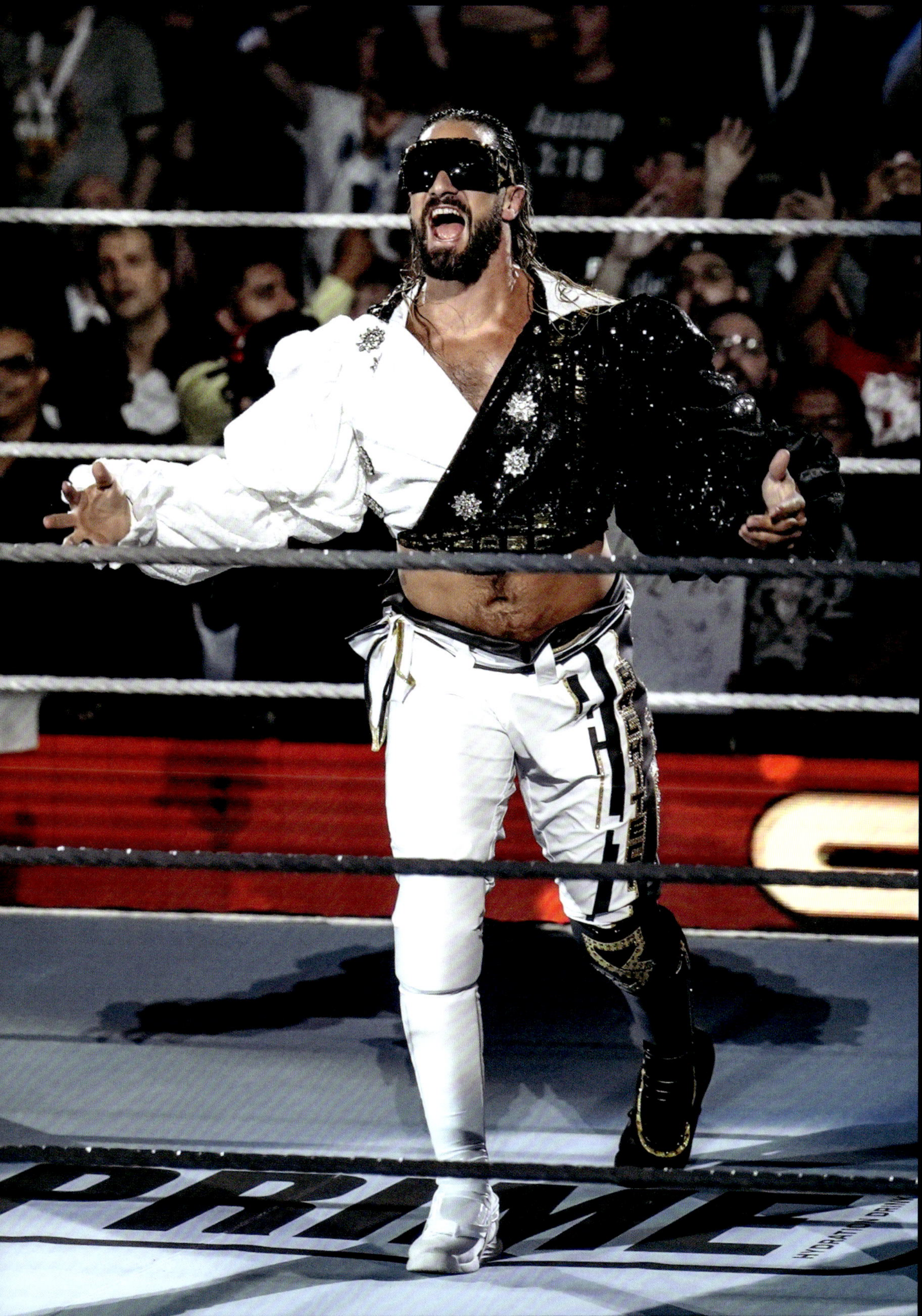

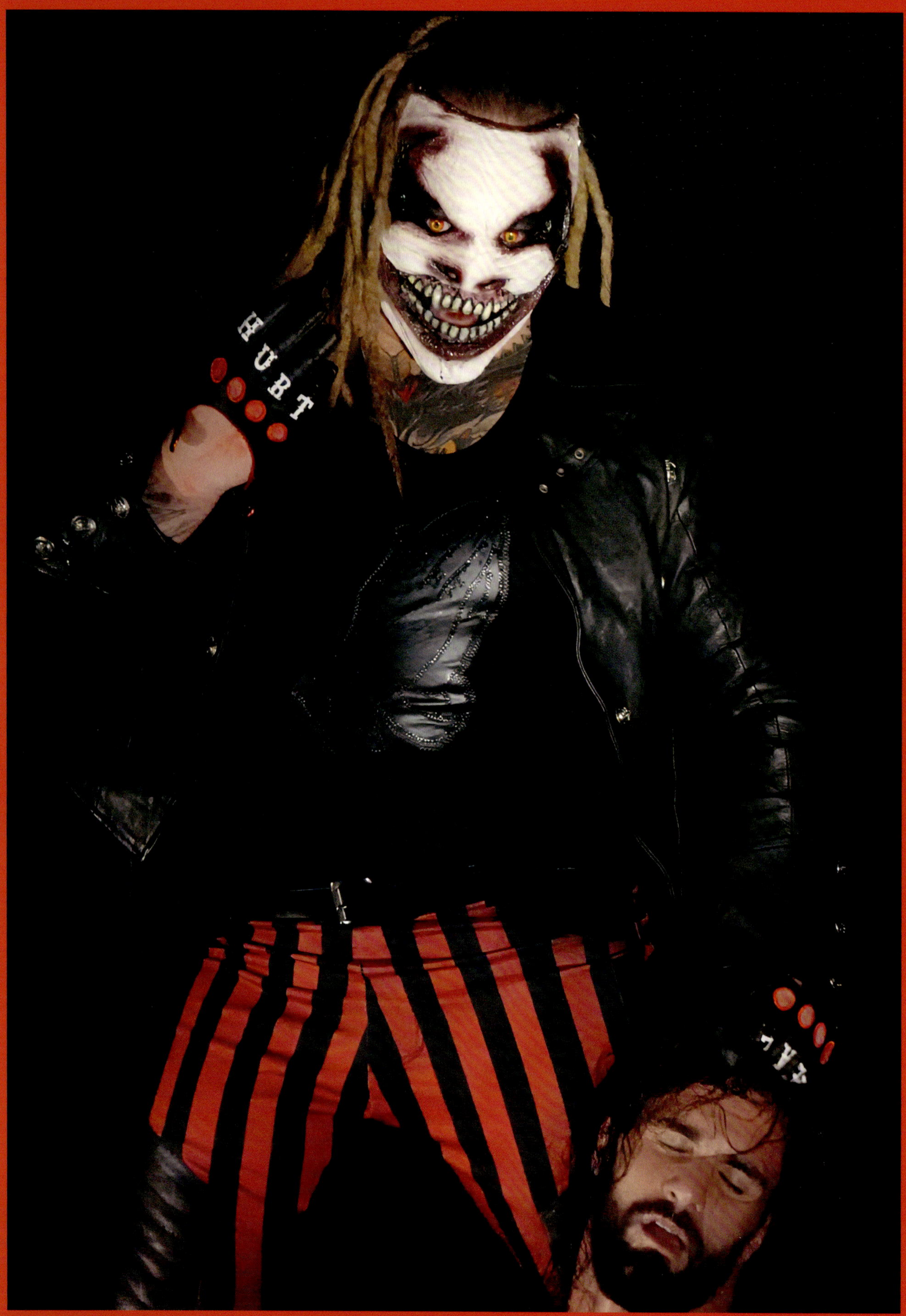
HURT

# WINDHAM ROTUNDA
## WWE'S "THE FIEND" BRAY WYATT

Active 2009–2023

WWE Champion

**Best known as** WWE Superstar Bray Wyatt, and by his alter persona The Fiend, Windham Rotunda will go down in history as one of wrestling's most creative superstars. Rotunda showcased his range with brilliant characters that fascinated viewers and felt authentic. Rob Fee, director of long-term creative at WWE, recalls Rotunda's commitment to crafting original characters. "The in-ring promo in his first SmackDown after his return at Elimination Chamber was really special," said Fee. "We sat on his bus trying to make it as genuine as possible. He'd try out a line, wouldn't feel it, and would say something like, 'Ugh, I'm just so nervous!' and I was like, 'Yes! That's just what you need to say!' We'd workshop different things but ended up using all the moments in between that were fully the real Windham. It was a special time, and I'm honored to have been a part of his lasting career."

Windham had a distinct talent for tapping into the emotion and feeling of each character with memorable looks. As the leader of The Wyatt Family, a wrestling faction that looked like a group of woodsmen who felt most at home in the swampland, Rotunda embraced his role as a backwoods cult leader with scruffy hair, disheveled attire, and deranged monologues. Lanterns became synonymous with Rotunda's persona as he guided his followers, including fellow wrestlers Erick Rowan and Luke Harper, through the swampy darkness. Rotunda also recognized the genius of the cinematic matches being created by Matt and Jeff Hardy over at TNA.

"The Fiend" Bray Wyatt ambushes Seth Rollins at Clash of Champions in 2019. Photo by Kimberly Morrell.

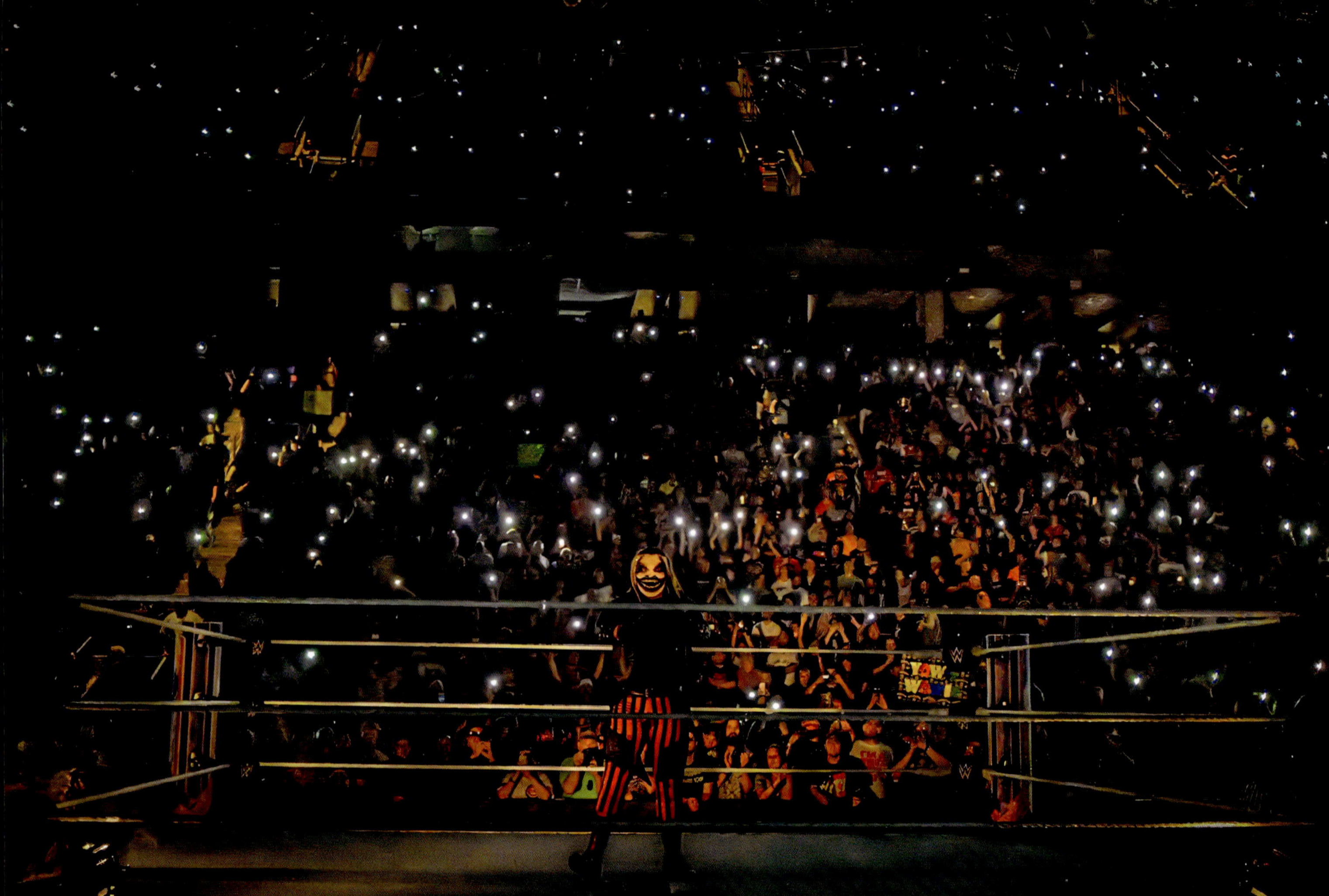

Bridging the gap between the rival leagues, Rotunda played a critical role in creating The Ultimate Deletion, WWE's first cinematic match. Matt remembers his friend and former colleague in a heartfelt way: "The ten months I spent working against and teaming with Bray Wyatt was one of the most fun times of my career. I loved him as a performer and a human being. I adored his out-of-the-box creative ideas and concepts. Bray was truly one of a kind."

Giving light to new creativity, Rotunda developed two very different personas that seamlessly contrasted, telling a larger story of character versatility. As a simple man with a childlike demeanor and neighborly attitude, Rotunda wore knit sweaters and khaki pants in the "Firefly Funhouse," a recurring segment for WWE.

## "Follow the buzzards."

–Bray Wyatt

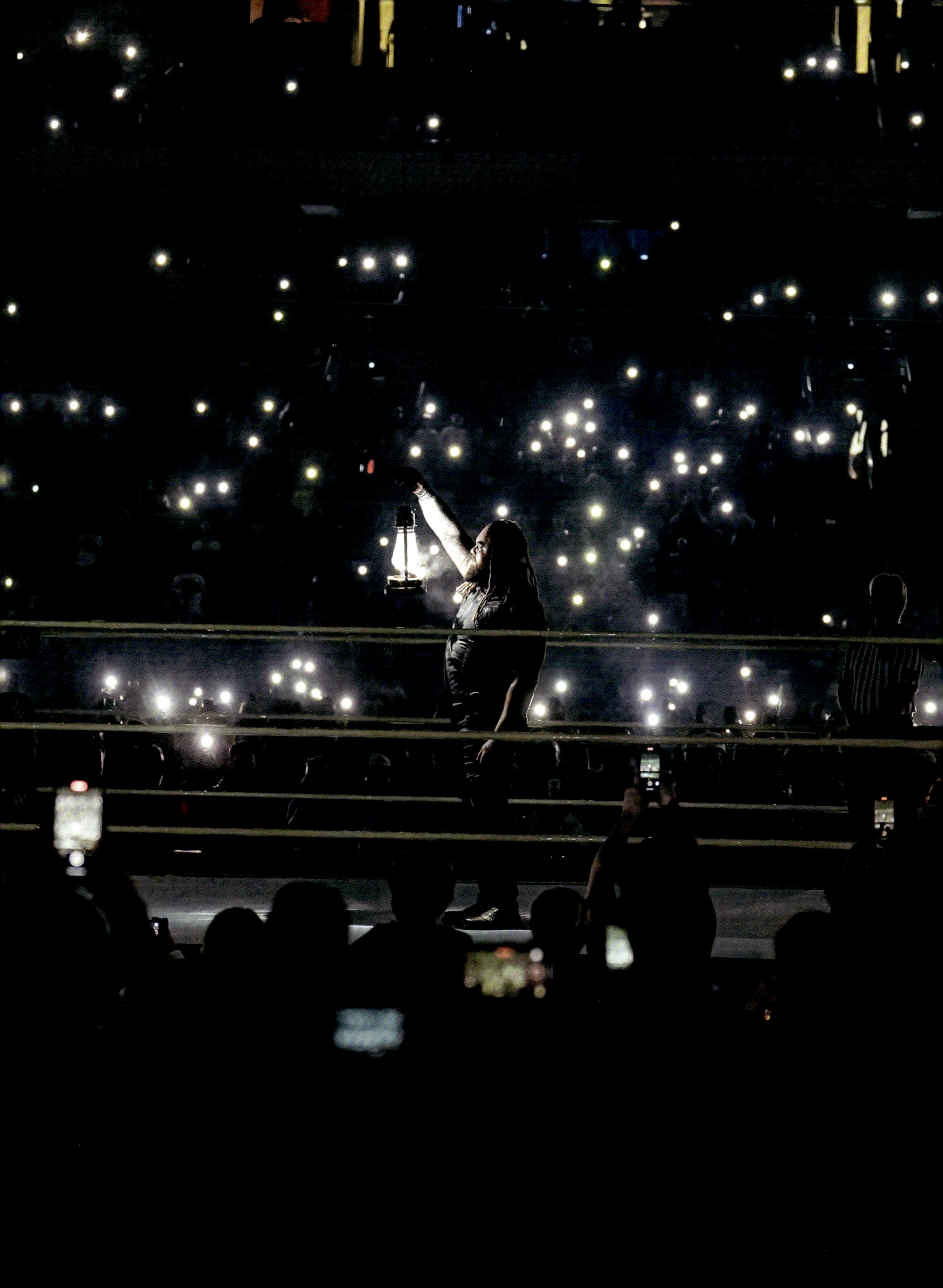

With a smile plastered across his face, he had a jolly presence, yet occasionally his actions would make way for his second persona to be unveiled. The Fiend unleashed Rotunda's scary side and catapulted viewers to another dimension. The extreme contrast between the two characters was exactly the purpose. "At one point, Windham wanted to create a documentary about his life that, halfway through, turned into a horror movie," said Fee.

WWE's The Fiend was successful in many ways, in large part because of his diabolical attire. The Fiend's crazed demonic mask invoked immediate fear in the audience. Creature-like body armor under a leather jacket portrayed an evil underworld creature. His striped pants resembled a rogue carnival clown. The Fiend told his story solely through sinister gear and stealthy wrestling. Other than muttering "Let me in" or mumbling phrases under his breath to his opponents, The Fiend never spoke at all. Instead, he believed in telling his story through his look, his cinematic movements, and his wrestling style.

Through each of his characters, Rotunda transformed himself to connect to the audience, and fans loved him right back for his out-of-the-box characters and unique perspective. Even after his untimely passing in 2023, Rotunda's legacy lives on through The Wyatt Sicks, a WWE wrestling faction started by WWE's Bo Dallas, Rotunda's real-life brother and fellow wrestler, that is inspired by Rotunda's genius, characters, and storylines. "No one would want their passing incorporated into the next story more than Windham," said Fee. "He loved blurring the lines of fiction and reality at such deep levels."

"The Fiend" Bray Wyatt in the Mountain Dew Pitch Black Match against LA Knight at Royal Rumble in San Antonio, Texas, in 2023. Photo by Kimberly Morrell.

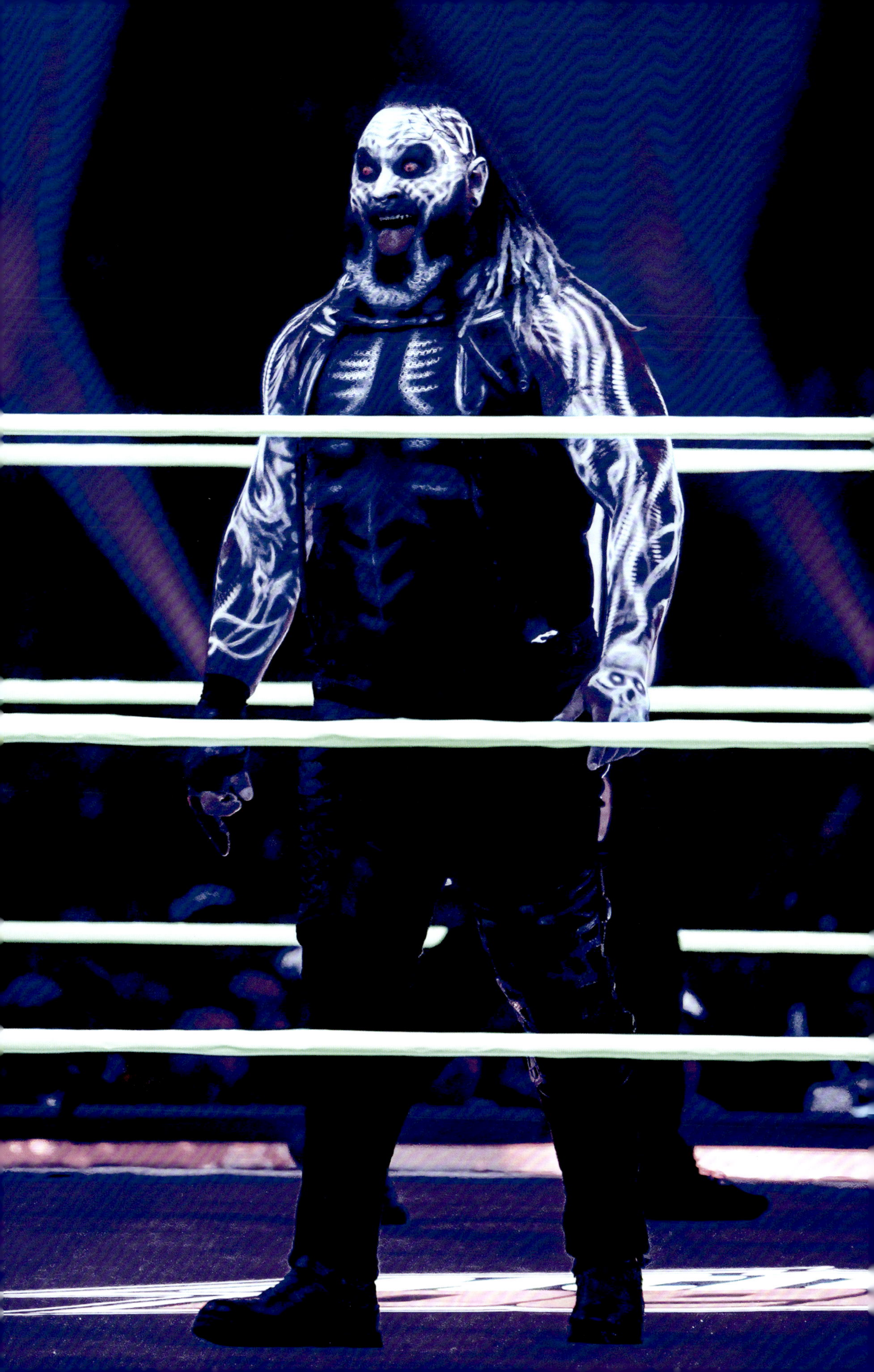

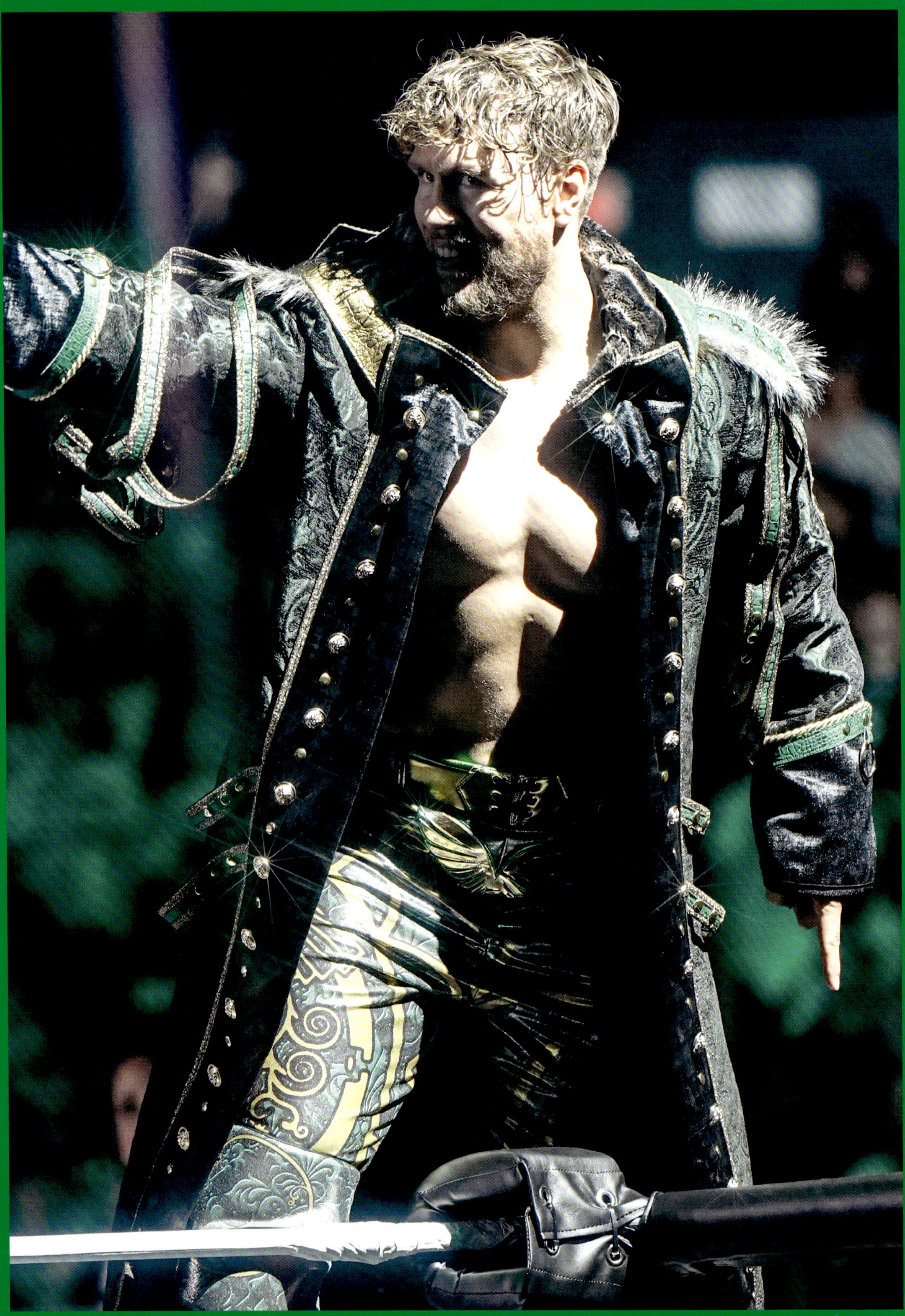

# WILL OSPREAY

Active 2012–present

IWGP World Heavyweight Champion
Three-Time IWGP Junior Heavyweight Champion

**Many wish for it**—Will Ospreay works for it. His renowned skill and elaborate style consisting of sweeping coats and exquisitely designed tights were honed during his time at New Japan Pro-Wrestling, where the British wrestler spent eight years early in his career. New Japan breeds a whole new caliber of athletes, and Ospreay is a direct product of this storied company. "The pageantry is really prioritized in Japan," said Ospreay. "Animation and the video games are a lifestyle because it's everywhere. It's in all the cities, and those companies are their major sponsors. So the more that you could look like a video game character, you almost cut corners to succeed far beyond what was being presented."

Known as The Aerial Assassin, Ospreay finds inspiration from his favorite video game, *Assassin's Creed*. Just as those in the game use their strength and high-flying moves to pummel opponents, Ospreay does so in the ring. His signature look includes intricate, long hooded jackets, oftentimes embellished with fur, feathers, metallics, and meaningful colors, like the memorable jacket Ospreay wore to the Wrestle Kingdom in Tokyo. "I remember the first time I ever felt like I found a look I wanted to go for," said Ospreay of that powerful look, which was created by Sarinah from Airhead Diva (a wrestling company) as he was beginning to embrace his new character: "It was January 2019, and I was in Wrestle Kingdom in the opening match against [Japanese wrestler] Kota Ibushi. I was the Junior Heavyweight, but I was also mixing with the heavyweight cards, so I wanted to show a little bit of maturity but still keep the assassin in there. Instead of something shiny, I wanted something deep forest green and dark to show a little bit of maturity. I also wanted to keep some color to show that I'm still growing up and learning things. We went for a Robin Hood–style *Assassin's Creed* look because I had a mentality of stealing from the rich to give to the poor. When I would go into those type of matches, I [would] think about serving the little man."

Clothes are more than just a way to tell The Aerial Assassin's story. For Ospreay, they're also a tool for personal growth that dates back to his foundational days as a wrestler. "I really felt like I discovered myself in my second jacket of 2019," said the wrestler, who wore a significant look to the final round of New Japan Pro-Wrestling's Best of the Super Juniors tournament: "At that time in my life, I was struggling so much with my depression and anxiety of moving my life over to Japan. I wanted to be accepted by the Japanese people—I wanted to be the adopted son. I always felt a level of anxiety because I couldn't speak the language very well."

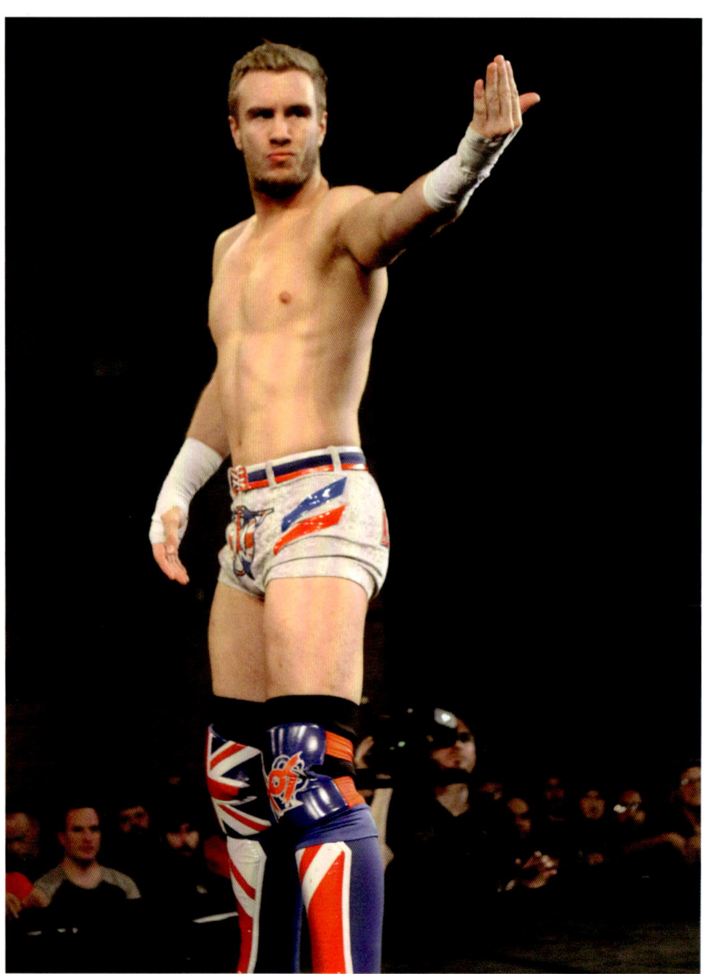

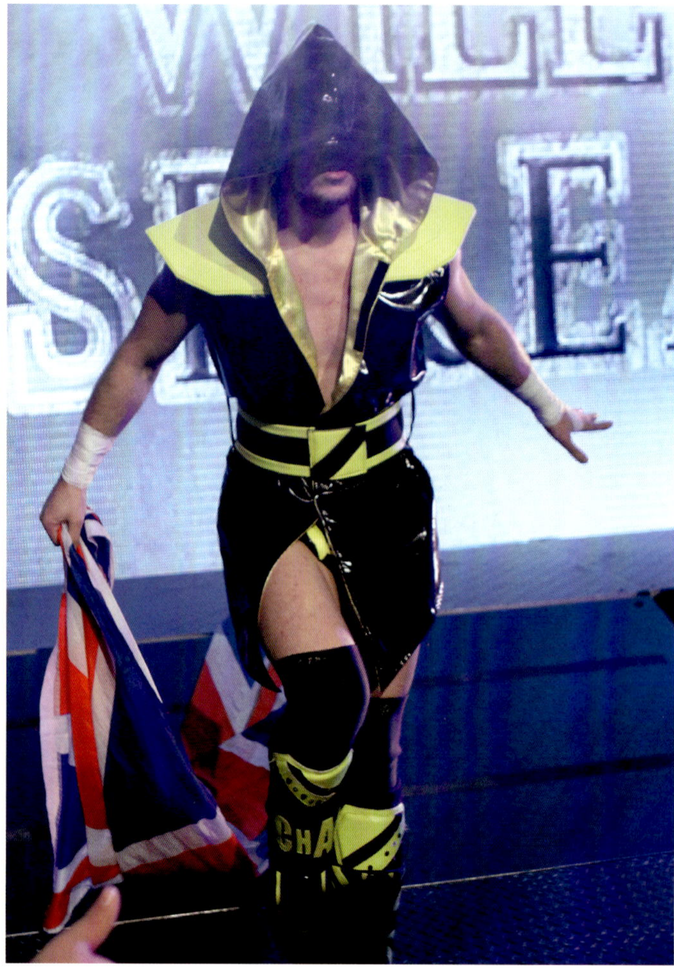

But in that high-pressure moment, Ospreay found strength in his commanding attire. "On the day of the Super Juniors, I was going to announce to everyone that I was officially moving to Japan, and I wanted to do it in Japanese," he said. "I dressed myself in this beautiful red, gold, and black gown, and it just fit the venue of the sumo arena [Ryōgoku Kokugikan in Japan] so well. It has red box seating; you can look up and see all the legendary sumo wrestlers, and there's a red round runway that I've walked down. . . . [I really wanted to] show people my commitment to their culture. I remember saying at the end of the match that I was moving to Japan, and the noise that they made, their reaction, made me feel like I was home. That is one of the most important jackets in my career."

In 2024, Ospreay lived out a fantasy at All In: London, a pay-per-view event produced by AEW at Wembley Stadium. "We started talking to Ubisoft [the company behind *Assassin's Creed*], and I was like, 'Look, this has been like a lifelong dream for me to have *Assassin's Creed* be part of my entrance.' I said, 'If you're going to make me a part of the brotherhood, it has to be the main character, Ezio, filling me up with emotion to bring me into the *Creed*.'" As the wrestler walked to the ring in a dramatic jacket inspired by the video game, Ezio's voice played on a voice-over clip. "I remember when they played it to me in rehearsals, and I was blown away," said Ospreay, whose life seemed to have come full circle: "The game inspired me to be a professional wrestler, and now that game is leading me out for the biggest moment of my wrestling career. I remember putting on the jacket and every single person that I walked past backstage turned their heads. It was just one of those moments where I generally felt like a superhero. I felt like I was about to go out there and become the man that I always wanted to be."

This powerful moment meant even more because it took place in London, where Ospreay grew up and began his wrestling career: "When I crouched down on that stage, I could hear everyone like popping for Ezio. It went so quiet, and [with] the beginning beats of my music, I felt goose bumps all over my body. Everybody says, 'Take it all in!' but you can't, because you're in a moment where you're surrounded by people that have watched you grow up. I thought there's probably someone up in the nosebleeds that has seen me wrestle in front of fifty people, and here I'm walking down this ramp at Wembley. It's one of those moments where I just felt like this is [the] coolest moment of my life to stand here with an *Assassin's Creed* jacket on. My mum's surname chanted throughout the arena, and I'm about to go and put on, like, the match of the year. You just can't write that."

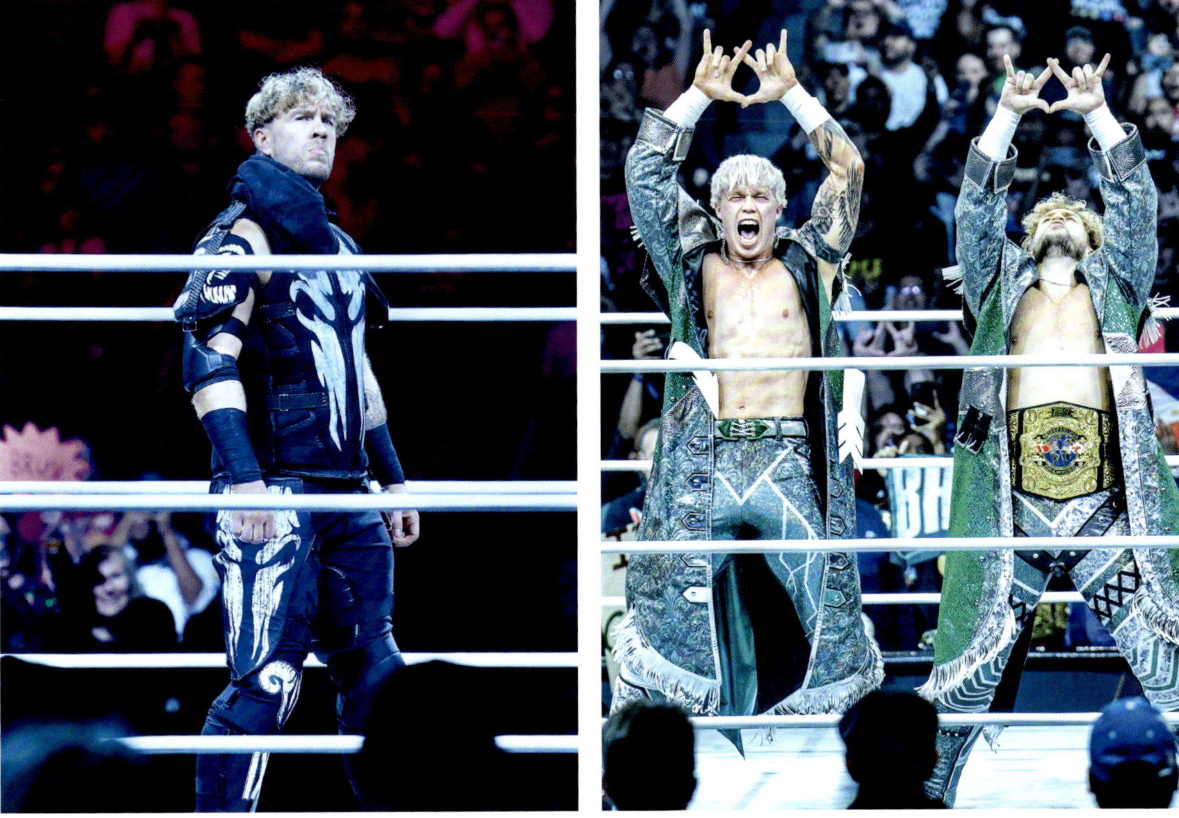

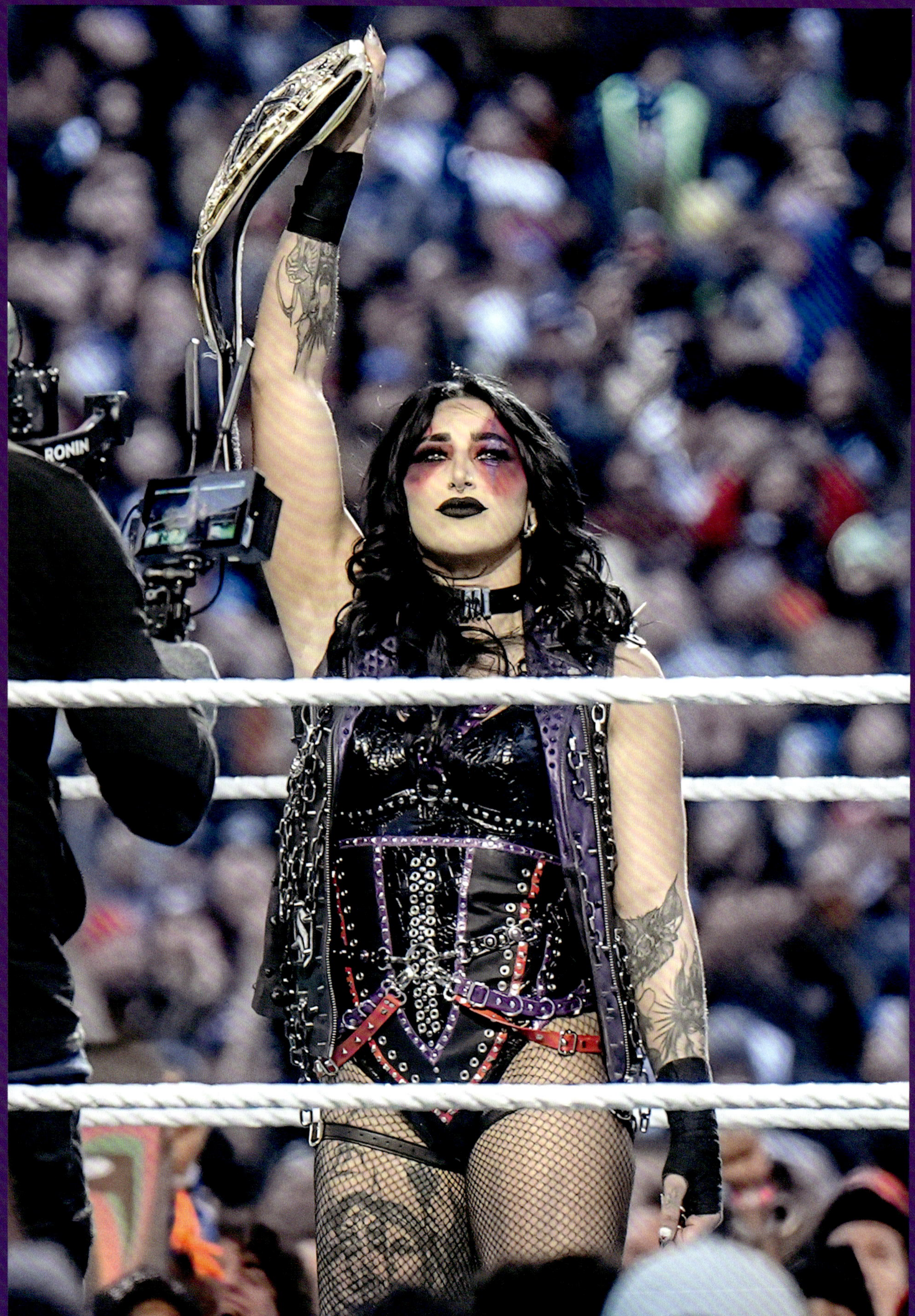

# DEMI BENNETT
## WWE'S RHEA RIPLEY

Active 2013–present

Three-Time Women's World Champion

**Better known as** WWE Superstar Rhea Ripley, Demi Bennett pursued a journey to the top that is an inspiring story in her commitment to self-love. After getting her start on the independent circuit in her native Australia, Bennett joined WWE in 2017 as part of the inaugural Mae Young Classic—and her career took off from there. But despite dominating the women's division and winning multiple championships before even turning thirty, Bennett didn't have an easy road. There was a point in her career when the young star was even ready to quit. "I went through a period in NXT between the first and second Mae Young Classic where I hated myself [and] wrestling, and wanted to go home to Australia," said Bennett. "I was getting bullied, and I didn't want to continue this dream of mine."

Bennett wondered if a new look might help her get out of her funk: "I asked Joe Belcastro, NXT's lead writer at the time, to cut my hair. He said no a few times, so I sent him a photo of me wearing a wig. It was the worst wig I could've tried on because the lady at the shop knew I wasn't going to buy any hair. Joe OK'd me cutting my hair, and I sat for twelve hours with the seamstress, watching her grandkids while she made my new gear. I didn't know what direction I was going to go in my career, so I went the simple route. That's why the attire was just white and black with a couple chains. I rocked up to the first day of the second Mae Young Classic, and one of the people that picked on me asked me about the new look. My response was 'This is the new Rhea Ripley.'"

Rhea Ripley against Becky Lynch at WrestleMania 40 in Philadelphia, Pennsylvania. Photo by Kimberly Morrell.

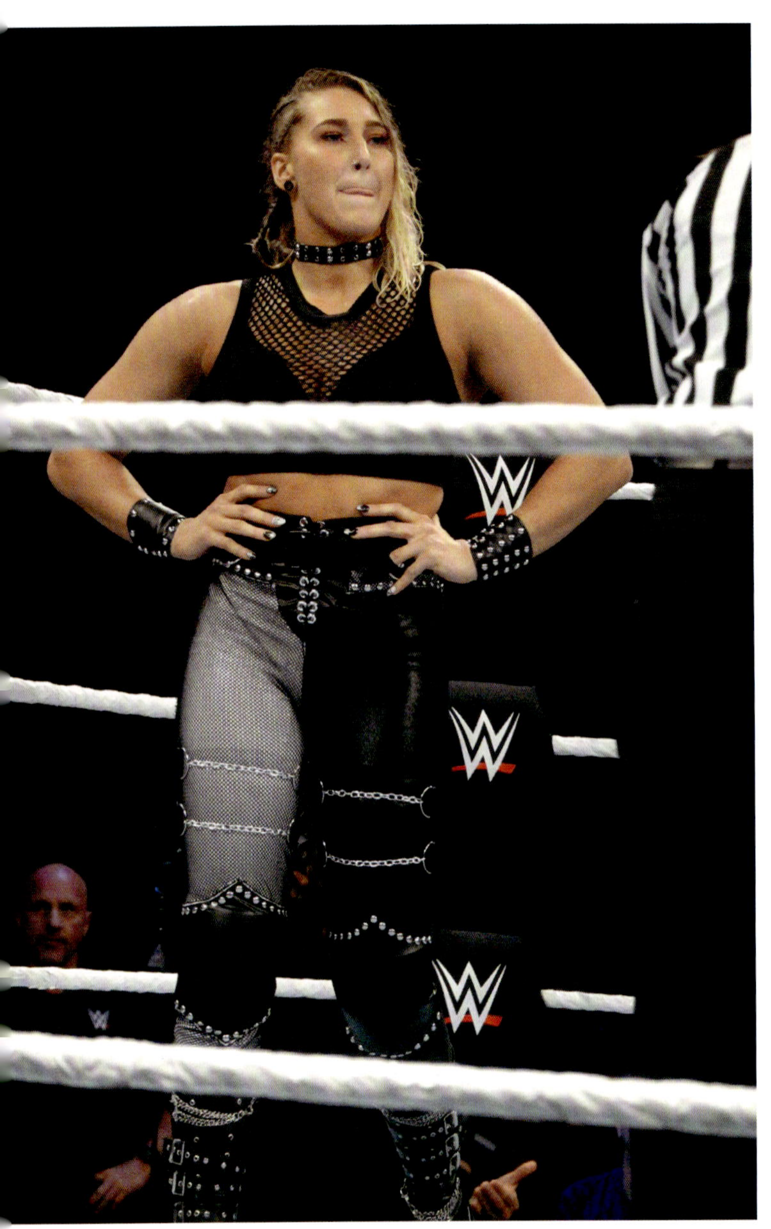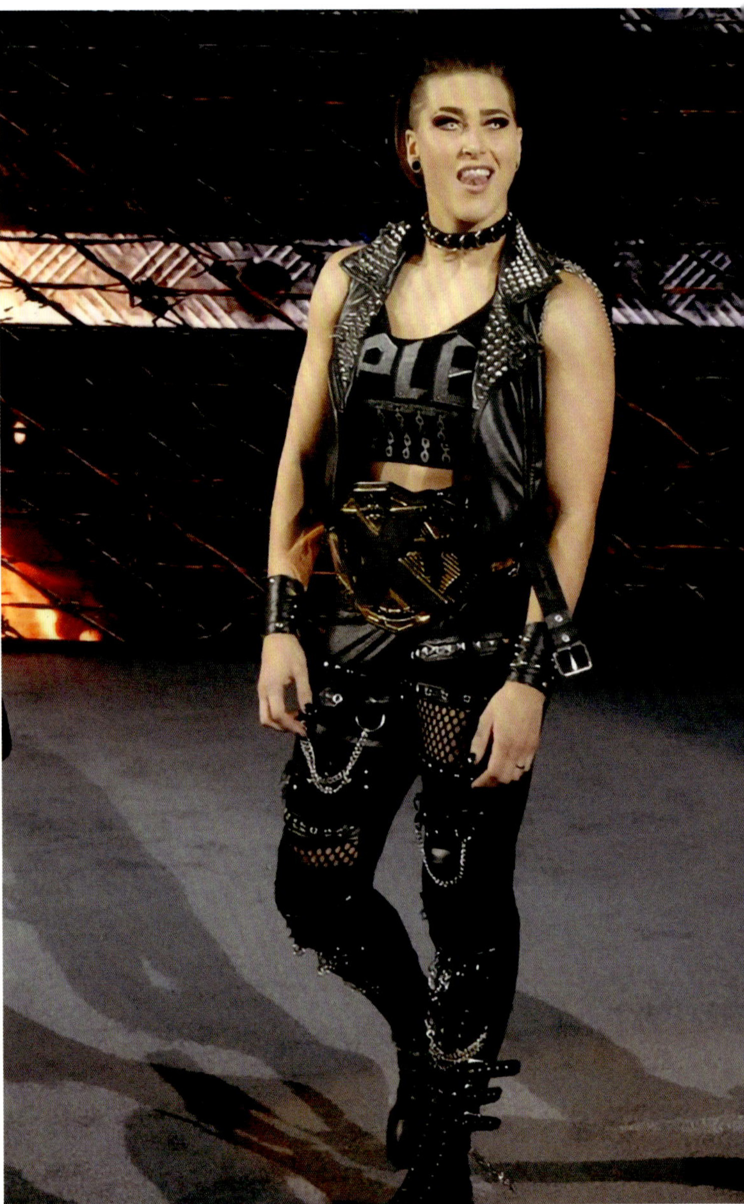

Bennett found renewed inspiration in her new look. "When I went out that night, I instantly felt more comfortable and confident," said Bennett, who had built up a lot of anger over the past year. But that night at the match, she relaxed into her new character. "I did what I thought was going to be good for me and I reacted in ways that felt natural to me," she said. "Something clicked, and I really feel like I connected. It felt like such a start for the Rhea Ripley name."

Now Bennett commands the ring with her dramatic goth and punk aesthetic. She wears hardcore looks made from black patent leather, mesh, and chains. She brings a heavy metal energy to the ring in studded harnesses, spiky shoulder coverings, and chokers proclaiming *MAMI* in big silver letters. Although she already had her footing as an individual competitor, joining The Judgment Day a few years into her career was an opportunity to grow and explore different parts of her character. "I always have some kind of purple in my gear for Judgment Day, which was such a pivotal point in my career. The purple reminds me of the growth within me. We were such a wild bunch of individuals from all over the country. When we all joined the group—me, Dominik [Mysterio], and Damian [Priest]—we were at

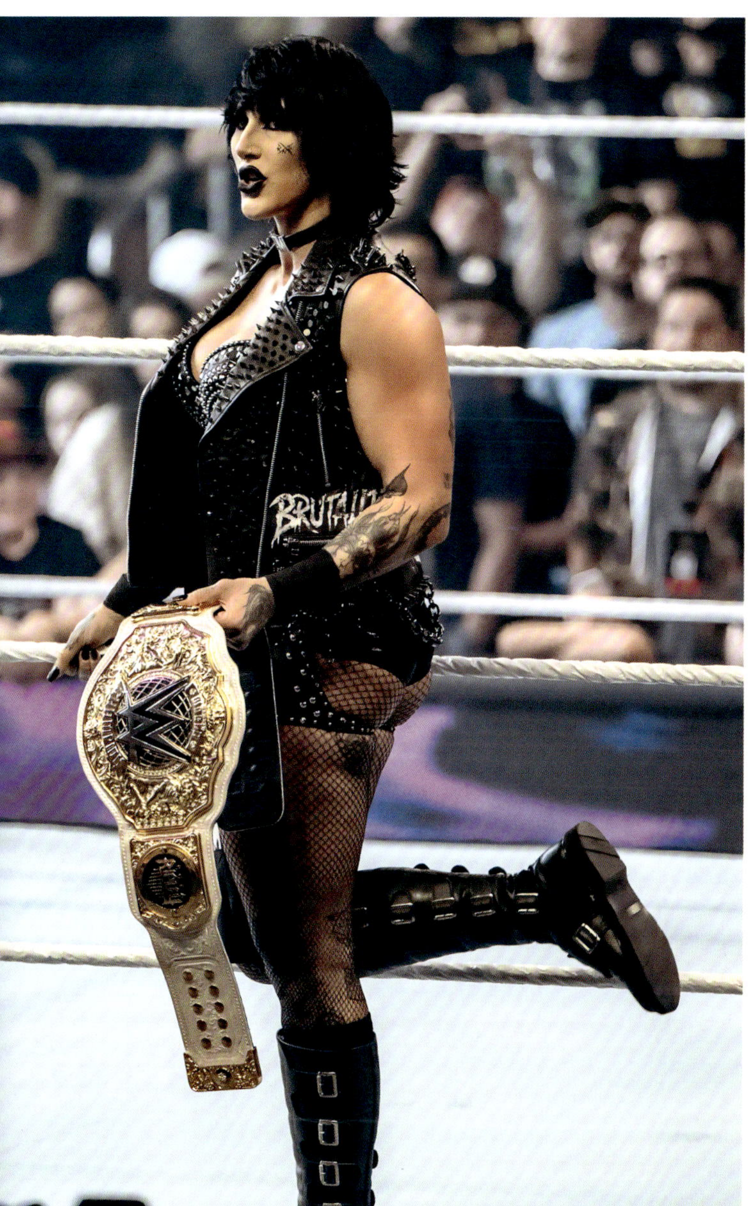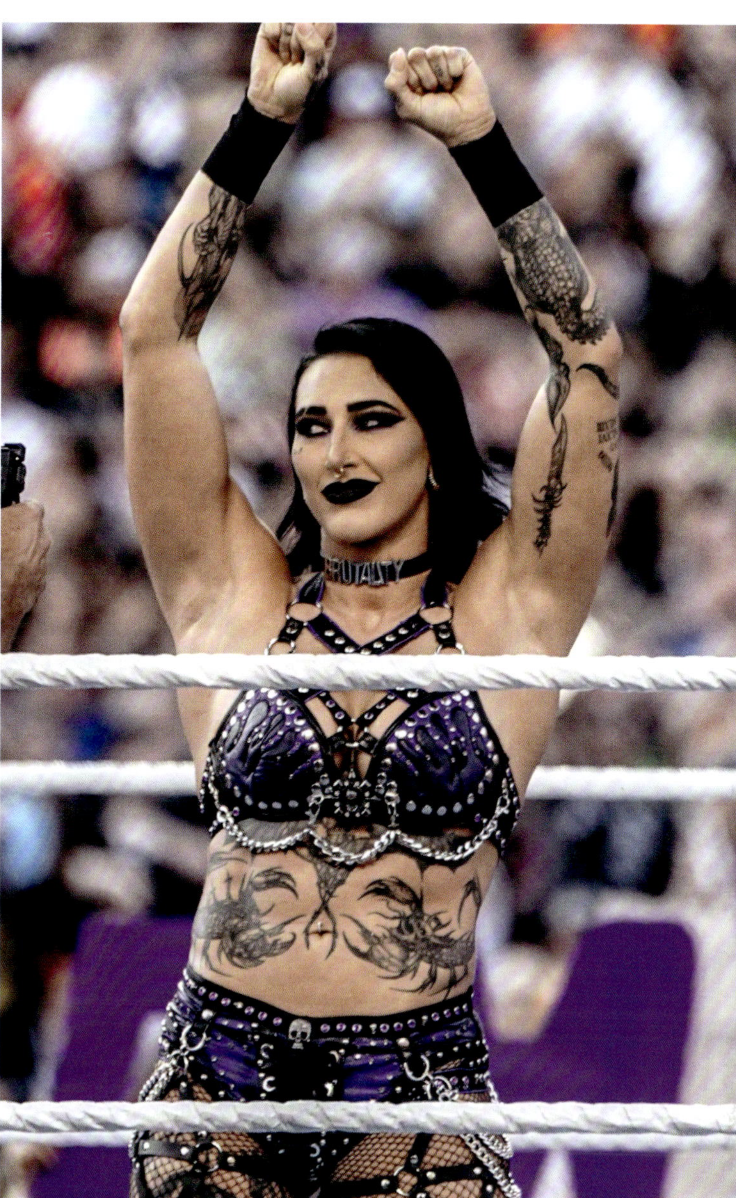



a stagnant place in our careers. Finn was a massive star in Japan and had all these accolades, but we all just meshed so well together and became a force to be reckoned with. There are sixteen total segments in *RAW*, and Judgment Day would be in nine of them, which meant it was working," said Bennett. "Each of the guys brought out a different side of me and opened all these different avenues for my character, which I got to show to fans. With Dom, I was strong yet soft and compassionate. With Finn, I was strong and strict, in a sister kind of way. And with Priest, I was strong, powerful, and forceful. In Judgment Day, there's just something inside of me that takes over, and I want to be the one in charge, which is so different than my everyday life. My alter ego that just takes over."

Bennett credits one of her best nights as an athlete partly to her attire: "One of my favorite nights was WrestleMania 39 versus Charlotte Flair. I was so damn nervous—I had a million things going through my head. I remember pushing through a crowd of people in gorilla and as soon as my music hit, I just threw everything in the air and went," Bennett recalled. When she stepped onstage, Rhea Ripley took over and crushed what would be remembered as the best match of 2023: "Stepping out in front of the crowd, I was instantly in the zone. It's this weird inner human thing for me that just unblocks where I'm shaking behind the curtains and then become a menace as soon as I see the first fan. I was wearing [husband and AEW wrestler Buddy Matthews] Matt's cloak that he wears with House of Black and had drips painted on my face as makeup that Matt and Priest had both done before. I was channeling all these different parts of my life in that moment. The only thing that could've made that night better was Motionless in White singing me out, which was one of the best experiences of my life when they sung me out the *next* year at WrestleMania 40."

Music has inspired many of Bennett's looks over the years: "When I first started working with [designer] Wicked Lester, she really just made rock-and-roll outfits for my favorite bands. The first gear I got from her was for SummerSlam, and I just bought something online, which wasn't customized or made for my body. Now I just ask, 'Can we use this as inspiration?' or 'I'm looking to tell this story,' and she knows exactly how to make it for me. The same goes for my jacket maker, Saints of The Undead. Music feeds my life, and I grew up idolizing a lot of bands, such as Black Veil Brides, Motionless in White, and Of Mice & Men. I'm now working with the same designer and wearing pretty much identically what Chris from Motionless in White is wearing. We have the same facial structure, and both wear purple eye makeup. Somehow, I have morphed into Chris Motionless."

Despite her rocky start, Bennett continues to confidently lead the charge of her own life. Her story is one to admire. "I honestly don't know how we got here, but I somehow became so many things all at once. I became someone that some think looks like a man, a brute, an eradicator, a sex symbol, and myself all in one. I go out there and am unapologetically me. As women, we get told so often what we should look like, what clothes to wear, how we should style our hair, act, and address ourselves, and none of that really matters. I don't like living under a false mold of what an insecure male thinks I should look like. Seeing people get confidence from the little things that I helped inspire them to do is awesome."

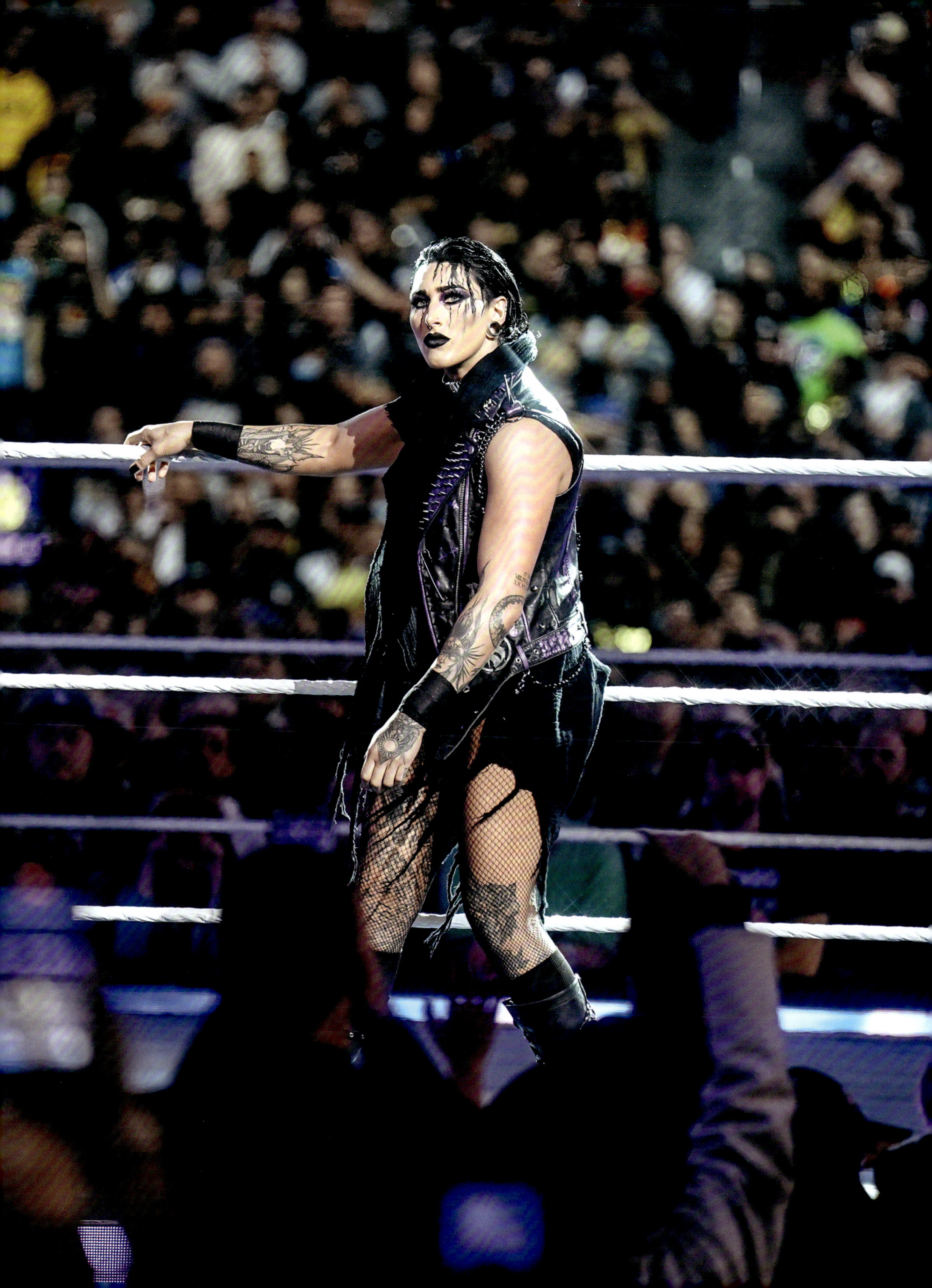

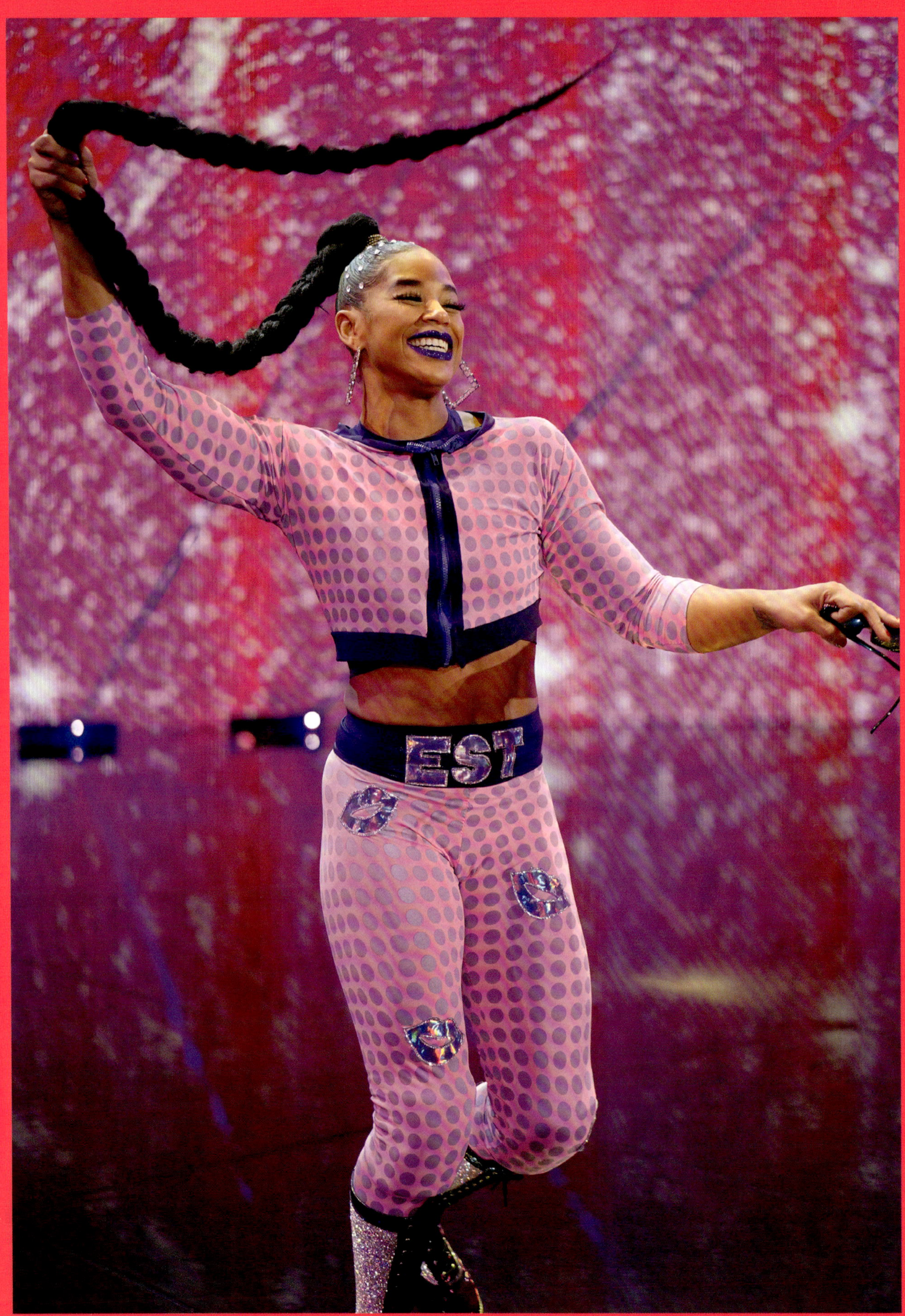

# BIANCA BLAIR
## WWE'S BIANCA BELAIR

Active 2016–present

Three-Time WWE Women's World Champion

**Bianca Blair isn't** just the fastest, the strongest, the quickest, the roughest, and the toughest competitor—she's also the boldest. Along with her impressive accolades, Blair—or Bianca Belair, as she's called in the ring—is known for her sparkling attire, which is often bedazzled in rhinestones and other glittering accents and highlighted by bright-red lips. The fashionable fighter credits her larger-than-life looks to her roots. "My grandmother was someone who always wore cheetah print, red lipstick, and she believed she should've been in Hollywood," said Blair. "So, growing up, I always pulled a lot from my grandmother because that's what a superstar means to me."

But Blair's style is about more than just making a statement; bold looks and flawless attire make her feel powerful, too. "When you look good, you feel good. I got that message from my mom and college coaches," said the wrestler, who's been running track and doing gymnastics since she was three years old: "My mom used to put me in track tournaments in my sparkly gymnastic leotards, and she would let me wear bright-red lipstick. My leotards always had rhinestones on them, and people would call me Little Flo-Jo. Today, I believe that Flo-Jo was the first sports fashionista because she was beautiful and unapologetically her. She wasn't just a beast on the track—she knew how to show up and show out. From childhood to running track at the University of South Carolina—where we were known as the Gamecock Divas—to WWE, I've carried that idea of 'look good, feel good' with me."

Bianca Belair at *Monday Night RAW* on November 22, 2021. Photo by Kimberly Morrell.

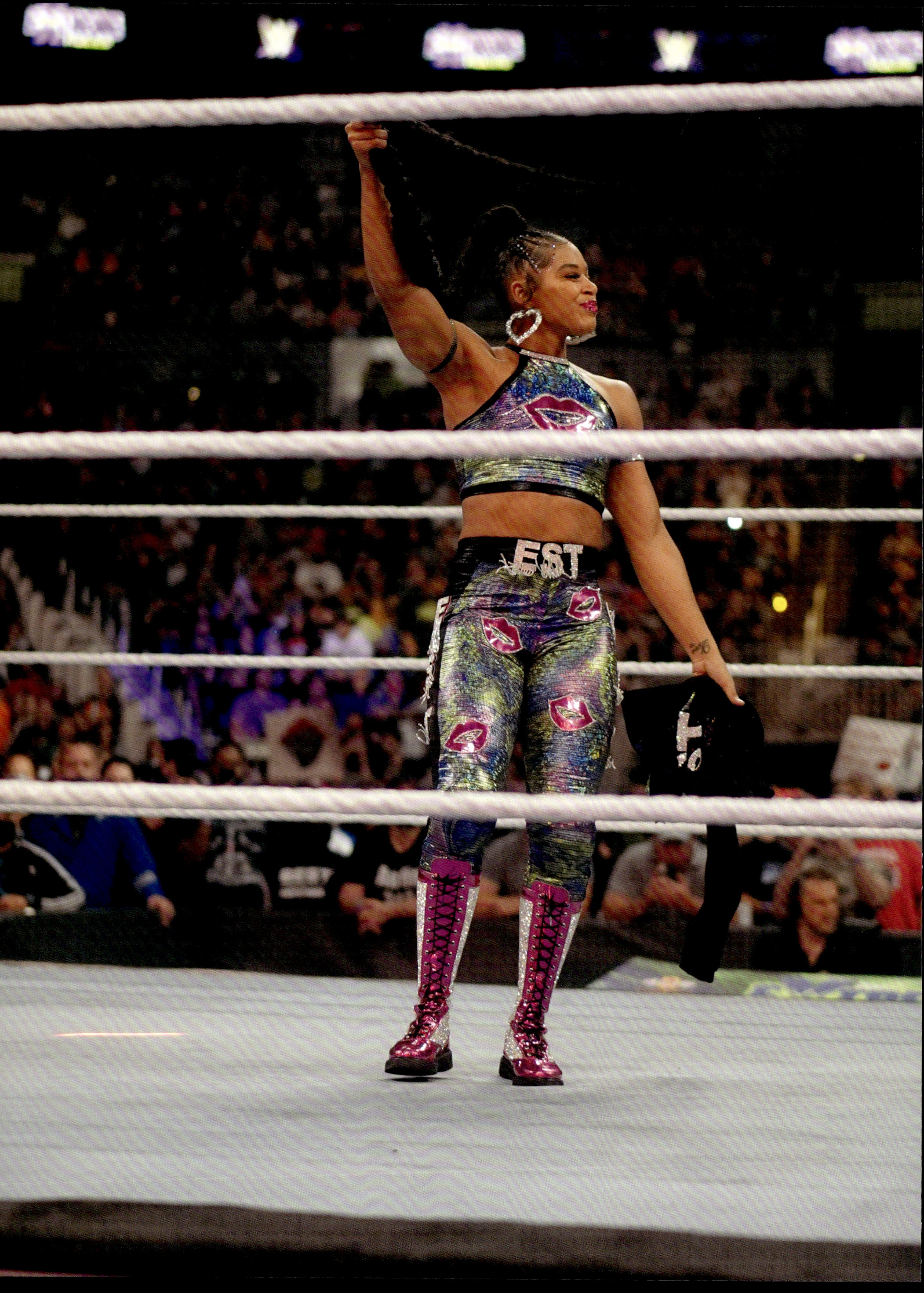

Blair's sense of style is so unique that she even sews her own garments. Learning to sew was difficult at first, but today she takes pride in creating her own gear. "When I first got into WWE, I recognized that everyone was getting their gear made from seamstresses. I'm very hands-on, a bit of a control freak, and with the creative process in my brain, it's hard for me to explain to people what I want. So, I decided to make my own," she said. "I made my first set of gear by hand, and I never actually ever wore it because it wasn't functional. Wrestling gear needs to be able to stretch, and I felt like it might split open. My husband bought me my first sewing machine, and I made another set. That gear is still sitting in my closet and has never been worn either. Maybe I'll revamp it and wear it to the ring one day."

Over the years, Blair has perfected her sewing ability—now fans eagerly wait to see what she's going to wear in the ring. For years, Blair's signature look included a sparkly two-piece ensemble of high-waisted tights with a matching crop top, topped off with glittery red lips: her hallmark symbol. The wrestler accentuated her look by wearing her hair in a long single braid that reached down past her knees. But it wasn't until WrestleMania 38 in 2022—by which point Blair had been in the WWE for six years—that the wrestler felt comfortable enough with her sewing to try a new design. "I have a design that I did for the whole time I was at NXT that I was very comfortable with because I don't use patterns," said Blair, referring to her trademark look, which she continued to replicate for years in NXT and beyond. "I was about a year and a half on the main roster, and I saw a fan post something online and there was this one design that I fell in love with. I originally thought, 'Maybe this will be the one set of gear that I have someone else make for me.' I put the idea in my back pocket, and then a year later I tried to make the look and completed it in two days. It's one of my favorite looks because I feel like it catapulted me in a different direction. Now, I will just put fabric on the floor and start cutting it up until it turns into something. That one gear broadened my horizons and creativity to try new things."



—Bianca Blair

Bianca Belair at WWE Extreme Rules in Columbus, Ohio, in 2021. Photo by Kimberly Morrell.

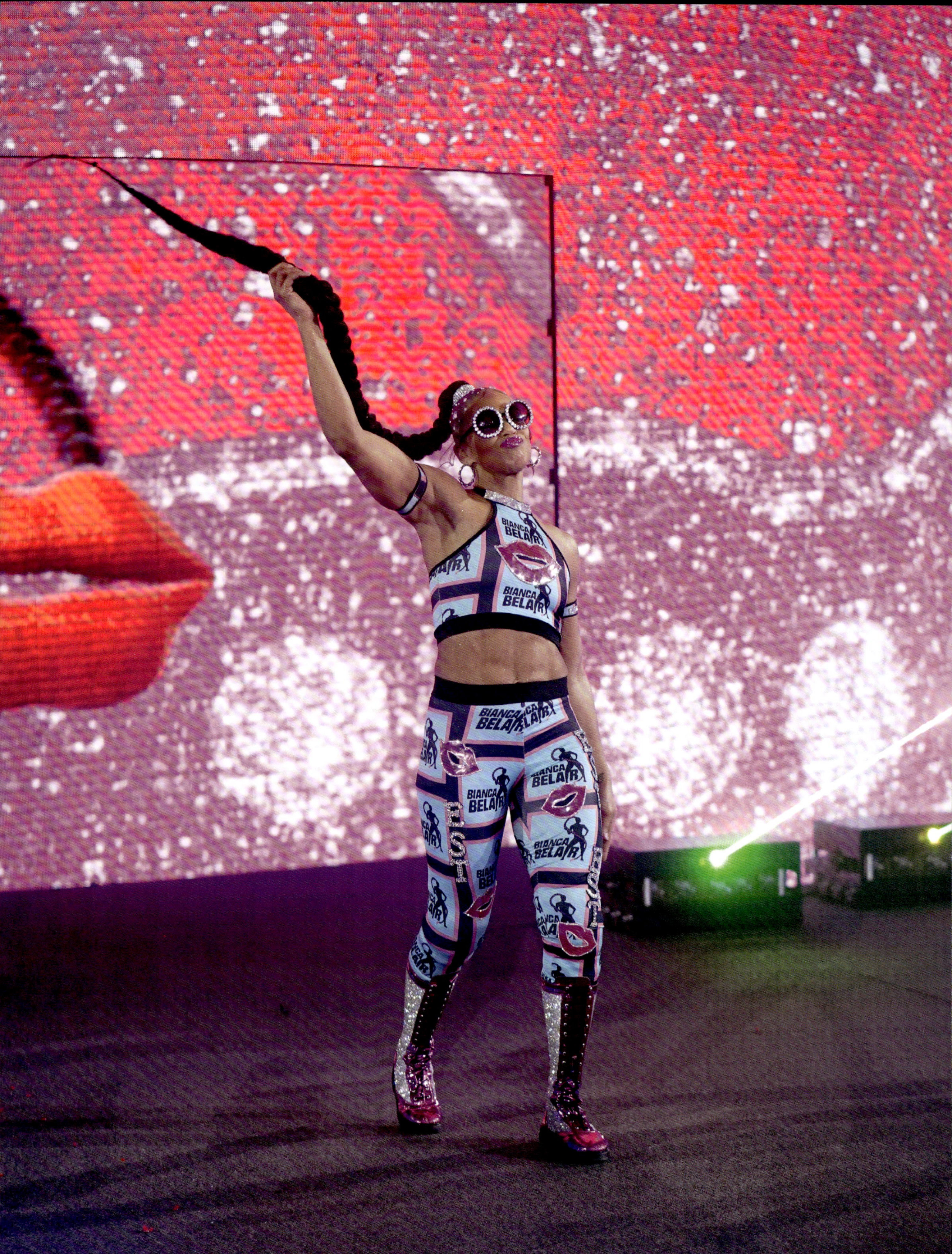

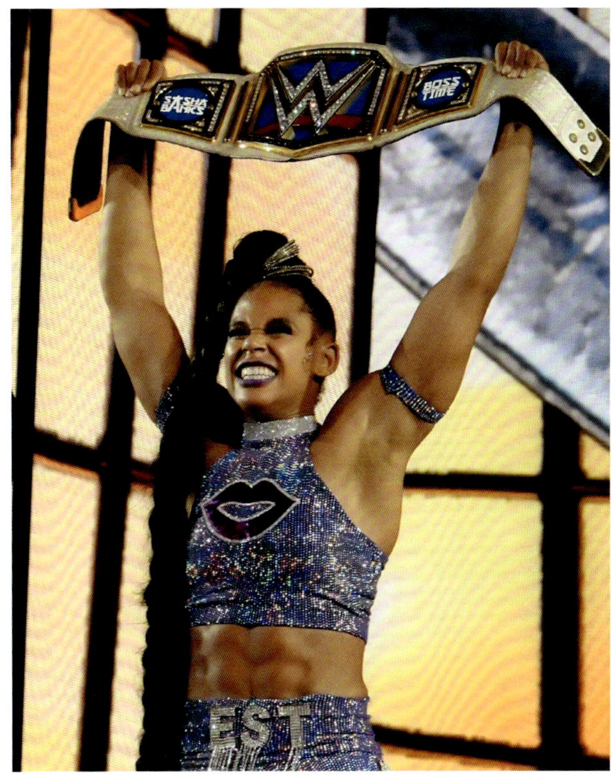

But though her sewing skills have progressed, crafting wresting gear isn't easy. "The gear process is very chaotic," said Blair, who works more quickly with a picture of the final look in front of her. "Sometimes all I have is a day or two before I go back out on the road, and if I don't finish it, I'll Instacart a sewing machine to the hotel. People have seen me backstage, on airplanes, or in the hotel sewing my gear. For WrestleMania [39] in Los Angeles, I actually didn't finish the look. [Fellow wrestler] Dakota Kai was in the locker room with me rhinestoning jewels onto the fabric. There's been times that I have gone out there with pins in my entrance jacket because I didn't have time to sew it. When that happens, the pins are poking me as I'm doing my entrance, but no one would know." Blair wore a shimmering purple crop top with matching leggings emblazoned with her name and signature lips to the historical match, where her bold look and confident style helped her become the SmackDown Women's Champion.

Despite years of making her own gear, Blair is still surprised by what resonates with fans: "I see fans all the time talk about their favorite look[s] of mine. Some of them surprise me. My gear from 2024 Elimination Chamber was maroon and gold, and many fans consider [it] a top gear. It blows my mind because that set of gear, I only had two days to make, and I actually forgot to order fabric that week. So I went into my closet and had to just pick something and make it work. I didn't put much thought into it. But a lot of the time, it's not about the design or how it looks—it's about the moment [in the ring]."

After nearly a decade in the ring, Blair remains proud of her singular style—because she never wants to be compared to anyone else. "I wouldn't say there's anybody in wrestling that influences me when it comes to gear," said the multifaceted wrestler. "I say that because I want to be Bianca Belair. The best way to stand out is see what everybody else is doing and go the complete opposite way." We will all be watching with excitement as she shines.

OPPOSITE: Bianca Belair at WWE Royal Rumble in St. Louis, Missouri, in 2022. Photo by Kimberly Morrell.

RIGHT: Bianca Belair becomes the new WWE SmackDown Women's Champion at WrestleMania 37 in Tampa, Florida. Photo by Kimberly Morrell.

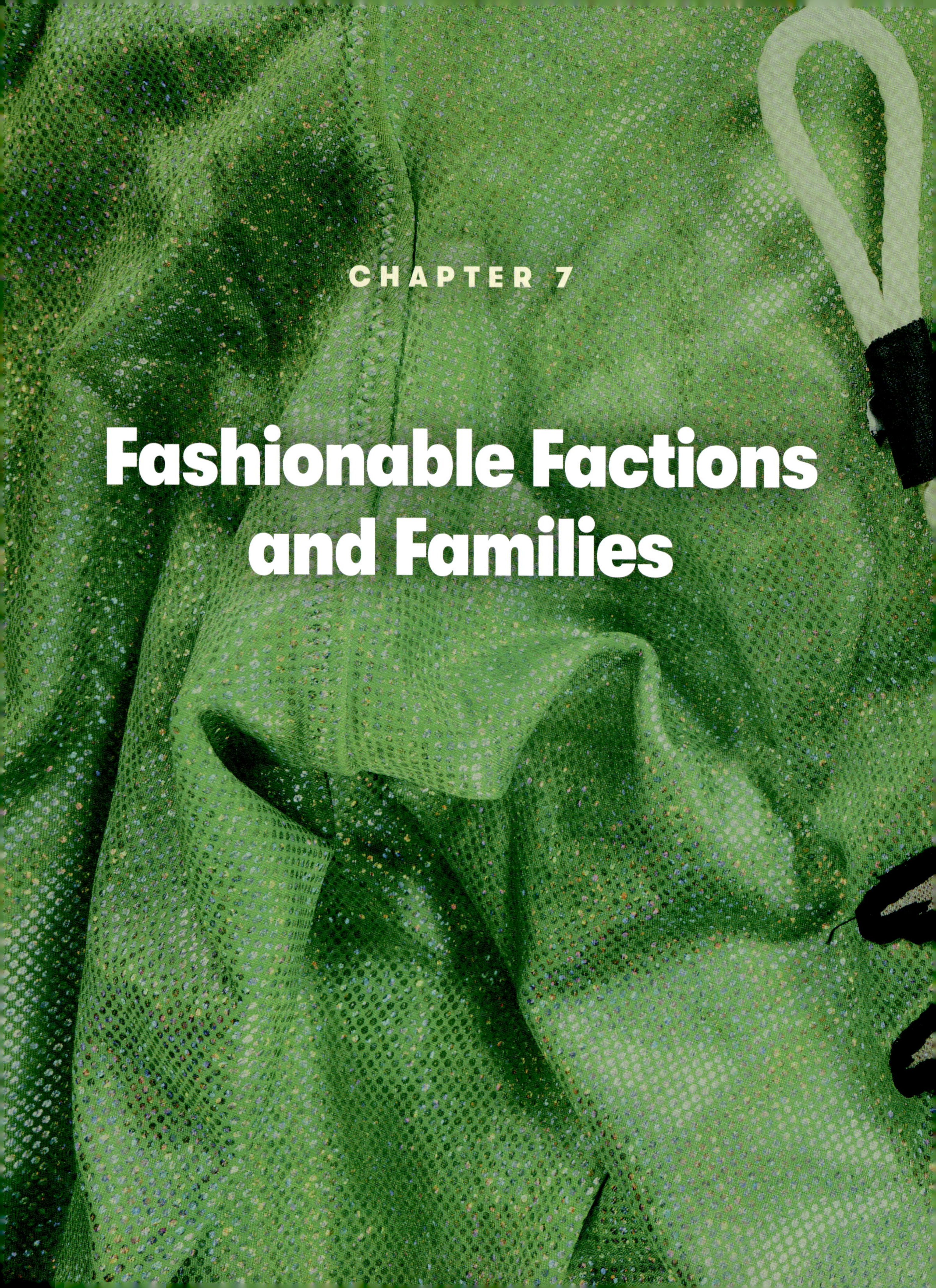


# Fashionable Factions and Families

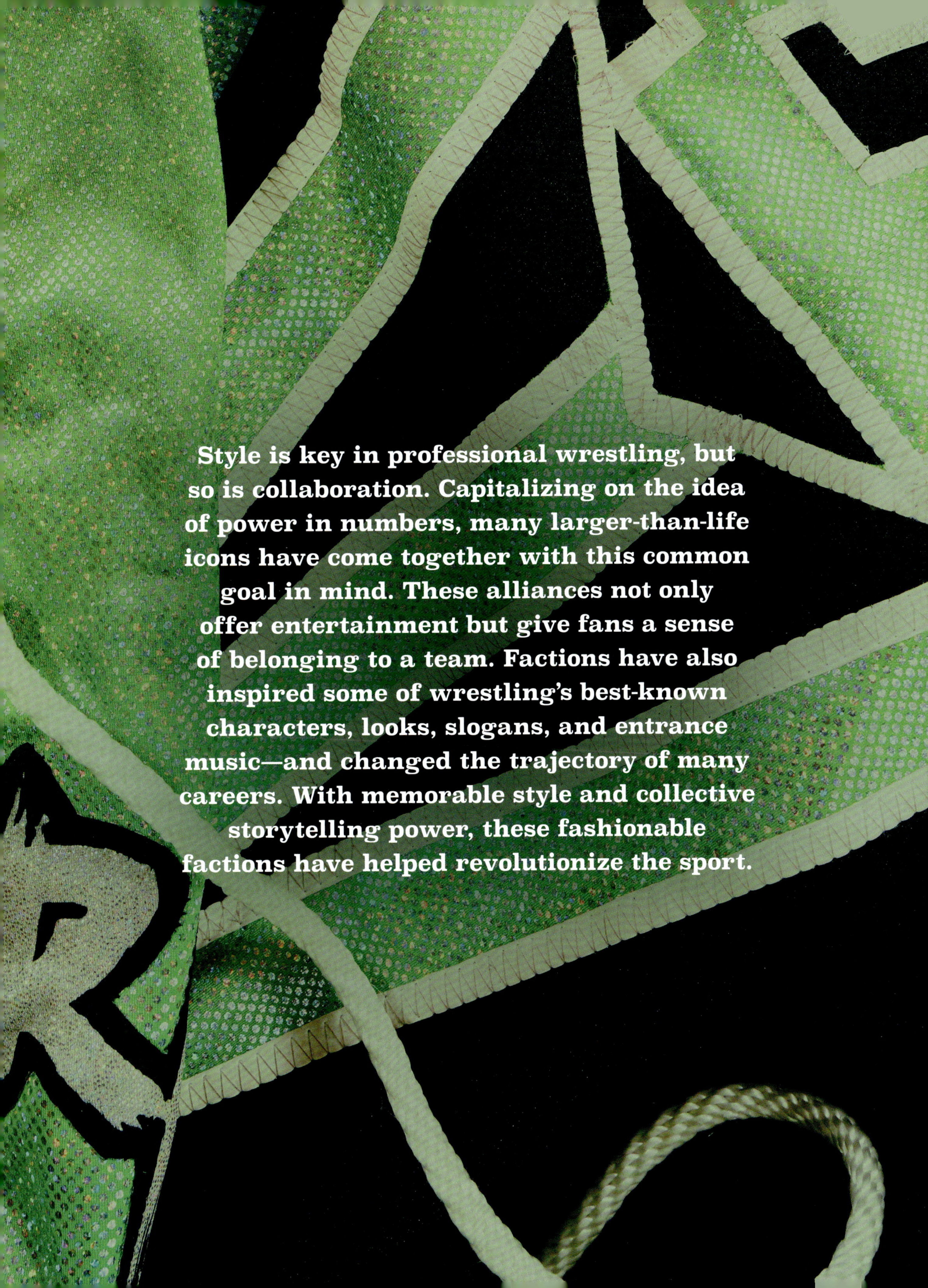

Style is key in professional wrestling, but so is collaboration. Capitalizing on the idea of power in numbers, many larger-than-life icons have come together with this common goal in mind. These alliances not only offer entertainment but give fans a sense of belonging to a team. Factions have also inspired some of wrestling's best-known characters, looks, slogans, and entrance music—and changed the trajectory of many careers. With memorable style and collective storytelling power, these fashionable factions have helped revolutionize the sport.

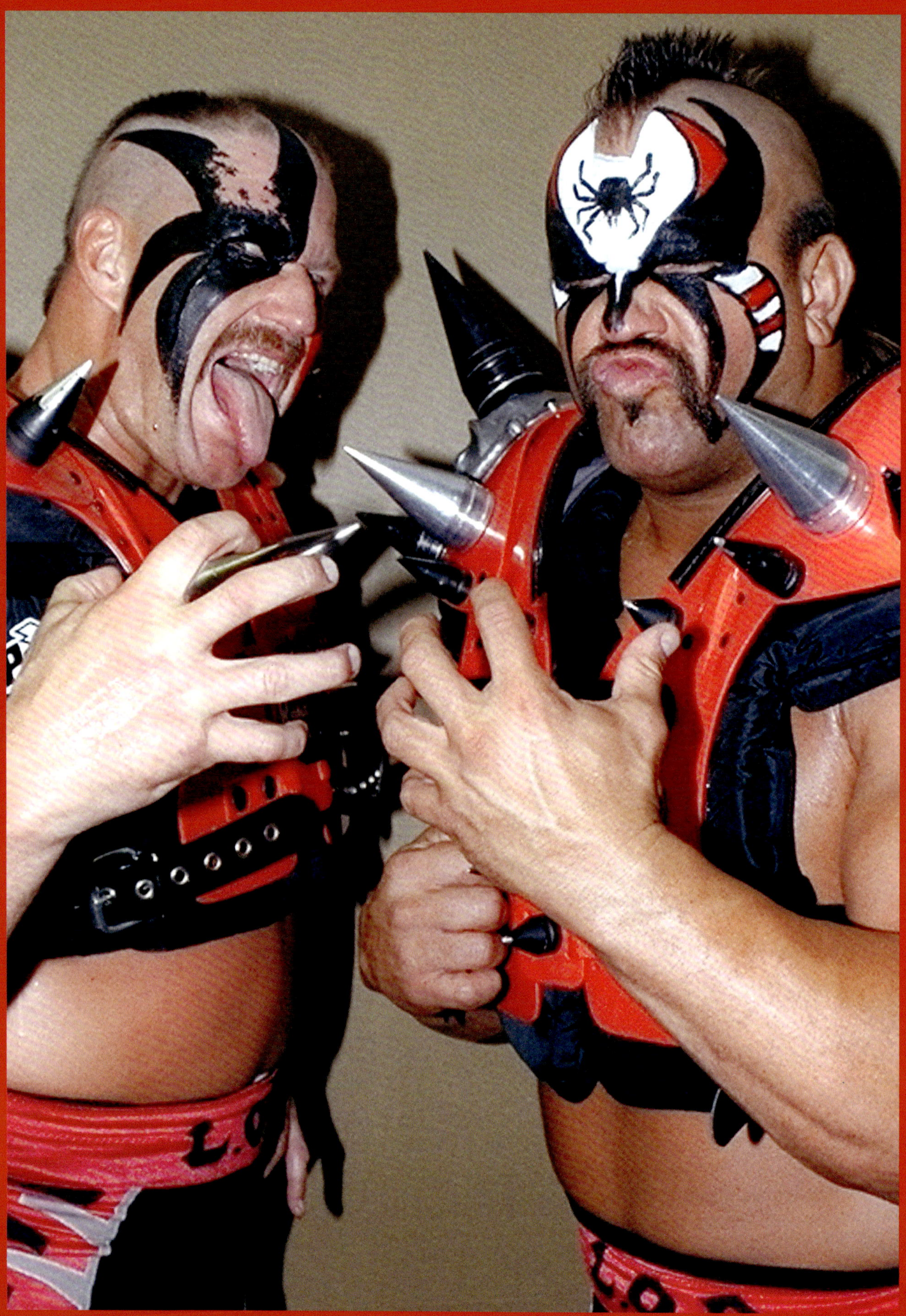

# ROAD WARRIORS
## A.K.A. *WWE'S LEGION OF DOOM*

Active 1983–2003

Only Tag Team to Win Championships in AWA, NWA, and WWE
WWE Hall of Famers

**A spectacle to behold,** the Road Warriors were designed differently. Also known as WWE's Legion of Doom, Animal and Hawk were intense, bold, and intimidating with their large statures and untouchable appeal. Arriving on the scene battle-ready, they sported footballer shoulder pads with massive, daunting spikes—opponents knew not to get too close. Most of the time, they wore red, yellow, and black, these colors playing a part in their distinctly bold impression. Before the Road Warriors ever hit the ring, the mere visual of the duo foreshadowed what an audience would soon witness: a combat-style fight. Because of their legitimacy and raw nature, they're one of the most accomplished tag teams of all time.

Terry Taylor, who wrestled as The Red Rooster in the '80s, remembers the fear Animal and Hawk inspired in their opponents: "We knew we were wrestling the Road Warriors, but back then, we were on one side of the building and they're on the other side, so there's no communication prior. The Road Warriors come out and they're head and shoulders taller than everybody in the arena. Brad [Armstrong] and I are in the ring and we're looking at them going, 'Holy crap, we're wrestling that?!' Brad goes, 'Who's gonna start?' I'm already on the outside with my hand on the tag rope. And I go, 'I guess you are!'"

Hawk and Animal before a match.
Photo by George Napolitano.

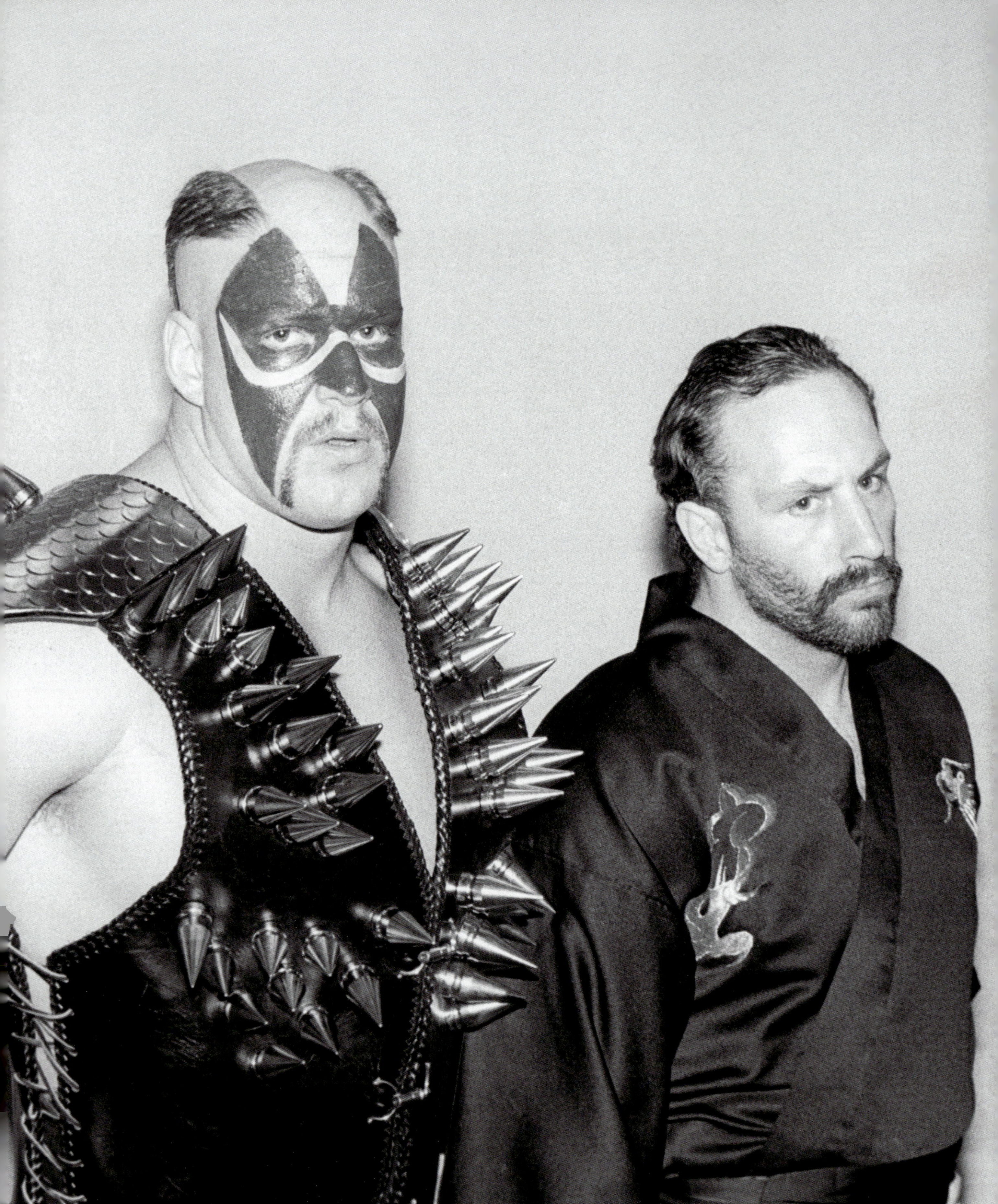

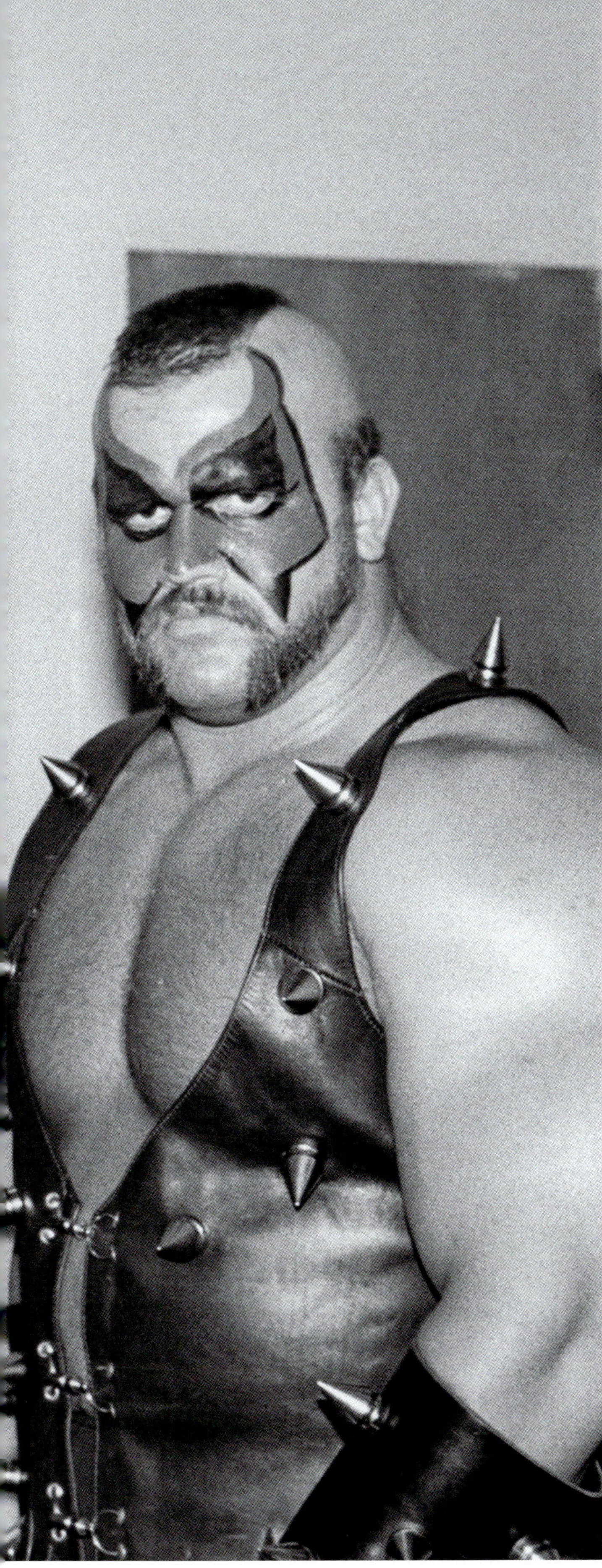

Legion of Doom also enhanced its punishing persona with face paint. Both Animal and Hawk wore intricate designs that told their story collectively and individually. Hawk's typical face paint incorporated one of two looks: either a bird's eyes, beak, or wings, or an inverted red triangle covering one eye. "Hawk started experimenting with two different looks," Animal wrote in his memoir, *The Road Warriors: Danger, Death, and the Rush of Wrestling*. "The first was what he called the joker, which was a giant upside-down red triangle under his left eye and then a giant spiral of black completely covering his right eye. Sometimes he played around with the colors and the spiral part would be blue or something, but the joker look became the design Hawk would be most recognized for over the years." Animal, meanwhile, usually painted a menacing spider on his face. No matter the look, they played up their face paint with snarls and wide eyes that made them seem almost feral to their opponents. As the Road Warriors, Animal and Hawk left an unshakable legacy. With symbolic gear and collective storytelling, they paved the way for other factions to succeed today.

Hawk (left), manager Paul Ellering, and Animal (right) pose backstage before a match. Photo by Bob Mulrenin.

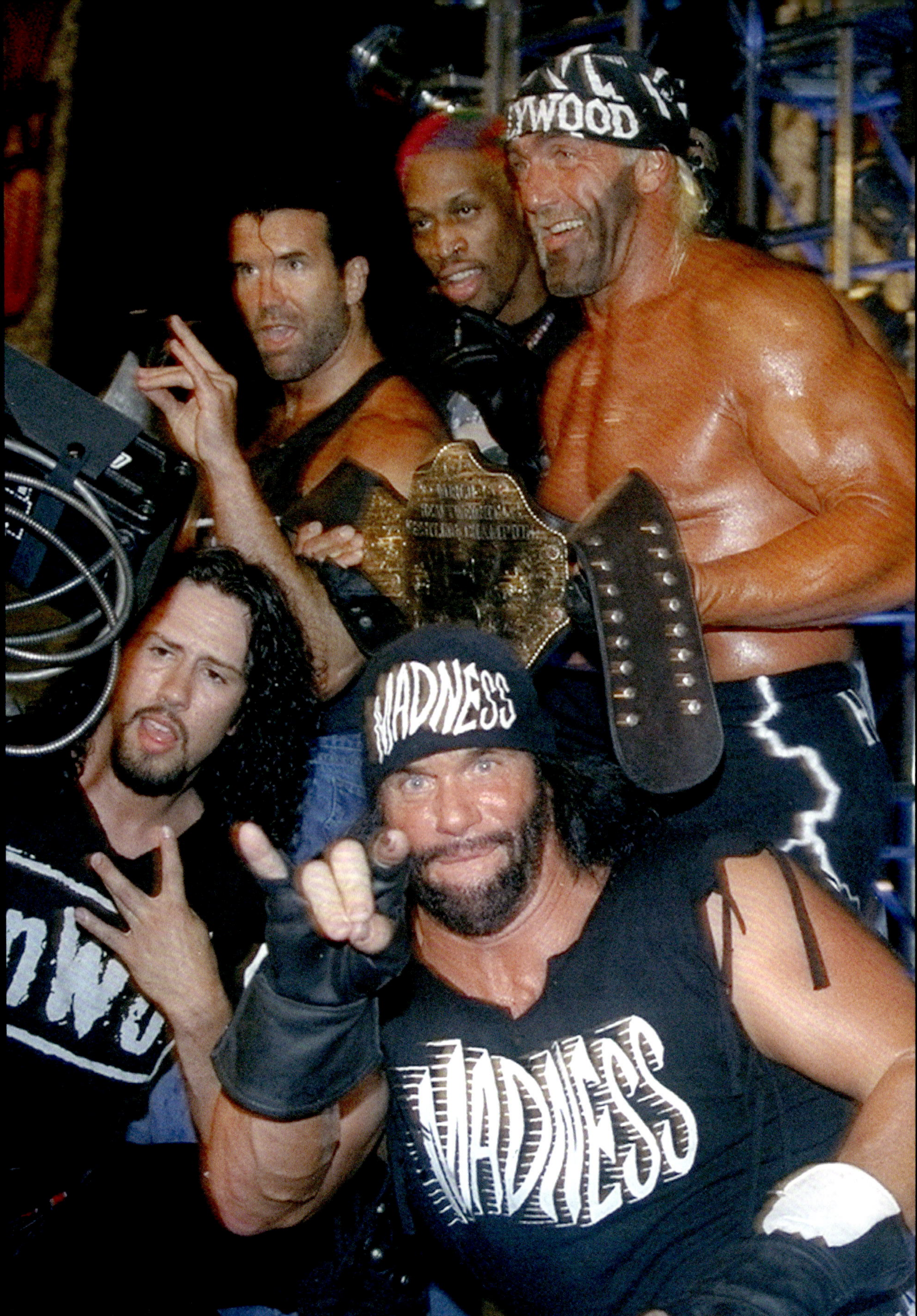
HOLLYWOOD
MADNESS
MADNESS

# WWE'S nWo (NEW WORLD ORDER)

Active 1996–2002

WWE Hall of Famers

**Professional wrestling changed forever** on July 7, 1996, when New World Order came together. Founded by wrestlers Hulk Hogan, Scott Hall, and Kevin Nash, the revolutionary faction made waves with its boisterous biker-gang style. Over the years, nWo featured a rotating cast of greats—from Ted DiBiase and Konnan to "Macho Man" Randy Savage and Dennis Rodman—but this original trio set the tone for what nWo would become. With his ripped T-shirts, bandanas, and spray-painted beard, Hulk Hogan established a villainous, trash-talking flair. Scott Hall brought the swagger in sleeveless vests and leather pants. Kevin Nash—the big guy—flaunted his muscles in tank tops and fingerless gloves.

Much of nWo's appeal lay in its realism, with edgy, minimalist style that incorporated everyday clothes regular people were wearing. "We wore a T-shirt, blue jeans, and high-tech boots, which were all the rage in the early '90s," said Sean Waltman, who joined nWo shortly after its formation in 1996. Soon fans were racing to buy the group's iconic look, leading to one of the most sold items on the market: a simple black T-shirt with nWo's logo stamped in bold white letters. "It was so different back then because wrestling shirts were just a picture of a guy, [but] the nWo T-shirt looked like something you could wear anywhere," said Waltman. "That logo is about as iconic as you can get." Of course, it didn't hurt that the T-shirts were worn by megastars who could pull off just about any look. According to Waltman: "I'm not saying we would have made anything [look] cool, but it was the personalities that made that cool."

nWo at WCW Nitro in Chicago, Illinois, at the United Center on June 16, 1997. Photo by George Napolitano.

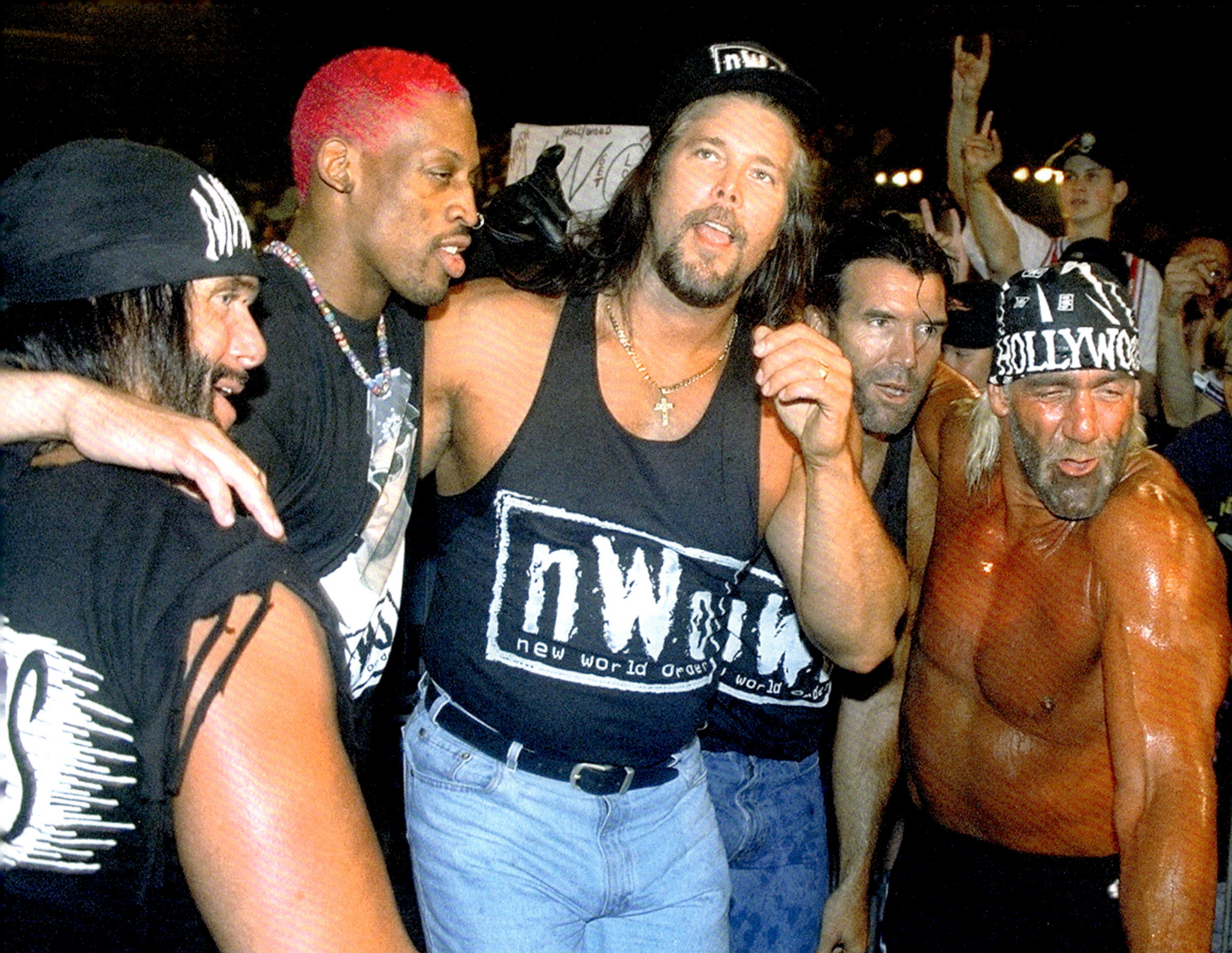



ABOVE: nWo at WCW Nitro in Chicago, Illinois, at the United Center on June 16, 1997. Photo by George Napolitano.

OPPOSITE: From left to right, Kevin Nash (back), Shawn Waltman as Syxx (front), Eric Bishoff, Scott Hall (back), and Big Show at WCW Nitro in Salisbury, Maryland, on November 25, 1996.

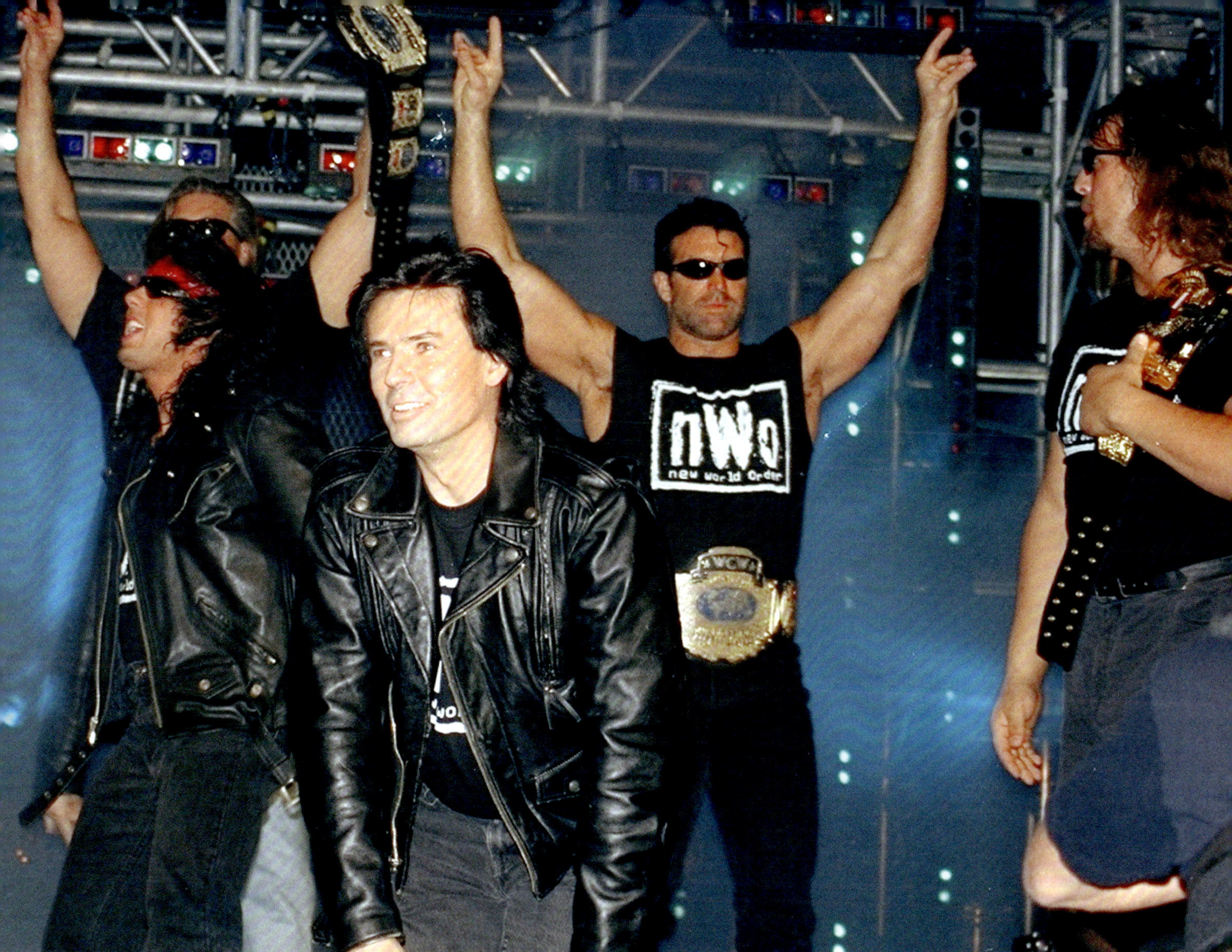

By incorporating streetwear into their act, nWo debunked the idea that wrestlers had to wear elaborate gear in the ring. Instead, the group fused elements from their everyday lives with cultural influences to create a look with widespread appeal. Some members—including Waltman and Hall, who donned Harley-Davidson jackets in the ring—were wearing their actual clothes. Other nWo looks were inspired by popular music at the time. "We took a lot from hip-hop," said Waltman, remembering how nWo was influenced by Ice Cube and Westside Connection. "If you listen to Westside Connection's album and go back and watch nWo, you can see where we got it from."

Decades later, nWo remains one of the most influential factions in wrestling history.

Not only did the group feature some of the sport's biggest stars, the "gang" also helped pave the way for new wrestling factions, including D-Generation X. "There's a big difference between the two groups but there's also a lot in common," said Waltman, one of the only wrestlers to belong to both groups: "nWo was like a street gang in the way we operated. In the DX that I came into, we were just happy dudes who liked to fight. I wouldn't say we were college frat boys, because mostly none of us went to college, but it was just different energy because we were having a lot of fun. Both were reality based with no bull- shit cartoon gimmicks, right? I wouldn't say we broke the fourth wall necessarily, but both [nWo and D-Generation X] felt bigger than everything else."

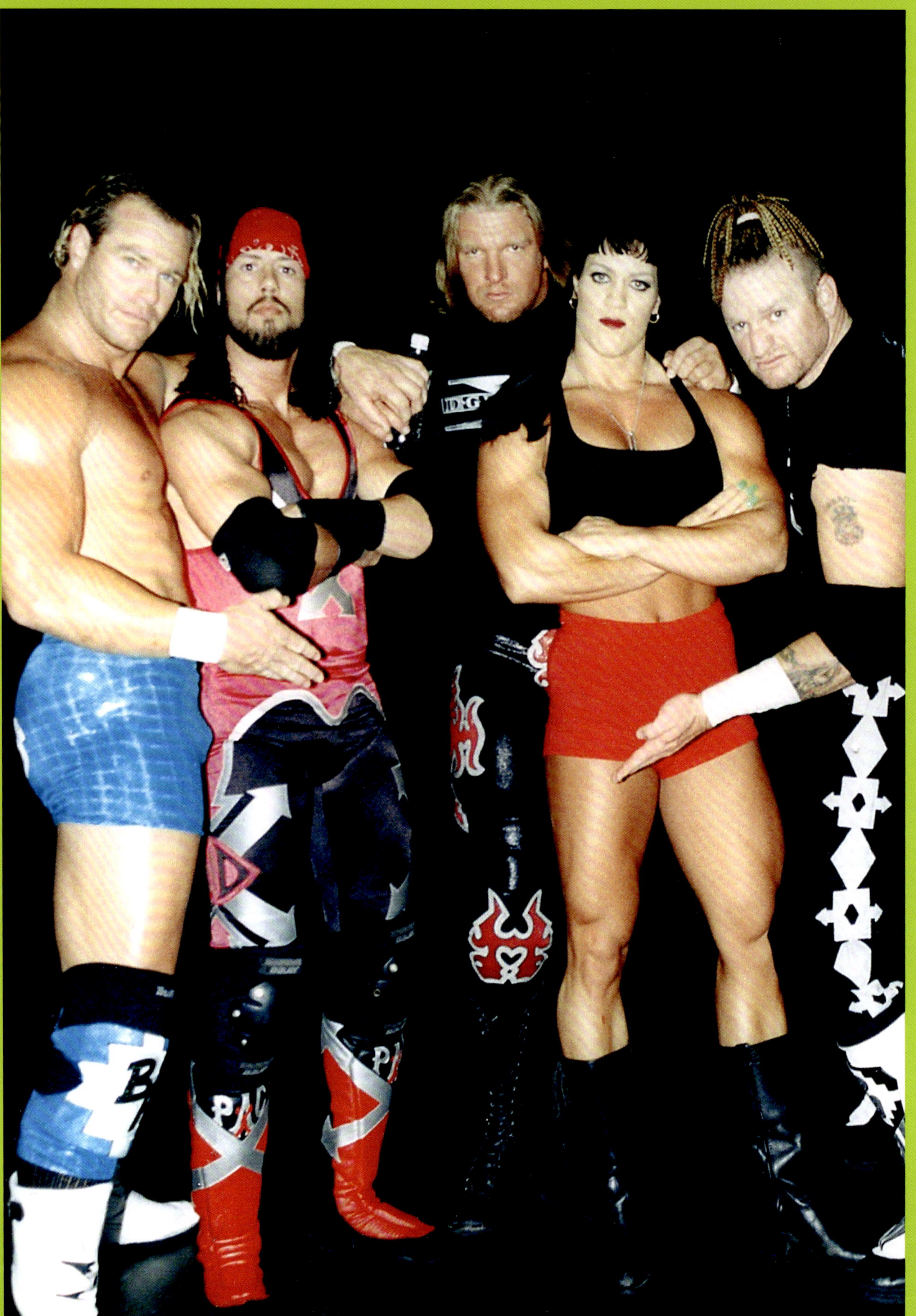

# WWE'S D-GENERATION X

Active 1997–2000

WWE Hall of Famers

**Just a year** after nWo burst onto the scene, another legendary faction began to take shape. Founded by Shawn Michaels, Triple H, Rick Rude, and Chyna, this rowdy faction of rule breakers embodied the rebellious style of a younger generation—and fans couldn't get enough. These younger wrestlers also brought Gen X sensibilities to the ring. This included a grungier, more defiant style incorporating streetwear, bandanas, sunglasses, and lots of neon green. "From a DX standpoint, the colors just kind of worked and we knew it," said Michaels of what would become DX's iconic look: black-and-green T-shirts stamped with their signature graffiti logo. "Believe it or not, the neon green was working for other people at the time, too, but with DX, the colors, the design, [and] the logo were new and innovative."

But even as DX epitomized the height of the '90s, members found ways to declare their own style. Triple H often wore leather jackets, demonstrating his grit as the group's backbone. Michaels wore mesh tops and chaps that signaled his bad-boy mentality. Chyna, the muscle of the group, dressed in black to reinforce her don't-mess-with-me attitude. Billy Gunn and Road Dogg—who joined DX in 1998—wore jean shorts and graphic tees to channel '90s youth culture. Sean Waltman—who also joined in 1998—leaned into baggier clothes with alternative skater style.

Each week, DX entertained fans with raunchy jokes and cutting-edge catchphrases. Their signature crotch chops riled up the crowds. Fans roared with delight when DX told their opponents to "suck it." "It was us just turned loose," said Gunn. "We wanted to be as off the charts as we could and see what we could get away with." Fans appreciated the group's unscripted dynamic, which felt fresh and authentic. "Oftentimes they would point a camera at us and say, 'Go,'" said Waltman. "There was no writing involved. Sometimes they would be five minutes short for the television show, and we just went out and shot the shit with the crowd. That's what helped and made people love us."

The group's rowdy style also mirrored society, which—in those early days of reality TV—was becoming more provocative. "We felt that with the birth of WCW and the Monday Night Wars, we were able to bring a lot of that to television," said Michaels. "It felt incredibly innovative in wrestling but even in society as a whole.

From left to right, Billy Gunn, X-Pac, Triple H, Chyna, and Road Dogg backstage in 1998 as D-Generation X. Photo by George Napolitano.

We wanted to be reality television before reality television was kind of the fad. At that time, the Jerry Springer, Maury Povich, and Jenny Jones shows were what we saw on television, where people are throwing chairs at each other. It was kind of a raunchy time, so to speak, in history. All of those things came at the right time and just clicked for DX."

Even back then, members knew they were blurring the lines between sports and entertainment. "We understood we were on a wrestling show, but we weren't wrestling, we were entertaining," said Gunn. "We would think, 'What's too far?'" This penchant for pushing the envelope led to the group's camaraderie. "Shawn and Hunter [Triple H] did it at first, and then it just evolved into something seen everywhere you would go," said Gunn. "From football fields to basketball courts, there was no place that somebody wasn't doing the Suck It." In those early days of the Attitude Era, fans appreciated DX's boundary-pushing persona—and couldn't wait to see what they'd do next. "The best thing about this era and when we were doing it was that nobody ever said, 'Turn it down,'" said Gunn. "It was always 'How much can you turn it up,' right? So that opened the door for a lot of fun."

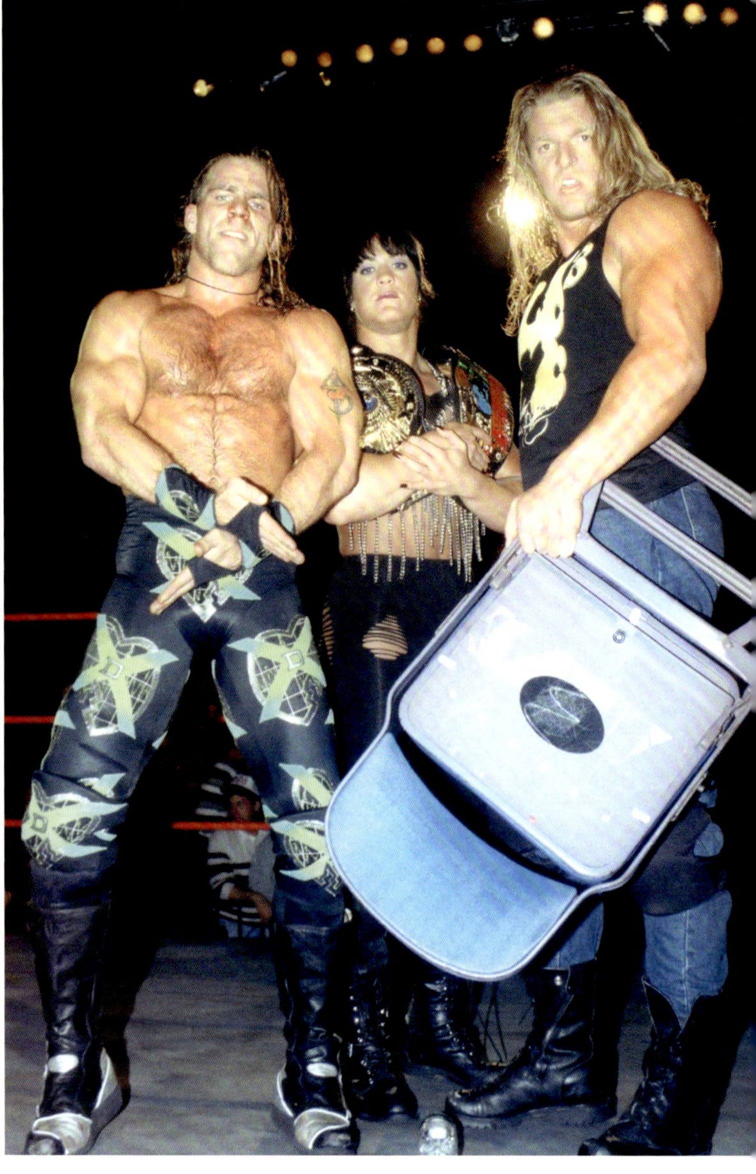

One shocking moment took place in 1998, when DX donned military gear and rode a tank to "invade" *WCW Monday Nitro.* Wearing combat boots, camouflage pants, war paint, and hard hats, DX did what they did best: brought the entertainment and drama in a never-seen-before way. Long before cross-promotions and forbidden doors became the norm, DX literally stormed the competition, changing the game. "That whole day, we knew we were doing something huge," said Waltman. "When we showed up on TV in the camo and army gear, we knew we had won the war. It was one of the biggest things in wrestling, and it's just amazing to be a part of that kind of show."

Decades later, D-Generation X still evokes a feeling of pride and nostalgia—because rebellion never goes out of style. "It puts a smile on my face because, let's face it, there's not very many people in this business that will have something that [everlasting]," said Gunn. "It's cool to point at your crotch and tell everybody to suck it no matter what generation we're in. It's very flattering and humbling knowing that we have done something that will never go away. DX just happens to be one of those things in wrestling that will stick forever, and I'm a part of that. People still come up and go, 'Hey, do they still call you Mr. Ass?' And I go, 'Yes. Yes, they do.' It's something I'll never get rid of, not that I would ever want to."

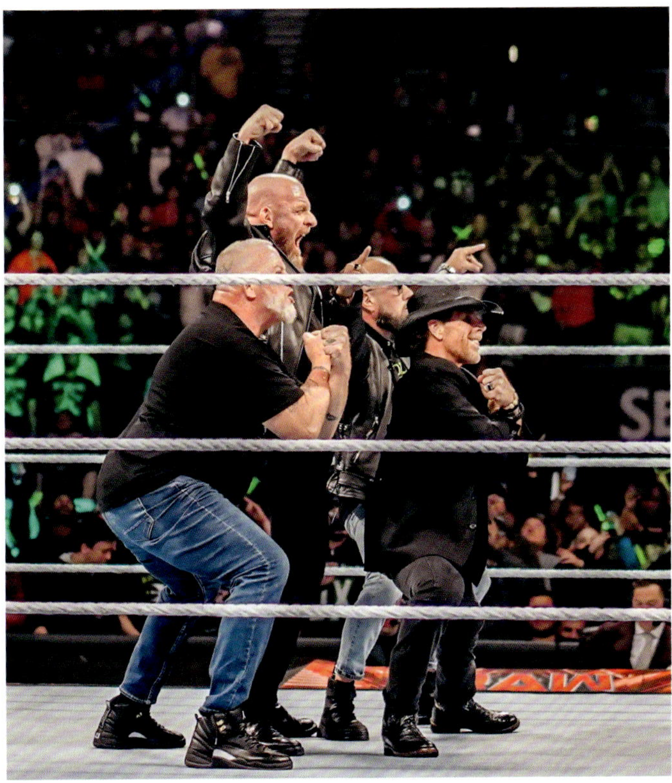

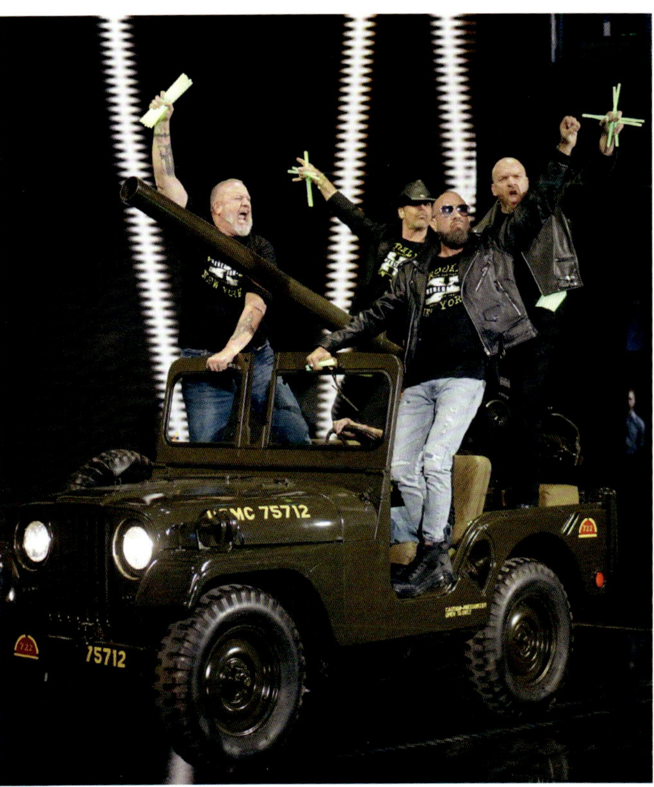

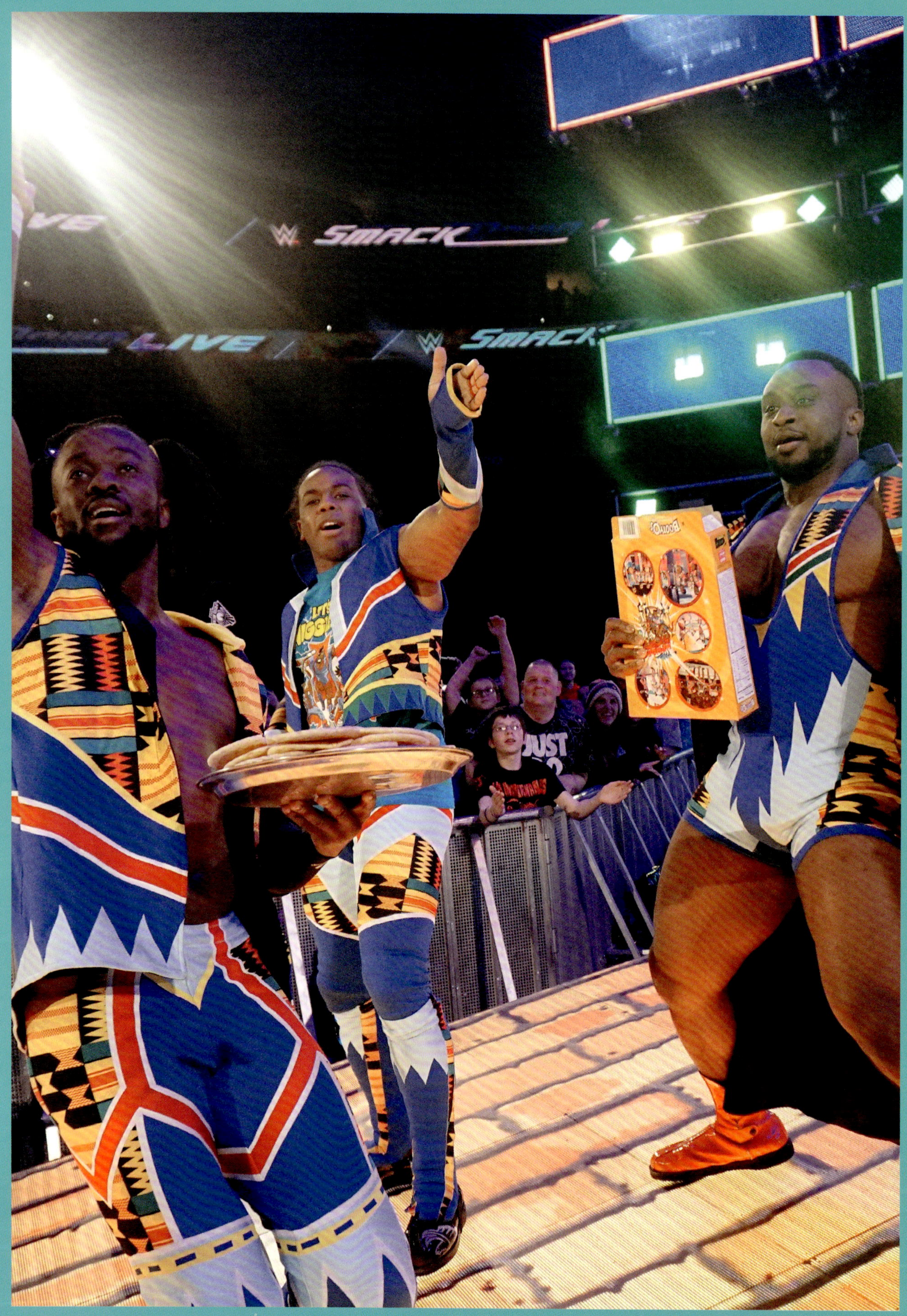

# WWE'S THE NEW DAY

Active 2014-present

Thirteen-Time WWE Tag Team Champions

**It's true, WWE's The New Day** does rock! Founded by WWE Superstars Kofi Kingston, Xavier Woods, and Big E, wrestling's most positive faction is known for its incredible skill, encouraging spirit, and ability to make just about anyone smile. This uplifting effect stems from The New Day's cheerful attire, which incorporates neon colors, playful patterns, and unicorns, comics, and other whimsical motifs to immerse the audience in a story-book wonderland. They've even been known to use trombones as accessories and invoke nostalgia through cereal box–inspired themes. By rewriting the rules of what wrestling gear can look like, The New Day wants fans to feel joy in their presence. Austin Watson, a.k.a. WWE Superstar Xavier Woods, explains how The New Day's gear relates to their work: "The visual aspect of storytelling is an extremely useful tool. We use our senses to interact with the world around us. They help us interpret a situation. We decide how we feel towards the thing being presented. So being able to use imagery to help tell a story gives just another rock for people to climb to as they scale the mountain that is our story. Using different colors or patterns to evoke certain emotions can help give context to a situation. This can help connect the dots for people, and that allows them to fall even deeper into our stories."

But The New Day's lighthearted looks also carry a double meaning, either by high-lighting a theme or supporting a greater goal. "I always aim to have wrestling gear that provides some kind of insight into my person-ality or motivation as a character," said Ettore Ewen, a.k.a. WWE Superstar Big E. "We have demonstrated our love for video games, anime, and nerd culture through our entrance gear and in-ring attire, but we've also used our gear as opportunities to champion causes like Feeding America."

From left to right, Kofi Kingston, Xavier Woods, and Big E at WWE Smackdown Live in 2018. Photo by Kimberly Morrell.

"I believe the only limits that we have are the ones that [we] put on ourselves. Just because someone hasn't done something before doesn't mean that it can't be done. My favorite wrestler as a kid was Flash Funk [2 Cold Scorpio]. He would come out and dance, and then when the bell rang he was incredible. Since seeing him, I've chased that same feeling of being able to mix fun and serious together. I think the secret is that if you're gonna do it, then you better be damn good at both."

—WWE Superstar Xavier Woods

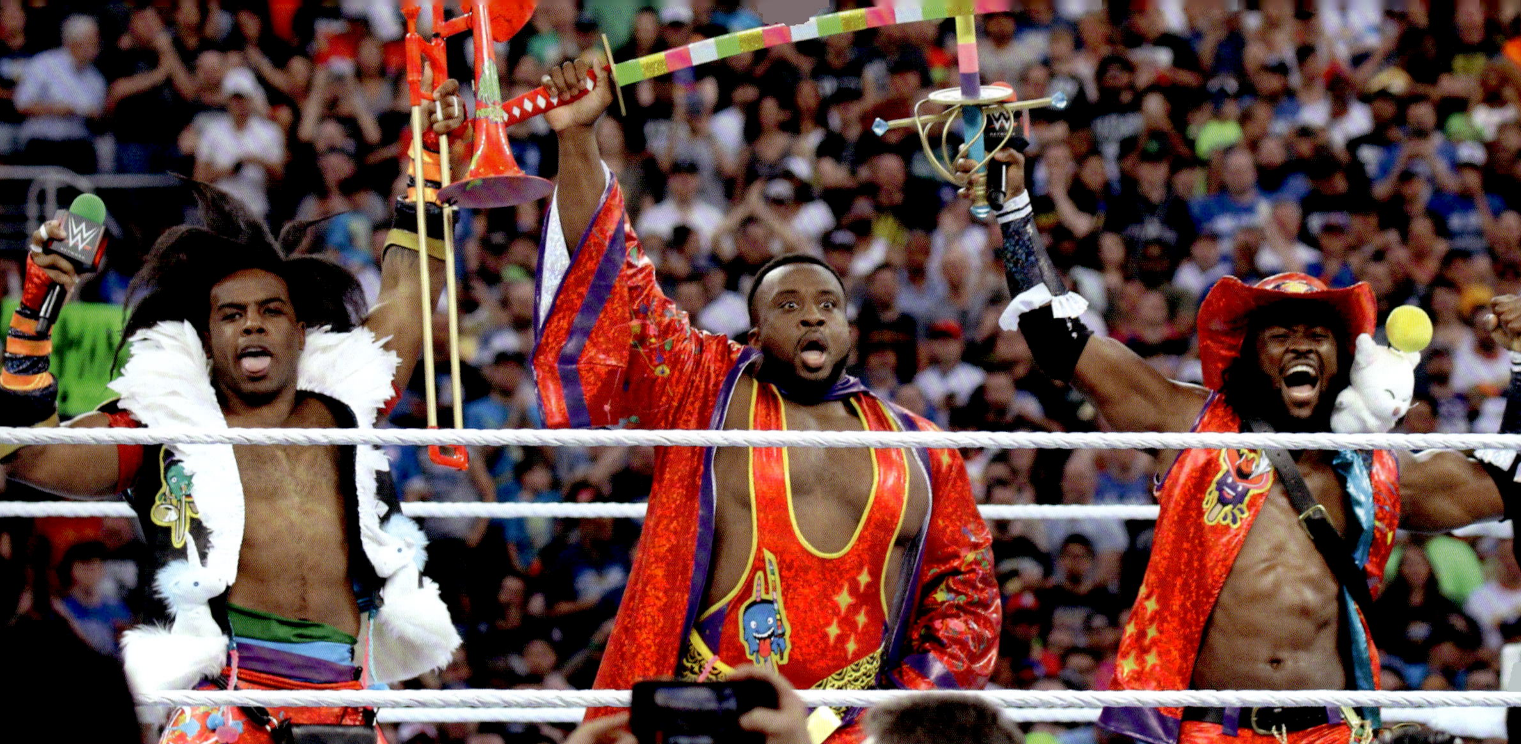

This layered storytelling approach is shared among the group—in fact, it's a point of pride among members. "When it comes to gear, we take utmost pride in the presentation aspect on several levels," said Kofi Nahaje Sarkodie-Mensah, a.k.a. WWE Superstar Kofi Kingston. "Even before joining New Day, I always infused my gear with my favorite comic-book characters, movies, or sports teams. When I met [Xavier] Woods, I quickly realized he was of the same mindset, but he was much more particular with the quality and details. The key for us [is] to always stay true to the theme while having a meaning behind wearing said theme."

The New Day showcased their distinctive style at SummerSlam 2017, where the faction wore Red Lantern–themed gear in a match against their archrivals, The Usos. "When we wore Red Lantern gear to face The Usos, it was because DC Comics' Red Lantern Corps represents rage in the comic books," said Kingston. "We were at a rage-filled stage in our rivalry. As silly as it seems a lot of the times, almost everything we do from a wrestling gear perspective has a specific reason behind it."

The New Day donned another memorable look for WrestleMania 35, where Kingston was vying for a long-overdue championship run. "One of my favorite experiences was designing gear for WrestleMania 35," said Ewen. "It was the year of Kofimania," the wrestler recalled, describing the overwhelming support for his teammate. "Kofi Kingston, my close friend and tag team partner of many years, was finally getting his well-deserved opportunity at the WWE Championship. We were brainstorming early 2019, and I really connected with the idea of Kofi being the uncrowned king. An extremely talented, hard-working superstar who had been passed over for opportunities like this time and time again." But Ewen wasn't thinking of just any old crown—he wanted a crown painted by Jean-Michel Basquiat, a contemporary of Andy Warhol who wasn't

**"We always wanted our looks to separate us from the rest of the pack. While others wore black and red to match their brooding, more serious characters, we wanted to introduce more pastels and brighter colors. As the group that espoused the Power of Positivity and proclaimed ourselves as the unicorns of pro wrestling (because we brought magic back to WWE), we wanted our gear to be bright, bold, and eye-snatching."**

–WWE Superstar Big E

truly appreciated by fans until after his death. "Basquiat had an unmistakable style and was known for his iconic paintings of crowns," said Ewen, who appreciated the parallels between the two stars. "We reached out to our friend and longtime gear maker, Johnny Davenport, and threw the idea his way. He perfectly encapsulated Basquiat's technique in our trio's wrestling gear for WrestleMania, and Kofi celebrated winning his first WWE World Championship in deeply meaningful wrestling gear."

But not all of The New Day's looks have landed with the audience at first. "It was a bumpy road to get onto television as a group," said Kingston, recalling an early look that fell flat with fans. "When we finally did, we were expected to play the role of positivity-preaching ministers. We were rejected heavily by the crowd, [as well as] several of our peers and coworkers." But these setbacks have only strengthened The New Day's resolve to be true to themselves—a sentiment they hope to share with the audience. "At any given time, we could have quit when we faced closed doors and difficulties," said Kingston. "Instead, we went against the grain, and we beat the odds. In doing so, we created something so special and legendary. Thinking about what we've done and how we defied the odds is the literal best feeling in the world. Striving for this feeling is the way that I believe we all should live our lives, and I want to motivate people to pursue that sentiment."

Creating friendship within partnership allowed fans to feel the authenticity of the group. "Our relationship means everything to me. Being a part of this has given me so many incredible memories that I'm nothing but thankful for," said Woods. "I've been around the world, I've gotten to make so many people smile, I've gotten to fulfill multiple life goals, and it's all because of this brotherhood. I'm there for them and they are there for me. That real understanding is what makes us us."

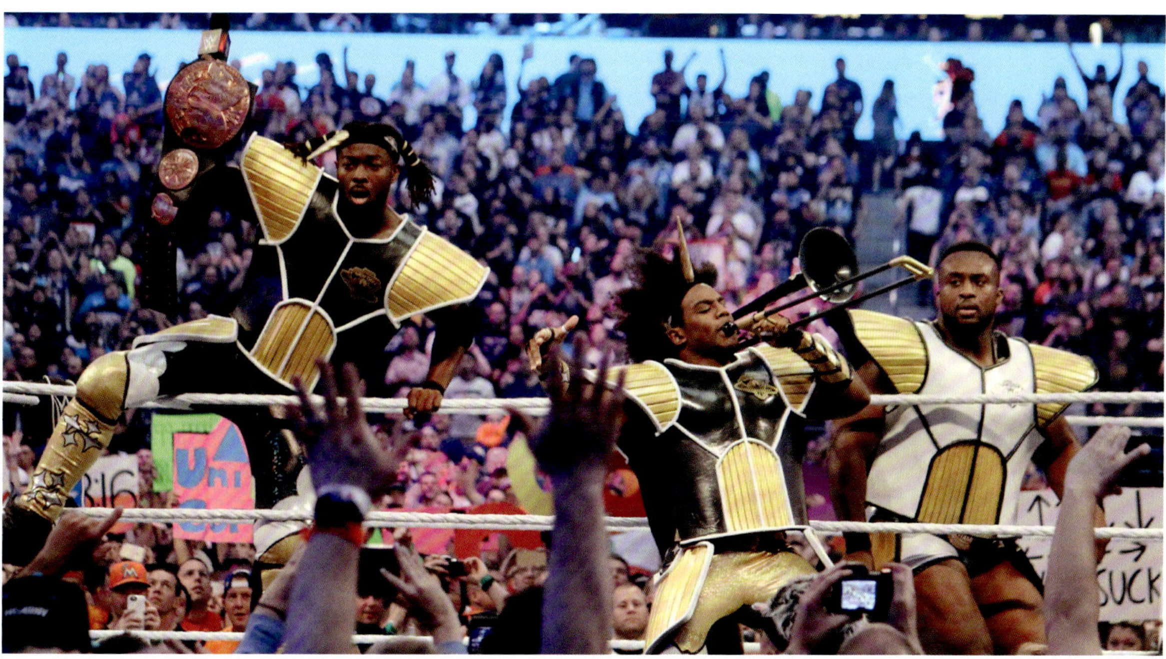



OPPOSITE: From left to right, Xavier Woods, Big E, and Kofi Kingston at WrestleMania 33 in Orlando, Florida, on April 2, 2017. Photo by Steve Argintaru.

ABOVE: From left to right, Kofi Kingston, Xavier Woods, and Big E at WrestleMania 32 in Arlington, Texas, on April 3, 2016. Photo by Steve Argintaru.

# THE HART LEGACY

Est. 1946

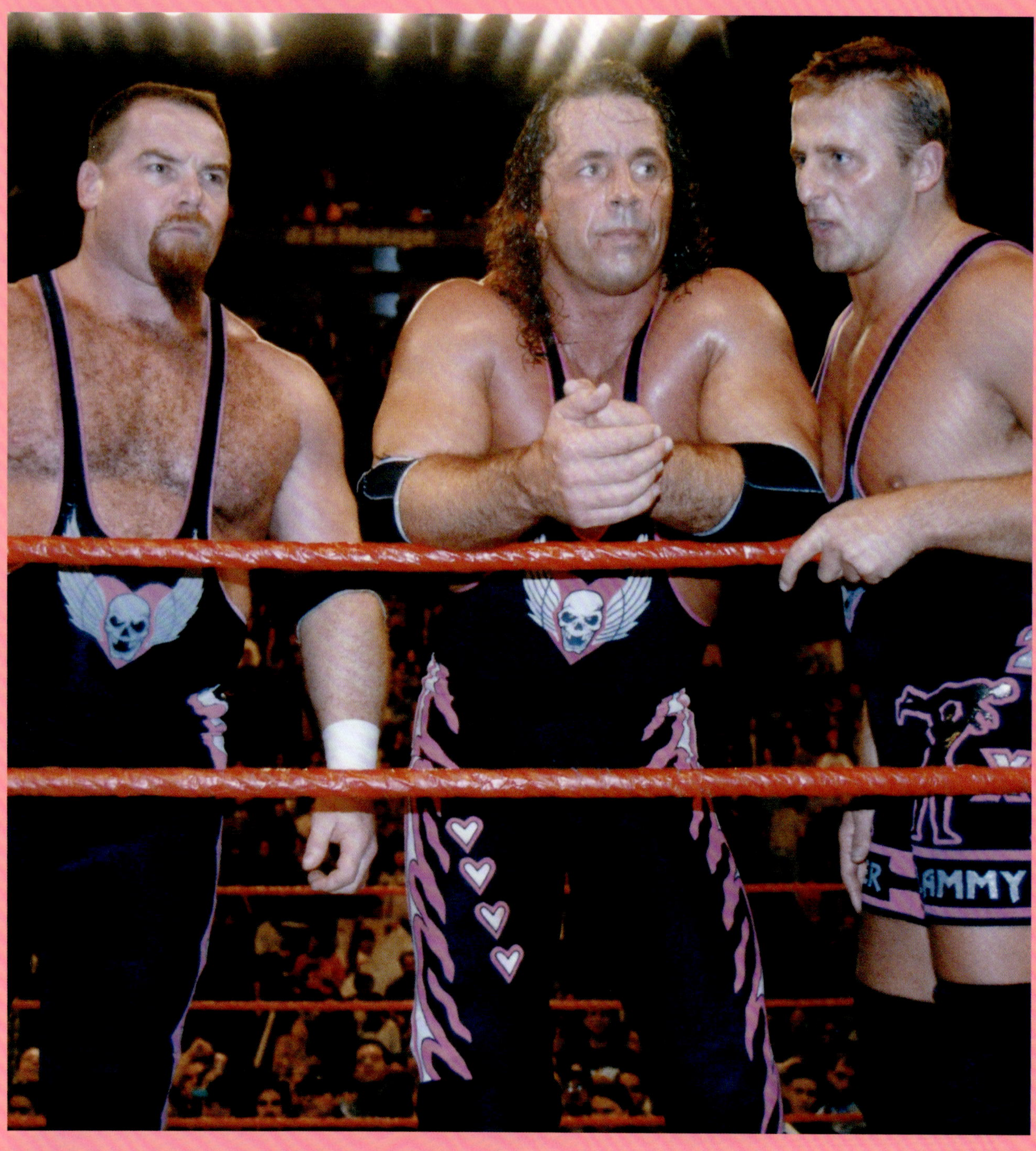

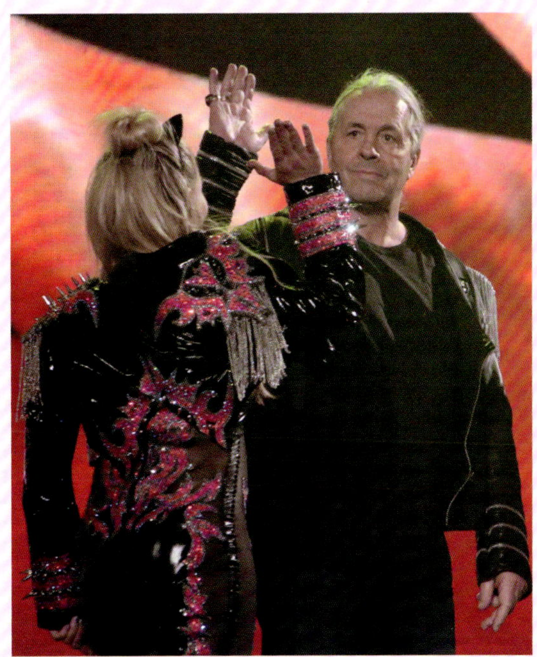

**This iconic wrestling family** includes eight decades (and counting!) of Harts in the ring. From "The Dungeon" to international television, the elements of their identity perfectly blend tradition and evolution. Shaping the very fabric of the wrestling industry, the Harts wore unforgettable pink-and-black attire that has become more than colors worn—it is their signature. The Harts symbolize excellence, grit, and unwavering dedication that is meant to be recognized as the best there is, the best there was, and the best there ever will be.

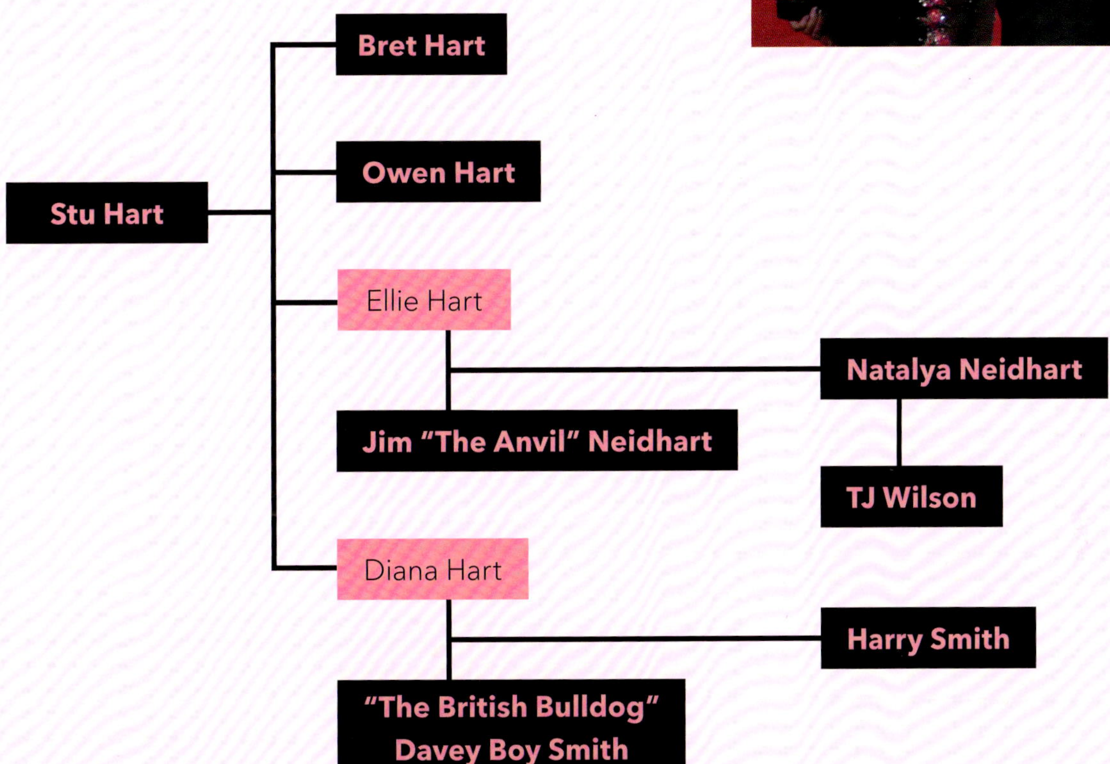


**"If I could design a Hall of Fame outfit that blends the entire essence of my family's wrestling legacy into one look, I think it would be a classic tuxedo. It would be a black tuxedo with a crisp white shirt and a hot-pink bow tie. It would have a little train in the back with a top hat. I think that look would embody tradition but also modern edge."**

—Natalya Neidhart

OPPOSITE: Left to right, Jim "The Anvil" Neidhart, Bret Hart, and Owen Hart immediately after the Montreal Screwjob at Survivor Series 1997. Photo by Steve Argintaru.

TOP: Bret Hart high-fiving Natalya before her match teaming with Beth Phoenix as the Divas of Doom at WrestleMania 35. Photo by Steve Argintaru.

**Stu Hart** laid the foundation for a wrestling dynasty built on discipline and grit, although its presentation and style would evolve. Making his own belts for his gear, he showcased his creativity with a minimalistic approach and believed in functionality rather than flash.

**Bret Hart** honored his father's precision-driven style but reimagined the way the look was delivered. By introducing and championing the color pink in the family wardrobe, he created sharp, intentional gear that mirrored his work in the ring.

**Owen Hart** carved his own path early on by eschewing the family hues to wear neon colors in tag teams like The New Foundation and High Energy. He made his way back to his roots a decade later, donning the family's trademark colors, but in a way that expressed his individual style and added his own unique spin on the family legacy in regal fashion.

**Jim "The Anvil" Neidhart** embodied power and strength, and his gear reflected his role as the muscle of the family. Whether he was wrestling alongside brothers-in-law Owen and Bret or on his own as a solo competitor, Jim wore pink with pride while relishing his role as the family enforcer.

**"The British Bulldog" Davey Boy Smith** served as an extension of the family's identity with utmost pride in his country of England. He was a complement to the group and married into the Hart family after training in the Hart Dungeon (the family gym and wrestling school), where he met and later married Stu's daughter Diana Hart. Alongside Bret and Jim in The Hart Foundation, he showed unity by donning the signature pink and black. Davey Boy didn't just fit in—he stood out in harmony.

**Natalya Neidhart** represents the third generation of the Hart family as Stu's granddaughter, Jim's daughter, and the first female in the family to step into the ring. Dressed in the family's iconic pink-and-black threads, she seamlessly blends femininity with toughness and holds her own as a competitor with countless accolades. As a torchbearer, Natalya proves legacy isn't just something you come from—it's something to live up to. She honors her lineage with a physical and visual representation and pays homage to her father and family by donning custom gear inspired by the family colors and wearing some of their most respected items to the ring.

**TJ Wilson** earned his place in the dynasty (and his pink-and-black threads) after becoming the last graduate of the Hart Dungeon, where he met and later married Natalya. After beginning his career as an individual competitor, TJ proudly wore the family colors with Natalya when they founded The Hart Dynasty, a tag team with her cousin, Harry Smith, to honor the family name.

**Harry Smith** connects the past and the future, representing the discipline and style that define the Hart family name. As the son of Davey Boy Smith and Diana Hart, he honors both sides of his family with pride, excellence, and tribute by sporting his dad's reds and blues when he wrestles solo and wearing pink-and-black gear when teaming up with Natalya and TJ in The Hart Dynasty.

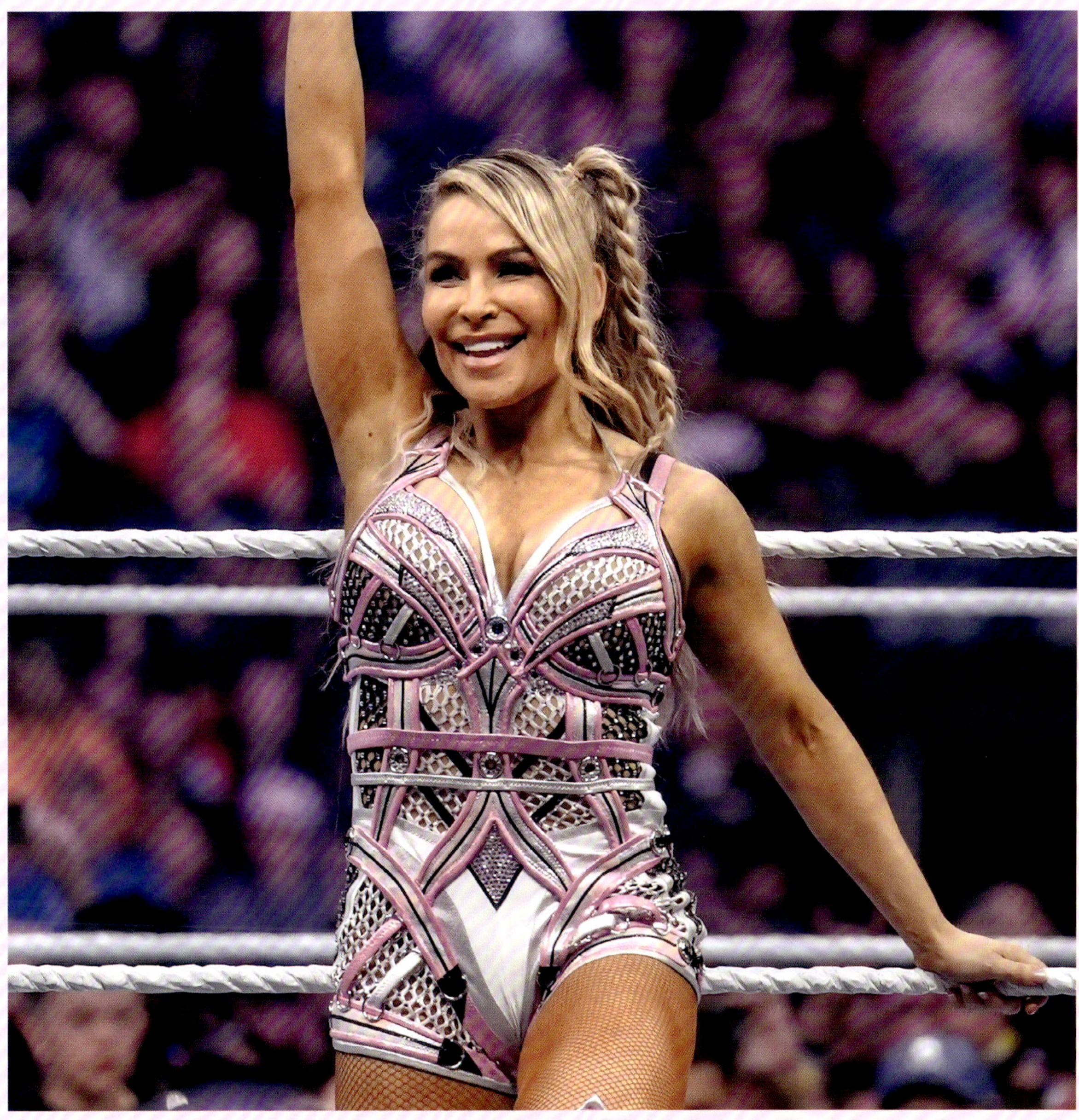

"The colors really do connect our generations. From Owen, my dad, and Bret to me, TJ, and Harry. They were wearing pink and black for two-plus decades of their careers before it got to us. It's very special, and it's nice to see guys [like Jey Uso or CM Punk] in this day and age paying homage to Bret, my dad, and Owen."

–Natalya Neidhart, WWE Superstar

Natalya Neidhart at the WWE Royal Rumble in 2024. Photo by Kimberly Morrell.

# THE SAMOAN DYNASTY

Est. 1960

**Also known as Anoa'i Family,** this dynasty spans fifty years of family lineage with strong ties to the Samoan Islands.

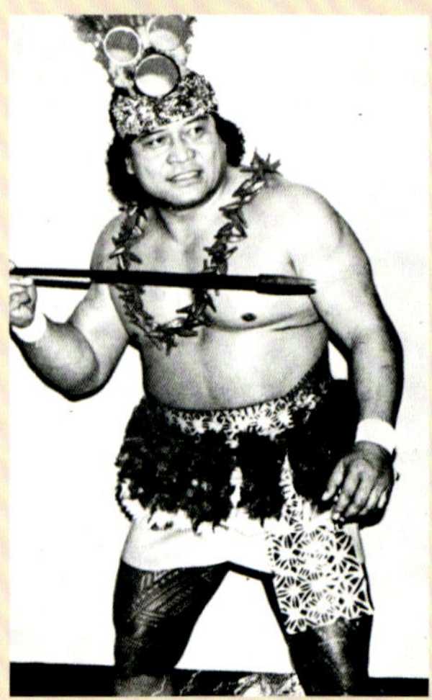

**Peter Maivia** laid the groundwork as the patriarch of what would become one of wrestling's most influential families. The High Chief radiated authenticity and cultural pride with gear inspired by traditional Samoan influences. With a warrior spirit and a heritage-driven look, he paved the way for generations of Samoan wrestlers to follow in his bare footsteps.

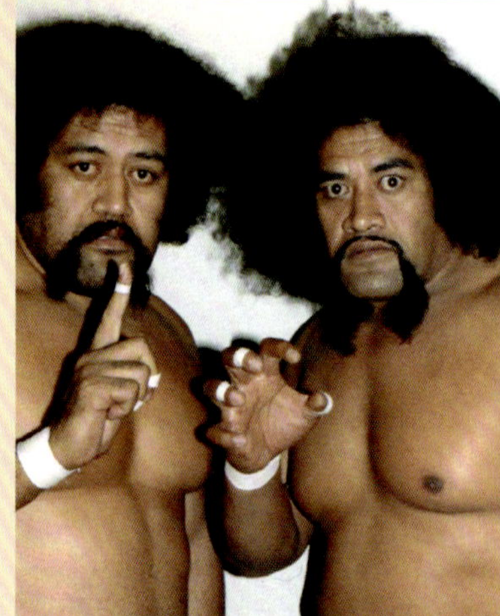

**The Wild Samoans** stormed the ring in cultural style with the volume turned up. Afa and Sika, nephews of Maivia, embraced chaos and unpredictability with spirited style. Their tribal attire paid homage to their homeland and showcased their powerful pedigree.

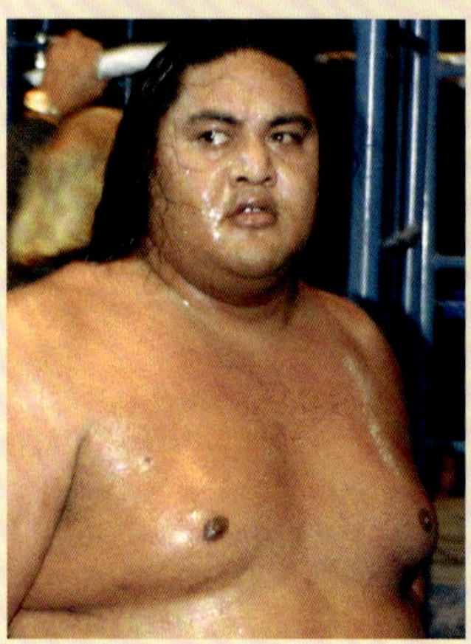

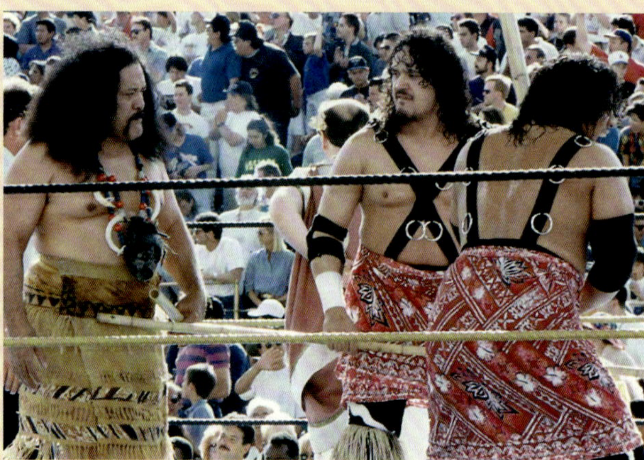

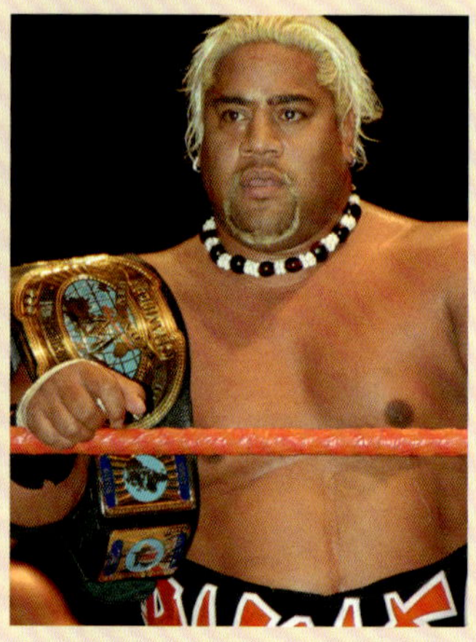

**Yokozuna** stood alone in presence but remained rooted in his Samoan heritage. Inspired by the art of sumo wrestling, he used his bare feet and massive stature to conquer opponents and win new fans for the family.

**The Headshrinkers** modernized what Samoan Dynasty tag team wrestlers could look like. With explosive moves, cultural tributes, and on-point acknowledgment patterns, Samu and Fatu, a.k.a Rikishi, cousins in tandem, bridged the gap between The Wild Samoans and future generations of The Samoan Dynasty.

**Rikishi** (a.k.a. Fatu) found his own footing through callbacks to Yokozuna and his sumo-inspired thongs and sarongs. Wearing bleached blond hair, ancestorial adornments, and lots of the color red, he expanded the family's wrestling lineage and unapologetically owned his massive frame.

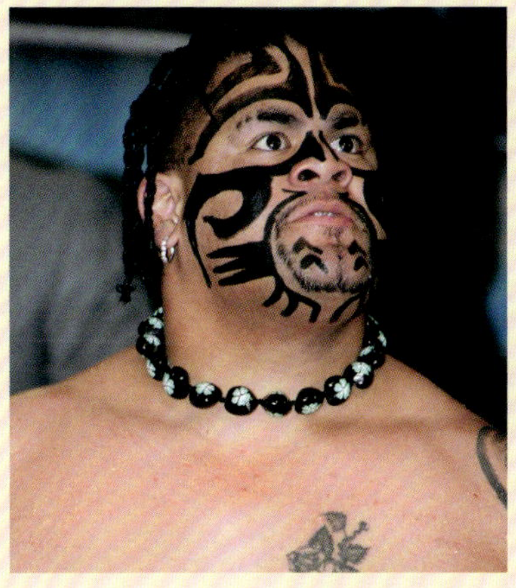

**Umaga** showcased his primal energy in his exaggerated use of tribal paint. He was an intimidating force, and his tattoos proclaimed his Samoan pride. Whether wearing a traditional lavalava skirt or a beaded necklace, he proved that the dynasty doesn't fade—it fights.

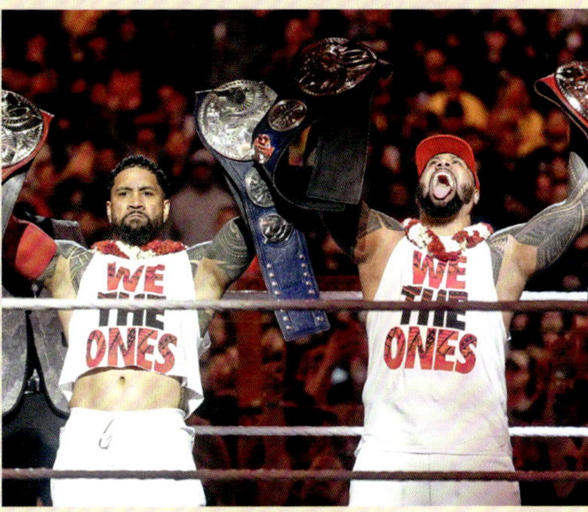

**WWE's Jimmy and Jey Uso** are the twin sons of Rikishi, and they proudly continue their father's legacy. They wear the color red to continue their story, especially as they develop their own personalities. The twins aren't just repeating history—they're making it with their skill, swagger, and unique spin on traditional Samoan references like tribal tattoos and expressions.

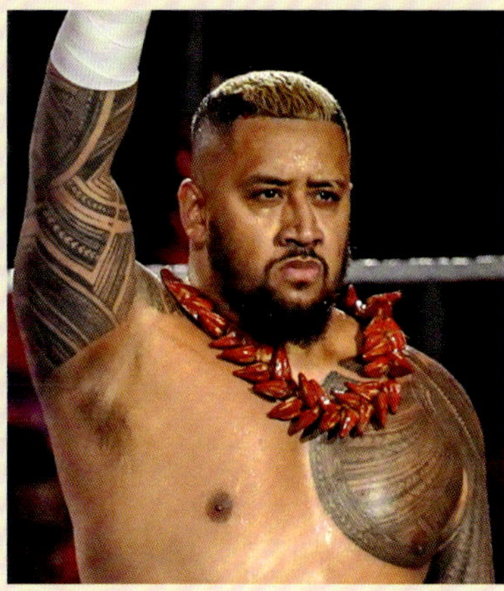

**WWE's Solo Sikoa** is as grounded as he is ruthless, and he serves as the perfect blend of those who came before him. A son of Rikishi, he has a barefoot stomp that signals his sturdy demeanor and recalls the roots of his past. With taped wrists and ankles, he is marked in warrior ink that directly correlates to his heritage.

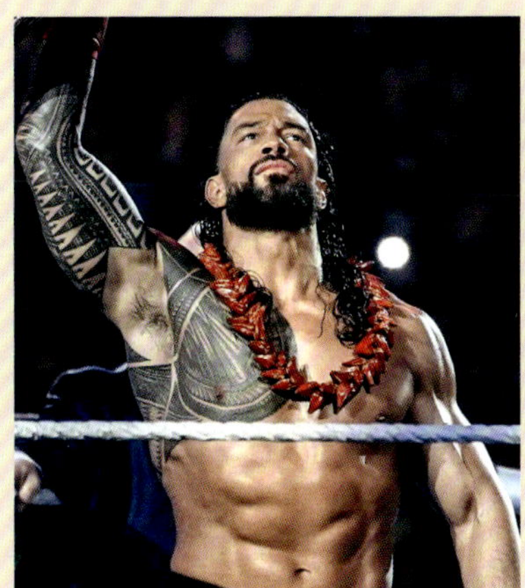

**WWE's Roman Reigns** is a culmination of all that The Samoan Dynasty holds. As Head of the Table and son of Sika, he commands attention that is deserved. He wears an 'ula fala with pride and has sacred designs etched on his body. His look and legacy are about being the ruler, backed by blood.

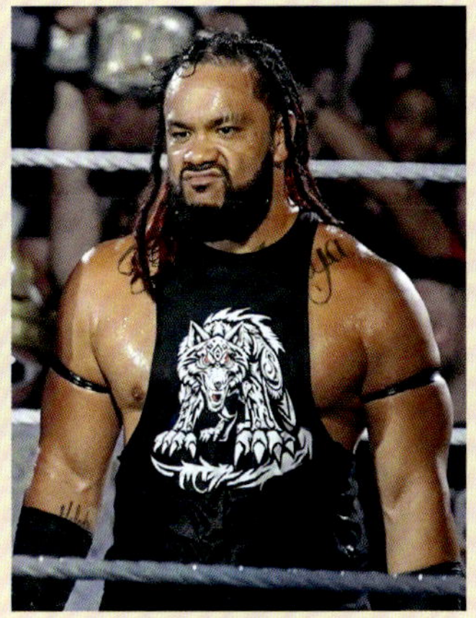

**WWE's Jacob Fatu** channels the intensity and chaos of past generations, becoming the rawest embodiment of The Samoan Dynasty. Cousin to Jey and Jimmy Uso, Solo Sikoa, and Roman Reigns, he has untamed hair that creates a visual throwback to the ancestors who came before him.

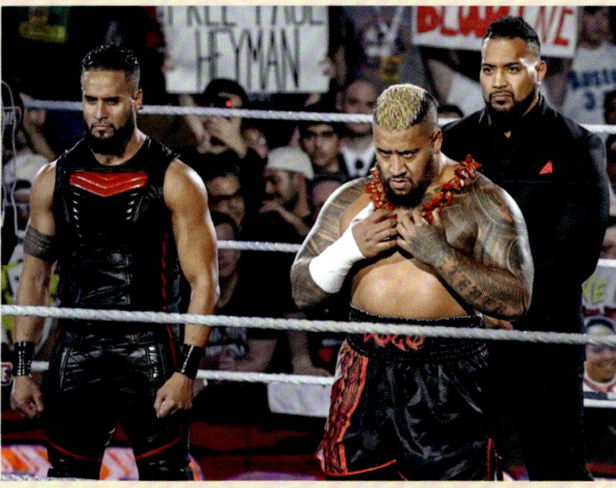

**WWE's Tonga Loa and Tama Tonga** present an extended connection to The Samoan Dynasty through their uncle and adopted father, Haku, whom The Rock also considers an uncle. The brothers bring defiant edge and fighting energy to the table and prove that family can be earned through loyalty. They serve up red-and-black gear, an enforcer approach, and tactical influences.

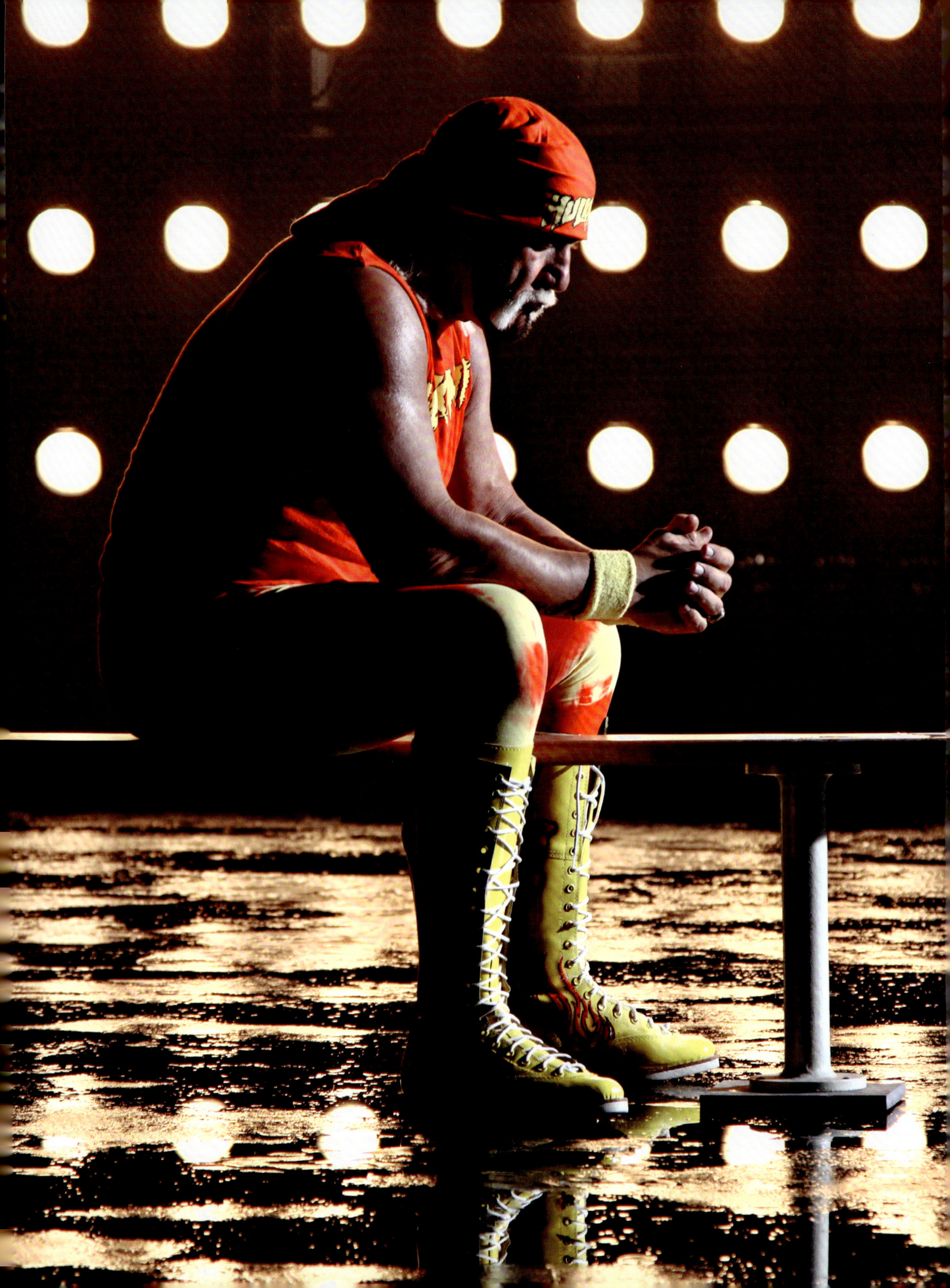

# ACKNOWLEDGMENTS

**This book wouldn't** have been possible without support from many people.

A big thank-you . . .

To Vic, my husband and tag team partner for life: I love you and this book wouldn't have been possible without you. To Ann-Marie and Kevin Mitchell, Helen Mitchell, and my entire family for believing in me and supporting my journey. To Johnny Russo, Jill Marsal, Brock Hartline, Lance Garrison, Ashley Snell, Adam Gee, and all my friends and colleagues who contributed thoughts. To Natalya Neidhart: Without your input, this book would have just remained a thought in my mind. To previous guests on *Threads with McKenzie Mitchell*: Matt Cardona, Chelsea Green, Kira Magnin-Forster, John Hennigan, Jessica McKay, Cassie Lee, Jordynne Grace, Torrie Wilson, Barbie Blank, Amanda Saccomanno, and Swerve Strickland. Thank you to all the talent, legends, and guests who inspired me to write this book and took the time to provide insight and knowledge, allowing the book to come to life.

Additional thanks to Malissa Lappas, Matt Bloom, James Curtain, Mickey Fitzpatrick, Keven Undergaro, Sam Roberts, Dixie Carter, John Gaburick, Charlie Lowery, Michael Dockins, Jason Mullen, Lynn Poffo and the Poffo Family, Steven Kaye and the Paragon team, Vic Martinez and the entire crew at BrandCrumbs, and to all of the amazing photographers who contributed to make this possible. To WWE for firing me and pushing me to follow my dreams, to TNA for giving me the knowledge I need to succeed in this business, and to everyone who contributed to this book, in big ways or small.

Thank you to the lineage of women in fashion in my family—finding four generations of businesswomen is hard to come by. You and your entrepreneurial spirit showed me how to be a strong, independent woman who isn't afraid to stand up for what she loves and believes in. My family gave me the roots, tools, and wings needed to fly.

And to myself and the young girl in me—through years of hard work, dedication, and genuine love for professional wrestling and fashion, my dream of blending both worlds has seamlessly come to life.

Hulk Hogan studio photoshoot at TNA in February of 2009. Photo by Lee South.

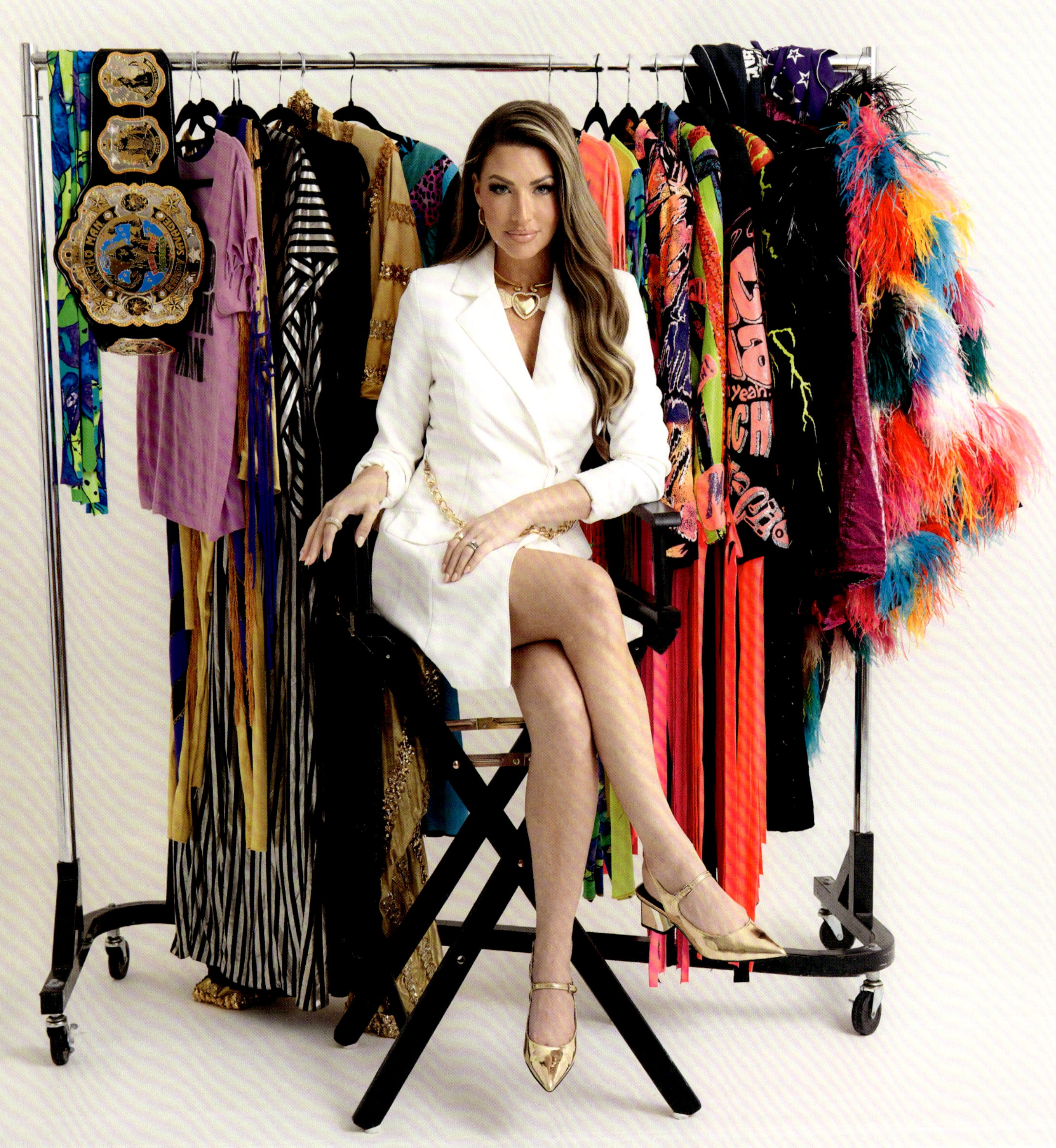

# ABOUT THE AUTHOR

**McKenzie Mitchell has worked** as an international on-camera host featured on some of the biggest networks, including Fox, USA Network, and Peacock. She is most known for her time in World Wrestling Entertainment (WWE), where she served for four years as a host, announcer, and backstage correspondent on WWE's weekly international television program, *WWE NXT*. Starting her career in TNA Wrestling in 2016 and making a triumphant return in 2025, McKenzie has collectively served as a host, reporter, and ring announcer for five years in the company under Anthem Sports & Entertainment.

McKenzie's love for being in the spotlight started at the young age of five, when she signed with her first modeling agency, and she has been represented ever since by multiple agencies. Throughout her acting and modeling career, McKenzie has been featured on multiple commercials, catalogs, television shows, and a billboard in three countries. Some of her most well-known work includes an SEC Network feature, as a guest host and expert on HSN, and a commentator and actress on *The Last Match: A Pro-Wrestling Rock Experience.*

McKenzie brings her vast experience and knowledge from television and social media to running and operating her business, Headline by MM, which carries on a seventy-five-year tradition of her family in the fine-jewelry industry. As a fourth-generation woman in business, McKenzie has entrepreneurship in her blood, and she brought Headline by MM's flagship store to Music Row in Nashville, Tennessee. With a love for fashion, sports, and business, McKenzie has created custom jewelry pieces for some of the biggest stars in professional wrestling, such as Seth Rollins, Roxanne Perez, and Trick Williams for capstone events like WrestleMania and SummerSlam.

Her curiosity and vision for fashion customization in the world of wrestling, combined with her knowledge in the space, helped conceptualize *Threads of Triumph*, a YouTube and podcast experience that dove into the closets of some of the most well-known stars in wrestling and music. *Threads of Triumph: Professional Wrestling's Most Iconic Looks* brings a fresh take on the sport and allows readers to go behind the seams of wrestling history.